Quantitative Research Methods in Translation and Interpreting Studies

Quantitative Research Methods in Translation and Interpreting Studies encompasses all stages of the research process that include quantitative research methods, from conceptualization to reporting. In five parts, the authors cover:

- sampling techniques, measurement, and survey design;
- how to describe data;
- how to analyze differences;
- how to analyze relationships;
- how to interpret results.

Each part includes references to additional resources and extensive examples from published empirical work. A quick reference table for specific tests is also included in the appendix. This user-friendly guide is the essential primer on quantitative methods for all students and researchers in translation and interpreting studies.

Accompanying materials are available online, including step-by-step walk-throughs of how analysis was conducted, and extra sample data sets for instruction and self study: https://www.routledge.com/9781138124967. Further resources for Translation and Interpreting Studies are available on the Routledge Translation Studies Portal: http://cw.routledge.com/textbooks/translationstudies.

Christopher D. Mellinger is Assistant Professor of Spanish at Walsh University, USA and the managing editor of the journal *Translation and Interpreting Studies*.

Thomas A. Hanson is Assistant Professor of Finance at Minnesota State University Moorhead, USA.

Quantitative Research Methods in Translation and Interpreting Studies

Christopher D. Mellinger and
Thomas A. Hanson

LONDON AND NEW YORK

First published 2017
by Routledge
2 Park Square, Milton Park, Abingdon, Oxon OX14 4RN

and by Routledge
711 Third Avenue, New York, NY 10017

Routledge is an imprint of the Taylor & Francis Group, an informa business

© 2017 Christopher D. Mellinger and Thomas A. Hanson

The right of Christopher D. Mellinger and Thomas A. Hanson to be identified as author of this work has been asserted by him/her in accordance with sections 77 and 78 of the Copyright, Designs and Patents Act 1988.

All rights reserved. No part of this book may be reprinted or reproduced or utilised in any form or by any electronic, mechanical, or other means, now known or hereafter invented, including photocopying and recording, or in any information storage or retrieval system, without permission in writing from the publishers.

Trademark notice: Product or corporate names may be trademarks or registered trademarks, and are used only for identification and explanation without intent to infringe.

British Library Cataloguing-in-Publication Data
A catalogue record for this book is available from the British Library

Library of Congress Cataloging-in-Publication Data
Names: Mellinger, Christopher D. (Christopher Davey), author. |
    Hanson, Thomas A. (Translator) author.
Title: Quantitative research methods in translation and interpreting studies /
    by Christopher D. Mellinger and Thomas A. Hanson.
Description: Milton Park, Abingdon, Oxon; New York, NY : Routledge,
    [2016] | Includes bibliographical references and index.
Identifiers: LCCN 2016007454| ISBN 9781138124950 (hardback) |
    ISBN 9781138124967 (pbk.) | ISBN 9781315647845 (ebook)
Subjects: LCSH: Translating and interpreting—Study and teaching—
    Research. | Translating and interpreting—Study and teaching—
    Methodology. | Translating and interpreting—Research. | Quantitative
    research.
Classification: LCC P306.5 .M455 2016 | DDC 418/.020721—dc23
LC record available at https://lccn.loc.gov/2016007454

ISBN: 978-1-138-12495-0 (hbk)
ISBN: 978-1-138-12496-7 (pbk)
ISBN: 978-1-3156-4784-5 (ebk)

Typeset in Times New Roman
by Swales & Willis Ltd, Exeter, Devon, UK

Contents

List of figures	vii
List of tables	ix
Acknowledgements	xi
Introduction to the volume	xii

Part I
Preparing   1

1 Research questions, hypotheses, and design	3
2 Sampling and ethics	9
3 Measurement	22

Part II
Describing   37

4 Descriptive statistics	39
5 Probability distributions	58
6 Statistical terminology and one-sample tests	70

Part III
Analyzing differences   85

7 Comparing two groups	87
8 Comparing multiple groups	110
9 Comparing groups on multiple factors	151
10 Testing categorical data	167

Part IV
Analyzing relationships **177**

11 Correlation and reliability 179

12 Linear regression 215

Part V
Interpreting results **239**

13 Interpreting results 241

References 249
Appendix A: Guide to selecting a statistical test 271
Index 272

Figures

3.1	Scree plot example	33
4.1	Graphical representation of the median and the mean	44
4.2	Histograms of unimodal and bimodal frequency distributions	45
4.3	Graphs of positive and negative skewness	51
4.4	Bar chart example	52
4.5	Histogram example	53
4.6	Box plot example	54
4.7	Scatterplot example	55
4.8	Line graph example	56
5.1	Normal (Gaussian) distribution	59
5.2	Quantile-Quantile (QQ) plot example	62
5.3	Left-skewed and leptokurtic QQ plot examples	62
5.4	The Anscombe quartet (adapted from Anscombe 1973)	67
6.1	Reported statistics for mean time on task example	81
6.2	Reported statistics for median test score example	83
7.1	Box plot of sample data for Russia and Canada elevation example	90
7.2	Histograms of sample data for Russia and Canada elevation example	90
7.3	Example of complete reporting of t-test results	109
8.1	Box plot of elevation example data	116
8.2	QQ plot of elevation example data	118
8.3	Null and alternative hypothesis models for ANOVA	120
8.4	Total and partitioned variation (within and between groups)	121
8.5	Box plot examples of ANOVA	124
8.6	Trend analysis example	143
8.7	Example of complete reporting of ANOVA results	148
9.1	Factorial ANOVA outcomes—no interaction	159
9.2	Factorial ANOVA outcomes—with interaction	160
11.1	Correlation example	180
11.2	Correlation example—outlier removed	182
11.3	The Anscombe quartet (adapted from Anscombe 1973)	183
11.4	Correlation example—restricted range	189

Figures

12.1	Simple linear regression raw data—scatterplot	219
12.2	Residuals vs. predicted values and independent variable—scatterplot	220
12.3	Scatterplots exhibiting heteroscedasticity—increasing and decreasing variance	220
12.4	Scatterplot with line of best fit examples	223
12.5	Scatterplots implying a need for transformation	227
12.6	Scatterplot example with outlier	233
12.7	Example of complete reporting of study results including regression results	237

Tables

4.1	Example data for zero-sum-deviation property of the mean	42
4.2	Example data for mode	46
4.3	Frequency table (absolute) example data (adapted from Ribas 2012, Table 6)	57
4.4	Frequency table (relative) example data (adapted from Ribas 2012, Table 6)	57
6.1	One-sample test for the median example data	82
7.1	Comparing two means: Examples from T&I literature	89
7.2	Mann-Whitney U-test example data with rank transformation	102
7.3	Wilcoxon matched-pairs signed-ranks test data with rank transformation	107
8.1	Summary statistics for elevation example	111
8.2	One-way ANOVA: Examples from T&I literature	112
8.3	ANOVA table with formulas	123
8.4	ANOVA table for elevation example	123
8.5	Example data adapted from Köpke and Nespoulous (2006)	127
8.6	Kruskal-Wallis example data	134
8.7	Repeated measures ANOVA example data	138
8.8	Repeated measures ANOVA table	140
8.9	Between-subjects repeated measures ANOVA	141
8.10	Repeated measures ANOVA table of example data	141
8.11	Repeated measures ANOVA with corrections for sphericity	142
8.12	Friedman's test example	146
9.1	Independent factorial ANOVA study design	152
9.2	Sums of squares, mean squares, and F-statistics	153
9.3	Factorial ANOVA with no significant effects	158
9.4	Factorial ANOVA with significant main effect	158
9.5	Adapted from Christoffels and de Groot (2004: 234, Table 1)	162
10.1	Testing categorical data: Examples from T&I literature	168
10.2	Chi-squared example data	168
10.3	Chi-squared example data—expected vs. observed values	172
10.4	Goodness-of-fit example data	174
10.5	Goodness-of-fit example data—expected values	175

11.1	Correlation: Examples from T&I literature	181
11.2	Correlation matrix example	188
11.3	Correlation matrix example—incorrect reporting	188
11.4	Test-retest reliability example data	200
11.5	Internal reliability example data	200
11.6	Cohen's κ example data	209
11.7	Cohen's κ example data, $\kappa = 0$	210
12.1	Linear regression: Examples from T&I literature	217
12.2	ANOVA table—linear regression	221
12.3	ANOVA table for regression example	222
12.4	Parameter coefficient estimates	224
12.5	Individual coefficient t-test example data	230

Acknowledgements

There are many people we would like to thank for their encouragement and support. We would first like to thank several friends and colleagues for taking time from their busy schedules to read and comment on various sections of the volume, including Brian Baer, Loubna Bilali, Jeff Child, Coral De Jesús, Alan Hanson, Adrienne Hollowell, Katie Lyman, Michael Mellinger, Jonathan Mellinger, Scott St. Amand, Valerie Reed, and Leslie Whetstine. Their suggestions challenged us to rethink and revise the manuscript. We would also like to extend our thanks to Walsh University's Library and Division of Languages and Letters for their support. Sara Laviosa and the anonymous reviewer of the manuscript deserve our thanks for their insightful comments on the initial proposal, which undoubtedly improved the final project. Lastly, a heartfelt thank-you to our families for their encouragement and support throughout the entire process.

Every effort has been made to contact copyright-holders. Please advise the publisher of any errors or omissions, and these will be corrected in subsequent editions.

Introduction to the volume

As translation and interpreting (T&I) studies evolve, investigators have incorporated novel research designs and methods to glean new insights on a broad range of research questions. Innovative data collection methods and their associated samples are drawn from a variety of sources for the purpose of describing specific phenomena and generalizing findings to larger populations. With the growth of quantitative data generated by new data collection tools—such as eye-tracking software, keystroke logging, corpus linguistics tools, and audio and video recording—it is not surprising that scholars have looked to statistical methods to make sense of the data. The science of statistics provides a wealth of tools and methods that can be used to address and analyze the proliferation of data. Scholars engage these tools in a number of areas to identify patterns, evaluate relationships and differences, and generate new research questions.

Yet the inclusion of quantitative data in a field often associated with the humanities has left some scholars without the requisite foundation to read, interpret, and use statistics in their work. Graduate-level translation and interpreting programs, traditionally housed in comparative literature programs, do not regularly incorporate quantitative research methods in their curricula, and opportunities for formal study using empirical methods are scarce. Oakes and Ji (2012) note, for instance, that corpus-based translation studies have suffered from a lack of quantitative analytical methods, despite burgeoning attention being placed on corpus studies. O'Brien (2009) describes the proliferation of data available when conducting eye-tracking studies that can prove unwieldly to the uninitiated. Likewise, Gile (2016) articulates the need for larger sample sizes in experimental research, though this requirement can prove problematic when attempting to recruit sufficient samples for T&I studies. Sun (2016) similarly describes growth in the use of quantitative data derived from survey instruments in the social sciences and its inclusion in translation and interpreting studies.

Systematic reflection on quantitative research methods has largely been limited to the types of statistical tests and analyses needed for specific studies and research projects. Some exceptions include articles by Balling (2008), Steiner (2012), and Balling and Hvelplund (2015), as well as several contributions to Oakes and Ji's (2012) edited collection. These works have described specific approaches to various aspects of statistical analysis, but no book-length treatment on the topic is available. Discipline-specific research methods volumes often mention quantitative research methods but remain silent on the specifics of statistical analysis, presupposing an understanding on the part of readers. Consequently, researchers instead turn outside the discipline to related works, such as those by Johnson (2008), Rasinger (2008), and Turner (2014). While these volumes provide a foundation of quantitative analysis, they do not recognize the challenges inherent to research in T&I studies, nor do they provide a comprehensive overview that can address its specificities. This volume endeavors to fill this gap.

This book approaches quantitative research methods with the explicit understanding that T&I studies pose unique challenges to data collection, analysis, and interpretation. Researchers are often faced with data feast or famine; either there is an overwhelming amount of data that can be unwieldy for even the seasoned researcher or else a dearth that leaves the researcher in want of additional data points. Moreover, experimental or quasi-experimental studies in T&I studies are not easily replicable, given the wide variety of participant and linguistic variables that are often under consideration. When working with professional translators and interpreters, there are limited participant pools, and every researcher must compete for their time. Results from these studies aim, in many cases, to generalize to a limited population (i.e., translators and interpreters), which further complicates research designs and analysis. Consequently, each situation must be approached based on the constraints imposed by the research design and data collection method. Therefore, the methods described in this book recognize the importance of the underlying assumptions of various analytic methods.

Of equal importance to the authors of this book is that its statistical advice is in line with current research in the field of statistics. Just as the discipline of T&I studies evolves, so too does the body of scholarship in statistics. Statistical methods are certainly portable across disciplines and domains, yet their constant evolution necessarily requires past recommendations to be revisited. By way of example, Osborne (2010: 64), in his offer of guidance on reviewing research that employs correlational analysis, states that several approaches to the calculation of a particular test are in fact "archaic." He continues his discussion as follows:

> Essentially, before massive computing power was available in every office, these formulae provided computational shortcuts for people computing correlations by hand or via hand calculator. Researchers using statistical software have no true use for them. [. . .] Reviewers seeing authors using archaic correlation coefficients [. . .] should be skeptical as to the authors' quantitative prowess, as this seems to be an indicator of outdated training.

While these strongly-worded comments are specific to one type of statistical analysis, the underlying sentiment should be heeded; researchers must stay up-to-date with current best practices in statistical analysis. These advances are, in part, the result of increased computing power and its availability to a larger population.

Greater ability to run simulation studies to test theoretical constructs in statistics has also enabled long-touted statistical measures to be critically examined. Of course, theoretical advances continue in the field as well.

The confluence of challenges in handling quantitative T&I data with advances in statistical analysis and design precipitates the need for a book of this kind. In particular, this volume serves as a primer with significant attention placed on data analysis and interpretation. Rather than re-hashing the statistical tests forwarded by similar works in related fields, we instead emphasize a theoretical understanding of particular tests. We also avoid adopting a more simplistic "more-is-better" approach to quantitative research design, and instead address challenges to T&I research with a more nuanced view of statistical analysis. The specific analysis techniques are grounded in the extant literature on statistics to provide ample resources for further investigation. This discussion draws attention to the underlying assumptions that are associated with each test, since these serve as the foundation upon which inferential statistics are based.

At the outset, statistical concepts are introduced and defined in general terms, which are then addressed more explicitly in subsequent sections. First, we differentiate between descriptive and inferential statistics, a commonly confused distinction in the field. The bulk of the volume is dedicated to inferential statistics, which can be broadly described in two categories: tests of differences and tests of relationships. Specific emphasis is placed on statistical tests that are most appropriate to the empirical work conducted in T&I studies, taking into account the varied nature of the studies conducted and the challenges inherent to data collection and small sample sizes. The final section returns to the original aim of the volume—to provide researchers with the foundation needed to interpret the data, while remaining cognizant of the limitations of statistical inferences and generalizability.

These sections allow the larger body of scholarship on statistical tests to be brought to bear on the field of T&I studies. Discipline-specific examples allow readers to relate the discussed statistical methods to potential T&I research projects. Likewise, this explicitly applied approach to the presentation of statistical tests will equip researchers with the necessary skills to investigate the wide range of variables involved in T&I.

In particular, the authors of this volume insist on the integration of nonparametric statistical analysis. Many introductory statistics handbooks and textbooks relegate nonparametric tests to the end of the volume with limited treatment or make scant reference to their usefulness. Nonparametric tests are often appropriate and useful tools for applied research, and they deserve ample attention and recommendation side-by-side with their parametric counterparts. Examples of successful empirical research are drawn from T&I studies to illustrate the implementation of these tests.

The objective of this volume, therefore, is three-fold: (1) to strengthen methodological and analytical rigor when working with quantitative data; (2) to empower T&I researchers to be critical readers of quantitative research; and (3) to improve the review processes as part of the process of dissemination of research incorporating statistical analysis. The focus on sound research design and appropriate statistical analysis aims to strengthen the arguments made using quantitative research methods and allow for greater generalizability of results. By the conclusion of the volume, readers should be informed consumers of quantitative research, being able to understand the methods and analyses reported in empirical work. Moreover, best practices are presented so that scholars will have the quantitative wherewithal to critique and improve research design, method, and reporting.

Structure of the volume

This volume is divided into five parts that encompass the various stages of quantitative research and analysis. This division spans the initial identification of a research question to the final reporting of results. Each part is then subdivided into chapters. Part I is dedicated to the preparation and planning of a research design and methodology that will employ quantitative methods. It describes some of the general principles that underlie best practices in research design. Here, we introduce methods by which researchers might identify research questions that are grounded in the existing literature in order to generate appropriate hypotheses that can be tested empirically. We also define key concepts that any researcher must consider during the design of a research project. Specific treatment is given to issues related to sampling and measurement, with an eye toward the specific challenges T&I researchers face in this area. Ethical considerations are presented as they relate to research design, data collection, and human subjects. The role of technology is also discussed in relation to the development of statistical analysis. The goal of Part I is to orient the researcher to these major considerations prior to data collection so that researchers are more likely to be successful in describing, analyzing, and interpreting data.

Part II introduces descriptive statistics. The measures introduced in this section are generally well known, such as the mean, median, and mode, as well as the range, variance, and standard deviation. It is crucial to understand these fundamental concepts before advancing to later sections of the volume. Confidence intervals are introduced in this section, since best practice dictates their calculation and reporting for almost all statistics. Data visualization techniques and outlier analysis are also presented. This section lays the foundation for more advanced inquiry into quantitative methods by introducing one-sample tests for the mean and median. These tests are basic inferential analyses that will serve as a bridge to more traditionally employed inferential statistics.

Parts III and IV are dedicated to inferential statistics and comprise the bulk of the statistical tests presented in this volume. In Part III, tests of difference are described in detail, along with their associated research designs. Widely recognizable tests such as the t-test, one-way ANOVA, and repeated measures ANOVA are presented in conjunction with their nonparametric counterparts: the Mann-Whitney U-test, Kruskal-Wallis ANOVA, and Friedman's test. The assumptions upon which each test is based are explicitly outlined so that any violations can be addressed through alternative statistical techniques, experimental control, or research design reconsideration. Each test also contains a section on reporting, so that researchers know both what information to report and how to interpret results for the reader. Recommendations on effect size, confidence intervals, and assumption testing are also provided.

Tests of relationships are presented in Part IV, which commences with a section on correlation, one of the quantitative methods for determining the strength of relationships. Recommendations are provided regarding which tests should be used in specific situations. Reliability also receives ample attention in this section given its overlap with correlation statistics and its regular use in research that focuses on assessment and survey design. The next chapter describes linear regression, a statistical method that is starting to be more widely adopted in T&I scholarship. More complicated regression models are presented toward the end of this part, together with recommendations on where additional information on these tests can be found.

Parts II–IV adopt a similar structure in their presentation of information. In addition to extensive discussion of the statistical tests and their relationship to translation and interpreting studies research, each section presents a condensed summary information box related to each test. Each box includes the purpose of the test as well as the associated hypotheses and experimental designs, the parametric and nonparametric versions, and the appropriate effect size. For most tests, two types of examples are provided. The first is a fictional example of generated data that serves as a basic illustration of the statistical method under discussion. The second set of examples is specific to T&I studies. These sample studies have been selected based on their research design and analysis and are briefly described in a separate table. These examples are then referenced throughout each chapter to help researchers tie specific statistical concepts to real-world research applications.

The volume concludes with Part V, dedicated to the interpretation and reporting of results. While the nuts and bolts of reporting are discussed in greater detail when each test is presented, this discussion centers on ethical reporting practices and the extent to which these results can be interpreted and generalized. Specific attention is placed on research integrity as it relates to quantitative research methods. Moreover, the interplay of effect size and statistical significance is explored. Design considerations such as robustness and triangulation are discussed here as well. Researchers must be mindful that quantitative methods are not the only tool in the T&I researcher's toolbox, and their application can often be strengthened in conjunction with qualitative approaches.

Each part provides ample references to additional resources so that readers can deepen their understanding of a particular test and critique its use in specific settings. An appendix is also provided in which a table can guide a researcher to select the appropriate test. References to the specific section that should be referenced appear in this format to facilitate quick reference within the work.

Using the volume

In writing this volume, we have assumed only a limited knowledge or background in statistics on the part of the readers. Conceived as an introduction to quantitative research methods in T&I studies, this book is most suitable for a graduate-level, first-year empirical research methods course or for use by advanced undergraduates. This volume will also be of considerable use to seasoned researchers who want to revisit some of the quantitative methods to see how advances in statistics could impact or enrich their current work. We encourage numerophobic readers (you know who you are) to use the plentiful examples as a way to understand the underlying mathematics involved in statistical analysis. The volume necessarily presents a fair amount of formal mathematics, but the main goal is to communicate the purpose and results of these statistical tests. A complete understanding of the assumptions, mechanics, interpretation, and limitations of statistics is necessary for them to be used to their full potential in research.

The overarching structure allows readers to advance from the initial stages of research design to the appropriate data analysis section and then to interpreting and reporting the results. If used as a textbook or for self-study, the chapters are presented in order of increasing complexity, such that a linear progression through the text is recommended. For readers interested primarily in a specific statistical test, these sections are somewhat self-contained and can be consulted individually. Where possible, intra-volume references have been provided so that readers can refer back to previous concepts. The appendix strives to provide another entry point into the book, such that quick reference is possible for a specific test.

Conclusion

Our hope with this volume is to provide researchers with a sound understanding of quantitative research and to equip investigators with the necessary tools to conduct research using these methods. The complexities of statistical design and analysis can initially seem daunting, but the aim in this volume is to make these analytical tools approachable. Quantitative methods are powerful and important tools, and when used appropriately, can help researchers investigate many of the intricacies of T&I.

Part I
Preparing

As described in the introduction to the volume, this book is divided into several parts that correspond to stages of the research project. Part I focuses on the initial preparation stage. The best research projects have as their foundation a well-motivated research question or hypothesis. Without understanding the nature of the research question(s) and purpose of the project, adequate samples or measurements cannot be obtained, data cannot be collected, and statistical tests cannot be appropriately selected or interpreted.

Therefore, Chapter 1 focuses on generating appropriate research questions and hypotheses. We also distinguish several common research designs. Chapter 2 is dedicated to sampling and ethics. For research involving human participants, ethical considerations related to the recruitment, selection, and inclusion of participants are intrinsically linked to sampling practices. Chapter 3 then addresses measurement and the notions of reliability and validity. Part I closes with a brief treatment of survey design and technology issues related to measurement.

1 Research questions, hypotheses, and design

This chapter introduces the basics of quantitative research methods. In order to conduct meaningful research, research questions and hypotheses require considerable thought and should be aligned with the extant literature. Personal experience or general observation may initially spark interest in a particular topic, and a review of the related scholarly work might reveal a potential area of investigation. Both research questions and hypotheses serve as the foundation of scholarly inquiry. Furthermore, research questions determine what data are needed to answer these questions and, by extension, how the data should be collected. These data will eventually determine the analytical method to be used and the types of conclusions that can be drawn.

Research questions

Investigators often begin to explore an area of research with a certain topic in mind. For instance, they may be interested in the impact of technology on the translation process or how a speaker might influence the performance of an interpreter. These questions are broad and do not make any predictions about the potential relationship between these two ideas; that is to say, they are *non-directional*. A broad question may also be broken down into related sub-questions that focus on more specific aspects of the overarching question.

To help structure the research project, researchers should identify a theoretical framework within which the research questions will be explored. At the highest level of abstraction, a research question involves a collection of *concepts* that are related to the area of interest. For the previous interpreting example, the investigator would need to explore various aspects of the interpreting task that are related to the research question. As meaningful relationships between these concepts are established, a *construct* begins to emerge. A rough definition of a construct is a group of concepts linked in a theoretical model. Constructs help researchers to refine their questions and provide structure to their investigations.

As the research process continues, investigators must further refine constructs into measurable and observable *variables*. To do so, constructs must be *operationalized* so that a research design or protocol can be developed to investigate the variables of interest. Operationalization entails a strict definition of the constructs so that they can be measured and tested. Researchers often draw on previous definitions of concepts or constructs to guide operationalization, and this linkage to previous research can help contextualize study findings in relation to other studies.

Two basic orientations to research can be adopted: *inductive* and *deductive*.[1] Generally speaking, deductive reasoning adopts a top-down perspective, in which a general theory leads to testable predictions (Evans 2013). In the interpreting example, a model on interpreting effort or performance might generate research questions that investigate specific aspects of the theory. Conversely, inductive reasoning attempts to use observations from a study as the foundation for theoretical development. Quantitative research tends to adopt a deductive line of reasoning since empirical and experimental observation can be used to test theories related to a specific object of analysis. This theory-driven approach to research allows investigators to evaluate the suitability of models or theories to describe specific aspects of translation and interpreting (T&I).

In a study, researchers must operationalize two types of variables: *independent* and *dependent variables*. In an experimental setting, independent variables are those that are manipulated or controlled by the researcher. The independent variable can also be referred to as the *treatment variable*. Returning to the interpreting example, if the investigator were to change the speaker's delivery rate and measure performance under different conditions, then the delivery rate would be considered an independent variable. It is important to distinguish between the independent variable, which is delivery rate, and the *levels* of the independent variable, which are the various rates. In this simple study, there is only one independent variable, but it includes several possible levels (e.g., slow, average, and fast speeds). More than one independent variable is possible in a study, but great care must be taken when introducing multiple independent variables. In non-experimental situations, the independent variable is not controllable by the researcher. In those cases, the independent variable often is referred to as a *causal*, *treatment*, *input*, or *explanatory* variable.

The dependent variable is the phenomenon that the researcher observes and measures but does not control. In many cases, the goal of research is to demonstrate a causal effect of the independent variable on the dependent variable. Causation, however, cannot be fully established in a single study. Outside of a fully-controlled experiment, researchers can establish that a correlation or relationship exists between variables, but a cause-effect relationship cannot be determined. In the interpreting example, some measure of the interpreter's performance (e.g., disfluencies) would be the dependent measure that is presumably affected by the delivery rate (i.e., independent variable).

The primary variables of interest in a research question are the independent and dependent variables; however, additional variables can affect their relationship. Terminology varies widely for these additional variable types, which are sometimes subsumed under the term *extraneous variables*. For instance, a *confounding variable* is one that potentially alters or influences the relationship between the independent and dependent variables. As an example, in a study of text readability and translation performance, environmental factors like noise or lighting could affect the participants' work. If performance differs among participants, but the noise level and lighting varied when they completed the task, then these variables will confound the results. Consequently, the researcher cannot determine what caused the change in performance—the independent variable of text readability or the variation in the experimental setting. To eliminate confounds, researchers can either control the experimental setting or introduce one or both of these as a *control variable* in the statistical analysis. Model selection and the inclusion of control variables is a topic that belongs primarily to linear regression (see Chapter 12).

Research hypotheses

The difference between research questions and hypotheses is largely a matter of degree. Research questions are phrased in a broader sense, postulating the possibility that a relationship exists between variables. In contrast, research hypotheses presuppose that a relationship exists between the independent and dependent variables and, in some cases, predicts the nature or direction of the relationship.

Research hypotheses can be either *non-directional* or *directional*. A non-directional hypothesis would state, for example, that faster rate of delivery has some effect on the number of interpreter false starts. In this case, the researcher suggests that a difference exists between these two conditions, but does not provide a prediction. In contrast, a directional hypothesis would predict the actual relationship, stating that a faster delivery rate increases the number of interpreter false starts.

The distinction between directional and non-directional hypotheses is important because it influences the way in which data are analyzed. Without compelling evidence from previous studies or without a specific theory to support directional hypotheses, non-directional analysis should be preferred. In this volume, the emphasis is placed on non-directional hypotheses. This decision is based on the predominance of this type of statistical analysis and for simplicity of presentation.

Researchers refer to the statistical tests of non-directional hypotheses as *two-tailed tests*, while directional hypotheses are called *one-tailed tests*. The underlying mathematical processes of these tests do not change based on the nature of the hypotheses. The only change occurs in the final interpretation of the results. Therefore, a researcher who desires to test a directional hypothesis can follow the guidelines of this volume with only a minor shift in interpretation. We stress, however, that such one-tailed tests are not as common as non-directional hypotheses, especially for exploratory research. Finally, thanks to statistical computer software, tests are easily adapted for a one-tailed test.

Null and alternative hypotheses

To this point, the focus has been on the development of a research question or hypothesis; however, these are not tested directly. Instead, quantitative research relies on the notion of *refutability* or *falsifiability* and uses this concept to test a second, related hypothesis known as the *null hypothesis*. Simply put, the null

6 *Preparing*

hypothesis states that no difference or relationship exists between the variables that are included in the research question or hypothesis. In the interpreting example, the null hypothesis would state that there is no relationship between the number of interpreter false starts and the speed of the speaker. Rather than setting out to prove the research hypothesis, statistical testing instead seeks to reject the null hypothesis.

This approach provides the starting point for statistical hypothesis testing. However, before proceeding to testing the null hypothesis, an important conceptual distinction needs to be made. Note that nowhere in this volume will we refer to *proving* a hypothesis to be true or false. Instead, we will discuss this in terms of "rejecting the null hypothesis" or "failing to reject the null hypothesis." One study can never prove the existence of a difference or a relationship between variables. Particularly in the social sciences, theories are developed through ongoing inquiry involving multiple studies on a topic.

Similarly, a null hypothesis is never proven nor accepted as true. Failure to reject a null hypothesis represents a lack of evidence against it, which is not the same thing as evidence for it. An analogy is often drawn to the legal system, in which lack of conviction in a court of law does not constitute proof of innocence, merely lack of enough evidence for conviction. The same idea is expressed in the pithy saying that absence of evidence is not evidence of absence. Being built upon probability theory, mathematical statistics is not designed to generate conclusive proof and always contains a probability of error. Therefore, particular language must be employed in reporting statistical test results to portray the evidence correctly.

Several conventions exist for the notation of statistical hypotheses. Throughout this volume, we will use H_0 (pronounced H-nought) for the null hypothesis and H_1 for the alternative hypothesis. The statistical notation related to inferential statistics that use the null and alternative hypotheses will be presented in each chapter.

Research design

The manner in which research will be conducted follows from the research questions or hypotheses; the type of research must be in support of the project. Several types of research are conducted in T&I studies, including experimental, quasi-experimental, and observational research. Researchers must weigh the advantages and drawbacks of each type of research to determine which design is best for their specific research questions or hypotheses. Alternately, researchers can employ several methods, known as *triangulation*, to provide a varied and complementary perspective. The use of several methods, measures, or theoretical frameworks to examine a particular phenomenon or behavior improves the *robustness* of study and can corroborate findings across the various measures (Keyton 2014).

Experimental research

Research that involves the specific manipulation of conditions or variables in a controlled environment would be considered experimental research. Two major aspects of a project characterize experimental research: *control* and *random assignment*. In an experiment, the researcher controls and manipulates the independent variables under specified conditions. Control of the independent variable(s) and the experimental conditions is one way for researchers to avoid potential confounding variables. A criticism of experimental studies is precisely the contrived nature of many experimental tasks and the artificial environment in which they are conducted. This potential disadvantage must be weighed against the benefits derived from controlling the variables.

Random assignment is the second characteristic of experimental research designs. When participants are enrolled in a study, researchers randomly assign them to various conditions. In some cases, the conditions would be a control or treatment group; in other cases, the participants receive various treatments or perform under different conditions. Random assignment aims at uniformity between the various groups and helps prevent confounding variables from affecting the results. Random assignment is distinct from random sampling, discussed in Chapter 3, but the two concepts work in cooperation to assert that observed effects in an experiment are the result of the experimental treatment or condition.

Two common experimental research designs are *independent* and *repeated measures* designs. The distinction between these two designs is whether participants take part in only one condition of the study or if they are measured under multiple conditions. A participant enrolled in an independent measures experiment would be placed into either the control or treatment group, and would only complete the task specific to that group. One benefit of this design is that participants are not unnecessarily burdened with multiple treatments, and attrition is potentially reduced. A drawback, however, is the need for a greater number of participants to enroll in each of the study groups.

Repeated measures designs, in contrast, enroll participants into multiple conditions or treatment groups. For instance, an experiment that is investigating interpreting in various settings may have the same interpreter perform a task in multiple conditions. Another variant of repeated measures design is to measure a participant at multiple points in time. A benefit of any repeated measures design is that the amount of variability is mitigated since each participant serves as his or her own control. Many factors are held constant when the same participant is measured more than once. Because of the lower variance, fewer participants are required for the study and statistical properties are improved in many cases. A drawback, however, is that participants need to complete multiple tasks; in this scenario, there is a greater likelihood of missing data as the result of attrition, or the possibility of additional confounding variables, such as fatigue, order effects, or carryover effects.

Quasi-experimental research

Researchers are not always able to control the independent variables; at times these variables vary naturally so that the researcher cannot manipulate them. At other times, the independent variable will also preclude random allocation. In such instances, the research can be classified as *quasi-experimental*. Research in T&I

studies often falls into this category since most investigators do not randomly allocate participants into specific experimental groups or are interested in variables that exhibit *natural variation*. For example, students who have different languages as their L1 can be naturally sorted into groups. Observed differences between groups would be quasi-experimental because the researcher neither controlled nor randomly allocated the independent variable of L1.

The difference between experimental and quasi-experimental research is not a clear-cut distinction. Depending on the philosophical bent of investigators, this differentiation may not even exist. Gile (2016) notes that the latter term is relatively new and that the designation varies across disciplines. The nature of research in the social sciences further blurs the line between these two categories and observational studies. For instance, research on novices and experts cannot neatly divide participants into these two groups, since the underlying variable of experience lies on a continuum. However, researchers may operationalize this variable and then develop experimental protocols to examine differences in participant behavior based on the levels of another independent variable. Consequently, research may not be easily classified as experimental, quasi-experimental, or observational.

Observational research

Research that does not involve the direct manipulation of variables within a controlled setting and does not allow for random assignment of participants is classified as *observational*. In certain contexts, the distinction from quasi-experimental research is largely a matter of degree. Quantitative research can still be conducted in observational studies, often when the researcher cannot feasibly or ethically manipulate the independent variable (Cochran 1965). These studies can also be of particular use when initially exploring correlations between two variables in a natural setting. One of the benefits of observational research is the ability to observe participants in a naturalistic environment. Researchers must weigh this benefit with the tradeoff of decreased control of extraneous variables that is possible in experimental designs.

Baraldi and Mellinger (2016) describe the incorporation of observational studies into T&I and some of the many ways that they have been used. Studies in T&I run the gamut of observational practices, from ethnographic studies of translator and interpreters to less-invasive observation of translator behavior via keystroke logging or eye tracking. Findings from observational studies may serve as the foundation of future experimental studies or, conversely, can corroborate results and triangulate experimental findings that lack a degree of generalizability.

Note

1 Other research approaches exist, such as *abductive* research. For a discussion of this line of reasoning in T&I studies, see Saldanha and O'Brien (2014:15).

2 Sampling and ethics

The goal of quantitative research is to make statements about a *population* of interest. The conclusions are based on data collected from a *sample*, which is any subset of the population. Once a researcher has formulated a research question and selected an appropriate design, the next task is to collect a sample. The first part of this chapter describes methods to obtain a useful sample for describing and making conclusions about the population, as well as some of the challenges of that process.

The chapter's second section is devoted to ethical considerations, which should be present in all aspects of a research project, from formulation of an idea to final reporting. A primary element of ethical research involves sampling procedures, particularly when human participants are involved. Researchers not only need to treat participants in an ethical manner, but they must also consider ethical principles when designing and implementing a research protocol.

Generalization and representativeness

The process of reaching conclusions about a population is called *generalization* of a study's findings. The first task is to specify the particular population about which a study hopes to learn. A population is an abstraction of all the people or objects that a researcher hopes to describe or understand better, often with an eye toward prediction. Populations, within the context of empirical research, do not exclusively refer to people. Rather, a population can be composed of a group of texts or objects. Members of a population must share some set of common characteristics; however, the exact size and composition of a population is only fully known in rare cases. For instance, a research project might hope to draw conclusions about students enrolled in interpreting programs at universities, while a corpus-based study might define a population as Tolstoy's entire oeuvre. Furthermore, populations can vary dramatically in size. Some study might try to draw conclusions for all multilingual individuals in the world, while another might describe the work of translators working from Chinese into Russian.

In the process of applying statistical methods, research estimates the value of a *parameter*. A parameter is an unknown value that measures or describes some aspect of the population. An example of a parameter is the average (i.e., the arithmetic mean) of a population: for instance, the average height of all the buildings in Munich or the average number of bananas eaten in a year by residents of London. Parameters are specific to the referenced population. Therefore, generalization can only be made to the population specified at the outset of the study.

Parameters can be abstract because they represent measurements that are difficult to define or measure. Average job satisfaction of conference interpreters and the average self-confidence of translation students are both parameters that might be of interest. Operationalization of these concepts allows for statistical estimation of the parameters. Parameters can also be mathematically abstract, including an extreme measurement or the variability of a measurement. For instance, the rate of the fastest human translator in terms of words-per-minute is a parameter, as is the variability of hourly wages for certified court interpreters.

The method of learning about parameters is studying and measuring a sample of the population and calculating a *statistic* that provides its estimation. A statistic is a number that describes a sample and is used as an approximation of a population's parameter. In many cases, the population's parameters are denoted by Greek letters (e.g., μ for the average, σ for the standard deviation), and the sample's statistics are denoted by Latin letters (e.g., $\bar{X}$ for the average and s for the standard deviation). A parameter will never be completely known and can only be estimated by a statistic.

When a population is small enough to be fully enumerated, researchers can conduct a *census*, in which every member of the population is included in a research study. Of course, constraints of time, money, and practicality make this impossible in most cases. Therefore, data are collected not from the entire population but from a sample drawn from the population. Formally, the first step in drawing a sample is to define a *sampling frame*, which is a list of all members of the population that might be included in the sample. In an ideal situation, the sampling frame can be formally specified and includes every member of the population. In practice, there is likely to be a mismatch between the sampling frame and the population because not every member of the population is known or it would be impractical to make a formal list of every potential participant in the sample.

The primary goal in selecting a sample is to maximize the generalizability of the research results to the population. This is accomplished by ensuring the *representativeness* of the sample, meaning that the sample is an unbiased and accurate reflection of the underlying population. The task of sample selection is constrained by resources of time and money, as well as the availability and willingness of members of the population to consent to participate in the study. Statisticians have devoted significant effort to defining probability-based methods of sampling, while the reality of applied research often results in the need for nonprobability methods. Several examples of each are described in the next section.

Generalization and representativeness are challenged by three main types of error. First, *coverage error* occurs when a sampling frame does not include every member of the population. Not every member of the population will have a chance of being included in the sample in that case. Second, *sampling error* is the inevitable difference between observing only a subset of the population and a full census.

A sample statistic is an estimate of a population parameter, but the estimate will have a degree of error because of the particular members in the sample. Finally, in some cases participants are unwilling or unable to participate in a study. Any problems with gathering data from members of the sample is labeled *nonresponse error*, which leads to missing data. Surveys are particularly prone to this type of error, and the missing measurements can lead to biased or incorrect estimates.

Sampling techniques

Since a sample is a sub-group of a population, a method must be determined to identify and recruit sample participants. Techniques for collecting a sample fall into two broad categories: probability sampling and non-probability sampling. The advantages of probability sampling include minimizing sampling error and maximizing generalizability. However, probability sampling can be impossible for several reasons. For instance, the research may require a targeted sample of participants that are difficult to recruit with probability methods. In such cases, non-probability sampling may be more appropriate. Non-probability sampling may also be appropriate should the researcher believe that the variables of interest are relatively stable throughout the population so that generalization is still plausible.

Probability sampling

The most formally mathematical way to ensure representativeness is to use some form of random selection. Probability sampling techniques ensure that every member of the sampling frame has a known probability of inclusion in the selected sample. Statisticians have defined various methods to accomplish this; for a full treatment, see Cochran (1977). For research involving human participants, the difficulty of defining a sampling frame can limit the use of probability techniques, though random selection should be encouraged to whatever extent it is possible because it generally maximizes representativeness. Due to the nature of the object of study, corpus-based research can more readily employ probability-based techniques (see Halverson 1998 and Biber 1993 for an overview of sampling in corpus studies). In this section, we will briefly describe the four most common types of probability sampling: *simple random*, *systematic*, *stratified*, and *cluster sampling*.

In simple random sampling, every unit in the sampling frame has an equal chance of being selected. The subjects are identified independently by random selection, likely with the aid of a computer's random number generator. This type of sampling is easily implemented but only when a complete, formal sampling frame is available. Therefore, it is more commonly employed in applied research that does not involve human subjects. Wu and Xia (1995) provide an example of random selection of words in an English–Chinese parallel corpus.

Systematic sampling describes the process of selecting participants from a sampling frame that are evenly spaced in the list. For example, every tenth name on the list could be selected. Rather than beginning with the first name, a random number is generated to identify the first participant, and systematic selection continues from that point. For example, in a thesis related to the translation of short texts, Cheung (2010) had access to a full list of the approximately 3,200 street names in Hong Kong and systematically selected every fifth item in the list for inclusion in the study. When the sampling frame is randomly ordered, systematic sampling is an easy way to draw an unbiased sample. If the sampling frame is ordered according to some scheme, it is important to check that the ordering does not result in a bias.

To collect a stratified sample, a researcher first identifies various subgroups of the population, called *strata*. Then a separate sample is drawn from each of the strata. This method helps ensure that various levels of a population are represented, even in a small sample and even if some of the levels are minorities. If a research project hopes to represent various perspectives adequately in a small sample, stratification may be necessary to ensure participation. For instance, Shaw, Grbić, and Franklin (2004) conducted a qualitative study that sampled lower-level students, upper-level students, and a recent graduate of interpreting programs.

Cluster sampling involves two steps: first, the selection of a certain cluster of a population and, second, a random sample of participants from within that cluster. Often, a population is geographically dispersed with a specific population being naturally grouped in clusters. An example would be first selecting a subset of all university-level translation programs in a country and then drawing a random sample only from the universities that were initially identified. A main benefit of cluster sampling is the cost savings of conducting a study in a few places. This method is useful when a population of interest is concentrated in distinct clusters.

Non-probability sampling

While we stress that probability sampling techniques are ideal for ensuring representativeness and maximizing generalizability, they cannot always be implemented. A researcher may be unable to sufficiently define a sampling frame. Identified participants from a random sampling technique may be unwilling to participate. Finally, translation and interpreting (T&I) studies often require participants with specific skills or traits so that *purposive sampling* is necessary.

Researchers may need to recruit individuals for participation in a study without identifying them randomly. Li (2004) argues that this kind of purposive sampling can more effectively ensure the inclusion of a variety of perspectives. While arguing in the context of qualitative research, this observation applies to quantitative studies as well. Conversely, Gile (1998) discusses the inherent challenges and potential bias of using small, targeted sampling techniques in interpreting studies. Researchers must take care to avoid bias in recruiting participants for a study.

Convenience sampling is particularly prone to concerns about possible biases or lack of representativeness. Sometimes convenience sampling is the only way to gain access to a population. If a researcher wants to gain access to observe or record conference interpreters working in a booth, he or she will need to develop contacts and relationships with a specific venue and group of interpreters.

The sample is the only convenient way for the researcher to access the desired data. Often, researchers have access to groups of students who can be incentivized or required to participate in research studies. This practice can be convenient, especially for pilot studies. However, the practice raises practical concerns about the representativeness of the population as well as ethical concerns about the level of coercion involved. Problems of convenience sampling of college students is not a recent phenomenon. McNemar (1946: 333) bluntly drew attention to the issue:

> The existing science of human behavior is largely the science of the behavior of sophomores. Too much research effort is expended on college students with subsequent waste of journal space devoted to speculation concerning whether the findings hold for mankind in general.

Convenience sampling is quite common in all social science research, but whether a better, more representative sample can be obtained through other means should always be a consideration of the planning process of any research project.

One way to avoid the concerns of convenience sampling is *volunteer sampling*. Advertising widely about a research study can bring in a sample of people for the study. Logistically, this process can be beneficial for a research project because people with an interest in the study and the time to participate self-identify. However, the motivation to participate can bring its own set of biases, and volunteer samples often result in participants with more extreme views on the topic of interest.

Another non-probability technique called *snowball sampling* is particularly effective for reaching minority or hidden populations. A population might be impossible to identify for purposes of sampling. Therefore, a researcher might recruit a known member of a community to identify and recruit other members for participation. The snowball sample grows as each participant identifies further potential individuals for recruitment. Snowball sampling is closely related to *network sampling*, in which a researcher uses an existing social network (real or virtual) to reach people who share a common trait. These techniques can help gain access by having members of the population help with recruitment. For instance, a researcher might want to study hearing children who grew up in a household with a deaf parent. Identifying such individuals would be difficult or impossible, but a snowball or network sampling technique might be able to tap into an existing community network to procure a purposive sample.

Ethics

As we noted in the introduction to this chapter, high-quality research is grounded in ethical practices through all phases of designing, conducting, and reporting research. Ethical research guidelines and practices span academic inquiry at the broadest level, but the focus of its treatment in this volume will be ethical considerations as they relate to quantitative research methods. Levin (2011: 465) describes the unfortunate reality that ethical practices espoused in research training programs do not necessarily coincide with the actual practice of professional research and writing. However, when they work in combination, ethical research practices and sound quantitative methods ensure that results are valid and generalizable to the greatest extent possible. Shortcuts in either area can impact the usefulness of the results.

This chapter focuses on ethical issues related to designing and conducting research. These phases typically fall within the realm of *research ethics*, while the later phase of reporting is often thought of as part of *research integrity* or *academic integrity*. This distinction is often more convenient than practical, since ethics and integrity need to be addressed throughout the research project (Israel 2015). Issues related to ethical reporting and academic integrity will be discussed in Part V of this volume.

Academic inquiry into ethics or moral philosophy can be divided into three major branches: meta-ethics, normative ethics, and applied ethics. In the context of research, the latter two are particularly salient; therefore, we will forego a theoretical discussion of different approaches to ethical inquiry (e.g., relativism, universalism, or non-cognitivism). Moreover, several of these perspectives on ethics can complicate the researcher's ability to determine a specific course of action when encountering an ethical dilemma (see Israel and Hay 2006: 12–22 for a more detailed discussion). Instead, the discussion of ethics here will be limited to the ways in which ethics have been codified into regulations. Likewise, the relationship of ethics to quantitative methodology and the application to research will be addressed.[1]

Regulatory bodies that oversee research are constituted at a number of levels, including the supranational, national, and university level. The overarching mandate of these bodies includes upholding ethical principles, ensuring the integrity of the research, and protecting the safety of human participants. These ethical principles appear in international agreements and declarations as well as some national regulations. The implementation of these standards is overseen by ethics review boards or committees that examine potential research projects and provide oversight of the entire research process.[2] In the United States, for example, the Office of Human Research Protections (OHRP) regulates the establishment and conduct of Institutional Review Boards (IRB) at research institutions, including academic institutions and medical facilities. These IRB committees rely on federal regulations to define their responsibilities and to empower them to review, approve, or reject research projects receiving funding of any kind from the U.S. government.[3]

The rationale for such stringent oversight is a reaction to historical improprieties involving human subjects. Consequently, the latter part of the twentieth century included the adoption and revisions of major agreements that govern the ethical treatment of research subjects, including the *Nuremburg Code*, the *Declaration of Helsinki*, and the *Declaration of Geneva*. The three major considerations enumerated in these documents are voluntary participation, autonomy, and respect for the individual. These principles took on added importance in reaction to human experimentation and war crimes that took place during World

War II.[4] Improprieties continued despite attempts at regulation, as made clear by Beecher's (1966) influential meta-analysis of ethical errors and questionable practices for research reports published in reputable medical journals. In particular, twenty-two examples are provided of papers in which a known effective treatment was withheld from patients. Only two of the fifty studies that Beecher reviewed mentioned participant consent. Beecher comments that a responsible investigator is the best safeguard.

In the United States, responsible and ethical behavior are guided predominantly by the *Belmont Report*, which was adopted into the U.S. Federal Register in 1979. This report highlights three central tenets that should be observed in research involving human subjects: *respect for persons, beneficence*, and *justice*. In addition, discipline-specific scholarly organizations often adopt specific codes of ethics for members of their academic community. Smith (2000: 5), for example, describes two supplementary moral principles that underlie psychology research involving human participants, namely *trust* and *scientific integrity*. Many of these concepts are related specifically to research involving human subjects, yet they are worth considering to the extent possible in all research projects.

As described in the *Belmont Report*, two ethical convictions are encompassed in the first principle of *respect for persons*: researchers should treat all individuals as *autonomous agents* and act to protect individuals with *diminished authority*. The notion of autonomy echoes the principles outlined in the bioethical declarations mentioned previously. Participants should be able to act independently and should be treated as capable of making their own decisions. The ability of a potential research participant to consider his or her participation in a research study is the foundation of *informed consent*, which is a commonplace feature of research involving human participants. Furthermore, the ability to withdraw from the study without penalty acknowledges the ability of a participant to act autonomously.

Likewise, researchers must ensure that potential research participants who are unable to act autonomously and voluntarily are afforded additional protections. Children and prisoners are traditionally cited as important protected classes; however, this protection extends to other constituencies.[5] Researchers in T&I studies, for example, should consider issues of limited-language proficiency and language access. By no means an exhaustive list, other aspects that may warrant extra care include the following: socioeconomic status, sex, gender identity, race, and ethnicity. The American Psychological Association (APA; 2010) *Ethical Principles of Psychologists and Code of Conduct* provides guidance on these considerations and how issues related to respect for persons might be resolved.

The second principle, *beneficence*, refers to the obligation to maximize benefits while minimizing risk and also to avoid harm to participants (called *nonmaleficence*). Smith (2000) describes the research risk–benefit binary as one that cannot be equated with a generic cost–benefit analysis. According to Smith, researchers should not weigh the risks of participants solely against the benefits for society, thus obviating the researcher's moral obligation. Instead, one manifestation of these principles is the adoption of a theory-driven approach to research so that human participants who take part in a research study are not unnecessarily exposed to risk from exploratory work. Research that adheres to higher standards of design and quantitative analysis will have conclusions that are grounded in the literature and will be more likely to satisfy the moral principle of beneficence (Rosnow and Rosenthal 2011: 51–2).

Researchers must take the necessary measures to help mitigate any risks that might arise from participants taking part in the project. As a part of sound research design and analysis, researchers should be mindful to design protocols in a way that fulfills the study's purpose without harming participants. Participants may not encounter considerable risk as the result of their participation in T&I research studies; however, this consideration should not be discarded. For example, researchers may propose a study that involves an element of deception. This type of research is appropriate within specific contexts and can be unavoidable if the researcher hopes to avoid confounds and maintain the integrity of the quantitative data.[6] Eyde (2000) provides insight on challenges inherent to research involving deception and outlines issues related to unforeseen problems, researchers' responsibilities, and the impact on participants. Hertwig and Ortmann (2008) review the literature on the use of deception in empirical studies and identify gaps between the prescribed rules of conduct and reality.

The third principle, *justice*, is often equated with the notions of fairness, equal treatment, or equal distribution of benefit for participants in a research study. This consideration is multi-faceted, since it involves both sampling practices and the treatment of participants. Inclusion criteria, for example, must consider whether the participants that are being recruited into a study have equal opportunity for inclusion. For instance, the recruitment of a particular population may be easy (e.g., students); however, the question must be raised whether other potential participants are unnecessarily excluded. Henrich, Heine, and Norenzayan (2010) describe behavioral science research that routinely draws on a very specific WEIRD population (Western, Educated, Industrialized, Rich, and Democratic). The authors identify potential bias in research that attempts to generalize the human population when the vast majority of participants are undergraduate students enrolled in behavioral science courses. As the authors describe:

> the high-socioeconomic status (SES), secular Western populations that have been the primary target of study thus far, appear unusual in a global context, based on their peculiarly narrow reliance, relative to the rest of humanity, on a single foundation for moral reasoning (based on justice, individual rights, and the avoidance of harm to others; cf. Haidt & Graham 2007).
> (Henrich, Heine, and Norenzayan 2010: 73)

In the case of students, researchers should also consider whether they are a vulnerable population since they are easily accessible. An implicit power differential exists between the professor-cum-researcher and students, which may result in latent coercion. Researchers ought to be mindful of whether the systematic recruitment of specific participants into studies is equitable and appropriate for the research project's object of study.

Research in T&I often investigates specific participant variables (e.g., years of experience, language combination, directionality), and many of these research questions will dictate sampling techniques. When designing research protocols, researchers should attempt to eliminate, to the extent possible, any potential confounds. Mark and Lenz-Watson (2011) suggest that biased research designs may decrease beneficence and justice. The sampling practices and research methodology, therefore, should be subject to considerable scrutiny prior to conducting the study. The interaction of beneficence and justice should be recognized, since the inclusion of certain participants in a study may provide certain benefit, while those excluded from participation are unable to derive the same.

Justice is also related to the equitable treatment of participants. This concept goes beyond the idea of being respectful of everyone involved in the study; instead all participants should have equal access to any potential benefits that could be derived. For example, participants occasionally are recruited with incentives, such as a gift card or payment. All participants should be able to receive this incentive, regardless of whether they complete the study or exercise their right to withdraw. Another common example is from medical sciences, in which placebo treatments are given. If a potential effective treatment is available, upon conclusion of the study those participants who did not receive a therapeutic treatment should have access to it in the interest of justice.

The requirements of justice can often be enhanced via *debriefing* of participants. Upon completion of the study (or withdrawal should the participant choose to do so), researchers should allow participants to know the purpose and eventually the results of the study. This debriefing can take many forms, including a conversation with the researcher, a handout with additional information, or contact information for later follow-up. Keyton (2014) describes a situation in which the experimental design offers training to only one study group before collecting outcome measures. The author suggests that the researcher should offer the same training to those who were initially denied this opportunity. Addressing the moral principle of justice would be particularly important in the context of pedagogical research in T&I studies. Lastly, debriefing is imperative when studies incorporate elements of deception. Eyde (2000: 69–71) provides guidance on the debriefing process for such studies.

Informed consent

When research involves human subjects, the concept of informed consent is a vital part of ethical design. In many countries, researchers are ethically (and at times, legally) bound to reveal information about a research project so that participants can voluntarily consent to participation. The requirements vary among regulatory bodies, but consent forms are often required to include information such as an explanation of the study's purpose and a general description of the project; the inherent risks and potential benefits of participation; contact information for questions or complaints; and participants' rights, including the right to withdraw from the study without penalty. Researchers who are undertaking research involving human participants should consult the guidelines provided by the overseeing regulatory body for specific information that must be included.

This component of a research project should be considered in the context of quantitative research methods for several reasons. First, quantitative data are often obtained from human subjects. Second, data obtained from human subjects are often analyzed and contextualized within a larger body of scholarship. As noted in the section on beneficence, theory-driven data help to avoid questionable research practices such as data dredging. Research projects are conceived with the aim of generalizing findings to a larger population. These results will naturally be compared with other scholarly works, which presupposes a discussion of participant behavior or data. In doing so, participants should be aware of how their data will be used.

To provide a fictitious example, quantitative data related to the translation process might be analyzed as a factor of translation quality. These participants might be asked to produce a translation while their production behavior is recorded using keystroke logging. Specific aspects of their behavior, such as translation speed, pauses, hesitations, and revisions, will then be related to translation quality markers. Without informed consent and an appropriate debriefing after the task, participants might be unaware that their behavior during the experimental task will be interpreted in this light. If results suggest that specific translation behavior is more prone to error production, participants may prefer not to participate or not to have their identity revealed. This preference may be an attempt to avoid any negative impact on their professional reputation. Informed consent about the research study allows for participants to understand any risks and benefits of the study. Faden, Beauchamp, and King (1986) provide extensive treatment on the history and development of informed consent, while the American Psychological Association (2010) provides practical guidance and ethical mandates on its use in human subjects research.

Of particular concern during the consent process is whether participants understand the consent process or any forms that they may sign. Researchers ought to provide the opportunity for participants to ask questions related to the study in order to improve comprehension of the various components of the informed consent document. In a meta-analysis of informed consent processes in biomedical research, Nishimura et al. (2013) indicate that extended discussions with participants and enhanced consent forms can improve participants' overall understanding without impacting recruitment.

Language usage can impact participant understanding. Cico, Vogeley, and Doyle (2011) highlight the importance of comprehension in the informed consent process and recognize the role played by language and terminology. This sentiment is echoed by Tamariz et al. (2013), in that inadequate health literacy of participants can be detrimental to the informed consent process. These considerations can be further compounded when informed consent is obtained in multiple languages. Kithinji and Kass (2010), for example, describe the challenge of assessing readability of non-English-language consent forms. Their case study of a Kiswahili translation of consent forms raised the question about the qualifications of the translators providing these renditions as well as the method of their delivery. In the case of Kiswahili and some other languages spoken in the region, the written format of informed consent may have hindered comprehension, given the oral tradition of these speakers. Differentiated delivery of informed consent documents may lead to differing levels of comprehension.

Research on interpreting has also provided insight on the informed consent process and should help shape T&I scholars' research practices when working with human subjects. Research and position papers on sight translation and its relationship to obtaining informed consent strongly suggest that researchers should create translations of informed consent documents. The temptation might exist to create an English language version of the informed consent document and then have this document sight translated for non-English-speaking participants. Reliance on an interpreter to sight translate informed consent documents, however, may prove problematic. For instance, Clifford (2005) describes the interventionist role that an interpreter may have to take in healthcare settings to obtain informed consent. Feinauer and Lesch (2013) also note challenges for interpreters when asked to perform sight translations of informed consent documents. The National Council on Interpreting in Health Care (NCIHC; 2009) has issued a working paper suggesting limits to the amount of sight translation, particularly for legal and consent documents. The Standard Guide for Language Interpretation Services (ASTM 2089: 2007) also states that healthcare providers are responsible for obtaining informed consent and that interpreters should not be asked to serve as a witness to the signed document.

Regulatory bodies may not always have the requisite expertise to address some of these issues related to T&I. Researchers who will require informed consent in multiple languages, therefore, bear the onus of responsible and ethical research practices. T&I scholars are well-positioned to lend their expertise to reflect upon these issues. Researchers are advised to consider translation and language issues of informed consent documentation prior to submitting any research protocol for review.

Anonymity and confidentiality

The process of informed consent can include a set of conditions under which the research will be conducted (Israel 2015). Among the more common and important conditions is a degree of anonymity or confidentiality. The terms *anonymity* and *confidentiality* are sometimes confused, and the researcher must indicate to potential participants how the data collected will be handled, used, and stored. A simplistic differentiation between these two ideas is related to identification—anonymous participants do not have their identity known by anyone involved in the research process, whereas confidentiality relates to the protection of identifiable information and data. Guarantees of anonymity may be restricted to relatively few research designs of interest for T&I scholars (e.g., online surveys). Therefore, the primary focus here will be on confidentiality.

Confidentiality in research has been a topic of interest to ethicists and researchers because it involves the ideas of trust and beneficence. The participant–researcher relationship implies a level of trust between both parties. On the one hand, the participant consents to participate in a research project. Researchers rely on the goodwill of participants to take part in good faith in following a specific set of instructions, guidelines, or tasks. On the other hand, researchers agree to meet the principles of ethical research by reducing potential risks to the participants and to avoid harming them. In doing so, research studies must identify and attempt to limit risks that could arise from sensitive information about participants being revealed. For example, an interpreting student might not want his or her opinion on a specific pedagogical practice to be directly attributable, to avoid offending a teacher. This meta-reflection on sensitive data are important since the researcher faces competing tensions of maintaining confidentiality and the dissemination of research findings.

As a general rule, researchers should outline specific protocols that will be followed during the research project to improve confidentiality. For example, data should only be accessible to the researcher or the research team. Only the information needed to examine the specific object of study should be collected. When collecting demographic information, researchers might consider collecting categorical information to avoid the collection of several data points that can be triangulated back to a specific person. For instance, knowing a person's age, gender, race, nationality, and working languages might be enough to identify a professional interpreter. Therefore, researchers should consider whether these data need to be collected or collect them as broader categories. Age could be divided into categories such as 18–30, 31–45, 46 and older. Alternatively, these demographics might be reported in the aggregate to eliminate issues of confidentiality.

When reporting data, researchers can use pseudonyms or participant numbers to avoid references to a specific person. Gender-neutral language can be used in research reports to further maintain confidentiality. Data should be stored in a way accessible only by the researcher and for a specific period of time and then subsequently destroyed. Grant-funded research projects occasionally require data to be publicly accessible in data repositories. In such cases, this *limited confidentiality* should be divulged to the research participant during the consent process. Moreover, the data should be de-identified as much as possible. Alternatively, participants may be given the option to exclude their information from these publicly accessible datasets.

The use of Internet-based research collection tools has required the concepts of anonymity and confidentiality to be re-examined, particularly with regard to safeguarding participant data. Mellinger (2015) in his discussion of Internet-mediated research in translation process research describes the possibility of identifiable information about participants being recorded during data collection (e.g., IP addresses). The collected dataset can be de-identified (i.e., the IP address removed) to avoid any potential links back to the participant. Similarly, Mellinger describes additional data security issues when data are transmitted via the Internet from the participant to the researcher. The way in which researchers plan to safeguard data must be taken into account when designing research projects to reduce possible breaches in confidentiality. In another setting, Gosling and Mason (2015) describe Internet research in the field of psychology and describe problems that can arise related to anonymity and data collection. Practical application of ethical principles is constantly evolving, and should be considered throughout the research process.

Notes

1 While it is impossible to provide a complete treatment of research ethics as they relate to quantitative methodology, see Panter and Sterba (2011) for a collection that addresses ethics and their role in research design, analysis, and reporting.
2 For an overview of research ethics and regulatory practices and their role in social science research, see Israel and Hay (2006). Israel (2015) provides an updated version of this volume, and both works provide geographically relevant, country-specific regulatory practices.
3 Institutional Review Boards are not without criticism. Schrag (2010) criticizes a universal approach to human subjects research that is derived primarily from biomedical entities to the exclusion of social scientists.
4 This commonly-adopted historical point of reference is perhaps an over-simplification. Israel and Hay (2006) note human experimentation was being conducted prior to WWII in several countries without the regulatory purview that is in place today. For information on medical research during this period in the U.S., see Lederer (1997).
5 In the U.S., 45 CFR 46 "Human Subjects Research," which constitutes part of what is often referred to as the *Common Rule*, provides special protections to several constituencies, namely children, prisoners, pregnant women, human fetuses, and neonates.
6 Sieber, Iannuzzo, and Rodriguez (1995) review various ways in which deception has been employed in research practices and identify seven types of non-informing of participants.

3 Measurement

Once variables of interest are identified and operationalized, an appropriate measurement process must be selected. In the abstract, measurement involves a systematic rule for assigning numbers to an observed characteristic. This formal definition encompasses simple demographic traits and easily measured variables such as a length of time. However, measurement also applies to more abstract or difficult-to-define concepts such as speech disfluencies, cognitive flexibility, job satisfaction, and task performance. Each of these concepts requires an objective, reliable, and valid measurement before it can be included as a variable in statistical analysis. Accurate numbers are the foundation of quantitative analysis; the cliché "garbage in, garbage out" correctly reflects the fundamental flaw in proceeding to analyze data that resulted from inaccurate measurement.

Measurement involves the entire process of assigning a number, including the measurement tool, its precision, and the skill of the administrator who determines the assigned number. When measuring physical distance, a tape measure is only useful for measuring centimeters if it is correctly marked. Furthermore, if the tape is marked in centimeters, it cannot be used to determine measurements denoted in millimeters. Finally, the measurement can be biased or completely incorrect if the person using the tape makes an error in handling the tool, reading the measurement, or recording the result. Of course, all of this presumes that the correct tool has been selected for the job. A tape measure will be of absolutely no use for measuring time or translation quality.

In this chapter, we address some of the basic issues of measurement.[1] We begin by describing the four levels of measurement and their relationship to the selection of appropriate statistical analyses. Then we introduce the general concepts of validity and reliability after which we discuss surveys as a tool for measuring abstract constructs. The chapter closes with a consideration of the effects of technology on measurement.

Levels of measurement

The measurement of different types of phenomena can require different tools and methods. The nature of the information that can be reflected in a measurement has been codified into four commonly recognized levels of measurement, based on the classification scheme devised by Stevens (1946): categorical (also called nominal), ordinal, interval, and ratio. The order of levels reflects the amount of detail encoded in the number, with categorical data being the simplest and ratio the most complex. In the operationalization of a variable, the measurement process will imply a certain degree of precision. It is important to recognize that the level of measurement applies to the data and not to the variable itself. Variables can be measured at different levels, and we will reinforce this idea after these levels have been described.

Levels of measurement are related to the selection of statistical analysis; however, the level of measurement does not fully determine the appropriate mathematical tools. Some influential papers and textbooks of the mid-twentieth century argued that parametric and nonparametric tests should only be applied to certain types of data (e.g., Stevens 1946; Siegel 1956). An early opponent of this idea pointed out in a satirical paper that the numbers themselves are unaware of their origin and level of measurement (Lord 1953). Furthermore, measurement theory and statistical theory are distinct (Gaito 1980). The valid implementation of inferential statistics does not rely on the level of measurement but on the mathematical assumptions of the particular test and the representativeness of the sample (Marcus-Roberts and Roberts 1987). Nevertheless, measurements are the inputs for statistical tests, and thus their levels influence both the choice of statistical test and its interpretation. Some of these considerations will be mentioned briefly in this section, but the purpose here is primarily definitional and descriptive for application in subsequent chapters dedicated to statistical analysis.

Categorical data

Some characteristics can only be identified, distinguished, and categorized but not otherwise measured. When such differentiation is the sole determinant of a measurement, the variable is called *categorical* or *nominal* level data. Such data are not intrinsically numerical because they represent qualities that are either present or absent. For ease of data management and analysis, though, categories can be assigned numbers. The biological sex of participants in a study might be assigned a value of zero for men and one for women, for example. When a categorical variable has only two levels, as in this example, it is sometimes referred to as a *binary* or *dummy* variable. Categorical data are mathematically discrete variables because only certain numerical values are allowed.

While a rule for assigning numbers to categories must be completely standardized and systematically applied, the numerical values are arbitrary. For instance, postal codes identify particular towns or neighborhoods in many countries, and athletes often wear a unique number on their jerseys. Similarly, participants in a study are often numbered, which also assists in maintaining confidentiality or anonymity of data. If an experimental design involves a treatment and a control group, members of the groups will be assigned different values of a nominal identifying variable.

Categorical level data can also be the result of answers to a questionnaire. Demographic information is a common source of categorical variables. A researcher might ask participants to identify their native language and assign values of one to German, two to French, three to Japanese, and so on. Because the numbers of a categorical variable are arbitrary, arithmetic cannot be conducted on the numbers. Therefore, no mathematical or logical reason exists to draw the conclusion that German plus French equals Japanese because one plus two equals three. The mathematical property of discreteness is also reinforced by this example, because there is no value of 1.5 that lies halfway between German and French; only the predefined categories and their associated numerical values are possible. Furthermore, while sequential numbering is often logical, the numbers could also have been assigned such that German was four, French was twelve, and Japanese was twenty. At no point should categorical data be used for arithmetic such as addition.

To allow consistent application of a systematic rule for assigning numbers, the categories of a nominal variable should fulfill two primary requirements. First, the categories should be *mutually exclusive*, meaning that every unit of analysis can be classified into one and only one category. Second, the categories should be *exhaustive*, meaning that every unit of analysis can be placed into an appropriate category. Categories should be defined and refined to meet these two standards and to measure the variable in a manner consistent with the research goals. For example, geographic information can be collected at various levels. In an international sample, a survey may ask for country of origin, while a country-specific survey might ask for a respondent's home state, district, or region. To be exhaustive, categorical variables often need to include a category labeled "other" or "miscellaneous" as a response for people, objects, or observations that do not belong to a listed category. Since respondents are usually requested to answer every question, this "forced choice" format requires an alternative category for impossible-to-classify items. In a well-designed categorical scale the miscellaneous category should not represent a large percentage of the responses. If it does, the scale should be re-examined for potential inclusion of additional categories.

The analytical value of categorical variables is three-fold. First, they allow for the creation of frequency tables in displaying descriptive statistics. In this way, categorical variables are useful in summarizing demographic and characteristic information, and frequency tables can be subsequently analyzed using chi-squared tests. Second, categorization is necessary for statistical tests that make comparisons between groups, primarily t-tests and analysis of variance (ANOVA). Third, dummy variables allow for categorical variables to be included in regression analysis. All of these uses will be described in subsequent chapters dedicated to the various statistical tests.

Ordinal data

The second level of measurement involves both identifying a trait and ranking the observations. The resulting data are said to be measured on an *ordinal* scale. For a physical trait, such as height, observations such as the tallest person, the second tallest person, and so on allow for easy ranking without the need for a more precise tool. Therefore, one advantage of the ordinal scale is that it can save time and effort in assigning numbers to observations.

Even more importantly, ordinal level data can be used to assign rankings to observations that would otherwise be difficult to quantify. In Dillinger (1994), participants interpreted two brief English texts into French in an experimental setting. An ordinal scale was used to assess the quality of the interpretation of linguistic features, with zero indicating absence, one indicating a semantic change, two indicating a paraphrase, and three indicating a verbatim interpretation. Language proficiency scales provide other examples of ordinal data by defining categories of language proficiency using a limited number of ranked levels.[2]

The previous two examples indicate a certain ambiguity in the use of ranks as the definition of ordinal level data. There is a difference between ranking every observation in the way that participants ranked every text in Dillinger's (1994) study and creating large groups with an inherent order as with ACTFL proficiency levels. When large categories are created by ranks so that many individuals or observations can receive the same rank, an ordinal level variable is often treated as a categorical variable. For instance, the identification of categories such as "novice" and "experienced" provide an example where a complex phenomenon such as translation skill is collapsed into two categories. Though the categories can be properly ranked, they are generally considered categories for the purpose of mathematical analysis. Conversely, when every observation is assigned a unique rank, such as ranking words by their frequency of use, the ranks are more similar to continuous numbers and treating them as such in statistical testing is more appropriate.

An important caveat of ordinal data are that the spacing between ranks cannot be assumed to be equal. In a race, the first place finisher might beat her nearest rival by only one second, while the third place finisher crosses the finish line fifteen seconds later. This nonlinearity was an initial cause for Stevens's (1946) concern regarding the application of certain mathematical tools. Nonparametric statistics can sometimes use this nonlinearity property to their advantage by limiting the influence of outliers and conducting valid inference for otherwise difficult-to-manage data. However, the application of parametric statistics to ordinal level data has continued to expand in the development of theoretical statistics.

Ordinal level data still constitute a forced choice response in many cases. For example, Bowker and Ciro (2015) had professional translators rank the translations of Systran, Reverso, and Google Translate. By the nature of the task, the respondents were forced to use the numbers one, two, and three in their ranking, even if a translator felt that two of the translations were very similar and one was unacceptable or incorrect in some way. In selecting ordinal level measurement, a researcher should consider if simple ranking could possibly mask large differences in quality. If such an outcome is a concern, more precise measurement might be preferable.

If ranks are approximately equally spaced, ordinal level data can begin to approximate the interval level of measurement. For instance, the ranking of machine translation output could be rated on a three-point scale of unsatisfactory,

satisfactory, and exemplary. The resulting figure is technically ranked and therefore ordinal, but the relatively equal spacing suggests a more precise level of measurement is attained. Therefore, the level of some measurement tools cannot be easily ascertained, and the four categories are neither strictly separated nor universally agreed upon. The next subsection will provide more examples of the challenges of drawing this distinction.

Interval data

When a measurement includes equal intervals, the data are said to be measured on an *interval* scale. Differences in the numerical values can be associated with real, observable differences with a high level of agreement between observers. The use of an interval scale also implies the existence of a measurement of zero, though the zero point can be arbitrary or impossible to observe in a practical setting. Interval data are mathematically continuous, because any real number can be assigned to an observation. The one shortcoming of an interval scale is that multiples and ratios are meaningless.

A classic example of data measurement at an interval scale is temperature. At this level of measurement, intervals do represent identical changes in the amount of heat. So a change in temperature from 10 to 15 degrees Celsius involves the same amount of heat as a change from 20 to 25 degrees Celsius. Calculating the difference between two observations is meaningful. Moreover, both the Fahrenheit and Celsius scales include the number zero, but in neither case does the zero indicate a complete lack of heat. The zero point is arbitrary.[3] Finally, the meaninglessness of multiples is also evident for temperature; there is no meaningful sense in which 80 degrees Fahrenheit is twice as hot as 40 degrees.

There is occasionally overlap and controversy in determining whether observations are ordinal or interval levels. Standardized tests such as the TOEFL or SAT are often considered to be measured on an interval scale. Similarly, IQ is often treated as interval level data, but a number of psychometricians argue that it should more properly be considered ordinal since the 10-point difference between 110 and 120 cannot be declared equivalent to the same interval difference between 115 and 125.

This same controversy over level of measurement applies to summative survey scales. If a respondent is asked to respond to a statement on a five-point scale from strongly disagree to strongly agree, the question is whether the answers are simply a ranking of the person's opinions or if the intervals between the answers are equivalent. If the difference between any two points is identical across the scale, then such instruments provide measurement at an interval level. In the next section on survey design we discuss Likert-type scales, which can usually be treated as interval level measurements. However, if a person is asked a similar question with categories of "never," "seldom," and "often," then the equality of intervals might be more questionable and the data considered ordinal. Once again, the four levels of measurement do allow for overlap and difficult-to-classify cases.

Ratio data

The final level of measurement is called the *ratio* level because it allows comparisons of division to be made; for example, three times as much or half as much of a given measurement is meaningful. Furthermore, the ratio level includes the recognition of a unique and meaningful definition of zero. Most physical quantities fall into this category: distance, volume, time, and weight, to name a few. Money can be measured on a ratio scale, because it is meaningful to say that someone has twice as much money as someone else, and the meaning of having zero euros is also uniquely defined.

Ratio-level data possesses all of the properties of the lower levels. The measurement is still capable of identification, ranking, and defining equal intervals. Thus, the ratio level is the most detailed of the four levels. Data measured at this level can be used in any mathematical operation.

Transformation of data

The level of measurement is not fully determined by the construct being measured; the chosen measurement method plays a significant role. The nature of the research question, the relative importance of a given variable, and constraints of time and expense can all influence the chosen level of measurement. Following data collection, the level of measurement can be transformed from a higher level to a lower one. In other words, ratio level can be transformed into interval level, both of which can be converted into ordinal data, and all three of which can be transformed into categorical data. But the reverse direction is never possible; for example, categorical data cannot be transformed into interval level data.

The same variable can be measured at various levels of measurement or transformed from one level to another after data collection. An example is the gas mileage of a motor vehicle. Perhaps the most intuitive measurement is to report the actual number of miles per gallon, which is measured at the ratio level. However, cars can also be ranked in terms of mileage, with one model getting the best mileage, another the second best, and so on. The same variable of gas mileage is thus measured at the lower ordinal level. The example can even be extended to categorical data by creating mutually exclusive and exhaustive categories such as 0 to 10, 11 to 20, and so on, with the last category perhaps being defined as any number greater than 50 miles per gallon. The nature of the research will determine the necessary level of precision in the measurement.

Transformations involving categorical variables are relatively common. One type of such transformations is the redefinition of categorical or ordinal variables for the purpose of assigning different groups for analysis. For example, a study conducted in Canada, the United States, and Mexico might ask participants for their home state or province, but the researcher could later reassign these categories to country-level data for use in analysis. A second example is the compression of a continuous variable into categories. For instance, certification exams generally result in a continuous score that is converted into the dichotomous pass/fail decision. A similar example is years of professional translation experience being reapportioned into the categories of novice and experienced.

Another common transformation is to convert interval or ratio-level data into ranks for use in nonparametric statistics. The continuous numbers are reassigned their corresponding ranks so that the observations 2.56, 3.3, 1.8, and 1.4 would instead by measured as 3, 4, 2, and 1, respectively. This rank transformation of the data can allow for robust estimation that avoids the influence of outlying observations. We will discuss its application in several nonparametric tests in subsequent chapters.

Reliability and validity

In order for a measurement tool to be useful during a research project, it needs to be able to produce consistent, repeatable results that accurately reflect the construct being measured. A measurement tool exhibits *reliability* when it provides stable and consistent results in repeated use. An instrument exhibits *validity* when it can accurately reflect the construct of interest.[4] In order for measurements to provide meaningful raw data for statistical analysis in a research study, they need to be both reliable and valid. If the data are flawed, no amount of statistical testing can overcome this confound. Therefore, researchers must be mindful of these concepts when selecting measurement tools to ensure that the object of inquiry will be appropriately measured.

This section will mostly provide brief definitions of various forms of validity. For a comprehensive treatment of the topic, see Newton and Shaw (2014) or Brewer and Crano (2014). Because reliability can be measured statistically, the topic is more fully developed in Chapter 11.

Before further description of reliability and validity, a concrete example will be used to illustrate their definitions. In a simple experiment, a researcher might be interested in determining the boiling point of water. Water is brought to a boil over a burner, a digital thermometer is used to record the temperature in degrees Celsius, and the temperature is recorded. The process is repeated four times. Three outcomes are possible for the four readings:

Case 1: 97.9, 98.0, 98.2, and 98.1° C.

Case 2: 96.8, 102.4, 98.3, and 101.8° C.

Case 3: 99.9, 100.0, 100.1, and 100.0° C.

In the first case, the thermometer is reliable but not valid. The reading is nearly the same every time, so it is consistent in repeated uses (reliable), but it is not accurately measuring what we know to be the true boiling point of water (100° C). Therefore, it is not a valid measurement tool.

In the second case, the thermometer is not reliable but appears to be valid. The numbers vary greatly, which makes it an unreliable tool. With any given measurement, the answer could differ dramatically from the true temperature. However, the temperature readings are scattered rather evenly around the true measurement, so the thermometer is at least valid in the sense that it is apparently attempting to measure the temperature correctly, and it is only the unreliable nature of the measurement that is preventing the true reading. A valid but unreliable instrument might be the result of user error.

The final case represents a reliable and valid measuring tool. The readings are all consistent with each other (reliable), and they are close approximations of the true construct (valid). Measurement tools can exhibit both, one, or none of these two important characteristics. The goal is to ensure research employs measures that possess both traits. Reliable and valid measurements provide useful data for statistical analysis.

Issues of reliability and validity arise in a number of areas of research in translation and interpreting studies. For example, Jääskeläinen (2011) describes reliability and validity in the context of think-aloud protocol (TAP) data when examining translation processes. In particular, the validity of TAP data may be called into question because the translation task is fundamentally altered when participants are asked to enunciate their processes while translating.[5] The relative approximation of an experimental task to real-life conditions is termed *ecological validity*.

The development of survey instruments and questionnaires must strive to establish validity. The easiest type of validity to attain in survey design is *face validity*, which refers to the sense that every question on a survey is related to the construct of interest. Face validity can be strengthened by conducting a thorough literature review on the topic and seeking feedback from experts in the field while developing the survey. Face validity is a necessary first step in creating a valid survey. For instance, one factor in Lee's (2014: 198) Interpreting Self-Efficacy Scale is self-confidence. Respondents are asked to what extent they agree with the statement, "I'm confident that I can paraphrase B language speech accurately." This statement exhibits face validity by using language that is clearly related to self-confidence.

Beyond face validity, measurements should possess *construct validity* and *content validity*. Construct validity is closely aligned with operationalization. In Chapter 1, we described operationalization as the process of defining a way to measure abstract ideas. Construct validity asks to what extent the measurement tool is capable and successful in capturing the phenomenon of interest. One way to demonstrate construct validity is through a comparison to other tools that measure similar things. Construct validity can never be proven but only developed over time through repeated application of a measurement tool in various settings. Content validity refers to complete coverage of the various aspects of the construct being measured. For instance, in Lee's (2014) self-confidence subscale there are a variety of questions, including some related to listening skills, speaking skills, and recognition of non-verbal communication. By examining the construct from multiple angles, Lee's survey more accurately measures an interpreter's self-confidence.

Another important type of validity is *criterion validity*, which occurs when an instrument provides measurements that align with other valid instruments. One way to demonstrate alignment is showing that two related measurements are highly correlated, which is called *concurrent validity*. For example, a large number of survey scales exist to measure introversion. The extent to which they agree is a measure of their concurrent validity. Criterion validity can also be established through *predictive validity*, which is the degree to which a measure provides information about other behavior, beliefs, or characteristics, possibly in the future. A person who scored high on an introversion scale, for example, might be less likely to introduce himself or herself to a stranger if presented the opportunity in the course of a study.

When considered in the context of research design and methodology, the importance of validity and reliability cannot be emphasized sufficiently. Angelelli (2004) and Lee (2014) provide two examples of instrument design. In both studies, the authors emphasize the importance of *internal reliability* of instrument items. Moreover, they outline the iterative approach needed to validate an instrument and demonstrate the considerable effort required to create a measurement tool. Similarly, Sawyer (2004) outlines the role that reliability and validity play in interpreting assessment, particularly with regard to interpreting performance. Various types of reliability are presented in more detail in Chapter 11, along with associated statistical tests.

Survey design

Surveys are a convenient method for collecting quantitative data about perceptions and opinions of participants. They can also be used to collect descriptive and demographic information as part of a larger study. The development of an instrument is a time-consuming and complicated process. While we cannot possibly provide a complete review of how every type of instrument is developed and tested, the fundamental principles will be discussed in relation to the concepts of validity and reliability so that researchers might be better positioned to analyze quantitative data.[6]

The first challenge in survey instrument design is writing the questions, called *items*, to elicit information from the study's participants, called *respondents*. Well-written and carefully-considered items are the first step in creating a valid survey instrument. Items should not be ambiguous or leading. If respondents are unable to understand the item or are biased in a particular direction, the study results will be biased or skewed. Likewise, items should not address two questions at the same time, which is sometimes referred to as being *double barreled*. When presenting categorical items, researchers should ensure that the available responses are truly exhaustive and mutually exclusive. Entire volumes are devoted to the art and science of item writing (e.g., Fowler 1995), and any researcher planning to develop a new survey is well-advised to consult one of them for considerably more coverage than can be provided here.

Employing or adapting a previously validated instrument is another approach that researchers may consider when planning to collect survey data. Lee (2014), for example, presents preliminary validation data related to the development of an Interpreting Self-Efficacy (ISE) scale. The researcher first collected 63 items that were drawn from self-efficacy and interpreting competence instruments. The items were then assembled and tested by collecting data from 413 respondents. The internal reliability measures and factor analysis allowed for the initial scale to be refined into a 21-item version with adequate validity and reliability for use in future studies related to the topic. This approach to instrument design reduces some of the challenges inherent in survey design by building on previous scholarship.

Previously developed instruments may, however, be unavailable in a specific language. The translation of an instrument into a foreign language seems like a natural option, but researchers should exercise considerable caution in this practice. In light of the considerable work required to write items, there may be linguistic features of items that can threaten the validity of an item or even the whole instrument when translated into another language. Translation of a survey instrument is a complex project that requires considerable attention to reliability and validity. A widely translated tool is the General Self-Efficacy Scale (GSE), which was first conceived in German by Schwarzer and Jerusalem (1995). A Spanish-language version was developed and validated by Baessler and Schwarzer (1996) among a total of at least 26 different versions to date. Proper development of validated scales allows their use in applied studies, such as Bolaños-Medina (2014), which employs the Spanish-language GSE in a study related to translation process-oriented research.

We close this section with a brief mention of the influence of the delivery mode on a survey's results. Self-administered questionnaires may yield different responses than interviews as a result of social desirability bias, in which the respondent provides answers that he or she believes (rightly or wrongly) are less likely to draw condemnation. The response rate can be skewed by the mode of administration, whether on paper, online, or over the phone. A full review of the possible biases is not feasible for considerations of space, but researchers should consider both best practices and the particular circumstances of the study.[7] For our purposes, these issues are of particular interest from a quantitative perspective since they may lead to missing data, differing sample sizes, or a potential confounding variable in the study if multiple design methods are used. Researchers should consider this step carefully when considering a survey instrument as part of their research protocol.

Likert-type scales

One of the most commonly used survey designs is the *Likert scale*, though the term is sometimes abused by use beyond its original definition.[8] First, a Likert scale contains multiple items that are part of a "structured and reasoned whole" (Carifio and Perla 2007: 109). That is to say, the items included in a Likert scale are not independent but rather aim to investigate a specific construct. Second, the items included in a Likert scale employ a *Likert responding format*. This format refers to items that have an interval or ratio scale in their responses. In Likert's (1932) formulation, these response formats consist of an odd-numbered scale from 1 (strongly approve) to 5 (strongly disapprove) that was intended to measure attitude by asking for the strength of agreement with statements on a bipolar scale. Likert's intent was that the language to describe the five points would cause the numbers to represent an evenly spaced, interval level of measurement. Additionally, the center point of the scale should represent a neutral opinion, which is distinct from having no opinion. Finally, Likert scales should include reverse-coded statements. If all of the statements are phrased in a positive direction, then a respondent can fall into a habit of agreeing or disagreeing with every statement. The item wording of reverse-coded statements needs to be carefully structured. Asking a respondent if they agree or disagree with a negative statement can be confusing. For example, agreeing with the statement "Spanish is easy to learn" can seem different from disagreeing with the statement "Spanish is not hard to learn," even though those responses would represent nearly the same opinion. Careful attention to item writing and pilot testing can combat this challenge.

When a survey scale is adapted in some way from the above description, it should properly be described as a *Likert-type scale*. Sometimes the five-point scale is replaced with another number of options. An extension to seven choices is one example, and a more substantial shift is a change to four or six possible responses. With an even number of choices, the respondent is not provided a neutral option, so he or she is forced to render a level of agreement or disagreement. This design should be used with caution for possibly introducing a bias toward stronger opinions. At the very least, surveys on the same topic, some of which used an odd number of responses and some of which used an even number, should not be directly compared.

While Likert-type scales are popular and widely used, alternative survey tools can be quite effective for measurement. Additional methods include Guttman scales, forced-rank lists, discrete visual analog scales, semantic differential scales, and ordered-categorical items. These lie outside the context of the present volume, but researchers should be aware that multiple tools exist before automatically developing a Likert-type scale. Should researchers wish to develop a rigorous survey with quantitatively meaningful data, they are strongly encouraged to investigate the literature on survey research methods, instrument design, and data analysis specific to these types of data.

Factor analysis

Every individual item in a survey can be viewed as a measurable or *manifest variable*. The goal of collecting survey data from a set of items is to build a model based on the inter-relationships among these variables. A set of variables whose responses tend to cluster with similar responses can be a reflection of an unobservable *latent factor*. The mathematical tools to estimate the correlations among the variables is *factor analysis*. The idea behind factor analysis is that observed variation in a larger group of variables is the result of differences in a smaller number of underlying factors.

An example is Lee's (2014) development of an ISE scale. Based on prior work in the literature related to self-efficacy, Lee anticipated that the ISE would be composed of three sub-component factors: self-confidence, self-regulatory efficacy, and preference for task difficulty. Thus, the 21 items on the ISE are in effect measuring these three constructs that comprise the overall measure of ISE.

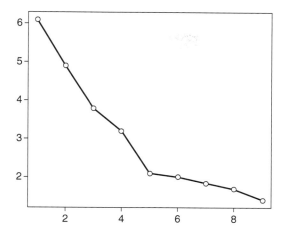

Figure 3.1 Scree plot example

Exploratory factor analysis (EFA) is a powerful tool for identifying the number of underlying factors and assisting in the elimination of less relevant items from a survey.[9] One important tool in interpreting EFA is a *scree plot*, which displays the *eigenvalues* of a correlation matrix. The mathematics of this procedure lie outside the scope of this volume, but the graph can be interpreted in a rather simple manner. In most cases, the points in a scree plot will have a sharply descending line followed by a nearly horizontal line. The number of factors corresponds to the last point before the bend in the graph. In Figure 3.1, the scree plot suggests that the data follow a four-factor structure. Additional and more formal model adequacy tools include examination of the eigenvalues that result from estimation of an EFA model, a consideration of the total variance explained by the factors, and several statistics of model fit.

Once the number of latent factors have been selected, model development is continued with factor rotation procedures to align the survey items as closely as possible with the factors. EFA can also be followed by *confirmatory factor analysis* (CFA), which imposes constraints on the mathematical model based on theorized relationships among the variables.

The mathematics of factor analysis are quite advanced, and proper survey development requires considerable time and effort in pilot studies and EFA. However, computing power makes the tools widely accessible without significant mathematical training. See Osborne (2014) for an accessible overview of EFA and Brown (2015) for a more rigorous treatment of CFA.

Technology and measurement

While the purpose of this volume is that of quantitative analysis and not data collection, we would be remiss if brief mention were not made of the data collection methodologies available to researchers. Evolving technologies and their potential benefits require that researchers consider the reliability and validity of the measurements provided by these tools. Translation and interpreting scholars rely on different measures when conducting research, and the hardware and software used to obtain this data must be taken into account. For example, time and keystroke logs are common measures used in translation process research. Translog is a regularly used keystroke logging tool that allows investigators to track the progression of target text production (Jakobsen 1999). This tool has also been used to track editing behavior, while TransCenter is a tool that allows researchers to investigate participant's behavior when post-editing machine translation (MT) output (Denkowski and Lavie 2012). Pupillometry and eye tracking provide insight into cognitive and behavioral processes (Seeber 2013). Survey data collection software, such as SurveyMonkey and Qualtrics, regularly feature in translation and interpreting studies.

Translation process data has also been collected online. Mellinger (2015) explores challenges related to data collection when working with Internet-mediated research methods and argues that some cognitive process data can be collected using keystroke methodologies. Mellinger (2014) demonstrates this practice by conducting an empirical study of computer-assisted translation that focuses on participant editing behavior when using a translation memory. Guerberof (2008) similarly uses online data collection to investigate post-editing. The breadth of research questions and the associated data collection methods related to translation as a cognitive activity are explored in Hurtado Albir, Alves, Englund Dimitrova, and Lacruz's (2015) overview of the TREC network. Investigation of these topics using Internet-mediated data collection tools may serve as another area for methodological innovation.

Any data collection tool is based on a set of underlying assumptions and requires appropriate set-up and implementation to obtain analyzable data. As mentioned in the survey design section, the mode in which an instrument is administered can impact measurements. If researchers or assistants improperly manage any step of the measurement process, there is an increased risk of unreliable and potentially invalid data being collected. The bottom line for technology and data collection is that researchers should use a method that they can expertly administer and that is capable of providing the measurements necessary to answer the research question.

Software packages for statistics

Just as technology has an impact on the measurement of research variables, so too does it affect statistical analysis and testing. Increased computing power and its availability to students, professors, and researchers have obviated the need for much statistical analysis to be performed with paper and pencil. Several statistical software packages include a wide variety of tests that allow researchers to process data efficiently without needing to know every formula. This ease of use is a double-edged sword. On the one hand, researchers are able to analyze data quickly and can select the most appropriate statistical test given the research question at

Measurement 35

hand. On the other hand, the researcher relinquishes full control of the formulas and algorithms implemented in these statistical packages.

The tradeoff of control merits consideration; statistical analysis software will only be as good as the formulas and algorithms on which they are based. The point-and-click approach to data analysis makes data processing more user-friendly, but the researchers still must know what tests to conduct, which variables to define, and how to interpret the results. Likewise, savvy methodologists might know which analyses are most appropriate, but will remain at the mercy of software developers to ensure that these tests are included in the software.

Likely the most commonly-used program is SPSS, which provides a user-friendly interface and the capability to calculate most of the statistical analyses in this volume. In contrast to the point-and-click approach, software packages such as R and SAS allow users to write the code that will process the data. This flexibility gives greater control to researchers to ensure that data analysis is conducted however they want. The considerable learning curve, however, can make this approach more challenging at the outset. Gries (2009, 2013) provides several volumes dedicated to teaching interested researchers how to use R. All statistical analysis and graphics in this volume were generated with R.

Notes

1 The treatment of measurement here is necessarily limited to an overview before continuing on to statistical analysis. For the interested reader, Allen and Yen (2001) provide more thorough coverage.
2 Three examples of commonly-used language proficiency scales are the Common European Framework of Reference for Languages (CEFR), the proficiency levels outlined by the American Council on the Teaching of Foreign Languages, and the Chinese Proficiency Test (Hanyu Shuiping Kaoshi, HSK).
3 We acknowledge the existence of the Kelvin scale and absolute zero, but these are of interest largely to quantum physicists. Furthermore, temperature is a widely used and classic example of an interval scale.
4 Alternately, some references consider the terms *reliability* and *validity* to be akin to *precision* and *accuracy*. In statistics, these terms have different meanings and therefore we will not use them here to avoid introducing confusion related to their use.
5 Jääskeläinen also notes that the reliability of these measures may be equally challenged, given the inconsistency of the verbal report.
6 A number of works dedicated to survey research methods and questionnaire design have been written by experts in the field. See, for example, Bradburn, Sudman, and Wansink (2004), Fowler (2013), Groves et al. (2013). Another important consideration is that of item response theory (see DeMars 2010). An overview of survey-based studies in translation and interpreting studies is provided by Sun (2016).
7 For a demonstration of social desirability bias in self-administered questionnaires that address potentially sensitive information, see Kreuter, Presser, and Tourangeau (2008).
8 Carifio and Perla (2007) address a number of misconceptions and misunderstandings about what constitutes a Likert scale.
9 A related but distinct methodology is *Principal Component Analysis* (PCA), which focuses its attention on the variables (survey items), considers all of their variability, and aims to reduce the dimensionality of the data to a smaller set of components. EFA is a more appropriate tool for measuring latent constructs because it inverts this assumption by considering the variables to be the result of underlying causes.

Part II

Describing

In Part I, we described the early stages of the research process: generating a research question, obtaining an adequate sample, maintaining ethical research practices, and planning appropriate measurements. The implementation of the research protocol is the next step, which results in the collection of data. We omit discussion of the data collection process itself because, while often being the most interactive step of the research project, it is always particular to the study at hand—whether it be observing interpreters at work, teaching translation students, or examining texts in a corpus. However, planning, describing, analyzing, and reporting are the supporting steps that ensure high-quality, useful results.

The immediate step following data collection is the assembly and cleaning of the study's sample data. Sometimes the task of data analysis is daunting given the sheer volume of data, as with fMRI or eye tracking data. Corpus studies can also involve a time-consuming, labor-intensive search process that results in large corpora. Process research involving human participants that are tested in specific quasi-experimental conditions can generate equally large datasets, comprising screen recordings, keystroke logs, and audio or video files. Summarizing and describing a large sample of data provides a deeper understanding of its structure, which guides the selection of further testing procedures. The mathematics that make up much of this volume are an important and necessary part of the overall process, but they are embedded between adequate preparation and correct interpretation. We strive to keep this overarching structure and purpose in mind throughout.

In Chapter 4, we present a discussion of descriptive statistics, which provide a basic understanding of the collected data, both numerically and visually. Chapter 5 discusses statistical distributions, which are an important foundational topic for further analysis. Distributions also allow for analysis of outliers and transformations of the data, if necessary. Chapter 6 more formally defines some important statistical terminology; the chapter also utilizes those terms and concepts in describing one-sample statistical tests. Therefore, the chapter serves as a bridge to the more complex statistics discussed in Part III.

4 Descriptive statistics

The first step in statistical analysis is the calculation of *descriptive statistics* that summarize the basic properties of sample data. The techniques presented in this chapter do not provide the conclusions of the study because they do not attempt to generalize the sample data to the underlying population. The task of deriving meaning and generalizing results to the population is accomplished by *inferential statistics*. However, descriptive statistics are an important first mathematical step because they serve three purposes in quantitative analysis.

First, descriptive statistics concisely summarize important characteristics of a sample. Providing a table of descriptive statistics in a research report is an efficient way to communicate basic properties of a sample. For instance, a study in which the participants were professional translators would likely provide a table that summarized some of their attributes, possibly including years of experience, gender, working languages, or any other traits that might be relevant to the research. The descriptive statistics provide an abbreviated summary so that a reader can quickly understand the characteristics of the data.

Second, descriptive statistics are useful for checking the assumptions of statistical tests. The validity of inferential statistics always rests on a set of assumptions about the sample data. Descriptive statistics can help verify that the data meet the assumptions or suggest when alternative procedures, such as nonparametric tests, might be better suited to analyze the data.

Third, the computation of descriptive statistics is part of the process of generalizing the sample data to make conclusions about a broader population. Appropriately generalizing results from sample statistics to the population requires an understanding of the population that the sample represents. For instance, words per hour in a translation task completed by students in Germany might provide interesting information about the performance of university students in Europe, but it might not be at all useful to understand the work of professional translators given the degree to which these populations differ.

Parameter estimation and hypothesis testing build upon the foundation of descriptive statistics. These procedures are the province of inferential statistics, which are described in Parts III and IV.

Overall, the goal of this chapter is to provide ways to describe the empirical features of data. Principally, descriptive statistics involve the measurement of five characteristics of sample data: the *frequency*, the *central tendency*, the *variability*, the *skewness*, and the *kurtosis*. The ability to condense a data set to five main numbers and still convey its essential features demonstrates the utility of statistics to describe data.

Frequencies

The most basic information to provide about a dataset is the sample size, typically signified by the letter n. When the data can be split into multiple groups, subscripts can be used to distinguish the size of each group. As an example, n_M and n_W might stand for the number of men and women in a sample or n_A, n_B, and n_C might represent the number of participants in each of three different treatment conditions in an experimental design.

The number of observations may not always correspond with the number of participants, because each participant can be measured multiple times. Observations can also be words or other units of text. Therefore, sample size needs to be based on the appropriate unit of analysis. Also, missing data may cause the sample size to differ from one statistic to another. Quality reporting carefully examines these issues and fully accounts for the number of observations in each case.

Frequencies are typically reported for three different reasons. First, frequencies can be included in a summary table of descriptive statistics. A research report should always include a description of the sample in its method section. Sometimes the sample size is simply reported in the text, but a table can be a concise way of summarizing sub-samples and various descriptive statistics. Timarová and Salaets (2011: Table 1) provide an example of this use of frequencies, breaking down their sample of 136 participants into three categories: conference interpreters, liaison interpreters, and a control group. They further subdivide those categories into the number of male and female participants. As part of a larger table of descriptive statistics, the frequencies of these categories help the reader to understand the nature of the participants in the sample. The purpose of their research is a comparison of traits and abilities between interpreters and a control group, and we revisit this study in Chapter 7 as an example of a t-test. Here, we focus on their use of frequency tables to describe the data before conducting analysis.

Second, beyond sample description, frequencies are sometimes worthy of analysis, particularly when dealing with categorical data. Knowing how rare or common various categories are can be useful in its own right. A translation or interpreting department at a university would certainly want to know how many students work in various languages. Furthermore, statistical analysis can examine whether the pattern of frequencies differs between groups.[1] For instance, Timarová and Salaets (2011: Table 5) itemize four complex patterns of learning styles. The reader is able to ascertain which categories are more or less common, and statistical analysis compares the interpreting students and the control group, finding no significant difference in the pattern of the frequencies. When frequency data are the result of counting a variable of interest, the numbers are frequently displayed in a table or bar graph.

The third and final situation in which frequencies should be reported is in conjunction with inferential statistics. Mathematical results can be influenced by the number of observations. Additionally, missing data can cause some tests to have a different number of observations than the overall sample. An example of inferential statistical tests with missing data is Table 4 in Timarová and Salaets (2011). In comparing interpreting students to a control group of students, they report the number of participants whose data allowed for inclusion in eight different statistical comparisons. The control group in their study did not participate in all phases of data collection, and the usable observations for the control group ranged from 28 to 103. Such variation is not inherently harmful to statistical analysis, but reporting the sample size is an ethical imperative and can aid interpretation.

A final comment on the presentation of frequencies is that they can be presented as *absolute frequencies*, meaning the number of observations in a category, or as *relative frequencies*, representing the percentage of the overall sample. Absolute frequencies are always appropriate, since they provide a reader with the exact number of observations. Relative frequencies are calculated as the number of observations divided by the total size of the category. The resulting percentage should be provided when relative size or relationship to the whole is of more interest in the context of the study. Both versions provide the same information; however, certain contexts can make one representation preferable. After all, describing a sample as consisting of 14 men and 36 women is identical to describing it as made up of 28% men and 72% women. Relative frequencies are more common with large samples and sometimes can be misleading in small samples, for which absolute frequencies should be preferred.

Measures of central tendency

The next way to describe a sample is by calculating a *measure of central tendency*, which is the single value that best represents a set of observations. If the data are numerical, a measure of central tendency suggests the location of the data on the number line. Another way to describe a measure of central tendency is that it expresses the most typical value in the sample. There are three common measures of central tendency: the mean, the median, and the mode. Throughout this section, we assume that data collection has resulted in a sample of size n and that we want to describe the central tendency of the sample.

Mean

The most familiar measure of central tendency is the *arithmetic mean*, often referred to as simply the *mean* or the *average*. Consider a simple example in which the number of students enrolled in five different university translation programs is found to be 28, 31, 32, 48, and 60. The calculation of the mean involves summing the observations and dividing by the sample size. In mathematical notation, the "bar" symbol over a variable represents the mean:

42 *Describing*

$$\overline{X} = \frac{1}{n}\sum_{i=1}^{n} x_i = \frac{x_1 + x_2 + \ldots + x_n}{n}$$

The formula makes explicit the notion that every observation is used in the calculation of the statistic. Consequently, if even one data point is changed, the mean changes.

For the example above, the average enrollment would be $\overline{X} = \frac{1}{5}(28 + 31 + 32 + 48 + 60) = 39.8$ students. This figure represents the central tendency of the number of students enrolled in translation programs. If the first program increased its enrollment from 28 to 38, the mean would increase to 41.8 students. Each observation is weighted equally, and a change in even one observation alters the mean.

One way to think about the mean is that it represents the theoretical result of an equal distribution. In other words, if the same total number of students were distributed equally to each university, the number of students at each would be equal to the mean. In this case, if all five universities in the sample had identical enrollment, there would be 39.8 students in each program. Of course, the notion of 0.8 of a student is nonsensical. This result demonstrates that the mean may not (and generally will not) be equal to any one observation in the sample data, nor is the average even required to be a feasible value in terms of the original units. The mean is a mathematical abstraction from the data.

A second way to think about the mean is that it serves as a balance point in the data; deviations from the mean on one side must be cancelled out by deviations on the other side. Therefore, the sum of the deviations is always zero. This property is illustrated using the example data set in Table 4.1. The mean value of 39.8 is subtracted from every observation, and those deviations are summed.

One problem that arises from this property of the mean is that one outlier can have an unlimited influence on the calculation of the mean. For instance, if the fifth school had 600 students instead of 60, the mean would be 147.8 students. One large observation can increase the value of the mean greatly, just as one negative observation can decrease it. This concept is described by saying that the mean is not robust to outliers. Therefore, even this familiar and simple statistic must be used with awareness of other qualities of the sample data. Other measures of central

Table 4.1 Example data for zero-sum-deviation property of the mean

Data	Deviation
28	−11.8
31	−8.8
32	−7.8
48	8.2
60	20.2
Sum	0

tendency may be needed to describe a particular sample. Some proponents of robust statistical methods suggest the *trimmed mean* as an alternative.

Median

The median is the second measure of central tendency, and it refers to the middle number of a sample. The process for finding the median is to rank the observations in order and select the midpoint. For the fictitious student enrollment numbers in Table 4.1, the median would be 32, because two universities have enrollments less than that number and two universities have greater enrollments. In situations with an even number of observations, the middle two scores are averaged. As an example, given the numbers 2, 3, 5, 6, 10, and 11, the median would be the average of 5 and 6, which is 5.5.

For a continuous variable, half of the data will be less than the median and half of the data will be greater than the median. For a sample that contains ties (i.e., observations of equal value), this relationship might be only approximate, and this approximation can be arbitrarily bad for discrete data for which only certain values are allowed. For a dataset containing the numbers 2, 3, 3, 3, 3, 3, 3, 3, 4, 7, 8, the median would be 3, and only one observation is less than the median. In general, it is safe to think of the median as the midpoint, with half of the data on each side, but that relationship can break down in extreme cases with many ties.

In contrast to the mean, the median is robust to the presence of outliers that tend be either large or small in a given dataset. In fact, up to 50% of the data can change before the median value will be affected. In the example of the mean, we noted that if the largest school had 600 students, the mean would increase dramatically to 147.8. However, the median would be unaffected, remaining at 32 students, which is a much better representation of the typical level of enrollment. Because of this robustness, the median is a better measure of central tendency for any dataset that contains outliers.

Some variables are more prone to outliers. In particular, measurements of time such as years of experience or task completion time tend to have many observations with shorter spans of time and only a few with longer periods. In other words, these data tend to exhibit *skewness*, a concept that is more fully described later in the chapter. When data contain outliers or exhibit skewness, the median generally represents the center of the data better than the mean. The reason for this is evident in Figure 4.1, which could represent observations of time needed to complete a task. The graph's horizontal axis depicts the measurement of time, with the height of the curve representing the number of participants who took that much time. The bulk of the participants finish in a relatively short period of time, as represented by the large number of observations (a relatively high humped shape) on the left side of the graph. Meanwhile, a few people take much longer, leading to a long tail on the right side of the graph.

The plot also shows the mean and median for this distribution. The few large observations cause the mean to be considerably larger than the median. The goal of a measure of central tendency, though, is to represent the typical value in the

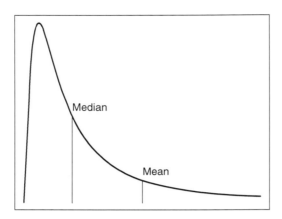

Figure 4.1 Graphical representation of the median and the mean

dataset. In this case, the mean has been influenced by outliers and no longer falls near the bulk of the observations.

In translation and interpreting (T&I) studies, one type of variable that is likely to benefit from the median is any measurement of time. An example can be found in O'Brien (2007), in which the median is used extensively for several different measures. The study compared the effort required for translation and MT postediting by English–German translators. In describing the participants, O'Brien provided the median number of years of experience. Reporting the median avoids bias that occurs in the mean if one participant has a considerable number of years of experience. Elsewhere in the paper, she compares the median rate of words per minute. In reporting a description of the data, O'Brien notes that one of the participants worked considerably faster than others, but use of the median appropriately represents a measure of center of the data. In their methodological paper, Balling and Hvelplund (2015) also mention the median as an appropriate measure of center for gaze time in an eye tracking study.

Count or quantity data is a second measurement type that can often be better described by the median. Like measurements of time, counts cannot be negative and can have a few large observations that bias the mean toward a higher value that would not be representative. In a meta-analysis of survey research of conference interpreters, Pöchhacker (2009) reports the median sample size, because the majority of the studies reviewed have fewer than 50 respondents while a few larger studies inflate the mean sample size calculation. A common example is median wealth in a country; a few very wealthy individuals in a sample will result in a high mean that does not represent the average experience. A joke among statisticians is that if Oprah walks into a corner bar, the average wealth will be in the millions of dollars. In T&I studies, the number of errors, keystrokes, and sentence length all fit into this category. Thus, machine translation (MT) studies often employ the median to describe data. For example, Doherty, O'Brien, and Carl (2010) report the median for a range of such variables, including fixation count, sentence length, and gaze time.

Finally, an important use of the median is for analysis and reporting of many nonparametric statistical methods. In Part III, we describe several examples such as the Mann-Whitney U-test, for which the medians of the groups being compared should be reported instead of the mean.

Mode

The final measure of central tendency is the mode, which is defined as the observation that occurs most often in a sample. To give an example with numerical data, if the sample consisted of 2, 3, 3, 4, 6, 7, 7, 7, 9, the mode would be 7 because it occurs most often. However, the mode is almost never used for ratio-level continuous data because identical measurements are not typically of interest. If the gaze time of 100 participants were measured, the fact that 5 participants had identical gaze time for one particular observation may not provide considerable insight into the task. The mode can also be determined from the highest point on a histogram or frequency distribution plot. In such cases, a continuous variable is divided into ranges and the number of observations within each range are plotted. Once complete, the mode is the highest point of the graph. Some frequency distributions can be *bimodal* or *multimodal*, meaning they have several local maximum points. Figure 4.2 displays a histogram with one clear mode (*unimodal*) on the left and a bimodal distribution on the right.

The mode is sometimes used for variables that are measured at the interval level, such as Likert-type scales.[2] Researchers may be more interested in knowing that the most common answer on a 5-point scale was 2, rather than knowing that

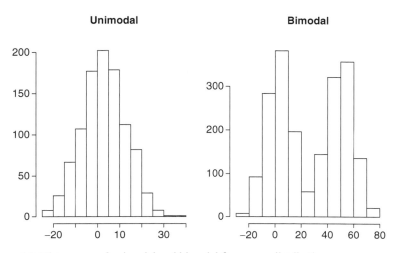

Figure 4.2 Histograms of unimodal and bimodal frequency distributions

46 *Describing*

Table 4.2 Example data for mode

	A	B	C
Judge 1	1	2	3
Judge 2	1	2	3
Judge 3	3	1	2
	1.67	1.67	2.67

the mean of the scores was 2.4, for example. Typically, the most common answer provides additional information regarding respondents' opinions.

Ordinal data can also be summarized by the mode. Whereas differences in interval scale data are relatively equal in size, differences of opinion expressed in ordinal data can vary substantially. Therefore, the mode of ranks can be informative regarding the strength of respondents' preferences, or the mode can be used to break ties in the mean ranks. Table 4.2 displays a simple case of rankings for which the mode is useful. The figures represent rankings of three different items (A, B, and C) as ranked by three different judges from best (1) to worst (3).

Item C is clearly the least favored by these judges. However, Items A and B have identical mean ratings. Looking at the mode of the ranks, Item A has a mode of 1 while Item B has a mode of 2, which suggests that Item A should be considered the highest ranked. This is not the only way to break such ties, but the mode can be used in this way to demonstrate strength of opinion. In a design very similar to this example, Bowker and Ciro (2015) asked three professional translators to rank MT output from three different programs: Google Translate, Reverso, and Systran. The mode of the ranks was suggestive that Google Translate was the superior tool.

The mode is particularly useful to describe categorical, non-numerical data, for which the mean or median cannot be calculated. For instance, a sample of conference interpreters could be asked to self-report languages in which they are conversationally proficient. Any attempt at calculating the mean or median of a group of languages would be senseless; however, it may be of interest that the most common response (mode) was French. Quite often the mode is listed first when reporting the list of responses or when listing the largest categories. For example, Zwischenberger (2015) describes the self-reported working languages of interpreters as French (24%), English (22%), and German (18%). The mode of this data is French, but listing the next several categories provides a better overall understanding of the data.

Measures of dispersion

At a minimum, descriptive statistics always require both a measure of central tendency and a measure of dispersion, sometimes called a *measure of variability*. A sample is more fully described by understanding both the most representative number and how closely the other observations are clustered around that point.

For example, the mean time it takes study participants to complete a task reveals nothing about how long you would have to wait for the slowest person, nor does it provide any indication of how fast this task could be finished. Another example is average reported translation speed of 510 words per hour among respondents in the American Translators Association (ATA)'s Translation and Interpreting Compensation Survey. A project manager, however, would also want to know that this figure ranged from 382 to 618 words per hour among the sampled professionals. Measures of dispersion indicate the data's spread or variability. Four measures of variability are reviewed in this section: the range, quantiles, standard deviation, and covariance.

Range

The most basic way to describe the dispersion of a sample is to calculate the *range*, which is the difference between the minimum and maximum values. For the enrollment data in Table 4.1, the maximum value is 60 and the minimum is 28. Therefore, the range is 32. Reporting the range as the difference of the endpoints is most valuable when the variable is limited in the values that can be observed. For example, percentage score on an exam must lie between zero and 100, and responses to a Likert-type scale are limited between the two extreme values, perhaps one and seven.

Ranges are also commonly reported by explicitly listing the values of the extreme observations. Providing these endpoints along with the range is especially common for demographic information, such as the age of participants. Reporting the mean (or median) and the range together provides a general indication of the overall shape of the sample data. Zwischenberger (2015) describes a sample with an average age of 52, with a minimum age of 30 and a maximum of 87, and Köpke and Nespoulous (2006) report years of experience among the interpreters in their study as ranging from 4 to 35 along with a mean of 16.9 years. These are descriptive variables and not the primary variables of interest in the respective studies. For quantitative data that are going to be subject to further analysis, the range is not as appropriate as the standard deviation.

Quantiles

Sample data can be separated into equal sized groups. *Quantile* is the generic name for such a division, with quartiles (four groups), quintiles (five groups) and deciles (ten groups) being the most common. Finding the cutoff points is similar to finding the median. Recall that the median is the middle observation, which implies 50% of the data are below and 50% of the data are above. That position implies that the median is the 50th percentile, and it divides the data into two quantiles. Similarly, the first quartile is halfway between the lowest observation and the median, with 25% of the data below and 75% of the data below.

The method for finding a quantile is to find the appropriate rank of the data by multiplying the sample size by the relevant percentage and rounding the result up

48 *Describing*

to the next whole number. If the result is a whole number, then one is added to the result. Then the data point that corresponds to that rank in the data is found. For example, if test scores were available from 22 students, their scores might appear as follows:

51, 54, 56, 56, 57, 64, 69, 71, 72, 76, 80, 84, 86, 87, 89, 90, 92, 94, 94, 96, 97, 99

The 25th percentile could be found by multiplying 22 (the sample size) by 25%. This calculation results in a rank of 5.5, which is rounded up to 6. Because the data are already in rank order, the sixth score can easily be seen to be 64. Finding the 75th percentile can, by similar process, be shown to be 92. This process is generic in the sense that it can be used to find any percentile of the data.

The *interquartile range* (IQR) is a measure of spread that combines two quantiles. The figure is calculated by subtracting the observation that represents the first quartile from the observation at the third quartile. Therefore, the IQR can be considered the range between the first and the third quartiles. One benefit of the IQR is that it does not include the most extreme (largest and smallest) observations, so it is not affected by outliers to the same extent as the range.

The IQR is a robust measure of variation in that it does not require any assumptions about the distribution of the population being sampled. In that capacity it can be used to identify potential outliers in a sample. To do so, the IQR is first multiplied by 1.5 and then added to the third quartile and subtracted from the first quartile; any point that lies beyond those extreme values is considered a potential outlier for further investigation. For example, if the IQR of a dataset is 14 with the first quartile at 18 and the third quartile at 32, then the extreme minimum value would be 18−14*1.5 = −3 and the maximum would be 32+14*1.5 = 53. Values greater than 53 or below −3 would deserve scrutiny.

The range and the quantiles are also commonly combined in a five number summary. The five numbers are the minimum, the first quartile, the median (the second quartile), the third quartile, and the maximum observation. Rarely is a five-number summary provided in-text, but those numbers are often used in the creation of boxplots, which we discuss in the last section of this chapter.

Standard deviation

The most commonly reported measure of dispersion is the *standard deviation*. The first step in calculating standard deviation is to find the *variance* of the sample data. The variance is not usually provided as a descriptive statistic because it is not in the same units as the original data; however, the variance is used in many statistical tests and is a necessary step in finding the standard deviation. The formula for variance gives a formal, mathematical definition of distance away from the mean. The sample variance is denoted s^2. The process involves, first, calculating the difference between each data point and the mean. That distance is then squared, summed, and divided by one less than the sample size:

$$s^2 = \frac{\sum_{i=1}^{n}(x_i - \bar{x})^2}{n-1}$$

The squaring is often described as being a necessary step to avoid negative values. While partly true, it is also related to mathematical technicalities beyond the interest of most non-statisticians. What should be clear is that the numerator of the variance formula is a measure of how much each observation differs from the sample mean. The denominator makes the variance a sort of average distance; the formal reason for dividing by ($n-1$) is that it represents the *degrees of freedom* of the variance. The concept of degrees of freedom is described in Chapter 6.

Variance cannot be negative, and a variance of zero can occur only when every observation in a sample is numerically the same. Samples with a small variance exhibit little variation in their scores; the observations are tightly clustered near the mean. By contrast, samples with a large variance are characterized by a great deal of variation. In that case, the observations will be more spread out and lie farther from the mean.

Once the variance is calculated, the standard deviation is found by taking the square root of the variance. Taking the square root returns the measure to the original units. So if the original data measure distance in meters, then the standard deviation is also measured in meters. The interpretation of the standard deviation is similar to the interpretation of variance described above. Standard deviation will always be positive, and larger numbers indicate that the data differ more from the mean than smaller numbers.

Covariance

All of the descriptive statistics to this point have involved only one variable. A measure of dispersion called *covariance* can be calculated for the relationship between two variables. The covariance represents *comovement* in two variables. If two variables are directly related, meaning that they tend to be large together and small together, then they will have a positive covariance. For example, height and weight have a positive covariance, as do years of education and salary. These covariances are general trends in that taller people generally weigh more and more educated people tend to earn more, but these are clearly generalities and not a strict association. For instance, we all know tall people who are slender and we all know of popular entertainment stars who are proof that a high salary is possible without a college degree.

By contrast, if two variables are inversely related, meaning that small observations of one are associated with large observations of the other, then they will have a negative covariance. A potential situation with negative covariance is the length of time spent simultaneously interpreting and the quality of the interpreter's rendition, implying the need for interpreters to work in teams and take breaks. It should be noted that covariance depends on the observed range of each variable. Observing an interpreter at work for ten minutes would be unlikely to lead to

50 *Describing*

any noticeable covariation between quality and time, but asking the interpreter to work for two hours without a break would very likely lead to an observed negative covariance. Similarly, returning to the example of height and weight, the positive covariance holds much more closely for children between the ages of 4 and 16 than it would for adults between the ages of 44 and 56.

As the name implies, the formula for covariance is related to the formula for variance. The numerator still includes the distance from the mean, but rather than a squared measure of distance, it is the product of the difference away from the mean for each variable:

$$s_{XY} = \frac{\sum_{i=1}^{n}(x_i - \bar{X})(y_i - \bar{Y})}{n-1}$$

The observations for the x and y variables must be paired as two measurements from the same unit of analysis. In the examples above, the height and weight measurements both come from the same person, and the simultaneous interpreters are each measured in terms of time and performance.

Covariance is related to the notion of *statistically independent variables*. Two variables are independent if the measurement of one is not influenced by or related to the measurement of the other. Hair color and weight, for example, have no obvious relationship and are therefore independent. Independent variables always have a covariance of zero. However, the converse is not always true. It is possible, though unusual, for two variables to have zero covariance but not be independent.

Other descriptive statistics

The most important descriptive statistics are the measures of center and spread. The mean and the standard deviation are the most commonly utilized measures, especially for continuous data. This section briefly describes two additional descriptive statistics that are useful to describe additional features that can be observed in some sample data.

Skewness

First, a distribution may exhibit asymmetries. The extent of the asymmetry is described by a *coefficient of skewness*, with a value of zero representing a symmetric distribution. Negative values imply that the data are skewed to the left, meaning that the left side of the distribution contains more extreme values than the right side. Positive skewness describes the opposite situation, in which more extreme values are particularly large observations. Figure 4.3 displays graphs depicting distributions with positive and negative skewness. A visual description is that a distribution with positive skewness has a long tail to the right, while a distribution with negative skewness has a long tail on the left side of the graph.

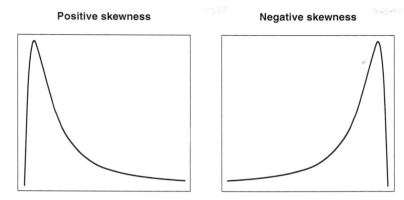

Figure 4.3 Graphs of positive and negative skewness

The median is a more appropriate measure of center when sample data exhibit skewness. The median is more robust to outliers, which is to say that the extreme values at the edges of the distributions result in a smaller change to the value of the median than to the mean. The mean is typically biased in the direction of the outliers or asymmetry. Therefore, with positive skewness, the mean will generally be greater than the median. Conversely, for a distribution that is negatively skewed, the median will be greater than the mean.[3]

Kurtosis

The final descriptive statistic covered in this chapter, *kurtosis*, measures the tails of a statistical distribution. The baseline for comparison is the bell-shaped standard normal distribution, which is probably familiar to most readers and is described more fully in Chapter 5. Typically, computer software calculates excess kurtosis, so that a normal curve represents a kurtosis of zero.

If excess kurtosis is positive (leptokurtosis), then the center of the distribution has a higher peak, and the tails are fatter and thicker. Conversely, negative kurtosis (platykurtosis) implies a shorter peak and narrower tails. Some disciplines, such as finance and insurance, pay great attention to the tails of a distribution because they can represent great financial losses. In applied T&I work, kurtosis is unlikely to need reporting except for extremely large samples with significant outliers. This situation may occur in some corpus studies.

Data visualization

The descriptive statistics described so far in this chapter provide a numerical summary of sample data. In some cases, the same information may be conveyed more conveniently or concisely in a graph, plot, chart, or table.[4] In an excellent tome on graphic design, Few (2012) argues that images are particularly valuable at displaying patterns, trends, and exceptions. Furthermore, graphs can demonstrate relationships among and differences between different variables.

The primary goal of data visualization techniques is to communicate information to the reader. When executed well, figures support the narrative of the literature review, hypotheses, and results of a research report. In this section, we identify some of the most common tools for data visualization. For extensions to the basic techniques provided here as well as a wealth of additional tools, see Yau (2011). Plots are also useful for understanding the structure of sample data and can be a good way to identify outliers (Gries 2010). Additionally, a researcher can examine plots as a way to check the assumptions of statistical tests.

Bar charts and histograms

When the purpose of a chart is to indicate relative size or describe a distribution, *bar charts* and *histograms* are useful tools. We discuss bar charts and histograms in the same subsection because their appearance and use are very similar. Both of these figures represent the frequencies of observations in categories. The primary distinction is that bar charts should be used for categorical or ordinal data, and histograms should be used for interval or ratio-level data. Therefore, bar charts have a natural number of bars, representing the various categories, while a researcher must decide the number of subsets of a continuous variable to use when creating a histogram.

A bar chart could display the native language of 100 people in a study's sample, for example. Figure 4.4 displays a possible distribution of this variable. The order of the categories in the figure is alphabetical, but there is no inherent ordering implied by categorical data. The horizontal axis could be reordered without changing the chart's meaning. The height of each bar represents the number of participants who fall into the various categories. The bars are separated by space to indicate that the groups are distinct levels of a discrete, categorical variable.

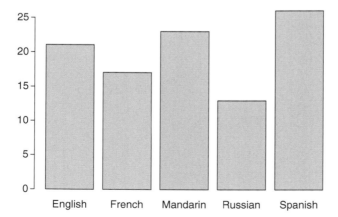

Figure 4.4 Bar chart example

Descriptive statistics 53

A histogram has no natural grouping because the horizontal axis represents a continuous variable. Consequently, the variable needs to be segmented into bins, which are represented by the widths of the rectangles in the figure. Because the histogram displays counts for a continuous random variable, the rectangles should touch, thereby acknowledging visually that the categories are artificial divisions of a continuous measurement. A number of formulas have been suggested for selecting the number of bins (or equivalently, selecting their width). The simplest formula is to use $\sqrt{n}$ bins, but more complex rules such as Sturges' (1926) formula are common defaults in statistical software. The final decision should always be to choose the number of bins that most clearly describes the salient details of the data.

To give an example, age is a simple demographic variable that might be displayed in a histogram. Figure 4.5 displays two possible histograms of the same dataset, representing the age of 100 participants. The histogram on the left uses 7 bins and nicely displays the data, while the histogram on the right arguably has too many bins (16) for the graph to convey useful information.

Box plots

The *box plot*, also sometimes called the *box-and-whisker plot*, is closely related to the five number summary discussed earlier in the chapter.[5] A number of variations exist on the box plot (McGill, Tukey, and Larsen 1978), but all box plots include a box shape that stretches from the first to the third quartile as well as a line to mark the median value inside the box. Figure 4.6 shows a box plot for two groups side by side. For group A, the first quartile, median, and third quartile are 3.7, 5.1, and 6.5, respectively. The same figures for group B are 6.8, 7.9, and 9.2.

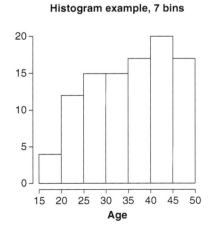
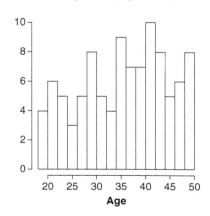

Figure 4.5 Histogram example

54 *Describing*

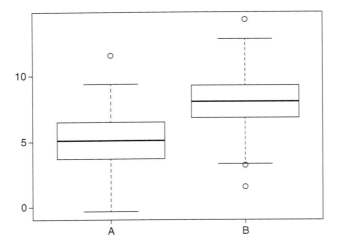

Figure 4.6 Box plot example

Not all box plots draw whiskers and outliers in the same way. In Figure 4.6, we have followed the most common convention, which is to calculate the IQR, multiply it by 1.5 and add it to the third quartile. Then the whisker extends to the level of the last data point within that range. The bottom whisker is drawn similarly, only subtracting 1.5 times the IQR from the first quartile to define the lower cutoff point. Any data points that lie outside the range defined by the whiskers are considered outliers. These are marked as individual points on the box plot.

The most valuable use of box plots is when more than one group is measured on a variable and box plots for each group are displayed side by side. Displaying multiple groups in this way allows for easy comparison of their relative levels. If the research question involves whether or not a difference exists, box plots can suggestively portray the results of the research. Based on Figure 4.6, Group B tends to have a higher value than Group A on the variable of interest.

Statistical testing for a difference between groups will formalize the suggested relationship. Therefore, box plots should often accompany the results of tests for differences between variables (which are the topic of Part III of this book), especially *t*-tests and analysis of variance (ANOVA). Box plots are also useful for providing a sense of the overall shape of a single distribution and the range of values of the variable. Additionally, they are useful for outlier identification in the early stages of data analysis, so it is advisable to create a box plot of most variables before proceeding to further analysis.

Scatterplots

While box plots are useful for displaying differences between variables, *scatterplots* are an excellent tool for showing relationships. Given two measurements

Descriptive statistics   55

from each participant, the data are presented in a two-dimensional graph. In an experimental research design, the horizontal axis should represent the independent variable and the vertical axis should represent the dependent variable.

A scatterplot is an excellent tool for exploring whether a linear relationship exists so that correlation coefficients or regression analysis are appropriate statistical tools to analyze the data. Two scatterplots appear in Figure 4.7. On the left is a linear relationship and on the right is a curvilinear relationship. Both graphs provide useful information for the researcher when planning and conducting statistical analysis and can help to convey results to a reader. However, the graph on the left can most likely be succinctly and adequately summarized with a correlation coefficient or regression line. Scatterplots that are nonlinear, like the graph on the right, can help explain more complex relationships.

If regression analysis is conducted, a regression line is often added to the graph. However, when drawing lines on a graph, it is important not to extend them beyond the sample data and thereby encourage unsubstantiated extrapolation. In most cases, lines representing a 95% confidence interval should also appear as a visual reminder that the line is an estimate. These concepts and issues related to linear regression are further discussed in Chapter 12.

Line graphs

When graphing variables, lines should only be drawn when all points on the line represent possible values of the two variables. *Line graphs* are particularly convenient for portraying trends over time and for showing relationships when the variable on the horizontal axis is intrinsically ordered. Stock charts are a well-known example of a line graph, in which time is on the horizontal axis and stock price appears on the vertical.

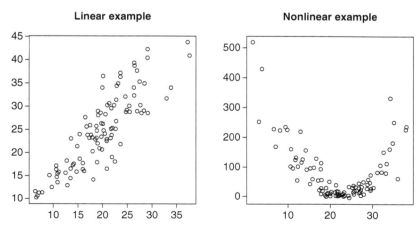

Figure 4.7 Scatterplot example

56 *Describing*

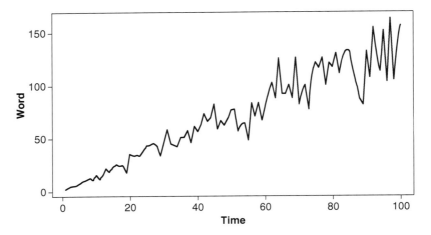

Figure 4.8 Line graph example

A graph with a similar appearance can be generated by eye tracking data. Carl and Jakobsen (2009: 131, Figure 10) provide one example of this kind of graph in which the horizontal axis represents time and the vertical axis represents the words in the source text. Eye tracking software records a translator's gaze as he or she works through the subject text. Carl and Jakobsen's graph simultaneously displays information regarding keystrokes. In Figure 4.8 we present a much-simplified line graph for a fictitious dataset as an example of how a line graph would appear. The line emphasizes the continuous nature of the data as the participant's gaze moves through time.

Frequency tables

The primary focus of this section is the use of figures like graphs and plots, but *frequency tables* can also be a convenient way to display categorical data. Ribas (2012) provides several examples of useful frequency charts in a comparison of the challenges in note taking during the interpreting task. The paper presents a number of tables in relative frequency form that compare responses from novice and advanced students. We illustrate the appearance of frequency tables with two examples inspired by that paper. The data in our tables are fictitious and the categories truncated and relabeled compared to Ribas (2012), but we want to draw the reader's attention to that paper as a particularly good example of data visualization. Table 4.3 shows what novice and advanced interpreting students might answer when asked to identify primary problem with production in a target language.

Because the table shows absolute frequencies, the total of each group in the sample is also provided. The table assumes that the actual numbers are of interest to a reader. In many cases, the comparison across categories or across groups

Table 4.3 Frequency table (absolute) example data (adapted from Ribas 2012, Table 6)

Problem	Number of Students	
	Novice	Advanced
Vocabulary issues	14	9
Nervousness	35	13
Unclear notes	22	21
Total	71	43

Table 4.4 Frequency table (relative) example data (adapted from Ribas 2012, Table 6)

Problem	Percent of Students	
	Novice	Advanced
Vocabulary issues	19.7	20.9
Nervousness	49.3	30.2
Unclear notes	31.0	48.8

provides more valuable information. The table would then be adapted to appear as in Table 4.4.

By converting the raw figures into relative frequencies (percentages), the table now clarifies that vocabulary issues account for a nearly identical proportion of the responses. The unequal sample size of each group concealed that information in the table of absolute frequencies. Frequency tables and other charts, graphs, and plots are deceptively simple to create, particularly with the point-and-click capabilities of computer software. However, thinking about the key information to present and considering the best means of communicating with the reader are excellent habits for any researcher to develop.

Notes

1 The chi-squared test described in Chapter 10 is the most common tool for analyzing categorical data.
2 Measurement levels are defined in Chapter 3.
3 These relationships between the mean and median are true for unimodal, continuous distributions that are quite common. However, violations can occur, most commonly for discrete distributions (von Hippel 2005). A plot of the data is always a good idea to check for such unusual situations.
4 Tufte (1990) provides numerous examples of creative artists dreaming up ways to convey an amazing range of complex concepts in images.
5 Some authors prefer the single word "boxplot."

5 Probability distributions

At the end of Chapter 4, we presented a number of graphs and plots for visualizing sample data. Histograms, for example, represent the frequency distribution of a variable. The uncertain outcome of any experiment can be modeled mathematically as a *random variable*. However, the probability of any given outcome can be predicted according to a *probability distribution*. Probability theory is built on this idea that the outcome of a random variable is unknown in advance, but the probability of any particular outcome can be modeled. The frequency distribution provides a model for the likelihood of outcomes of an experiment.

A distribution assigns a probability to every possible outcome of an experiment. The simplest probability distribution describes the result of a coin flip. The only two outcomes are heads and tails, and we typically assign 50% probability to each outcome. The probability distribution defined by this example is the *binomial distribution*. The simplicity of the example makes evident that all possible outcomes must be assigned a probability and all of the probabilities must sum to one. We could not, for example, assign a probability of 80% to one side of the coin and 10% to the other. All probability distributions share these two qualities.

The binomial distribution is an example of a *discrete probability distribution*, meaning that every possible outcome can be listed. Another example of an event that can be modeled by a discrete distribution is rolling a die. On a standard, six-sided die, the only possible outcomes are the numbers from one to six; each value is assigned an equal probability if we assume a fair die. Another type of probability distribution is a *continuous distribution* in which a range of numerical outcomes is possible. The height of a person is an example of a continuous random variable because any number is possible within a reasonable range. An easy way to remember the difference between discrete and continuous variables is that discrete variables involve counting or categorizing while continuous variables involve measuring.

Statistical testing often assumes that the shape of the population's probability distribution is known. In addition, test statistics are always built upon the null hypothesis in such a way that the statistics follow a theoretical distribution. The goal of this chapter is to provide a working vocabulary and familiarity with basic information about the most common probability distributions. This background knowledge will aid comprehension of the inferential statistics presented in later chapters.

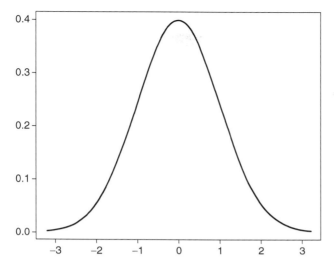

Figure 5.1 Normal (Gaussian) distribution

Normal distribution

By far the most important distribution in statistics is the *normal distribution*, also sometimes called the *Gaussian distribution*. The shape of the normal distribution is the well-known bell curve, which is higher in the middle and lower in the tails of the shape (see Figure 5.1). The peak of the distribution occurs at the mean of the variable. Measurements that are close to the mean are very likely, and measurements that differ greatly from the mean are less likely.

Many actual measurements and observations naturally follow the normal distribution. In the eighteenth century, de Moivre developed a version of the normal curve based on the odds involved in gambling. Galileo was among the first to note that measurement errors are normally distributed. In a final historical example, Adolphe Quetelet measured the chest circumference of over 5,000 Scottish soldiers and showed that the data approximately followed the normal distribution. All of these observations have in common independent, random errors that as a whole will follow the normal distribution. This section describes the importance of the normal distribution and a minimal set of facts needed for applied statistical research.

Normality assumption

All of the parametric statistical tests in this volume require the assumption that the variable of interest follows the normal distribution in the population. Therefore the mean and standard deviation fully describe the distribution, and a plot of the data follows the classic bell-curve shape. Moreover, extreme observations are very unlikely.

60 *Describing*

The normality assumption is the foundation for the statistical theory of hypothesis testing. In particular, normality guarantees control of the level of Type I error and the proper estimation of statistical power. Additionally, confidence intervals require the assumption of normality in order to match their stated level of confidence.

Due to the importance of the normality assumption, numerous tests exist to check formally whether sample data approximately follow the normal distribution. On the whole, these tests for normality suffer from two problems. First, for large samples, the tests tend to reject the null hypothesis too often. Therefore, the test will incorrectly conclude that the distribution is non-normal, when the distribution truly is normal. Second, the tests tend to have low power for samples smaller than 50, which means that the tests will fail to detect non-normality, even if the distribution truly is non-normal. Of the available tests, the Shapiro-Wilk test is superior to the Anderson-Darling test and the nonparametric Kolmogorov-Smirnov test in almost all cases (Ruxton, Wilkinson, and Neuhäuser 2015).[1]

Shapiro-Wilk test

Among the best and most commonly used tests for normality is the Shapiro-Wilk (1965) test. The null hypothesis of this test is that the distribution of the sample is normally distributed, while the alternative hypothesis states that the distribution is non-normal.

Statistical computer packages quite easily calculate and report the Shapiro-Wilk statistic, denoted W, as well as its associated p-value.[2] Hypothesis testing is introduced more fully in Chapter 6, but for the purposes of this discussion the result of the test can be interpreted in a simple manner. If the calculated p-value is less than .05, then there is sufficient evidence that the sample data are not normally distributed. If the calculated p-value is greater than .05, then there is not enough evidence to reject the null hypothesis of normality. In no case can the test definitively prove that the sample data or the underlying distribution follows the normal distribution. The test can only fail to find enough evidence to reject normality.

Pre-testing the sample data for normality in order to determine the appropriate inferential statistical procedure is now widely shunned among statisticians, as discussed in Chapters 7 and 8. Therefore, the Shapiro-Wilk test should be used sparingly. In some cases, it may be necessary to conduct the test following other statistical analyses as a double check of the assumptions. Another situation would be if a research project is conducted for the purpose of showing that a given variable is normally distributed in a population. Again, however, this research question would be quite rare.

z-scores

If a population is known or assumed to be normally distributed, then individual observations can be converted into *z-scores* (also called *standard scores*). The

Probability distributions 61

transformation of raw data into a z-score is also referred to as *standardizing* the observation. The process involves a simple calculation of subtracting the sample mean and dividing that result by the sample standard deviation:

$$z = \frac{x_i - \overline{X}}{s}$$

When sample data are transformed using this formula, the resulting numbers are measured in units of standard deviation. Thus, a z-score of 1.5 means that the original observation is one-and-a-half standard deviations above the sample mean, and a z-score of –2 means that the original observation is two standard deviations below the sample mean. By replacing the units of measurement with standard deviations, a z-score allows comparison to the hypothetical distribution of an entire population.

For instance, a professional translator might respond to a job satisfaction survey on which the scores range from 6 to 30 based on six questions that are measured on a 5-point Likert-type scale. If the translator's reported job satisfaction is 18, the raw data point provides relatively little information to interpret because there is no way to compare the figure to the larger population. However, it might be known from previous pilot studies developing and implementing the survey instrument that the mean of the distribution is 16 with a standard deviation of 1.56. In that case, the z-score would be (18–16) / 1.56 = 1.28. Using a z-table, the probability of observing a score that is 1.28 standard deviations above the mean is approximately 90%. Therefore, this translator reported a higher job satisfaction than 90% of the population. Put another way, this person scored at the 90th percentile for job satisfaction.

Quantile-quantile plots

One method for visually assessing the normality of a sample is to create a *quantile-quantile (QQ) plot*. The term QQ plot is technically generic for the quantiles of any distribution, though in practice it almost always refers to the normal distribution. When the distinction is important, the QQ plot is also referred to as a *normal probability plot*.

The creation of the plot involves ranking the sample observations and then graphing them against the expected values of the observations. The approximations of the expected values are based on the assumption that the population from which the sample was drawn is normally distributed. Therefore, if the sample truly follows the normal distribution, the observed values and the expected values should be equal to each other. Graphically, this situation would result in the graph of a straight line with an upward slope of 45 degrees. For a normally distributed sample, the results would look something like Figure 5.2 in which the observations are almost perfectly lined up on the 45 degree line drawn on the graph.

A QQ plot is also useful for assessing the skewness and kurtosis of sample data. For skewed distributions, the shape will tend to curve in the same direction

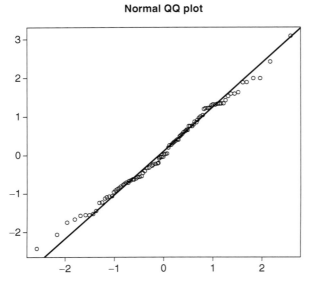

Figure 5.2 Quantile-Quantile (QQ) plot example

on both ends. The shape resembles the letter *c* or a portion of a circle. The plot on the left side of Figure 5.3 displays the result for left-skewed data. For right-skewed data, the curve would be inverted.

For distributions with fat tails (leptokurtic), the QQ plot will be in the shape of the letter *s*, going up on one side and down on the other. The plot on the right of Figure 5.3 shows such a plot for a leptokurtic distribution.

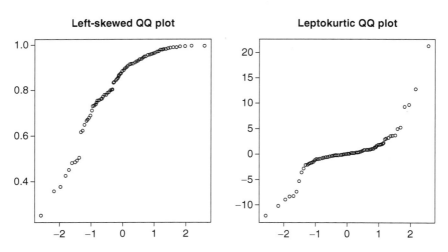

Figure 5.3 Left-skewed and leptokurtic QQ plot examples

Data transformations

If the sample data are not approximately normal, a data transformation may be necessary before proceeding with any parametric statistical tests (Micceri 1989). The need for data transformations will usually be evident from an obvious curve in a scatterplot of the data. Among the more common transformations are taking the square root or the logarithm of every observation; in some cases, these transformed values more closely approximate the normal distribution. One drawback of data transformations is that interpretation can be more difficult. Some of the advantages and challenges of transformations are presented by Osborne (2002).

Datasets that exhibit significant differences from the basic assumptions of parametric statistical tests may require additional care and may require the assistance of a skilled statistician. The interested reader would be well-served by beginning with Tukey's (1977) classic text on exploratory data analysis. However, we also note that the use of nonparametric analysis and other robust estimation techniques often include a component of data transformation. If outliers are dealt with appropriately, the necessity of a transformation may be less common thanks to modern statistical procedures.

Central Limit Theorem

One of the most powerful and widely used theorems in the field of statistics is the *Central Limit Theorem* (CLT). The theorem describes the behavior of the sampling distribution of the sample mean. This very abstract statement can be made more tangible by considering a basic experiment.

Imagine that a measurement is made on a random sample of independent observations, and the mean value of the sample is recorded. For example, a phone survey could be conducted in which 40 households were asked how many children under the age of 18 lived in the home. Some respondents would answer zero, but the answers would vary. The mean number of children might be 2.4 in the sample. The process is then conducted repeatedly: randomly sampling 40 households, asking for the number of children, and calculating and recording the mean value of the responses.

Think of each of these means as being a piece of raw data in a new sample. That is to say, a sample now exists in which every observation is itself an independently created sample mean. According to the CLT, for large sample sizes (of the original experiment, 40 households in this case) the distribution of this new data is normal with the exact same mean as the original population but with a smaller standard deviation.[3] Specifically, the standard deviation of the distribution of sample means is the population standard deviation divided by the square root of the sample size. The important point of this experiment is that statistics follow underlying probability distributions in the same way that random variables follow underlying probability distributions.

Two important points should be made about this heuristic and informal statement of the CLT. First, the distribution of the original population does not need to be normal. In this case, the number of children in a household is not required to be normal for the theorem to be true. The sample size, however, does need to be large, typically meaning at least 30 observations. Second, the standard deviation of the sample mean is usually given a special name, the *standard error*.

To return to mathematical notation, we can create a *z*-score for the sample mean with the standard error in the denominator:

$$z = \frac{\bar{X} - \mu}{\sigma / \sqrt{n}}$$

This formula is another statement of the CLT. The numerator is the difference between the sample mean and the population mean, while the denominator is the standard deviation of the sample mean, which is known as the standard error and is smaller than the population standard deviation by a factor of $\sqrt{n}$.

The CLT is the bedrock of many test statistics. The formula clarifies the impact of a larger sample size in decreasing the standard error. The theorem holds in the mathematical limit as the sample size increases. A common guideline suggests that a minimum sample size of 30 or 40 observations is required for the CLT's conclusion of approximate normality to be employed.

Other distributions

Parametric tests assume that variables used in statistical analysis follow a normal distribution in the underlying population. However, test statistics and confidence intervals involve mathematical computations of the sample data. When data that are assumed to be normal are manipulated, the underlying theoretical structure is altered, and the shape of the distribution changes. Therefore, the three distributions in this section can be thought of as transformations of the normal distribution for the purpose of conducting inferential statistical analysis. Familiarity with the terminology used to describe theoretical distributions is helpful to understand the inferential statistics that are discussed in later chapters. Likewise, the descriptions provided here may help the reader to see the relationships and mathematical structure that form the foundation of statistics. A complete understanding of these theoretical distributions and their derivations, however, is not necessary.

t-distribution

For small sample sizes, the CLT cannot guarantee the normality of the sample distribution of the sample mean because it is built on an assumption of large sample sizes. Furthermore, the formula for the CLT requires knowledge of the population's standard deviation. This parameter is always unknown and must be estimated by the sample standard deviation. The following statistic follows a *t*-distribution, which is very similar to the normal distribution. The *t*-distribution has a symmetric bell shape, but also has fatter tails. That is to say, it has more probability in the tails and a larger chance of observations further away from the mean.

$$t = \frac{\bar{X} - \mu}{s/\sqrt{n}}$$

The shape of the *t*-distribution depends on a figure called degrees of freedom. This concept will be presented in greater detail in Chapter 6; for now, suffice it to say that the degrees of freedom in this case are $(n-1)$, one less than the sample size. As the sample size increases (and the degrees of freedom increase), the shape of the *t*-distribution grows closer to the normal distribution.

The *t*-distribution is used primarily for making inferences about the mean of a distribution and, more usefully, about the difference between the means of two groups. This application is discussed extensively in Chapter 7.

χ^2-distribution

When a number of standard normal distributions are squared and summed, the resulting distribution is called a *chi-squared distribution*,[4] which is denoted by the second power of the Greek letter chi: χ^2. The distribution is used almost entirely for hypothesis testing and not to model any naturally occurring phenomena. The shape of the distribution depends on the number of degrees of freedom, which from statistical theory is based on the number of standard normal variables that are squared and summed. The chi-squared distribution is always greater than zero and is asymmetrical with a right skew.

The calculation of variance is closely tied mathematically to the chi-squared distribution. Therefore, inferences related to the variance often employ it as the underlying theoretical distribution for the test statistics. This test procedure and other chi-squared tests are covered in more detail in Chapter 10.

F-distribution

The *F*-distribution is defined as the ratio of two χ^2-distributions divided by their degrees of freedom. The shape of the distribution requires two numbers for degrees of freedom, called the numerator and denominator degrees of freedom. The names refer to the fact that each of the chi-squared distributions involved in the computation has its own degrees of freedom.

The *F*-distribution is another example of a theoretical distribution that is used almost entirely for hypothesis testing. The distribution is used in Levene's test and other statistics used to test the ratio of two variances (see Chapter 7 for an overview of Levene's test). The primary uses of the *F*-distribution, however, are for analysis of variance (ANOVA) and regression modeling. The mathematical model in both cases is the same; Chapters 8, 9, and 12 make extensive use of the *F*-distribution.

66 *Describing*

Poisson distribution

If a process involves counting the number of times some event occurs in a period of time or space, then the probability distribution of the variable follows a *Poisson distribution*. The events (or *arrivals*, as they are sometimes described) must be independent from one another. The counting process must involve whole numbers only, and it is generally impossible to determine non-occurrence of the event.

Some classic examples include the number of phone calls arriving at a switchboard or the number of hits to a website. The number of people who cross a certain street or the number of cars that travel through a given intersection would also be expected to approximate a Poisson distribution. In each of these cases, the average number of events is stable for a given time period or location, the arrivals are independent, and the events are whole number occurrences only. The distribution is most useful for relatively rare events, and it is naturally skewed to the right because the variable can never be less than zero. For instance, the number of people crossing a given street in an hour could never be negative, but there is a slight chance that a large number of people would cross in a given hour, skewing the distribution to the right.

Translation and interpreting (T&I) studies would likely benefit a great deal from more frequent employment of the Poisson distribution. Relative frequency of type and token lengths follow a Poisson distribution (Baayen 2001; Patton and Can 2012). Therefore, the method is appropriate for a number of applications in corpus-based studies. Furthermore, any research project that involved counting the occurrence of some phenomenon (e.g., interpreter disfluencies, translator typos or pauses) could potentially be modeled with a Poisson distribution. Variables of this kind could even be used in advanced regression models in which the dependent variable is a counted process (Gries 2010). Chapter 12 of this volume includes a brief introduction to Poisson regression.

Outlier analysis

Understanding statistical distributions and the expected shape of sample data can assist in the identification of *outliers*.[5] Various definitions of outliers exist in the statistical literature, but there are two main perspectives. First, outliers can be identified by the unusual nature of the data itself; this perspective focuses on the measurements or inputs to statistical models. Any observation that lies a considerable distance away from the mean or from the majority of the sample data can be defined as an outlier. Second, outliers can be identified by the strong influence they have on the calculation of test statistics (e.g., Stevens 1984). This perspective focuses on the output of inferential statistics, and an outlier is identifiable by the effect its removal has on the conclusions of hypothesis tests or parameter estimation.

The importance of outliers is demonstrated by the famous Anscombe (1973) quartet, displayed in Figure 5.4. The quartet consists of four sets of data that have nearly identical descriptive statistics but dramatically different appearances.

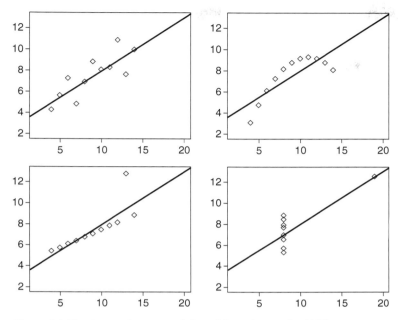

Figure 5.4 The Anscombe quartet (adapted from Anscombe 1973)

The appropriate model and understanding of the data is obvious once they are graphed, but in two of the four cases outliers cause significant errors in the statistical analysis.

Outliers exist for a variety of reasons. Anscombe (1960) describes three sources that contribute to the variability that leads to outliers. Two of the categories, *measurement error* and *execution error*, represent problems with the data collection process. For example, Balling and Hvelplund (2015) argue that eye tracking studies with fixations below 40 milliseconds or pupil diameters greater than 9 mm are highly unlikely to produce valid data. Seeber (2013) also discusses pupillometric measures and the impact that external factors may have on physiological eyetracking data. For these kinds of errors, the best solution is often to remove the observation from the dataset. Anscombe's (1960) third category is *inherent variability*. Random sampling will sometimes result in the inclusion of a more extreme measurement that is unusual but perfectly valid. Researchers are tasked with the challenging problems of identifying outliers and selecting the best strategy for dealing with them.

Identification of outliers can be univariate or multivariate. The simplest method for recognizing univariate outliers involves graphical techniques (Gries 2010). Box plots and scatterplots reveal obvious errors and draw attention to potential problems (Coleman, Galaczi, and Astruc 2007). Univariate outliers can also be recognized by calculating the z-scores of each data point. If the data follow the

68 *Describing*

normal distribution, z-scores greater than three (or less than negative three) represent observations with a very low probability. The generalization of this process to multivariate data is called *Mahalanobis distance* (1936), and an important related measure in the context of regression analysis and residual errors is *Cook's distance* (1977). The actual computations lie beyond the scope of this volume, but in all of these cases outliers are detected by their unlikely large distance from an expected or predicted value.

Once outliers have been detected, there are several possible ways of dealing with them. For obvious cases of data error, outliers should be removed from the sample data, a process sometimes referred to as *trimming* the data. For example, Leijten, van Waes, and Ransdell (2010) chose to omit data from seven participants in their experiment involving keystroke logging and reaction time measurement; some of the omissions were due to technical errors and others were due to outlying observations of the measured variables. Manually trimming large datasets can be time-consuming and potentially subjective (Balling and Hvelplund 2015). Therefore, in corpus or eye tracking studies in particular, outlier removal must be done automatically according to some rule, such as the omission of any data point that lies more than three standard deviations away from the mean.

An alternative to trimming is *winsorizing* the outlying observations. The process involves replacing extreme observations with a pre-specified percentile of the sample data. For instance, all outliers beyond the 95th percentile might be recoded to have the same value as the 95th percentile observation or some other maximum allowed value. This clipping process does not require removal of a participant, which can be valuable for smaller samples, but it does prevent extreme measurements from skewing the analysis.

In some cases, trimming or winsorizing can obscure the most interesting observations in a dataset. Outliers should not be discarded without careful regard for any information they might contain. Osborne and Overbay (2004) mention the unexpectedly long lifespans of some women living with untreated HIV in Africa. Those cases likely represent an excellent source for future research, rather than data to be discarded. Examination of extreme cases, such as the best practices of fast-working translators, the learning strategies of extreme polyglots, or the more significant décalage of some professional interpreters, might eventually yield particularly interesting results.

Instead of altering the sample data directly, alternative statistical techniques can be selected that are more resistant or robust to outliers. For instance, the median can be used as a measure of center rather than the mean, as in Leijten, van Waes, and Ransdell (2010). Data transformation can also be included in the testing procedure—for example, nonparametric tests often use a rank transformation. Wilcox (1998) is a staunch advocate of other modern techniques such as the trimmed mean, M-estimation, and robust regression.

The best approach for dealing with outliers is multi-pronged. Outliers should be identified by graphical, statistical, and practical methods. Statistical models should be estimated both with and without identified outliers in the dataset. Residual checks should be a routine part of inferential statistical procedures. Finally, the research report should document the procedures used. A good example in the literature is O'Brien's (2007) treatment of the variable words per second. The measurement was skewed significantly by outliers when, for example, one participant completed a passage of eight words in two seconds without making any edits. The author excluded five such extreme cases, but she also reported descriptive statistics both with and without the outliers in order to show their influence. Well-executed, fully-described procedures demonstrate the researcher's recognition and proper handling of outliers, thereby building confidence in the meaningfulness of the quantitative results.

Notes

1 The Kolmogorov-Smirnov test has been the subject of particular criticism (e.g., Tukey 1993).
2 Technically, almost all popular software implements Royston's (1992) approximation of the Shapiro-Wilk test, but the distinction is not important to use or interpret the test.
3 This presentation of the CLT foregoes mathematical formality to provide a heuristic understanding for applied statistics. To be slightly more formal, the theorem assumes that the sample size grows toward infinity. Therefore, it does not hold exactly in small samples.
4 Some authors prefer "chi-square." However, the notation and derivation are both related to raising standard normal variables to the second power, so they have been "squared."
5 Aggarwal (2013) provides a comprehensive treatment of the topic of outliers.

6 Statistical terminology and one-sample tests

This final chapter of Part II serves as a bridge between descriptive and inferential statistics. We begin by defining a number of statistical terms and concepts. These terms are important in describing research designs and understanding statistical analysis, so comprehension of this vocabulary will help to establish the conceptual foundation for inferential statistics. Discussion of these terms is necessarily limited; we instead aim to provide a working vocabulary and a brief synopsis of the major ideas for quick reference should the need arise. Several of the presented concepts, such as effect size and confidence intervals, are treated in greater detail in subsequent chapters.

The one-sample tests at the conclusion of this chapter provide easy-to-understand examples of how to conduct inferential statistics. The tests themselves are of modest utility compared to the more powerful and commonly-employed tests later in the book. However, we describe these basic tests in a step-by-step manner to clarify the process of hypothesis testing with these examples, in order to build the foundational knowledge that will allow for learning more complex tests.

Introduction to statistical terminology

In Chapter 4 we covered descriptive statistics, which are used to summarize sample data. In Chapters 7–12, we will explain the application of inferential statistics, which attempt to reach conclusions about the underlying population. In other words, the goal of these analyses is to generalize the findings from the observed sample data as a way to understand the larger population from which the sample was drawn. Statistics provides the tools and structure for making those inferences, and this section is devoted to a minimal set of definitions that will assist in understanding that process. Some of these terms have already been introduced and rough definitions suggested; however, this section provides more formal definitions along with some examples and discussion of the various terms.

Definition of a statistic

The formal definition of a *statistic* (as opposed to the discipline of statistics) is any function of the sample data. Therefore, a statistic is a numerical value that is calculated from measurements in the collected sample. The calculation can involve all of the sample data, in the way that the sample mean consists of adding all of the observations and dividing by the sample size. The calculation can involve fewer pieces of data, however, such as the median, which uses only one or two of the observations, depending on whether the sample size is odd or even. A statistic might also simply be one data point such as the maximum observation.

A statistic can serve three purposes. First, it can serve as a descriptive statistic of the sample. For example, the sample mean serves as a descriptive measure of center. The use of various descriptive statistics was covered in Chapter 4. The remaining two purposes are needed for inferential statistics. The second use of a statistic is as an estimator, in which the number provides an approximation of the unknown population parameter. For example, the sample mean is an estimator for the unknown population mean. The next subsection of this chapter is devoted to the topic of parameter estimation. The third application of a statistic is for hypothesis testing, in which the calculated figure is used to compare the sample data to a theoretical distribution. This comparison is made in order to determine whether to reject the null hypothesis. Hypothesis testing is described more fully below.

Parameter estimation

One purpose of inferential statistics is *parameter estimation*. A *parameter* is an unknown property of a population that is estimated by the collection of sample data and calculation of a statistic. The parameter thus serves as the target quantity when thinking in terms of validity and reliability. A parameter is considered fixed for a given population at a given time. Conversely, a statistic varies based on several sources of error. The reasons for variability include sampling error and measurement error. Theoretically, if an entire population could be measured simultaneously (a *census*), then the parameter could be known with certainty.

An example of a parameter is the average height of all the adult women in Norway. At any moment in time, this is a fixed number. If we could measure every single woman in the country simultaneously, we could calculate the true average height of the population. Of course, this data collection process is impossible; by the time we gathered and processed the data, the population would have changed (e.g., people grow or immigrate) so that the number would no longer be the true parameter. To overcome this challenge, we collect a random sample and use the average height of the sample as an estimate of the population parameter.

Just like the previous height example, we could hypothetically calculate the average hourly wage of every person in the country to obtain a single average. This number would encompass all of the variability that exists with respect to professions, years of working experience, and any other variable impacting how much a person earns. We could do the same if we were interested in the average wage of a certified court or medical interpreter in a given country. However, all of these scenarios are impractical, and we would instead calculate an estimate. Data could be collected from a random sample of interpreters by means of a survey on wage information in order to estimate this unknown parameter.

72 *Describing*

Thinking of a parameter as a fixed goal of estimation is appropriate only after careful definition of the population. A parameter is fixed only for a well-defined population at a given moment in time. The parameter of average wage of court interpreters in one country is different from the average wage of court interpreters in another country. Moreover, parameters can and will change over time. The quality of a parameter estimate also depends on the quality of the sample, the validity and reliability of the estimator, and various other errors that can introduce variability. One of the main tasks of statistics is to provide high-quality parameter estimates.[1]

Confidence intervals

Parameter estimation results in a single number estimate, called a *point estimate*. This estimate can be thought of as a best guess approximation of the population parameter. However, different samples will result in different point estimates; there remains uncertainty about how far our sample estimate lies from the population parameter. Rather than estimating with a single number, therefore, it is possible to construct an interval estimate called a *confidence interval* around the point estimate. The goal is to define the confidence interval in such a way that the parameter lies within the interval.

If we think again about calculating the average height of women in Norway, one sample of 30 women might give an estimate of 165 cm. If we repeat the experiment with a new sample of 30 different women, we might get a sample mean of 169 cm instead. Theoretically, we could repeat the process over and over again: collecting a sample of 30 women, calculating the sample mean, and constructing a confidence interval around the mean. In every case, the confidence interval would be a particular function of the sample data. Therefore, in each case the confidence interval either contains the parameter or it does not. By repeating the process many times and by constructing the confidence intervals in a particular way based on probability theory, we can predict how often the confidence interval contains the parameter.

In almost all cases, confidence intervals are constructed for 95% confidence and symmetrically around the point estimate. Therefore, the formula for the endpoints of a confidence interval can be compactly written as the point estimate plus or minus a distance determined by the sample's variability and a number from the appropriate probability distribution. Examples that accompany each statistical test in this volume will clarify the exact procedures necessary, and most software packages provide appropriate confidence intervals automatically around point estimates. For the primary tests of a research project, a confidence interval should always be reported to improve interpretation beyond the simple point estimate.

The best way to think of a confidence interval is as an interval estimate based on the sample data. Imagine you were offered a prize if you could guess how many marbles were in a jar. The number of marbles in the jar is a parameter, a fixed but unknown trait. If you were allowed only to guess one number, say 210, you would be very unlikely to be correct. However, if you could guess an interval, perhaps guessing that the number of marbles was between 170 and 250, then you would be more likely to win the prize. The estimate would be more likely to include the parameter. Of course, your guess is either right or wrong; you are not 95% likely to win the prize. A 95% confidence interval means that if the sampling and calculation process was repeated an infinite number of times, then 95% of the confidence intervals would contain the true parameter. Over-interpretation beyond that should be avoided.

Hypothesis testing

Null and alternative hypotheses were introduced in Chapter 1. The two hypotheses represent different models or structures of the underlying population. In the process of hypothesis testing, the null hypothesis is assumed to be true unless the sample data provide convincing evidence otherwise. In that case, the sample data would suggest that the alternative hypothesis is a better description of the sample data. For instance, a very simple statistical model might have a null hypothesis claiming that the average hourly wage of a conference interpreter is $1,200. Obviously any collected data would reject this null hypothesis as a poor model of the actual hourly wage of conference interpreters (though it would be nice!).

The process of conducting a hypothesis test involves the determination of two numbers. First, a test statistic is calculated from the sample data. The test statistic could be the same as a descriptive statistic, such as the variance, or a statistic with a more complicated formula. Second, a critical value is found from a theoretical distribution, such as the F-distribution. Then, the magnitude of these two numbers is compared. The comparison leads to a decision about the null hypothesis. Test statistics that are more extreme (more negative or more positive) than the critical value lead to rejection of the null hypothesis. This section describes various terms related to hypothesis testing and closes with a discussion of some criticisms, strengths, and weaknesses of the procedure.

Errors, power, and p-values

In reaching the decision of a hypothesis test, two different errors could occur. Type I error describes the situation in which the null hypothesis is rejected, even though it is true. A Type I error corresponds with a false positive, wherein the sample suggests a relationship or a difference exists, even though no such effect is present. In contrast, a Type II error describes the opposite situation, in which the test procedure fails to reject the null hypothesis, even though it is false. The probability of a Type I error is denoted with the Greek letter alpha, α, and the probability of a Type II error is denoted with beta, β.

The simile of a Type I error as a false positive is often clear in a medical context. If a person tests positive for a disease they do not have, they might be subjected to unnecessary treatments. If a pill is incorrectly proclaimed to be able to cure a disease, many people might waste time and money (not to mention risking side effects) with no benefit. In translation and interpreting (T&I) studies, a simple corresponding example might be pedagogical studies. In that setting a Type I error would be an announcement that a new method of instruction or studying would increase the speed of language acquisition, when in fact, there is no measurable benefit when applied to the whole population. A Type I error provides false information that can lead to bad results, wasted resources, and misdirected research efforts based on incorrect decisions.

The level of Type I error is set in advance by the researcher by choosing a significance level for the statistical test. In every statistical test in this volume, the significance level is set at 5%, which is a nearly universal standard in applied social science research. The statistical testing procedures are designed to maintain this chance of rejecting the null hypothesis when it is true (committing a Type I error). Keep in mind that the level is arbitrary and that interpretation of statistics needs to include more than one piece of information.

A Type II error is the failure to reject an incorrect null hypothesis. This type of mistake would rarely result in any announcement of the findings or action taken, so a Type II error is considered less severe than a Type I error. When the level of Type II error is subtracted from one, the resulting number is referred to as *statistical power*. So a 20% probability of Type II error implies 80% statistical power. Power is the probability of correctly rejecting the null hypothesis when it is false. The level of power is not directly controlled by the researcher, but larger sample sizes always lead to increases in power. Balanced designs that have the same number of participants in each group also generally increase power. Finally, several different statistical procedures will exist for testing any given research design; selection of the best test is often driven by power considerations.

Power considerations should always occur before any statistical procedures are conducted. Estimating a minimally meaningful effect, selecting the best test statistic, and determining the necessary sample size are all related to statistical power and should be part of the planning stage of any research project (Lenth 2001). Post hoc power considerations are not useful and do not convey any additional information beyond the p-value and confidence interval (Hoenig and Heisey 2001; Colegrave and Ruxton 2003).

When a test statistic is calculated, the result can be compared to a theoretical probability distribution. The distribution implies the likelihood of observing that particular result. An important probability in this context is called the p-value. In calculating the p-value, it is assumed that the null hypothesis is true, and the probability distribution of the test statistic is developed under that assumption. Then the computed test statistic from the sample is compared to the distribution. The probability of getting a more extreme test statistic (larger in absolute value) is the formal definition of the p-value. Therefore, the p-value represents the probability of an even more unusual result than the particular sample. If that probability is low, meaning less than 5%, then the sample would appear to violate the assumption that the null hypothesis is true. Thus, the null hypothesis would be rejected.

For example, we might compare the means of two groups with a null hypothesis that they are the same. When a difference is observed, the appropriate question is whether the difference is large enough to constitute a significant difference or whether the difference is small and due simply to random experimental error. Thanks to modern statistical computing software, a *p*-value provides a fast way to make a decision regarding a statistical test. If the *p*-value is less than .05, the null hypothesis is rejected. Otherwise, there is not enough evidence to reject the null hypothesis at the 5% level of significance.

A result should be declared either statistically significant or not statistically significant only at the pre-determined level. The significance level is almost always 5% in social science, but this level is traditional and arbitrary. The determination that a result is meaningful should be provided by a measure of effect size,[2] reporting of the descriptive statistics, and a discussion of how the results fit into the larger body of scholarship on the particular topic. Strictly describing *p*-values in terms of "statistical significance" rather than just "significance" can help prevent this misunderstanding.

The precise numeric value should not be over-interpreted.[3] An all too common, although incorrect, practice is attempting to use a *p*-value to demonstrate the importance of a statistical result. Asterisks sometimes appear in tables for tests that result in different levels of *p*-values with an implication that smaller p-values are somehow more significant. Rasch, Kubinger, Schmidtke, and Häusler (2004) argue strongly against this practice, despite its wide adoption by statistical software and its use in many publications. An equally erroneous practice is the suggestion that a *p*-value larger than .05 somehow "approaches" significance or is "nearly significant." A final caution regarding *p*-values is that simple comparisons between them are not appropriate (Gelman and Stern 2006). This issue is discussed further in the final chapter of the volume on the topic of reporting.

Degrees of freedom

For many people who have survived an introductory statistics class, *degrees of freedom* (often abbreviated *df* in reporting) is a poorly understood concept that amounts to rote formulas needed for certain statistical tests and distributions. We cannot hope to provide a complete formal understanding in a brief treatment, but a definition in simple language and some examples will hopefully clarify the main intent. Degrees of freedom in general can be thought of as how many additional facts or pieces of data are required so that everything about the relevant variable is known. For example, imagine that you are told that a sample contains 50 people, who all speak either Mandarin or Korean as their primary language. If you are then also told that 35 people in the sample speak Mandarin, then it is automatically known that the remaining 15 people speak Korean. This example has only one degree of freedom because learning one piece of information (i.e., that 35 people speak Mandarin) allowed for complete knowledge about the distribution of language in the sample.

We can extend this example to multiple languages. A sample of 100 citizens of Switzerland could contain people who have as their L1 one of its four official languages: German, French, Italian, or Romansh. If it is known that 38 people have German as their first language, 27 French, and 23 Italian, then it automatically follows that 12 people speak Romansh as their L1. Knowing three pieces of information provide complete information about the variable in this case. Consequently, there are three degrees of freedom. This pattern that the degrees of freedom are one less than the number of categories holds true in many cases, particularly for analysis of variance (ANOVA; see Chapter 8). In many situations the degrees of freedom are one less than the sample size, based on a similar argument.

A bit more formally, we mentioned in Chapter 4 that the denominator in the sample variance calculation ($n-1$) is the number of degrees of freedom for the estimate. The reason is that the normal distribution has only two parameters: the mean and the variance. In order to calculate the variance, the mean must first be estimated, and this estimation creates a restriction in the relationships among the sample data. Therefore, another way of thinking about degrees of freedom is that you start with the sample size and subtract one degree of freedom for every estimated parameter. This way of thinking aligns well with regression design and more complicated ANOVA models.

The reason degrees of freedom matter when conducting inferential statistics is that they determine the shape of the theoretical distribution that is used for finding the critical value. In particular, the t-distribution and the χ^2-distribution have different shapes based on the related degrees of freedom, and the F-distribution requires two different measures of degrees of freedom, called the numerator and denominator degrees of freedom. For the non-mathematically inclined, the degrees of freedom are usually easy to find in computer output and should always be reported in parentheses or brackets behind the name of the distribution in any research report. For instance, if a t-statistic was 1.85 with 24 degrees of freedom, it would be reported as $t(24) = 1.85$.

Residual errors

Hypothesis testing always involves the consideration of statistical models to describe data. Once a model has been estimated, the predictions of the model can be compared to the observed data. The difference between the predicted values and the actual values are referred to as *residuals* or *residual errors*.

The sample mean is an example of one of the simplest statistical models. If the average height of American men is approximately 177 cm, then the best guess for any randomly selected man is that he will be 177 cm tall. If a randomly selected man is 180 cm tall, then the residual error for that observation is 3 cm. More complicated models can make better predictions using more information. For instance, a regression model could use a person's gender, weight, shoe size, and age to predict his or her height. The model's equation would make a prediction that could be compared to sample data and the residual would be the difference between the prediction and the observed measurement.

Residuals are useful for checking the adequacy and accuracy of statistical models. For most models, the residuals should be random and approximately follow the normal distribution. Obvious patterns or outliers in the residuals can suggest problems with the chosen statistical model. Therefore, we will discuss residual errors often in Chapters 7 through 12.

Adjustments to hypothesis tests

The validity of null hypothesis significance testing (NHST) always rests on a set of assumptions about the sample data and the underlying population. In practice, these assumptions are never fully met, only approximated. Furthermore, a research project often involves conducting multiple tests with the same set of data. Statistical adjustments can be made in an attempt to correct for these issues.

Any adjustments made to NHST procedures are typically made in the service of two goals: controlling the probability of a Type I error at a specified level (usually 5%) and maximizing the power of the test (which is equivalent to minimizing the probability of a Type II error). Adjustments can be made in three ways. First, the computation of the statistic itself can be changed; taken to the extreme, a different test statistic can be used. Instead of the mean, we can use the trimmed mean or the median, for example (Wilcox 1995). Second, the degrees of freedom can be computed differently. Lowering the degrees of freedom is one way to acknowledge a greater degree of uncertainty, thereby creating a more conservative test in order to reduce the chance of a Type I error. Third, the p-value cutoff can be reduced below a nominal 5% level. The second method corresponds to Welch's adjustment to the t-test and the third method to the Bonferroni correction, both of which are discussed in Chapter 7.

Effect size

NHST can provide information on the probability of observing a given result, but *effect sizes* provide an understanding of the strength and practical impact of a difference or relationship. Ellis (2010: 5) describes this difference between two types of significance, by noting that "[p]ractical significance is inferred from the size of the effect while statistical significance is inferred from the precision of the estimate." Although the shortcomings of NHST have been debated for decades, only in recent years has the reporting of effect sizes come to the forefront as a primary supplement to statistical testing. The *Publication Manual* of the APA (2009: 33–34) now emphasizes the importance and need for reporting of effect sizes to convey the full results of a study. However, the published literature still lags in providing effect sizes (Ferguson 2009; Fritz, Morris, and Richler 2012). Even rarer is the reporting of a confidence interval for the effect size (Algina and Keselman 2003). In our description of test statistics, we focus on raw effect sizes with only occasional references to confidence intervals surrounding them. Applying the lessons of confidence intervals, however, would improve interpretation, especially for smaller effect sizes.

The reporting of effect sizes communicates the practical impact or meaningfulness of a study's results. Therefore, an effect size should be included for every statistical test, whether or not it is significant. Knowing the relative importance of variables assists in the accumulation of knowledge and theory development (Lakens 2013).

There are three primary ways to report effect sizes. The simplest is to use the same units of measurement as the study and describe the actual difference. For instance, a study could report that post-editing MT output was, on average, 5 minutes faster (95% CI [2.5, 7.5 minutes]) than human translation of the same passage. The advantage of this approach is that it communicates the relevant difference in meaningful terms. However, the original units do not allow for comparison to other studies, so the two alternative approaches involve standardized effect sizes.

Standardized effect sizes come in two primary types, known as the d family and the r family. Although almost any test can be described by an effect size from either group, the d family measures the standardized difference between groups, so it is appropriate for the tests of difference that we report in Part III. Meanwhile, effect size in the r family focuses on the strength of relationships and are most appropriate for the tests in Part IV. For each of the tests we discuss, we include a section on the relevant effect size. For a more thorough but approachable treatment, see Ellis (2010).

Parametric and nonparametric tests

The distinction between *parametric* and *nonparametric* tests lies principally in the assumptions that are made about the underlying population. To begin with, a parametric test typically assumes that the variable of interest follows a normal distribution in the population. Nonparametric tests make fewer assumptions (though, it should be noted, they are not assumption-free). In particular, nonparametric tests do not assume normality of the sample data.

The two reasons for preferring nonparametric tests in certain cases is to maintain control of the probability of a Type I error and to increase statistical power. Whenever the assumptions of a parametric test cannot be met, there is generally a nonparametric procedure available that will meet these two criteria. In this volume, we present nonparametric tests side-by-side with their parametric counterparts, rather than relegating them to their own chapter, as is common in previous books.[4] The smaller sample sizes and unknown population distributions that characterize much of T&I research suggest that nonparametric procedures deserve a more prominent placement and wider adoption.

With large enough sample sizes, a claim is often made that the Central Limit Theorem (CLT) provides assurance of approximate normality. Therefore, nonparametric tests are used primarily for experiments with smaller sample sizes. Nonparametric tests are valid for any sample size, but their advantage in terms of power and Type I error are generally slight with larger sample sizes. We stress that the decision between parametric and nonparametric methods should be based on an assessment of the assumptions. Both can be valid for small or large sample sizes, but generally nonparametric tests are more common for sample sizes smaller than 40. This number serves as a guideline only, and the final decision should be multi-faceted.

Reporting results

The treatment of the terminology covered in this chapter serves two purposes. First, knowing the definitions will help in understanding the presentation of the statistical tests in later chapters. Second, the headings should serve as a checklist for reporting the results of statistical analysis. Reporting the results of the main test procedures of any research paper should include the following:

1. An estimate of the population parameter of interest, including a confidence interval;
2. A description of the statistical test procedure, including whether it was parametric or nonparametric and the reason that the test's assumptions are adequately met;
3. The results of the statistical test, including the value of the test statistic, its degrees of freedom (if appropriate), and its exact p-value;
4. A measure of effect size.

Descriptive statistics, graphs, and tables should also be included when they improve interpretation. All of this information can be concisely reported in a few paragraphs at most, as we will illustrate in later chapters of this book. The responsibility of the researcher is to interpret these numbers in a meaningful way in terms of the research hypothesis.

One-sample test for the mean

This section will demonstrate the procedure for the statistical test of the value of the mean. In doing so, we will illustrate many of the terms described so far in this chapter and transition from preparing and describing data to testing and making inferences, topics that dominate Parts III and IV. To test whether the mean value equals a numerical constant we employ a one-sample t-test.[5] The null hypothesis is that the mean of the underlying population equals a specified number, and the two-sided alternative is that the mean does not equal that number.

The one-sample t-test examines a simple research question. For instance, we might investigate whether the average time needed for to translate a 500-word passage was 120 minutes for a sample of 100 translators. The null and alternative hypotheses would be the following: $H_0: \mu = 120$ and $H_1: \mu \neq 120$. We generated fictional data for this situation and calculated the following descriptive statistics: $M = 122.6$ minutes, $SD = 10.9$ minutes, with observations ranging from 101.6 minutes to 156.8 minutes.

The one-sample t-test assumes that the sample data are continuous and drawn from a population that is normally distributed. In this case, given a fictitious sample size of 100, we can argue that the CLT promises approximate normality. Additionally, the data must be independently collected. Other tests have more restrictive assumptions, but this particular test is used in this chapter precisely because it is a simple test for introducing the general procedure.

The appropriate test statistic is built on the sampling distribution of the sample mean (see Chapter 5) and is calculated by dividing the difference in the estimated and hypothesized mean by the standard error:

$$t = \frac{\overline{X} - \mu}{s/\sqrt{n}} = \frac{122.6 - 120}{10.9/\sqrt{100}} \cong 2.37$$

This test statistic follows a *t*-distribution with 99 degrees of freedom (one less than the sample size). The appropriate critical value for this situation is 1.98; therefore, because the test statistic exceeds the critical value, the null hypothesis can be rejected.

When the test is conducted with statistical software, a *p*-value will also be provided. In this case, the *p*-value is .0197, which is less than the 5% cutoff. Notice that the decisions based on the critical value or on the *p*-value will always be identical, but rejection occurs when the test statistic exceeds the critical value and, equivalently, when the *p*-value is below the 5% level.

The point estimate of the population mean is simply the sample mean, and a confidence interval can be built around the sample mean with the following formula:

$$\overline{X} \pm t_{crit} * \left(\frac{s}{\sqrt{n}} \right)$$

The critical value from the *t*-distribution appears in this formula. For the example data, the 95% confidence interval would result in the following:

$$122.6 \pm 1.98 * \left(\frac{10.9}{\sqrt{100}} \right) \cong [120.42, 124.76]$$

The final step is to calculate the effect size. Because we are making a comparison of the degree that a sample potentially differs from a hypothesized mean, we use the formula for Cohen's *d*:

$$d = \frac{\overline{X} - \mu}{s} = \frac{122.6 - 120}{10.9} = .239$$

A more substantial discussion of Cohen's *d* appears in Chapter 7. For now, it is sufficient to understand that .239 is a rather small effect size.

We have now completed all of the necessary calculations to report the results of this experiment. In practice, most of them would be conducted by statistical software, but effect sizes in particular often require some hand calculation. Furthermore, knowing the process allows for better interpretation of computer output. Complete reporting would look something like that shown in Figure 6.1.

To test whether the average time-on-task was 120 minutes, a one-sample *t*-test was conducted. Results imply that the average time is greater than the hypothesized 120 minutes (*M* = 122.6, *SD* = 10.9, 95% CI [120.42, 124.76], *t*[99] = 2.37, *p* = .02). However, the effect size was small (Cohen's *d* = .239). The observed mean time exceeded the hypothesized time by only 2.6 minutes.

Figure 6.1 Reported statistics for mean time on task example

This reporting includes all of the required information listed above. The purpose is to allow the reader to understand not only the statistical significance but the practical impact of the study. The particular example here is statistically significant. However, with a small effect size and a 95% confidence interval that nearly includes the hypothesized mean of 120 minutes, the meaningfulness of the results would be rather low. Further discussion of the results and how they relate to the literature would appear in the discussion and conclusion of the research report.

One-sample test for the median

Our first example of a nonparametric test is the *Wilcoxon signed-ranks test* (1945) for the median, also called simply the *signed-ranks test*. The procedure is relatively simple and introduces some of the most common issues related to nonparametric statistics. Assume that a professor assigns a translation exam to 100 students but only takes 10 of the completed exam papers home to grade and forgetfully leaves the rest in her office. She grades the 10 exams and observes the following scores:

55, 64, 69, 71, 74, 82, 85, 86, 89, 98

She now wants to determine whether the class median is 70. The sample median is 78 (the average of 74 and 82). The statistical test can determine if this difference is unusual or extreme enough to be statistically significant or if the difference between 70 (the hypothesized median) and 78 (the sample median) is due to random error.

As with all statistical tests, the first step is to check that the data meet the assumptions. The signed-ranks test has relatively few assumptions, and they are easily met:

1 The sample is randomly drawn from the population of interest;
2 The population is symmetric around the median for the variable of interest;
3 The variable of interest is continuous and measured at least at the interval scale;
4 The observations are independent.

The null hypothesis of the test is that the median is equal to some specified value, and the most common alternative hypothesis is the two-tailed version that the median is not equal to the specified value. In mathematical notation, $H_0 : M = c$ and $H_1: M \neq c$ where c represents some number. In the example, $c = 70$, the hypothesized median score.

82 *Describing*

The test statistic is completed in four steps. First, the hypothesized median is subtracted from every observation. Second, the absolute values of the differences are ranked. The smallest value is given a rank of one with any differences of zero ignored. If ties occur, all of the tied observations receive the same rank, which is the mean of the rank positions they would have occupied. This rank transformation procedure is very common in nonparametric statistical tests. The ranking eliminates the outliers and effectively moves the data from a higher level of measurement to the ordinal level of measurement.

Third, each rank is assigned the same sign as the associated difference score. Fourth, the ranks of the positive and negative scores are summed separately and labeled T^+ and T^-. The smaller of these two sums is the final test statistic, denoted T.

The procedure sounds more complex than it is in practice. Like many nonparametric procedures, the work can be completed quite easily by hand or with Excel. Of course, most statistical software packages will also do these calculations automatically. Table 6.1 illustrates these steps for the sample exam scores.

The first column displays the raw scores. The "Difference" column is the raw scores minus the hypothesized median value of 70. Notice that the data have been ordered according to the absolute value of this difference. The "Ranks" column provides the ranks of the differences, with ties recorded as the average of the associated ranks. The "Signed ranks" column contains the same number as the "Ranks" column with the same sign (positive or negative) as the "Difference" column. Finally, the two sums are calculated. The smaller sum is 12, and this value is the final T-statistic for the test.[6]

The final decision regarding the null hypothesis requires comparing this value to a table of critical values to obtain a critical value and/or p-value. Published tables are available for sample sizes up to 30. For a sample size of 10, the critical value of the two-tailed test is 8. Test statistics that are less than 8 result in rejection of the null hypothesis. Since the calculated test statistic in the example is 12, we

Table 6.1 One-sample test for the median example data

Scores	Difference	Ranks	Signed ranks
69	−1	1.5	−1.5
71	1	1.5	1.5
74	4	3	3
64	−6	4	−4
82	12	5	5
55	−15	6.5	−6.5
85	15	6.5	6.5
86	16	8	8
89	19	9	9
98	28	10	10
	Sum of positive ranks: T^+		43
	Sum of negative ranks: T^-		12

cannot reject the null hypothesis. There is not enough evidence that the population's median is different from 70.

The remaining statistics for the signed-ranks test demand more complicated formulas. Therefore, we will omit their details and refer the reader to Daniel (1990) for general details. Of course, most applied researchers will rely on statistical software. Output from the program R provides a 95% confidence interval of [67.5, 87.0] and a *p*-value of .131.

The effect size will often need to be calculated by hand until statistical software begins to more regularly incorporate such estimates into its procedures. Kerby (2014) provides a method for calculating an effect size measure in the *r* family. First, calculate the total sum of the ranks for the given sample size: $S = \frac{n(n+1)}{2}$ and then use that figure in the final calculation:

$$r = \frac{(S-T)}{S} - \frac{T}{S}$$

For our sample, $S = \frac{10*11}{2} = 55$ and $r = \frac{55-12}{55} - \frac{12}{55} = .56$. As we mentioned previously, the interpretation of effect sizes is discussed further in later chapters, but an *r* value of .56 would be considered a large effect. Notice that the null hypothesis could not be rejected but the effect size was large. The implication is that further research is needed. Replication with a larger sample size or better experimental controls will likely lead to statistical significance. However, the practical impact of the difference can also be interpreted directly without the need for statistical significance. The relevant question is whether a class median of 78 instead of the hypothesized value of 70 is meaningful in this case.

The nonparametric test described here exhibits many common features, beginning with the rank transformation of the data. Complications in confidence intervals and *p*-values are also common. In some cases, nonparametric tests employ large-sample approximations and correction factors for tied observations. These corrections complicate the numerical procedures but not the final interpretation. It always remains the case that *p*-values less than 5% imply rejection of the null hypothesis. However, confidence intervals and effect sizes are also necessary and arguably more important than the simple decision of whether to reject the null hypothesis. Finally, reporting of the results (see Figure 6.2) would be similar to the parametric case:

To test whether the median test score was 70, a one-sample Wilcoxon signed-ranks test was conducted. The observed median (78) exceeded the hypothesized value. However, the results were not statistically significant ($T = 12$, $p = .131$, 95% CI [67.5, 87.0]). The effect size was large ($r = .56$), which suggests that the difference may have practical meaning for this application.

Figure 6.2 Reported statistics for median test score example

Notes

1 In theoretical statistics, estimators are evaluated based on a set of criteria that includes *unbiasedness*, *efficiency*, and *consistency*. For reasons of space, we must omit formal definitions of these and other properties. However, a significant portion of theoretical statistics has historically been devoted to the creation of statistics that possess desirable properties. Communicating some of the results of ongoing development in the field is one motivation for this volume.
2 Effect sizes and p-values are mathematically related. However, the sample size plays a role in the calculation of each, so a small effect can be significant and a large effect can be nonsignificant. For this reason, researchers should always report both an exact p-value and a measure of effect size.
3 See Nickerson (2000) for a comprehensive discussion of interpretation fallacies related to p-values.
4 Space considerations allow for the selection of a limited number of nonparametric tests and relatively brief treatments. For a more comprehensive overview see Daniel (1990).
5 Some introductory statistics books and classes also teach the similar z-test, which can be used when the standard deviation is known. Since this will almost never be the case, we omit a description of this test.
6 There are a number of different ways to combine the final ranks. Depending on the procedure, the test statistic is sometimes denoted by W or V. Also, take careful notice that this T-statistic does not follow Student's t-distribution.

Part III
Analyzing differences

In Part III, our attention shifts from preparing and describing to analyzing quantitative data. All of the statistics that we discuss in this section depend on adequate preparation, proper sampling techniques, reliable and valid measurement, and ethical data collection. No amount of statistical expertise can overcome problems with the foundational issues discussed in Part I. Furthermore, the descriptive statistics of Part II provide the mathematical and terminological basis for further analysis with the inferential statistics covered in these chapters. The one-sample tests that concluded Part II represent transitional techniques from description to inference.

The particular focus of Part III is using inferential statistics to analyze differences among groups. We discuss the procedures for hypothesis testing, confidence intervals, and effect size measurements. We also provide guidance in selecting the right test, interpreting results, and reporting the findings from the statistical analysis.

In Part III, we present four chapters related to analyzing differences. In Chapter 7, we describe the statistical tests for comparing two groups, beginning with the parametric t-test and the nonparametric Mann-Whitney U-test, followed by the paired t-test and Wilcoxon matched-pairs signed-ranks test. Chapters 8 and 9 describe the main applications of the many varieties of analysis of variance (ANOVA), all of which allow for comparisons among multiple groups and multiple variables. In Chapter 10, we describe chi-squared tests, which are used primarily with categorical data.

7 Comparing two groups

The purpose of the inferential statistics in this chapter is the identification of statistically significant differences when comparing two groups to each other on some measurement. Research in translation and interpreting (T&I) studies often pose questions structured around the examination of two groups. For instance, Carl et al. (2011) report on the results of an experiment that compares human translation to post-editing of machine translation (MT) output. One group of participants translated British newspaper texts into Danish, while another group post-edited a machine-translated version produced by Google Translate. Their results suggest several benefits of post-editing, including slight improvements in quality and time savings. In another example, O'Brien (2007) compared two groups of English-to-German translators, one set of participants translating the text and the other post-editing a machine-translated text. Among the findings was a faster speed and lower technical effort for the post-editing group.

In both of these examples, two distinct groups of participants performed a task under different conditions and were measured using continuous-level variables. These situations illustrate the basic data template for a test of differences: two groups (a binary independent variable) are scored on some measurement (a continuous dependent variable). For Carl et al. (2011) and O'Brien (2007) the independent factor had two levels—i.e., human translation and post-edited MT—and in each of these studies one of the dependent variables was the time needed to complete the translation task. The goal of the statistical analysis is to determine whether the groups differ in terms of the mean value of the dependent measurement. The statistical tools described in this chapter provide a formal method to distinguish whether group differences are statistically significant. The basic inferential statistic for this situation is called Student's *t*-test, and its nonparametric counterpart is the Mann-Whitney *U*-test.

A variation on this research design is to use the same sample and measure the dependent variable twice under different conditions. For instance, Roziner and Shlesinger (2010) examined the differences in the working conditions of remote and on-site conference interpreters. The design involved participants working

Comparing Two Means: Overview

Purpose: To determine whether there are statistically significant differences in the means of two independent groups.

Null hypothesis: The means of the two groups are the same (H_0: $\mu_1 = \mu_2$)

Alternative hypotheses:

1. The means are different (non-directional, H_1: $\mu_1 \neq \mu_2$)
2. The mean of one group is larger than the mean of the other (directional, either H_1: $\mu_1 > \mu_2$ or H_1: $\mu_1 < \mu_2$)

Experimental designs:

1. A single dependent variable is measured for two independent groups (*t*-test)
2. A measurement is made twice from the same group of subjects (paired *t*-test)

Parametric tests: Student's *t*-test, Welch's *t*-test

Nonparametric tests: Mann-Whitney *U*-test, Wilcoxon matched-pairs signed-ranks test

Effect size: Cohen's *d*, Hedges' *g*

and being measured in both environments. The researchers used participant self-reporting, medical data, and observation to compare a number of measures of working conditions and performance. The results provide practical suggestions to improve the remote interpreting environment, thanks to this side-by-side comparison. In a similar design, Braun (2013) conducted an experimental study to compare the performance of French-English legal interpreters in remote and face-to-face settings. She concluded that remote interpreting (RI) is associated with greater challenges for interpreters, including "message content, linguistic items, paralinguistic features and coordination of talk, and a faster decline of performance in RI over time" (Braun 2013: 219). This type of design, in which each participant is measured twice, calls for either a paired *t*-test or the nonparametric Wilcoxon matched-pairs signed-ranks test.

The remainder of this chapter focuses on the details of these four tests: the *t*-test, the Mann-Whitney *U*-test, the paired *t*-test, and the Wilcoxon signed-ranks test. We also discuss a variation of the *t*-test conducted on the ranks of the original data. For each test, the assumptions are examined, as well as adjustments and alternatives when those assumptions are violated. We also describe the hypothesis tests and measures of effect size for each. Throughout the chapter, we utilize fictitious datasets to illustrate the testing procedures and published T&I research to show how the tests have been implemented. Four such examples are briefly summarized in Table 7.1. The chapter concludes with an example of reporting results.

Table 7.1 Comparing two means: Examples from T&I literature

1 Carl et al. (2011) compare the process of post-editing machine translated text to the work of human translators. The use of Translog allowed the authors to compare keystroke and gaze data. In comparing the two groups, the authors found slight improvements in quality and faster translation time for post-editing.
2 O'Brien (2007) also considered the work of human translators and post-editing of machine translation. Post-editing effort was reported to be lower, on average.
3 Timarová and Salaets (2011) assess the difference in various traits and abilities between interpreters (a group that includes both conference and liaison interpreting students) and a control group of students in the third year of an applied language undergraduate degree program. Among a number of dependent variables, they use the Wisconsin Card Sorting Test (Grant and Berg 1948) to measure cognitive flexibility. They conduct t-tests to determine whether the two groups differ and determine that the interpreting group makes fewer errors ($M = 15.8$) than the control group ($M = 20.1$), on average.
4 Marlow, Clough, Recuero, and Artiles (2008) assign 12 participants several search terms in various languages (four each in an appropriate L1, L2, and L3 for each participant) and ask them to identify and bookmark three relevant web pages in five minutes. The search terms were divided into "hard" and "easy" categories, based on the ability of Google Translate to translate them correctly. Among several dependent variables, the researchers noted the number of pages bookmarked for each task. The mean number of bookmarks for the easy topics (2.105) differed significantly from the hard topics (1.559).

To demonstrate the use of the statistical tests covered in this chapter, we describe an example related to measuring the elevation above sea level in two countries. The simple research question is whether Russia or Canada has the greater average elevation. Both countries are geographically large and exhibit substantial variation in their terrain. Therefore, it would be difficult to make a confident prediction of the outcome of the study. A two-tailed t-test provides a method to conduct a formal comparison.

To make a determination, a random sample of locations is identified in each country, and elevation data are collected at those locations. The first step in analyzing the data is calculating the descriptive statistics and creating plots. For this fictitious example, we generated a sample of 28 observations in each country. A comparison boxplot of the data appears in Figure 7.1. For the sample data, the mean elevation in Russia is 739.4 meters, and in Canada it is 594.3 meters. The associated standard deviations are 353.3 and 380.4 meters, respectively.

From the descriptive statistics and the boxplots, there is suggestive evidence that the average elevation in Russia is greater than in Canada. However, the difference could be caused by the sampling error, due to the particular randomly selected points, rather than a true difference. Furthermore, the relatively large standard deviations cause a great deal of overlap in the boxplots. To show the danger of making decisions based on comparison of the means and examination of the plots, consider the histograms of the same data in Figure 7.2, drawn

90 *Analyzing differences*

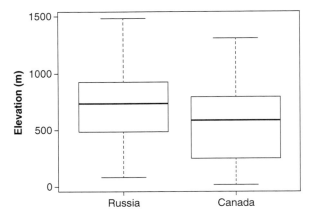

Figure 7.1 Box plot of sample data for Russia and Canada elevation example

with estimated normal curves. The difference does not appear obvious in these figures, even though Russia's mean elevation of 739.4 exceeds Canada's 594.3 meters. The histograms highlight the need to consider variability in addition to the sample means.

Inferential statistics provide a probability-based method for determining whether the mean elevations of the two countries are different. As we shall see in the description of Student's *t*-test, there is not enough evidence in these data to conclude that a difference exists. The testing procedures described in this chapter provide the basis for a conclusion that goes beyond simple observation of the descriptive statistics.

Student's *t*-test

The classic parametric test for comparing two groups is called the *t*-test. Gosset (1908) initially published the test under the pseudonym "Student," which led to

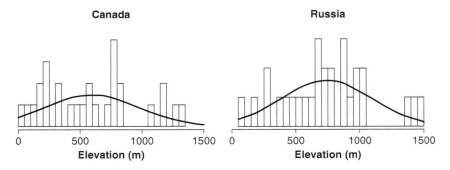

Figure 7.2 Histograms of sample data for Russia and Canada elevation example

the test being referred to as Student's *t*-test. We will sometimes follow the shorter naming convention. In terms of research design, the *t*-test is appropriate for the comparison of a post-test only experimental design with two independent groups. Therefore, the test is utilized to compare two different groups that complete the same task in a controlled environment, such as comparing novices to experts or language learners and native speakers on a translation task.

The test determines whether the means of the two independently measured groups differ at a statistically significant level. The null hypothesis is that the means of the two groups are the same: $H_0: \mu_A = \mu_B$. The alternative could take any of three forms: $\mu_A > \mu_B$, $\mu_A < \mu_B$, or $\mu_A \neq \mu_B$. The last of these, the two-tailed test, is the most common; as we discussed in Chapter 6, there should be a good theoretical reason or prior expectation to suggest the use of a one-tailed test. Otherwise, the two-tailed test should be preferred. The decision of analytical procedure should be made prior to any statistical analysis.

Assumptions

The assumptions of any statistical test provide the ideal conditions under which Type I error is controlled and power is maximized. Violations of these conditions do not automatically imply incorrect decisions regarding the null hypothesis, but they do suggest less-than-optimal performance and an increased likelihood of errors. An analogy is a motor vehicle that performs best when it is properly maintained. Worn out mechanical parts or poorly inflated tires will make any journey less efficient, and the vehicle may not reach its destination. In an analogous way, using a statistical test without its assumptions being met results in lower power and an uncontrolled chance of Type I error.

For the *t*-test to be valid, three assumptions must be met:

1 The observations are *independent*;
2 The variance of the two groups are identical, known as homogeneity of variance or *homoscedasticity*;
3 The underlying population must be *normally distributed*.

The once-standard advice was to pre-test the assumptions of the *t*-test by employing a set of additional hypothesis tests. However, statisticians have reconsidered the effects of this process, and many papers in the statistics literature now argue convincingly against this idea of pre-testing (e.g., Rasch, Kubinger, and Moder 2011). The problem arises from the introduction of multiple decisions in the testing process; the preliminary test determines what test to use in the second stage of analysis. Simulation studies show that Type I and Type II errors are affected by this conditional application of the *t*-test. Direct application of the correct test is the best procedure.

The quandary for applied research is that the test's assumptions must be considered, even though statisticians no longer recommend the use of preliminary tests. The solution is multi-faceted. First, samples should be of equal or nearly equal size, because this maximizes power in all situations. Inferential statistics are thus not divorced from the planning and sampling procedures. Second, boxplots and histograms should always be examined for obvious violations of the assumptions and the existence of outliers or problems in the data. Third, if similar studies or a pilot study have been conducted, the evidence of those results should be considered in selecting a statistical test. Finally, when faced with uncertainty, more robust procedures should be preferred.

Independence

The first assumption is that all observations are independently collected. In other words, the response or performance of one individual is unaffected by others in the sample. This is not tested statistically, but is instead achieved through good research design. Careful thought should be given to the research protocol and any potential confounding variables. For instance, Marlow, Clough, Recuero, and Artiles (2008) assigned participants to various web search tasks in an experimental setting. Every participant worked individually on the assigned problems and the performance of each participant had no bearing on what the others did. In doing so, the researchers could ensure independence of the observations.

Equal variance

Student's t-test requires an assumption of equal variance in the two groups. Previously, the standard advice was to check this formally with a preliminary test called Levene's test (1960). The null hypothesis of Levene's test is that the variances are equal, so a p-value less than .05 is evidence that the two groups have unequal variances. A now-outdated practice was to conduct Levene's test first and subsequently use Student's t-test only if Levene's test failed to reject the null hypothesis of equal variance.

The primary reason to shun the two-stage analysis of Levene's test followed by a t-test is the resulting distortion in the probability of a Type I error. Simulation studies have demonstrated that the problem is further exacerbated by small sample sizes and that the situation is worse when the two sample variances are numerically close (Zimmerman 1996, 2004). Furthermore, simulation studies have raised concerns about possible issues with Type I error properties of Levene's test itself, particularly for small samples and non-normal populations (Neel and Stallings 1974). Therefore, application of Levene's test as a pre-test for the equality of variances is no longer recommended.

Situations with unequal variances are quite common, since the two groups being compared are composed of people who differ on some trait or who are working under different conditions. To give one practical instance, comparisons of experts and novices will many times result in a different range of performance on some task. The performance of experts will generally cluster much more tightly, while novices display a range of outcomes. Timarová and Salaets (2011) provide an example of this kind of study by comparing individuals with more interpreting training to a control group. Variance can also differ due to different types of tasks being completed by the two groups. An example is the different kind of work required for translation and for post-editing, as in O'Brien (2007). In these types of situations, unequal variances should be expected.

Because inequality of variances for two groups is so common, a number of statistical papers now recommend the use of a modification called *Welch's t-test* as the default method for comparing two groups (e.g., Moser and Stevens 1992; Zimmerman 2004). If the assumptions can be met, Student's *t*-test technically provides slightly higher statistical power. The assumption is most likely to be met when each group has an equal number of participants of at least 30, the tasks being completed are relatively equivalent, and the populations do not differ greatly in their training or other personal traits. We present the details of Student's *t*-test because they are a more easily understood statistical procedure that is appropriate for this idealized situation. The test provides a baseline against which other tests can be compared and understood, though in practice Welch's *t*-test (described in a later section) should be preferred. When equal variance cannot be assumed, Student's *t*-test should not be used.

Normality

The final assumption for the *t*-test is that the sample data come from a population that is normally distributed. As we discussed in Chapter 5, the normality of a sample can be tested by using the Shapiro-Wilk test. However, as was the case with the equal variance assumption, pre-testing the normality assumption is no longer recommended as an acceptable practice, following a deluge of evidence from statistical simulation studies (e.g., Arnold 1970; Rao and Saxena 1981; Moser, Stevens, and Watts 1989; Zimmerman 2011).

Pre-testing the normality assumption causes a number of issues, the worst of which is a distortion of the probability of Type I and Type II errors. Schucany and Ng (2006) recommend great caution in applying normality pre-tests. In their simulation study, pre-testing does not solve the problems of Type I errors and actually worsens them in some cases. By creating multiple layers of testing, pre-testing introduces multiple opportunities for errors, which weakens the final results.

Additionally, the performance of pre-tests for normality are particularly weak when distributions are skewed, a finding that is reinforced and extended by Rochon and Kieser (2011). Therefore, graphical methods are important to screen for obvious evidence of non-normality. Rank-based tests such as the Mann-Whitney *U*-test should be preferred in the situation of non-normality.

Another problem with using the Shapiro-Wilk as a pre-test is that failure to reject the null hypothesis does not guarantee normality. The test's null hypothesis states that the data do come from a normal distribution. However, failure to reject a null hypothesis does not prove that the null hypothesis is true, simply that the evidence is not strong enough to reject it. Therefore, it is illogical to use a pre-test as an argument in favor of the normality assumption (see Schucany and Ng 2006). It is also important to remember that the assumptions must apply to the underlying

94 Analyzing differences

population and not to the sample data. The normality or non-normality of the sample may be due to the sampling procedure, confounding variables, or random error. None of these are properties of the actual population of interest.

Selecting the right test

When the assumptions of Student's *t*-test are violated, alternative procedures are recommended. Each of the alternative tests addresses the violation of a specific assumption. Welch's *t*-test is designed to counteract the effects of unequal variances, and the Mann-Whitney *U*-test is preferable when the underlying populations are not normally distributed. When both conditions are violated simultaneously, all of these tests can have unacceptable levels of Type I error. In such a case, estimation using outlier detection and trimmed means may be the most appropriate course of action (Zimmerman 1998). However, one straightforward method has been shown to perform well: conduct Welch's *t*-test on the rank transformation of the raw data (Ruxton 2006; Zimmerman and Zumbo 1993).[1] The ranking procedure reduces the influence of outliers while Welch's procedure compensates for heterogeneity of variance. This underutilized test procedure would be of great value for small-sample studies that do not appear to meet the three assumptions outlined in this section.

Hypothesis testing

If the assumptions of the *t*-test are met, the first step in conducting the hypothesis test is to calculate a combined measure of standard deviation that incorporates data from both samples. This estimate is called the *pooled standard deviation* (s_p). Because Student's *t*-test assumes that the two samples come from populations with equal variances, all of the data can be combined in one estimate of the pooled standard deviation:

$$s_P = \sqrt{\frac{(n_A - 1)s_A^2 + (n_B - 1)s_B^2}{n_A + n_B - 2}}$$

In the formula, the groups are indicated by subscripts, with sample sizes n_A and n_B and standard deviations s_A and s_B. The resulting figure is a weighted average of the standard deviation of the two groups. For the elevation example comparing Russia (group A) to Canada (group B), the pooled standard deviation can be calculated using the sample sizes for each (n_A and n_B both are 28) and the individual groups' standard deviations ($s_A = 353.3$ and $s_B = 380.4$):

$$s_P = \sqrt{\frac{27*353.3^2 + 27*380.4^2}{28 + 28 - 2}} = 367.1$$

The second step is to use the pooled standard deviation in the calculation of the *t*-statistic. All *t*-tests have the same general structure: a ratio in which the numerator includes the means and the denominator is a measure of standard deviation. To test for the difference in means between two independent samples, the *t*-statistic takes the following form:

$$t = \frac{\overline{X}_A - \overline{X}_B}{s_P \sqrt{\frac{1}{n_A} + \frac{1}{n_B}}}$$

Researchers will not need to calculate this equation by hand since statistical software packages will perform this task. Seeing the formula, however, helps clarify that the test relies both on the difference between the means and the variability, represented in the formula by the pooled standard deviation. Lower levels of variability allow for the detection of smaller differences in the means. For the Russia and Canada comparison, the calculated *t*-statistic is approximately 1.48.

To determine statistical significance, the calculated statistic is compared to a critical value from the *t*-distribution. The proper critical value depends on the degrees of freedom for the test, as determined by the sample size. For Student's *t*-test, the degrees of freedom are given by the total sample size minus two, because the mean from each group is estimated and one degree of freedom is lost for each estimate. Therefore, the formula for the degrees of freedom is $df = n_A + n_B - 2$. For the elevation data, there are 28 observations from each country so there are 54 degrees of freedom: $df = 28 + 28 - 2 = 54$.

The significance level is also a determinant of the critical value. For the comparison of the elevation of Russia and Canada, the two-tailed 5% critical value is 2.005. Because the absolute value of the test statistic is less than the critical value, the null hypothesis cannot be rejected. Restated, there is not enough evidence that the means of the two groups differ significantly. Computer output of this analysis would also include a *p*-value of .1449, which exceeds the 5% cutoff. Therefore, the results are not statistically significant.

To review, the process of conducting a *t*-test can be summarized in a few steps:

1 Calculate descriptive statistics: sample means and sample standard deviations for each group.
2 Verify that the assumptions of the test are satisfied using boxplots.
3 Combine the standard deviation measures into a pooled standard deviation.
4 Compute the *t*-statistic.
5 Find the critical value, using the pre-selected significance level.
6 Make the decision of the hypothesis test by comparing the *t*-statistic to the critical value, or equivalently, reject the null hypothesis when the *p*-value is less than .05.

All six steps are conducted simultaneously by computer software, and the final decision is to reject the null hypothesis if the *p*-value is less than .05.

Confidence intervals

When reporting a *t*-test, a confidence interval for the difference in the means should always be provided. A 95% confidence interval is standard in most cases, and it gives the reader a better understanding of the likely difference in the parameters of the two groups. The endpoints of the confidence interval are calculated with the following formula:

$$(\bar{X}_A - \bar{X}_B) \pm t_{n_A+n_B-2} * s_P \sqrt{\frac{1}{n_A} + \frac{1}{n_B}}$$

The *t*-value in the equation (2.005 in the case of 54 degrees of freedom) comes from the calculated values of the *t*-distribution with the appropriate degrees of freedom. The pooled standard deviation (s_p) comes from the earlier formula. For the elevation data, the 95% confidence interval for the true difference in elevation between Russia and Canada can be calculated as follows:

$$(739.4 - 594.3) \pm 2.005 * 367.1 * \sqrt{\frac{1}{28} + \frac{1}{28}}$$

The formula gives a 95% confidence interval of [−51.6, 341.8]. The results provide 95% confidence that the true difference in the means lies in this range. Since this particular interval includes zero, there is not sufficient evidence to state that the parameters are different.

Effect size

As we discussed in Chapter 6, the results of statistical tests should include a measure of effect size. For the results of a *t*-test, some authors (e.g., Field 2013) advocate correlational measures (referred to as the *r* family) for use with *t*-tests. However, the most commonly reported measures of effect size for Student's *t*-test are standardized measures of difference (the *d* family).[2] The most well-known measure of this type is Cohen's *d* (1962), which is defined as the difference between the sample means, scaled by the pooled standard deviation:

$$d = \frac{\bar{X}_1 - \bar{X}_2}{s_P}$$

Depending on the order of the means, *d* can be positive or negative, but the absolute value is usually reported, along with descriptive statistics that make it clear which mean is larger.

The denominator of Cohen's *d* requires an estimate of the pooled standard deviation, which can be calculated several different ways. Among the most common choices is to use the same pooled standard deviation estimate as for the *t*-statistic calculation. In that case, the statistic is more properly called Hedges' *g*

(1981) or Cohen's *d* with Hedges' correction. For large samples, the difference is negligible, while for small samples the correction factor is important. The correction factor prevents overestimation of the effect size.

Because small sample sizes are often employed for translation and interpreting (T&I) studies, we advocate the use of Hedges' *g* in reporting effect sizes for all *t*-tests. The measurement provides information related to the difference between the means, which is the purpose of a *t*-test procedure. Furthermore, Hedges' *g* is an unbiased version of Cohen's *d*, and the numerical difference is generally small.[3] For the example data comparing the elevation of Russia and Canada, the effect size is calculated as follows: $g = (739.39 - 594.29)/367.1 = .395$.

Interpreting the magnitude of the effect size is context specific. If a study compares multiple solutions to a problem, the existence of alternative solutions and cost–benefit analysis are necessary to gauge the importance of the effect. For instance, a study of classroom pedagogy that showed a statistically significant but very slight effect size might still lead a researcher to recommend adoption of a new practice if it were inexpensive and easily implemented. Specifically, a small improvement in vocabulary acquisition with the use of flash cards might be more valuable for students than a slightly larger improvement that requires purchasing computer software. Effect size must be weighed, described, and interpreted in terms of meaningfulness in a practical setting.

As a general guideline, Cohen (1988) suggested that an effect size of 0.2 should be considered small, 0.5 medium, and 0.8 large (and these standards are applicable for either *d* or *g*). However, the benchmarks were offered along with a caution that effect sizes always need to be considered within the context of the study. Blindly applying these guidelines is not good practice. Instead, a researcher should describe the practical implications and approximate magnitude of the observed change. Additionally, effect sizes from similar studies in the literature provide a comparison. The ability to compare results and aid replication efforts are two more reasons why research reports should always report effect sizes.

Cohen's guidelines are widely cited but are not immune from criticism; nor is this the only available standard. Ferguson (2009) gives much higher figures for Cohen's *d*: .41, 1.15, and 2.70 for the recommended minimum practical effect (RMPE), moderate, and strong effect sizes, respectively. This more stringent standard means that the practical impact will be greater, but it also requires stronger evidence. Beyond the numerical controversy, language of small, medium, and large has been criticized as generic T-shirt sizes that are removed from the practical setting. In a survey article of various effect size estimates, Fritz, Morris, and Richler (2012) offer the terms merely statistical, subtle, and obvious as candidate replacement terms.

At a minimum, some measure of effect size should be provided in all research reports. Further reporting of effect sizes can be provided when they are useful in convincing a reader of the practical impact of a difference in means between two groups. Confidence intervals for the effect size estimate can be calculated (e.g., Cumming and Finch 2001; Bird 2002). However, a description in terms of practical significance is likely more useful for a reader than additional statistical

98 *Analyzing differences*

analysis. The purpose of reporting effect size is to show the meaningfulness of a study's result, so pro forma presentation of statistics should be eschewed in favor of a broader discussion of the results.

Sample size determination

All researchers have heard repeatedly that bigger sample sizes are always better. For T&I studies, collection of a larger sample size can be thwarted by lack of resources or access to members of the population. In a qualitative study on cognitive processing of translation memory proposals conducted by O'Brien (2008), only five participants were ultimately included in the study. O'Brien recognizes the possibility that results may change given a larger sample size, but notes that due to challenges inherent to participant recruitment and attrition, data collection sometimes requires researchers to make do with limited sample sizes. Researchers might also be frustrated by the vague notion of the maxim that bigger is better. This subsection discusses the benefits of a larger sample size and helps in determining an estimated number that is in line with the research goals.

The advantages of a larger sample size are increased power in hypothesis testing and narrower confidence intervals. Mathematically, the benefit arises from the presence of the sample size in the denominator of the sample variance estimation. Both advantages imply the ability to detect smaller effect sizes between two groups. Thus, selecting an appropriate sample size requires a predetermination of a minimum effect size that would constitute an interesting or meaningful result.

The multiple factors to be weighed (both statistically and practically) create challenges in the planning of a study and estimating an appropriate sample size (Lenth 2001). For a *t*-test of two independent groups, an estimate of the necessary sample size is a function of the confidence level, the estimated power, and the minimal effect size of interest. Traditionally, the confidence level is 5%, the power is set at 80%, and a researcher can select Cohen's *d* at various levels to determine the sample size (Dupont and Plummer 1990). A rough estimate of the relationship is that the minimum sample per group is given by $n = \dfrac{16}{d^2}$, which is rounded up to the nearest integer.

For the traditional .2, .5, and .8 measures of Cohen's *d* representing small, medium, and large effect sizes, the respective minimum sample sizes are 400, 64, and 25. Identifying a small effect size requires a large increase in sample size, because the relationship is not linear. For many studies involving human subjects, the power to detect small effect sizes will be quite low because recruiting enough participants for the two groups is impossible, unduly expensive, or prohibitively time-consuming.

Recall that these are estimated relationships to be used in planning. The numbers provide a useful guideline but must be considered in terms of the study's goals and the expectations regarding effect size and meaningfulness. If such figures are reported at all, they would be discussed in the methods section of a research report, while describing the sampling procedure. Post hoc calculation of power is unnecessary and ill-advised (see Lenth 2001 for an extended discussion of this issue).

Welch's *t*-test

In almost all cases, the strict assumptions of Student's *t*-test are not met. To compensate for the situation of unequal variances, two adjustments can be made to the procedure outlined above. First, the pooled variance is replaced with a weighted figure of both sample variances. Second, the degrees of freedom used to find the critical value are altered. When modified in these ways to account for unequal variances, the *t*-test should properly be referred to as Welch's *t*-test (1947).

In practice, researchers often generically report the use of a *t*-test, without any reference to Student or Welch. Many are likely running Welch's *t*-test, because it is provided by default in several computer programs. An astute reader can determine which test was used by examining the degrees of freedom, since the degrees of freedom are always (n–2) for Student's test but smaller for Welch's. Still, reporting should strive for clarity in exactly which test is employed.

In almost all applied T&I research, Welch's *t*-test is the superior choice. In terms of interpreting computer software output, the test statistic without assuming equal variances should be reported. Rasch, Kubinger, and Moder (2011) present a simulation study supporting this point. First, they reinforce the negative results of pre-testing for equality of variances and normality before selecting a test for the difference between two means. Second, they propose that Welch's *t*-test should be considered the default test. Zimmerman (1996) gives the same recommendation of unconditional use of Welch's *t*-test because of its superior performance. Furthermore, Moser, Stevens, and Watts (1989) report that Student's *t*-test is more powerful than Welch's *t*-test only in certain situations, such as vastly different sample sizes, which are unlikely to be of interest in well-designed research projects. Even then the power advantage is typically less than 5%, so the loss in power is negligible. Therefore, researchers should strongly favor the use of Welch's *t*-test when comparing the mean values of two groups.

The first change in procedure for conducting Welch's *t*-test is the omission of a pooled estimate of the variance. The example below again uses data from the comparison of elevation in Russia and Canada. The test statistic consists of the difference between the means divided by a measure of standard deviation, but the estimate of standard deviation involves both sample variances rather than a pooled variance.

$$t = \frac{\bar{X}_A - \bar{X}_B}{\sqrt{\frac{s_A^2}{n_A} + \frac{s_B^2}{n_B}}} = \frac{739.4 - 594.3}{\sqrt{\frac{353.3^2}{28} + \frac{380.4^2}{28}}} = 1.479$$

In most cases, the value of Welch's *t*-statistic will be similar in magnitude to Student's *t*-statistic (Student's *t* was 1.48 for these same data). Many statistical programs will either report both versions or choose between them automatically, based on the variances of the two samples. However, researchers should never allow computer software to do their thinking. Welch's test is almost always preferable and should be the default method unless convincing evidence is available that the variances are equal.

100 *Analyzing differences*

The second difference when using Welch's *t*-test is calculating the degrees of freedom using Satterthwaite's correction (also called the Welch-Satterthwaite formula):

$$df = \frac{\left(\dfrac{s_A^2}{n_A} + \dfrac{s_B^2}{n_B}\right)^2}{\dfrac{\left(\dfrac{s_A^2}{n_A}\right)^2}{n_A - 1} + \dfrac{\left(\dfrac{s_B^2}{n_B}\right)^2}{n_B - 1}}$$

Based on this formula, Welch's test will not have an integer number of degrees of freedom. In the example problem, the formula results in 53.71 degrees of freedom. When critical values had to be looked up on tables, the degrees of freedom were rounded down to the nearest whole number. Using any good statistical software, however, makes such advice obsolete, and research reports should include two decimal places for the degrees of freedom in reporting results of Welch's *t*-test.

The effect size of Welch's test is still most commonly calculated by Cohen's *d*, with identical interpretation to Student's *t*-test. The confidence interval calculation is also similar, with only the standard deviation changing from the pooled version to the inclusion of the standard deviation of each group:

$$\left(\bar{X}_A - \bar{X}_B\right) \pm t_{n_A + n_B - 2} * \sqrt{\dfrac{s_A^2}{n_A} + \dfrac{s_B^2}{n_B}}$$

In the case of our example data, the confidence interval is hardly changed by this alternate calculation. The reason is that the variances of the two groups are not dramatically different.

Mann-Whitney *U*-test[4]

Whereas the problem of unequal variances can be overcome with the modifications of Welch's test, violation of the normality assumption can seriously undermine the validity and performance of the *t*-test (Delaney and Vargha 2000). In statistical parlance, the *t*-test is not robust to departures from non-normality. When the relevant underlying distribution is not normal, nonparametric tests generally have better statistical properties (Bridge and Sawilowsky 1999). This section provides information on the Mann-Whitney *U*-test, which is a nonparametric test analogous to the *t*-test.[5]

In the situation of non-normality, the Mann-Whitney *U*-test can have greater statistical power than parametric methods (Blair 1981), and simulation studies consistently demonstrate the advantages of the Mann-Whitney *U*-test in a range of conditions (e.g., Blair, Higgins, and Smitley 1980; Sawilowsky and Blair 1992).

The Mann-Whitney U-test is often used with relatively small samples (fewer than 30 observations per group), in which case the Central Limit Theorem (CLT) does not apply for approximate normality. Penfield (1994) showed in a simulation study that for non-normal distributions with equal variances, the Mann-Whitney test outperformed the t-test in terms of power for a number of sample sizes up to 20 per group.

Notice that sample size is not the sole determinant of which test to use. Rather, the underlying population's normality (or lack of normality) is the key issue. Furthermore, the t-test can be effectively used on small samples, as long as the test's assumptions are strictly met.[6] Therefore, we stress that the primary motivation for using the Mann-Whitney test is presumed non-normality of the population. The Mann-Whitney test is not appropriate in the case of unequal variances, only for the situation of non-normality.

A number of variables in T&I studies are likely to be non-normal due to the nature of the phenomena studied. For example, word usage is often shown to follow Zipf's law (1949), in which the frequency of a word's usage is inversely proportional to its rank. Furthermore, individual work performance is often described as following a stable Paretian distribution, in which extreme outliers are much more likely to occur (O'Boyle and Aguinis 2012). T&I studies regularly combine measures of language and measures of individual performance with small sample sizes, thereby compounding the problematic nature of assuming normality in statistical analysis. The Mann-Whitney U-test is appropriate in these situations where a normality assumption is untenable.

Nonparametric methods of analysis have been utilized by some researchers in T&I. For instance, in her comparison of translation and post-editing, O'Brien (2007) had a sample of 12 translators, and descriptive statistics displayed a number of outliers. Therefore, the Mann-Whitney U-test was used for group comparisons. Similarly, Rosiers, Eyckmans, and Bauwens (2011) used the Mann-Whitney U-test to compare the performance of students of T&I on several measures, namely communication competence, language anxiety, motivation, and self-perception of linguistic competence. The paper does not discuss the motivation for their choice of method explicitly. However, given a sample of 35 participants and several performance measures that are unlikely to be normally distributed, the Mann-Whitney test appears to be an appropriate choice.

The procedure for calculating the Mann-Whitney statistic involves the ranks of the observations, rather than the raw data. The rank transformation is common in nonparametric statistics, as we described in Chapter 6. The test makes the following assumptions to compare two independent samples on some continuous random variable:

1   The data are two random samples from populations with unknown medians.
2   The samples and observations are independent.
3   The dependent variable is continuous and capable of being ranked.
4   The distributions of the underlying populations differ only with respect to location.

102 Analyzing differences

The final assumption requires the distributions to have a similar shape and measure of dispersion, as discussed in Chapter 4. Therefore the distributions can differ only by a shift in their location. This assumption implies that the Mann-Whitney U-test compares the medians of the two groups. Therefore, the sample data should be visually inspected for similarity in the distributions. If a significant difference between the two groups is apparent, alternative test procedures should be used, such as Welch's t-test on the rank-transformed data.

The calculation of the U-statistic involves, first, calculating the sum of the ranks in each group. The larger of these two sums is denoted S, which is combined in a formula with the sample size of each group to calculate the final statistic:

$$U = n_1 n_2 + \frac{n_1(n_1+1)}{2} - S$$

For small samples, this statistic is readily understood and easily calculated by hand. Consider a fictitious sample of the time (in minutes) that it takes to complete a translation of a brief passage. Group 1 might consist of students in a translation program and Group 2 of professional translators. The time needed to complete the task is measured and converted to ranks. The data for our fictitious example is shown in Table 7.2.

The slowest time (9.08 minutes) is assigned a rank of 1, while the fastest time (1.21) is assigned a rank of 12, and all other times are ranked accordingly. The ranks are then summed. The larger of the two sums is taken to be S in the computation of the test statistic. So in this example, $U = 6*6 + \frac{6*7}{2} - 53 = 4$. The U-statistic can then be compared to the 5% critical value from statistical tables in making a decision whether to reject the null hypothesis. Values of U that are smaller than the critical value imply rejection of the null hypothesis in favor of the alternative hypothesis. For the example data, the critical value is 5, so we conclude that the medians of these two samples differ, at the 5% level of significance.

Three modifications can be made to the Mann-Whitney U-test. First, when the sample size in either group is larger than 20, an approximate z-statistic can be calculated, based on the CLT (Daniel 1990). Second, if the large-sample approximation is used, a continuity correction can be applied to account for the alteration

Table 7.2 Mann-Whitney U-test example data with rank transformation

Group 1	Rank	Group 2	Rank
9.08	1	4.81	5
5.12	4	1.42	10
3.94	6	3.02	8
6.59	2	1.33	11
6.29	3	3.34	7
2.28	9	1.21	12
Sum	25	Sum	53

from the discrete Mann-Whitney U-statistic to the continuous normal distribution. Finally, if there are ties in the observations, a correction factor can be included in the calculation.

These three adjustments will likely all be made by computer programs, rather than by hand calculation, but Bergmann, Ludbrook, and Spooren (2000) point out that several popular programs actually use different algorithms in conducting the Mann-Whitney test. This difference is a strong argument in favor of using software over which the user has more programming control, such as R. At the very least, researchers are urged to check the documentation of their preferred program for information and to report what software was used. Modifications due to adjustments will result in slightly different p-values, depending on the software used and the correction methods employed.

A confidence interval for the difference should be provided along with the results of the Mann-Whitney test and the median of each group. Statistical software packages generally provide these figures. However, researchers should be aware that many programs employ a measure of center called the Hodges-Lehmann (1963) estimator rather than the median.

Effect size

When calculating the effect size, either the exact U-statistic or the approximate z-statistic for large samples can be used. In the first case, the effect size is measured by the rank-biserial correlation formula provided by Wendt (1972):[7]

$$r = 1 - \frac{2*U}{n_1 * n_2}$$

Alternatively, the large-sample approximation is given by the following formula:

$$r = \frac{z}{\sqrt{N}}$$

These effect sizes can range from zero to one, and the effects are generally considered small at .1, medium at .3, and large at .5 (Ellis 2010). Effect sizes should be considered in the larger context of the study and the practical impact of the observed difference.

Rank-transformed Welch test

We have now presented the three most common tests for comparing the measure of center of two groups. The t-test is the baseline parametric test, and it requires the strictest set of assumptions. When the assumption of equal variance is violated, Welch's t-test has superior performance. When the underlying populations are not normally distributed, the Mann-Whitney U-test provides more power to compare the medians of the two groups. There remains the more complicated situation in which both of these assumptions are violated simultaneously.

It is a common mistake to use nonparametric methods, such as the Mann-Whitney test, even in the presence of distributions that are not similar. The test was definitely not designed for use with groups that exhibit unequal variances. Zimmerman (1996) provides statistics and plots that convincingly portray the problems with Type I and Type II error of the Mann-Whitney U-test when the variances are unequal. The Mann-Whitney test has been shown to underperform in the presence of skewness and non-homogeneous variance (Fagerland and Sandvik 2009). Furthermore, Rasch, Kubinger, and Moder (2011) show that the Mann-Whitney U-test has lower power than Welch's t-test when the variances of the two groups are not equal.

An alternative procedure is to rank-transform the sample data and perform Welch's test on the ranks (Zimmerman and Zumbo 1993). This rank-based procedure has the advantage of being conceptually straightforward and relatively easy to implement. No additional formulas or new tests are necessary, and the procedure performs better in the case of both unequal variances and non-normality.

The combination of parametric tests on rank-transformed data has been known among statisticians since at least Conover and Iman (1981) described such tests as a bridge between parametric and nonparametric procedures. The test can be described in a research report as Welch's test conducted on the ranks of the data. Depending on the computer software, it might be necessary to conduct the test in multiple steps: first, converting the data into ranks, and second, calculating the results of Welch's t-test. In a comparison of several tests, Fagerland and Sandvik (2009) found that this procedure provided qualitatively similar performance to other, more complicated tests.[8]

The challenge of comparing two groups grows quickly in complexity from the disarmingly simple example of comparing the elevation of Russia and Canada. The reason so many methods exist is that each set of sample data potentially comes from populations with different distributions, so different assumptions are made in the course of calculating the test statistics. Wilcox and Keselman (2003: 272) summed up the problem: "No single method can be expected to compete well in all possible situations that might be encountered simply because different methods are sensitive to different features of the data." The rank-transformed Welch test is one more useful tool for comparing the means of two groups when the assumptions of the t-test are violated.

Paired t-test

All of the tests discussed so far involve the comparison of two independent groups, meaning that each group involves different participants, objects, or corpora. Another comparison can be made in which the same participants are tested at two different times or for two different treatments. A corpus study might compare stylistic, textual features of authors who also work as translators. In that case, each individual would have two measurements, one from translation work and one from an original-authored work. This design goes by many names. We will refer to it as a paired t-test, but it is also commonly referred to as a *repeated measures t-test*. When the design involves pairs of participants that are tied through completion of a similar task, the test can also be referred to as a *matched-pairs design*, a *dependent samples t-test*, or a *test for related samples*.

The main benefit of a paired *t*-test is a decrease in variability due to extraneous factors. For instance, Roziner and Shlesinger (2010) and Braun (2013) both compared interpreters as they provided on-site and RI services. In both studies, the researchers had the same group of interpreters complete interpreting tasks in the two conditions. Had the studies used two different groups of participants, the data would potentially be influenced by the participants' ages, education, years of work experience, or language facility. By using the same participants in the two situations, these factors are held constant. Each participant serves as his or her own control, thereby eliminating nuisance factors in the observed data. The result of this decrease in variability is an increase in the power of the statistical tests.

An increase in power is equivalent to a decrease in Type II error. The *t*-test is therefore less likely to fail to reject the null hypothesis when a significant difference exists. The gain in power also comes without an increase in the sample size, which can save on the costs and time involved in finding an appropriate sample.

A paired design does have three drawbacks. First, a participant may be unable or unwilling to complete both phases of the research. If multiple participants leave a study the results can be skewed. Researchers should always strive for good sampling and research design to prevent attrition. When it does occur, the reasons for the lost data should also be examined, because a trend in attrition may be interesting in and of itself. To give an extreme example, if a medical study originally intended to test two treatments for a disease, but the first treatment cured half of the patients who failed to come back for the second treatment, then the planned comparison is meaningless but the attrition is obviously of interest.

A second problem is carryover effects that take place between the measurements. Carryover can occur due to repeated practice of a task. Sometimes a study is designed to measure learning, but the research must ensure that participants are not merely improving due to completion of the same task or test. A common use of the paired *t*-test is a pre- and post-test design, in which participants are measured before and after a treatment such as training or education. In one example of this design, Scott-Tennent and González Davies (2008) had participants examine a passage for cultural references both before and after training. Their protocol included a four-month gap between measuring performance on the same test. The research report included four ways by which they ensured carryover effects were not significant: the length of time between measurement, lack of access to the test material, no provision of feedback from the first measurement, and not telling participants during the pre-test that they would be tested again with the same task. Such careful attention to research protocol can help overcome the problem of carryover effects.

The third and final problem of a repeated measures design is the potential for the order of the measurements to matter. This order effect is closely related to the carryover effect. The distinction is that the carryover effect occurs in a situation in which the order of the measurements cannot be changed. Pre- and post-test designs that involve a treatment, training, or intervention of some kind cannot have the order of the measurements reversed. By contrast, participants can sometimes be assigned two tasks in random order. For instance, consider a study in which researchers are investigating differences between the tasks of simultaneous interpreting and sight translation. The order in which these two tasks are undertaken can easily be changed; half of the participants could perform the sight translation first and then a simultaneous interpreting task, while the remaining participants could perform these tasks in the reverse order. Randomly assigning half of the participants to each of the tasks and then proceeding to the other is called *counterbalancing*, and it is a good method to overcome order effects.

Assumptions

An advantage of the paired *t*-test is the relative paucity of assumptions. The observations must still be independently collected, meaning that each participant's performance is unaffected by every other participant. However, the paired data are purposely dependent across measurements, because each pair of measurements is collected from the same participant. Furthermore, equality of variances is less likely to be problematic because the same participants are measured in both cases. The assumption of normality applies only to the differences in scores between the paired data. Serious violations of the normality assumption indicate the use of the nonparametric Wilcoxon signed-ranks procedure.

Hypothesis testing, confidence intervals, and effect size

The statistical significance of the paired *t*-test is determined by computing the difference in measurements between all of the pairs. The original data are thus transformed into a new set, denoted D. The difference scores should be normally distributed. This assumption allows the differences to be analyzed using a one-sample *t*-test, as first discussed in Chapter 6.

The test statistic requires the descriptive statistics of the mean and standard deviation (s_D) of the difference scores. The other figure to appear in the computation of the test statistic is the sample size, n:

$$t = \frac{\bar{D}}{s_D / \sqrt{n}}$$

The critical value for this test comes from a *t*-distribution with $n-1$ degrees of freedom, and computer software easily provides the test statistic and associated *p*-value. A 95% confidence interval is also usually provided, using the following formula:

$$\bar{D} \pm t_{(n-1)} * s_D / \sqrt{n}$$

The effect size is typically measured using Cohen's *d* or Hedges' *g*. Overall, the paired *t*-test requires little in the way of new material. The data are transformed to difference scores and analyzed using the same procedures as the one-sample *t*-test described in Chapter 6.

Wilcoxon matched-pairs signed-ranks test

The nonparametric counterpart to the paired *t*-test is often referred to in shortened form as the Wilcoxon signed-ranks test or sometimes even simply the Wilcoxon test. The primary conceptual difference of the Wilcoxon test from the paired *t*-test is that it compares the median of the two groups, rather than the mean. As the full name implies, the test does so by examining the rank transformation of the data.

For the Wilcoxon test, the data should come from paired measurements taken on the same set of participants on a continuous variable, just as with the paired *t*-test. The assumption of independence between observations is still required. The two distributions should also be symmetric around their medians. Examining box plots and descriptive statistics can allow assessment of this assumption. The data do not need to follow a normal distribution, which is the main advantage of the test over the paired *t*-test.

The computation of the test statistic begins similarly to the paired *t*-test by finding the differences in the scores between the pairs of observations. The absolute value of those differences are then ranked, and the sign of the difference is assigned to the rank. So, for instance, if differences of 3, 5, and −6 were observed, then the ranks of the absolute values would be 1, 2, and 3 respectively. The signed ranks, however, would be 1, 2, and −3 because the last rank in the example is for a difference that was negative. Table 7.3 provides an example dataset to demonstrate the procedure. The scores are for a fictitious pre- and post-test experiment, so that each participant has two scores. The computed differences and the signed ranks also appear in the table.

The final step is to sum the absolute value of the positive and negative ranks separately, with the resulting two test statistics referred to as T^+ and T^-, respectively. For the two-tailed alternative hypothesis, the appropriate test statistic for the final decision is the smaller of these two figures. In the example data, $T^+ = 1$

Table 7.3 Wilcoxon matched-pairs signed-ranks test data with rank transformation

Before	After	Difference	Signed rank
83	82	1	1
85	87	−2	−2
78	81	−3	−3
78	89	−11	−4
65	84	−19	−5
66	89	−23	−6

and $T^- = 2 + 3 + 4 + 5 + 6 = 20$, so the former is the final statistic T, which is compared to the critical value. For sample sizes less than 30, exact tables are available for comparison to make the decision of whether to reject the null hypothesis. For larger sample sizes, a normal approximation is used, and a z-statistic is reported in place of T.

Computer software packages that compute the Wilcoxon test statistic will generally include a p-value as well as a confidence interval for the median. The calculation of the confidence interval is a rather involved mathematical process involving all of the possible paired averages (Daniel 1990: 158). Alternatively, the normal approximation can be used to construct a confidence interval for larger samples.

The effect size of the Wilcoxon test has two different formulas, one for the exact test and one for the normal approximation (as was the case for the Mann-Whitney test as well). For the exact test, both T^+ and T^- are needed in the calculation:

$$r = \frac{4 * \left| T - \left(\left(T^+ - T^- \right) / 2 \right) \right|}{n(n+1)}$$

For the large-sample z-approximation of the test statistic, the formula is simplified:

$$r = \frac{z}{\sqrt{n}}$$

A discussion of alternative derivations of this formula and intuitive descriptions are provided by Kerby's (2014) simple difference formula. Sizes of .1, .3, and .5 are traditional benchmarks for small, medium, and large effect sizes, respectively. Such guidelines come with the usual proviso that interpreting effect size should be done in terms of the observed difference in medians and the nature of the research question. The median difference should be considered for its practical impact, and the effect size figure should be used to substantiate claims of meaningfulness, rather than simply using the cutoffs as the basis for decision making.

Reporting

We conclude this chapter with an example of reporting the results of statistical tests that compare the measure of center of two groups. A thorough report will always include descriptive statistics, such as the sample size, the mean, and the standard deviation of each group. The test statistic and an exact p-value should be provided. Finally, a confidence interval for the difference between the groups and an effect size should be included. Some of these numbers may already be provided elsewhere in the research report. For example, the sample size should appear in the methods section, and the descriptive statistics may appear in a table, rather than in-text. Figure 7.3 shows one way of reporting the outcome of our research on the elevations of Canada and Russia.

Elevation above sea level was measured for 28 randomly selected points in both Russia and Canada. The observed elevation was higher in Russia (M = 739.4, SD = 353.3) than in Canada (M = 594.3, SD = 380.4). However, the difference was not statistically significant ($t[54]$ = 1.48, p = .145, 95% CI [–51.6, 341.8]). Furthermore, the effect size was small (Hedges' g = .395).

Figure 7.3 Example of complete reporting of t-test results

Notes

1 Modern methods, such as M-estimation, trimmed means, and bootstrapping lie outside the scope of this book but can also be useful for multiple violations of assumptions (Wilcox and Keselman 2003).
2 A third category of effect size, the odds ratio, is less commonly used.
3 The computational difference is so slight that software programs sometimes calculate Hedges' g but label it Cohen's d. Confusion around this issue is unfortunately common. Thankfully the magnitude of the two numbers typically differs by only a small amount.
4 The nonparametric version of the independent sample t-test is known by several names due to the nature of its historical development. Wilcoxon (1945) developed the test for a restricted set of cases, while Mann and Whitney (1947) expanded the treatment to cover most cases employed in practical research today. The test is commonly referred to as the Mann-Whitney U-test in the literature, though it is also sometimes described as the Mann-Whitney-Wilcoxon test or the Wilcoxon rank-sum test. The moniker of Mann-Whitney appears to be most common, and we shall follow this convention, which has the added benefit of distinguishing it from the Wilcoxon signed-ranks test discussed later in the chapter.
5 Two alternative procedures modify the Mann-Whitney test are given by Fligner and Policello (1981) and Brunner and Munzel (2000). Simulation studies show that these tests perform well in a range of situations, but the results are not uniform in recommending one test over all others (e.g., Feltovich 2003; Hyslop and Lupinacci 2003). The performance of the tests can depend heavily on sample size and the assumed underlying distribution of the data. We choose to focus here on the basic Mann-Whitney test as the most commonly used and easily understood nonparametric test that performs well in most situations.
6 Gosset (1908) examined applications of the t-test on samples as small as four observations.
7 Kerby (2014) gives an alternative and intuitive formula for this effect size.
8 Alternative procedures not discussed further here include the Brunner-Munzel (2000) and Fligner-Policello (1981) tests.

8 Comparing multiple groups

The previous chapter described tests to determine whether two groups differ in terms of their means or medians. Our fictitious example data compared the average elevation of Russia and Canada. We also presented a number of translation and interpreting (T&I) studies that compared two groups: on-site and remote interpreters; post-editing of machine translation (MT) and human translation; and novices and experts. For situations in which two groups are compared, the most basic parametric test available is the t-test.

This chapter extends the concept of testing for differences to the comparison of three or more groups. The canonical test for this scenario is *analysis of variance* (ANOVA), which is a powerful statistical procedure that can be used in a broad set of situations and experimental designs. However, the best way to understand ANOVA initially is to consider it to be an extension of the t-test. We extend the hypothetical study from the previous chapter to clarify this concept.

This chapter's structure is similar to that of Chapter 7. First, we provide a summary of the vital terminology, an overview of ANOVA, and an extension of the example. Then, we describe the assumptions and procedures of the parametric ANOVA tests: Fisher's F-test and Welch's F-test, which are analogous to Student's t-test and Welch's t-test. When the assumptions of the parametric test cannot be met, it may be preferable to use a nonparametric version of ANOVA, the Kruskal-Wallis test. Subsequently, we describe the use of ANOVA in repeated measures designs and its nonparametric counterpart, Friedman's test. We conclude with guidance in proper reporting of ANOVA results.

ANOVA: Overview

Purpose: To determine whether there are statistically significant differences in the means of three or more independent groups.

Null hypothesis: The means of all k groups are the same ($\mu_1 = \mu_2 = \ldots = \mu_k$).

Alternative hypothesis: The mean of at least one group is different from the others. (NB: This is different from claiming that all of the means differ.)

> *Experimental designs:*
>
> 1 A single dependent variable is measured for 3 or more groups (one-way ANOVA);
> 2 A measurement is taken 3 or more times for the same participants (repeated measures ANOVA, also known as within-subjects design);
> 3 Multiple independent variables (two-way ANOVA and factorial ANOVA, as discussed in the next chapter).
>
> *Parametric tests:* Fisher's F-test, Welch's F-test
>
> *Nonparametric tests:* Kruskal-Wallis test, Friedman's test
>
> *Effect size:* Eta squared (η^2), Omega squared (ω^2), Epsilon squared (ε^2)

In Chapter 7 we presented a case in which the means of two samples were compared: the average elevation of Russia and Canada were compared using a t-test. Suppose that a researcher now wants to extend the study to determine if the average elevation differs among five countries: Nepal, Switzerland, Ethiopia, Russia, and Canada. A number of points are randomly selected within each country's borders (28 points for each country in this example), and each site's elevation is measured. The dependent variable is the continuous measure of elevation, while the nominal, independent variable is the country in which the measurement was made. There is only one independent variable in this situation, and it has five different levels. Summary statistics for this fictional experiment appear in the Table 8.1.

It would be natural to conclude that the average elevation in Nepal is greater than that of Canada. The summary statistics, coupled with direct observation and common sense, are strongly suggestive of this conclusion. In contrast, a comparison of the means for Switzerland and Ethiopia shows virtually no apparent difference in average elevation; we cannot tell just how different each country's elevation is based solely on visual inspection. The statistical procedures presented in this chapter allow proper inference from these data to determine if the average elevations are different.

One-way ANOVA

Statisticians use the term *one-way ANOVA* to describe experimental designs in which there is one categorical independent variable; this variable is sometimes

Table 8.1 Summary statistics for elevation example

	Mean	*SD*	*N*
Nepal	2,862.3	1,146.4	28
Switzerland	1,377.0	732.7	28
Ethiopia	1,221.3	764.6	28
Russia	739.3	353.3	28
Canada	594.3	380.4	28

112 *Analyzing differences*

referred to as the *independent factor*. In the elevation example the independent variable is country. Since this variable is categorical, we refer to the possible observations as the *levels* of the variable (i.e., the five countries included in the example). Researchers must carefully distinguish between the number of independent variables and the number of levels in order to select the appropriate statistical test. For one independent variable with two levels, a *t*-test is suitable, while for one independent variable with three or more levels a one-way ANOVA is appropriate. Four examples from the research literature given in Table 8.2 represent situations in which ANOVA can be useful.

Once the independent variables and levels have been identified, the mean and standard deviation of the dependent variable can be calculated separately for each group. In the elevation example, the descriptive statistics in Table 8.1 present each country's mean elevation and its associated standard deviations. ANOVA is the statistical procedure used to determine whether the mean values of the

Table 8.2 One-way ANOVA: Examples from T&I literature

Four published studies in the T&I literature that employ ANOVA are briefly described below. They are summarized here to provide practice recognizing the structure of ANOVA, especially identifying the variables. These studies will be referred to throughout the chapter as useful illustrations.

1. Köpke and Nespoulous (2006) investigate working memory capacity among (1) professional interpreters, (2) interpreting students, (3) multilinguals, and (4) students with no multilingual competence. The study encompassed several tests of working memory capacity and made three predictions, each involving the expected relative level of performance. They can be generally summarized as predictions that professional interpreters and interpreting students would outperform the control groups of multilinguals and students. In this study, therefore, the dependent variable is working memory capacity. The independent variable is experience in interpreting, and it has four levels.
2. Kruger (2012) utilizes ANOVA a number of times in a broad study of mediation effects in translated and edited texts. The texts in the study are three subcorpora: (1) an English translation of Afrikaans, (2) edited English text, and (3) unedited English text. One of the hypotheses involves the ratio of full and contracted forms that appear in the text–e.g., use of "I'll" versus "I will." In this example, the dependent variable is the ratio of contracted to non-contracted forms, while the independent variable is text type, comprised of three levels.
3. In a similar ANOVA design, Redelinghuys and Kruger (2015) describe differences among three kinds of texts: (1) texts that have been translated by experienced translators, (2) texts produced by inexperienced translators, and (3) non-translated texts. The authors test for differences between the groups on a number of measures, including Flesch Reading Ease score. Hence, the study involves a one-way ANOVA with three levels of text type serving as the independent variable and the Flesch Reading Ease score as the dependent variable.
4. Yudes, Macizo, and Bajo (2011) explore differences among (1) simultaneous interpreters, (2) bilinguals without training in simultaneous interpreting, and (3) monolinguals in their performance on the Wisconsin Card Sorting Test (as a measure of executive process). Data from the experiment are analyzed with a one-way ANOVA in which the dependent variable is task performance and the three levels of the independent variable are defined by the language experience of the participants.

groups differ to a statistically significant degree. Thus, it is vital to remember that ANOVA is a procedure for comparing means, despite the fact that the name of the test refers to variance.

Before discussing the mathematics underlying ANOVA, we next describe the inherent problem with performing multiple comparisons of two means, and this discussion also clarifies the null and alternative hypotheses of ANOVA. Following that, the assumptions of ANOVA are explained, including their relative importance and procedures for assessing their validity. Finally, the remainder of this section is devoted to the details of implementing the three main tests for one-way ANOVA: Fisher's F-test, Welch's F-test, and the Kruskal-Wallis test, including several associated procedures for each of them such as post hoc testing, effect size, and power.

The problem of pairwise comparisons

When multiple groups need to be compared, it would be tempting simply to conduct all of the pairwise comparison tests between groups using t-tests—i.e., t-tests could be used to test the difference between Nepal and Canada, between Nepal and Ethiopia, and so on. This analysis, however, would be incorrect for at least three reasons. First, and most importantly, running multiple tests raises the probability of a Type I error. Recall that Type I error represents a false positive, in which a test erroneously reports a difference between two groups. Researchers generally select statistical procedures that limit the probability of a Type I error to 5%. Because every test that is conducted has a 5% chance of error, then by running multiple tests, the researcher greatly increases the possibility of a false result being reported.[1]

As an analogy of inflated Type I error from multiple testing, imagine if a doctor tested a patient for some disease with a test that has a 5% probability of a false positive. If the test came back positive for one patient already suspected of having the disease, there would be relatively little reason for skepticism. However, if the same doctor were to test 100 patients without any symptoms of the disease, five positive test results would not be surprising, due solely to testing error. This would be the case even if every one of the people were healthy.

A second reason to avoid pairwise testing is the number of tests that would be required as the number of groups increases. The number of necessary pairwise tests is given by the expression $\frac{k(k-1)}{2}$, in which k is the number of groups. Had Köpke and Nespoulous (2006) used t-tests to compare the performance of all four groups of interpreters, they would have required six tests. For studies with five groups there are ten possible pairs, and for six groups the number is fifteen. Each new group has to be compared with every other group, so the computational requirements quickly get unwieldy. The large number of comparisons inflates the probability of a Type I error and complicates the interpretation of results.

A final reason to reject pairwise testing procedures is that this practice is one form of data mining. Instead of relying on a theory-driven approach, the

114 *Analyzing differences*

researcher is sifting or dredging through the data to find statistically significant results. This concern is particularly troublesome when large sets of data can be easily collected. If enough variables are measured and enough tests are run, groups will always differ in some way. However, these results have little practical meaning. Therefore, such a practice is poor research design and, in some cases, can be considered unethical. As we discussed in Chapter 1, researchers ought to situate their research question within the existing literature and develop hypotheses and research questions prior to data collection and analysis. This practice helps to prevent numerical analysis from leading to false conclusions.

In light of the drawbacks of exhaustive pairwise comparisons, ANOVA instead tests the equality of the means in an omnibus null hypothesis, which states that every one of the means is identical for k groups included in the study:

$$H_0: \mu_1 = \mu_2 = \ldots = \mu_k$$

Therefore, the null hypothesis states that the mean of every group is equal to the grand mean (i.e., the mean of all of the data). The alternative hypothesis is that at least one of the groups has a different mean. In terms of the elevation example, the grand mean for all 140 observations is approximately 1,358.8 meters. The null hypothesis states that the mean within every country is equal to this overall mean, while the alternative hypothesis states that at least one country differs.

An important distinction is that the alternative does not claim that all of the groups have different means, but rather at least one of them does. All of the means may differ, but the actual relationships become clear only through further testing. In ANOVA, the alternative hypothesis is non-directional: the mean of the differing group could be larger or smaller.

The null hypothesis allows for statistical analysis of the data. In the case of Köpke and Nespoulous (2006), the null hypothesis would be that that working memory capacity does not differ among the different participant groups: professional interpreters, interpreting students, multilinguals, and students with no multilingual competence. The alternative hypothesis is that at least one group performs differently. In the Redelinghuys and Kruger (2015) study, the null hypothesis is that the Flesch Reading Ease score is the same for all three texts, and the alternative is that at least one of the texts is different.

Assumptions

Before conducting ANOVA, the test's assumptions should be considered to ensure that Type I error is controlled. Furthermore, any violations can diminish statistical power, nullify confidence intervals, and invalidate conclusions. The classic parametric ANOVA test, which we will refer to as Fisher's F-test,[2] requires the same three assumptions as the t-test. The only difference is that equality of variances must hold for all levels of the independent factor. The three assumptions that the data must meet for proper application of Fisher's F-test are as follows:

1 The observations are *independent*.
2 The variance of each group must be identical (*homoscedasticity*).
3 The residual errors must be *normally distributed*.

These conditions should be considered before selecting the appropriate test. However, statistical software packages will often automatically check the assumptions simultaneously with ANOVA calculations. This can erroneously lead to a two-step analysis in which the assumptions are formally tested and then the appropriate main analysis is selected. Preliminary statistical testing is no longer considered a proper approach by most statisticians (Wells and Hintze 2007); a better solution is to utilize more robust statistical tests.

The assumptions generally come closest to being met in a controlled scientific experiment due to random assignment of participants as well as substantial control over experimental conditions. These conditions are not always possible in T&I research; researchers cannot always carefully control the experimental environment, manipulate the independent variable, or randomly allocate participants into groups. In addition, regularly employed measurements in T&I research—e.g., time, counts, or Likert-type scales—can cause violations of the equal variance and normality assumptions. Therefore, T&I researchers must be cognizant of the assumption violations that are rampant in practical research settings.

Tests that are not unduly affected by departures from the assumptions are termed robust. Fisher's F-test is robust only to mild violations of these three assumptions, which motivates the later discussion of the more robust Welch's F-test and the nonparametric Kruskal-Wallis test. Ongoing research in statistics continues to seek more robust techniques,[3] but we present here the most well-known and widely used tests.

Independence

The first assumption of independence is the most vital because it cannot be overcome with the use of alternative statistical techniques. Independence must be implied by a well-designed research protocol with adequate planning and controls. Mathematical technicalities assume that the residual errors are independent from each other and from the independent variable. In the elevation example, random selection of observation points assures independence.

Of the previously-described T&I studies, most involve independent observations of participants undergoing identical testing procedures. An exception is Kruger's (2012) corpus study. In a corpus setting, creating a representative sample of independent observations can be a more challenging task. One method Kruger (2012) employed to accomplish independence was to procure original and edited versions of the same text and randomly assign one version to either the edited or unedited subcorpus. In general, independence must be assessed heuristically through adequate sampling design and/or experimental procedures. Retrospectively, once an ANOVA model has been estimated, assessment of

116 *Analyzing differences*

independence can be conducted by examining a runs plot of the residuals, which should exhibit no obvious pattern.

Equal variance

The second assumption of ANOVA is that the variance of each group is equal. Many earlier introductory textbooks recommended a formal pre-test for the assumption of equal variance. However, this suggestion for a two-step testing procedure has now been rescinded, based on statistical theory and simulation studies (e.g., Moser and Stevens 1992; Albers, Boon, and Kallenberg 2000; Zimmerman 2004; Ng and Wilcox 2011). The two main reasons these tests have fallen out of favor are their low power and the inflated Type I error that can arise from a two-step procedure (Caudill 1988; Moder 2007; Rasch, Kubinger, and Moder 2011). Unfortunately, the old way of thinking persists in much applied work and even some textbooks, but statisticians have become blunt in arguing against pre-tests for homoscedasticity. For instance, Oehlert (1990: 118) writes, "There are formal tests for equality of variance—*do not use them!*" (emphasis original).

In a list of practical recommendations, McGuinness (2008) expresses a growing consensus among statisticians that formal testing should be shunned in favor of graphical methods to check for equality of variances. A box plot of the data for each group should show approximately equal vertical distance within each box-and-whisker for the different categories. A box plot of the elevation data appears in Figure 8.1.

The graph reveals problems with the assumption of equal variance. For example, the variance in Nepal is considerably larger than in Canada or Russia,

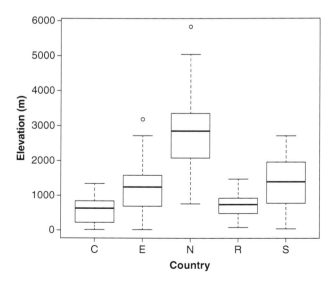

Figure 8.1 Box plot of elevation example data

and both Ethiopia and Nepal have an outlier. Fisher's F-test may not be appropriate with this sample because of the large differences in variance from one group to another.

Reasons do still exist to be familiar with the statistical tests for equality of variance. For one thing, there are cases in which variability is the parameter of interest (though this is rare in T&I research). An additional reason is that prior literature may make reference to tests for equality of variance, and a reader should be able to understand the purpose and procedure of these tests. Finally, they can be provided as post hoc confirmation of assumptions when presenting research results.

Indeed, this last justification may be necessary to pacify peers who have not been trained in modern statistical methods. Meta-analyses of prior research often look for evidence of pre-testing as a marker of quality (e.g., Keselman et al. 1998). A researcher will occasionally encounter a reader or reviewer with a similar bias for formal tests. For this reason, it might be necessary to justify statistical decisions with formal tests after the fact.

The most commonly encountered test for equality of variances is Levene's test (1960), which is standard in some statistical software programs. Two competing tests that may be encountered are Bartlett's test (1937) and the Brown-Forsythe test (1974). However, the former is known to be very sensitive to the normality assumption, and studies have shown few instances when the latter is superior (Conover, Johnson, and Johnson 1981). Therefore, although there is no universally best test for the equality of variances, Levene-type tests are generally recommended as the strongest available test in most settings (e.g., Parra-Frutos 2009). All three of these tests (i.e., Levene's, Bartlett's, and Brown-Forsythe) use a null hypothesis of equality of variances, so the preferred outcome is a p-value greater than 5% because non-significance implies relative equality of variances. Because these tests are no longer recommended by most statisticians as a pre-test step in ANOVA, we will not describe their mathematics in more detail.

In practice, the assumption of homogeneity of variances will always be violated to some extent. If the differences among the variances of each group is not too great, the ANOVA F-statistic may still yield the correct inference. In other words, the test is robust to mild violations of this assumption (Olejnik 1987). This robustness property is stronger when the groups all have an equal number of observations. Therefore, in designing and conducting research, it is recommended to have the same number of participants in each group whenever possible because it improves the performance of the statistical tests.

However, this mild robustness property should not be relied on when superior methods are available. Because unequal variances are almost always in evidence, Welch's F-test or some other robust method should be used instead of Fisher's F-test in almost all cases (Clinch and Keselman 1982).[4] Conducting ANOVA under the condition of heterogeneous variances remains a challenging statistical problem. The current consensus is to shun Fisher's F-test in almost all cases in favor of Welch's F-test, just as we saw in the last chapter Welch's t-test should be preferred to Student's t-test.

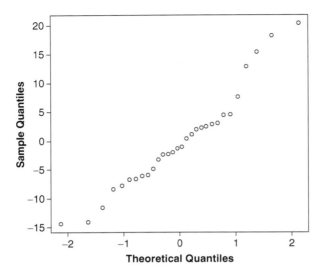

Figure 8.2 QQ plot of elevation example data

Normality

Preliminary visual inspection for outliers or skewness is also a good first step to look for obvious departures from normality (McGuinness 2008). Fortunately, the normality assumption does not have a serious effect on the standard F-test, so long as the variances are homogeneous and the sample size of each group is the same. Most statistical software will easily produce a QQ plot[5] of the ANOVA residuals. If the resulting graph shows most of its points on or near a 45 degree line, then the normality assumption is adequately met. A QQ plot of the elevation example data appears in Figure 8.2.

If inspection of the plot suggests significant departures from normality, nonparametric tests should likely be used to analyze the data. Additionally, non-normality should lead a researcher to consider the possibility of data entry errors, weaknesses in the experimental design or procedures, and the potential need to transform the raw data before conducting statistical tests. The shape of a QQ plot can help detect the type of departure from normality and identify outliers.

Beyond visual inspection, formal testing of the normality assumption is possible. As was the case with homogeneity of variances, pre-testing is no longer recommended in the statistics literature. Läärä (2009), for example, lists seven reasons for why normality pre-testing is inappropriate. Therefore, such tests should be provided only as descriptive information and post hoc confirmation of assumptions.

The formal tests can utilize either of two different procedures. The first method would be to test the raw data of each group for normality using a procedure such as the Shapiro-Wilk test, which was described in Chapter 5. Notice that it is necessary to test each group separately because each group will have a different mean if the null hypothesis is rejected. In practice, studies in T&I would often lack an adequate sample size to test each group separately. For instance, Köpke and Nespoulous (2006) have a sample size of 35, and Yudes, Macizo, and Bajo (2011) have 48 participants. Dividing these samples into subgroups for normality testing will result in too few observations for valid testing. The preferable second procedure is to conduct a normality test of the residuals from the ANOVA testing procedure. This method allows the entire sample to be used in one test so that the number of observations is adequate.

Lack of normality is not a serious problem for inference when the variances and sample sizes of each group are equal. Furthermore, if samples are large enough, an appeal can be made to the Central Limit Theorem (CLT) to suggest approximate normality. For cases of serious departure from normality, the Kruskal-Wallis test is an alternative nonparametric procedure that does not require the assumption of normality.

Fisher's F-test

If the three assumptions above are met, the hypotheses of ANOVA can be tested with the parametric test developed by Fisher (1921). This seminal test has been largely supplanted by more recent ANOVA tests, but an understanding of Fisher's F-test remains important for at least two reasons. First, the test procedure is the clearest for explaining the logic behind ANOVA, and second, the procedure can be expanded to more complicated research designs in a way that other procedures often cannot. Most modified tests can be thought of as variations on this original design. Therefore, this section describes the logic and calculation of Fisher's F-test in order to provide an understanding of the ANOVA process. A thorough knowledge of the hypotheses and logic of the model will aid in good research design, statistical analysis, and comprehension of results. Understanding the pitfalls and advantages of the baseline model will also guide the selection of alternative tests, when necessary.

In ANOVA, the null and alternative hypotheses describe two competing models for the structure of the population. According to the null hypothesis, the means of each group are identical. In other words, the dependent variable does not differ significantly when measured for each group. This is equivalent to the claim that the independent variable does not help in understanding or predicting the dependent variable. By contrast, the alternative hypothesis states that at least one group differs in its mean value. Hypothesis testing can determine the more likely model to explain the structure of the observed sample data.

Consider a very simple example of twelve data points that have been collected from three different groups with four participants in each group. Figure 8.3 displays the visualization of the competing hypotheses. In Panel A, the null hypothesis claims that the data are best explained using just one mean parameter, called the

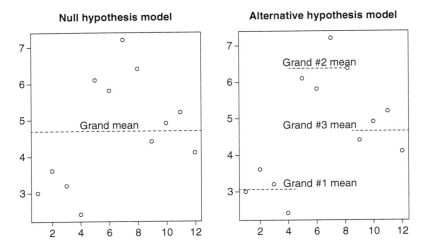

Figure 8.3 Null and alternative hypothesis models for ANOVA

grand mean and denoted $\overline{x}_{grand\ k}$, while the alternative hypothesis depicted in Panel B asserts that the data are better described by each group having its own mean, denoted $\overline{x}_{group\ k}$. In the example, visual inspection suggests that the alternative hypothesis does a better job of explaining this particular data set. From the way the data points cluster at three different levels, it appears that the data are better explained by multiple means (the alternative hypothesis) rather than by the grand mean (the null hypothesis).

ANOVA formalizes the intuition that the groups are different by examining the variability between and within the groups. It begins with the total variance of the sample data, which is calculated using the sample variance equation:

$$s^2 = \frac{\Sigma \left(x_i - \overline{x}_{grand}\right)^2}{n-1}$$

Recall that this can be thought of as a measure of how spread out the sample points are from their mean. The logic of ANOVA testing is that this total variation stems from two sources. On the one hand, the differences could simply be random and unexplainable: within-group variation. On the other hand, the observed differences could be partially explainable due to the level of the independent variable: between group variation. In terms of our country elevation example, a randomly selected point in Nepal would be expected to have a high elevation, because the average elevation in Nepal is high, but there would also be a random component due to variation within the country. Comparing the variation between groups and within groups is the purpose of Fisher's F-test.

Graphs can illustrate the concept of how total variation can be partitioned into two kinds of variation: between-group and within-group.

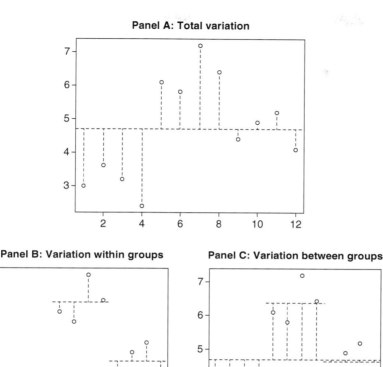

Figure 8.4 Total and partitioned variation (within and between groups)

Panel A depicts total variation, with the deviation of each data point from the grand mean drawn on the graph. Those deviations are used in the calculation of the total sample variance. Panel B depicts how variation occurs within each group, while Panel C depicts the variation among the group means.

Summarizing the mathematical relationships of ANOVA formalizes the relationship depicted in the graphs. The process begins with the numerator of the sample variance $\Sigma\left(x_i - \bar{x}_{grand}\right)^2$, which is called the total sum of squared deviations. The term total sum of squared deviations is often shortened to the total sum of squares and abbreviated SS_T by most authors.[6] To understand both the terminology and the mathematical derivation, consider the formula as consisting of three steps. First, $\left(x_i - \bar{x}_{grand}\right)$ is the deviation of a given data point from the mean, or how much that particular observation differs from the average. Second, the deviation is squared, which is necessary for mathematical reasons, in part because it eliminates negative values. Finally, the squared deviations are summed to give the total sum of squared deviations. Sums of squared deviations are a measure of variability among the data, and their calculation lays at the heart of ANOVA.

SS_T is partitioned into two terms: the error sum of squared deviations (SS_E, the unexplained variation or residual error) and the model sum of squared deviations (SS_M, the explained variation). SS_M is the squared difference between the group means and the grand mean, multiplied by the number of observations in each group: $SS_M = \Sigma n_k \left(\bar{x}_{group\ k} - \bar{x}_{grand} \right)^2$. This is the amount of variation between groups and can be thought of as the amount of variation attributable to the alternative hypothesis. SS_E is the squared difference between each data point and its associated group mean $SS_E = \Sigma \left(x_i - \bar{x}_{group\ k} \right)^2$, which measures variation within groups. By these definitions, the following identity holds: $SS_T = SS_M + SS_E$.

Returning to the country elevation data might clarify these concepts in a more easily visualized example. If one of the observations came from a location in Nepal, it would likely have a large squared deviation from the grand mean and make a sizeable contribution to SS_T. However, it might be close to the average elevation of Nepal and therefore make very little contribution to SS_E and relatively more to SS_M. Meanwhile, an observation collected from a mountain top in Canada could also have a large contribution to SS_T. However, because it would likely be different from the average elevation of Canada, it would make a larger contribution to SS_E than SS_M.

Directly comparing SS_M and SS_E would be misleading because there are a different number of terms in each sum. For SS_M, there is only one deviation per group (a total of k terms), while for SS_E there is one deviation per observation (a total of n terms). Therefore, each sum of squares is divided by the appropriate number of degrees of freedom, and the resulting figures are known as mean squares for the model and for error (MS_M and MS_E). The number of degrees of freedom come from partitioning the total degrees of freedom in the sample variance calculation. There are $k-1$ degrees of freedom for the group effect, which results in $n-k$ degrees of freedom for the error, because $(n-1) = (n-k) + (k-1)$. Therefore, $MS_M = SS_M / k - 1$ and $MS_E = SS_E / n - k$. These figures represent the average amount of variation that can be attributed to the model in the alternative hypothesis and the unexplained, residual error, respectively.

The final step in the calculation of an ANOVA is to compute the F-statistic as the ratio of MS_M to MS_E. Recall that the purpose of the computation is to determine whether the null or alternative hypothesis provides a better model of the data. If the alternative hypothesis is the better model, then MS_M will be large relative to MS_E and the F-statistic will be large. Conversely, a small F-statistic would imply that the null hypothesis provides a better fit for the observed data. Determining whether the statistic is large or small requires a critical value from

Table 8.3 ANOVA table with formulas

Source	SS	df	MS	F	Sig.
Model	$\Sigma n_k (\overline{x}_{group\,k} - \overline{x}_{grand})^2$	$k-1$	$SS_M / k-1$	MS_M / MS_E	p
Error	$\Sigma (x_i - \overline{x}_{group\,i})^2$	$n-k$	$SS_E / n-k$		
Total	$\Sigma (x_i - \overline{x}_{grand})^2$	$n-1$			

the appropriate F-distribution. Computed values that exceed a critical value result in rejection of the null hypothesis. The critical values are based on the level of Type I error (usually 5%) and the two numbers of degrees of freedom, one for the numerator MS_M and the other for the denominator MS_E.

All of the computations outlined in this section can be summarized in an ANOVA table such as in Table 8.3. Statistical software packages generally provide results in a similar format. The abbreviation in the final column stands for significance, which is a common heading for the p-value. A decision regarding the test's hypotheses can be made solely from the p-value. If it is less than 5%, the null hypothesis should be rejected in favor of the alternative. However, the F-statistic and degrees of freedom are also necessary for complete reporting of results.

The ANOVA table of the elevation example data appears in Table 8.4. Generally, a research report will not include a complete ANOVA table because the results are fully summarized by the F-statistic, its associated degrees of freedom, and the p-value. Thus, the table can be summarized quite briefly by stating that the ANOVA revealed a statistically significant difference ($F[4, 135] = 41.18$, $p < .001$).

To summarize this section, we reiterate the logic of Fisher's F-test for the one-way ANOVA. If the null hypothesis were true, then each group in a given experiment would actually be coming from the same population. Any subdivision of the observed variation into explained and unexplained variation would be random because the variance between the groups and the variance within the groups would be identical. If, however, the alternative hypothesis were true, then its model would do a better job of summarizing the variation. In that case,

Table 8.4 ANOVA table for elevation example

Source	SS	df	MS	F	Sig.
Country	90,192,824	4	22,548,206	41.18	<.001
Error	7,924,576	135	547,589		
Total	98,117,400	139			

124 *Analyzing differences*

introducing group means would increase the amount of explained variation, and the *F*-statistic would be larger. If the calculated *F*-statistic is large enough, the null hypothesis can be rejected. The decision can be made either by comparing the statistic to the critical value or by comparing the *p*-value to the .05 cutoff.

Post hoc tests

If the ANOVA *F*-test is statistically significant, the null hypothesis is rejected in favor of the alternative. Therefore, at least one of the means is different. However, the pattern and relationship among the groups is still left unclear by this conclusion. The situation might be that one group has a much higher measure on the dependent variable than the others, as in Panel A of Figure 8.5 or all three might differ as in Panel B.

Determining the relationship among the sample means requires follow-up statistical tests, regularly referred to as either *post hoc tests* or *pairwise comparisons*. In most cases, tests are conducted for all pairwise comparisons among the groups. Such calculations would seem to violate the earlier argument that strongly advocated against just such a process. Recall that we provided three reasons in the earlier discussion: the inflated probability of a Type I error, the large number of tests, and the potential for data mining. However, once the null hypothesis of the ANOVA has been rejected, the situation regarding pairwise comparisons has changed.

The concern of potential data mining no longer proves problematic since the ANOVA *F*-test has rejected the null hypothesis of equal means. In other words, the charge of data mining is invalid once the overall ANOVA test is shown to be statistically significant. There is already evidence that a difference exists for at least one group; the post hoc tests help in understanding the source of that difference.

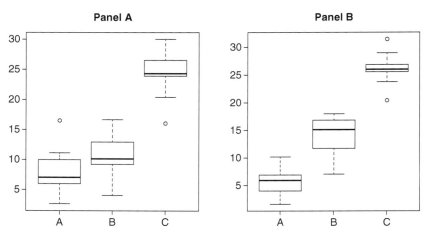

Figure 8.5 Box plot examples of ANOVA

However, the issue of inflated Type I error probabilities remains a potentially serious problem.[7] Post hoc tests address this concern by modifying the *t*-test procedure to limit false conclusions. The goal of these modifications is to maintain a 5% probability of total Type I error across all pairwise tests, which is referred to as the *familywise error rate*. A number of post hoc test procedures exist to accomplish this goal, and this section will discuss some of the most common procedures: the Bonferroni correction, Tukey's Honestly Significant Difference (HSD) test, and Dunnett's test.[8] Occasionally, studies in the published literature refer to follow-up *t*-tests without any reference to modifications. Such results are either inaccurately described or poor statistical practice. We suspect the former in many cases because software will often automatically select an appropriate follow-up procedure, but complete reporting of appropriate statistical techniques is important in communicating results.

The simplest possible adjustment is the *Bonferroni correction*. To control the total probability of a Type I error for all simultaneous pairwise tests, the Bonferroni correction alters the traditional 5% *p*-value criterion for significance by dividing it by the number of pairwise comparisons. As an example, for an ANOVA in which the independent factor has four levels, there would be six possible comparisons, so the *p*-value cutoff would be .05/6 or approximately .0083. Therefore, the Bonferroni correction consists of first calculating the standard *t*-statistics and their associated *p*-values, but the results are compared to this modified cutoff. Any *p*-value below this figure would represent a statistically significant difference between the two groups.[9]

The Bonferroni correction has the benefit of being conceptually straightforward because it uses the traditional *t*-test with a simple adjustment made to the *p*-value cutoff. A drawback of this approach is that it is unnecessarily conservative, often making it difficult to detect significant differences between groups. This represents a significant reduction in statistical power, and the problem is particularly acute for large numbers of comparisons or small sample sizes. For that reason, Bonferroni corrections could be especially problematic for the kind of small samples that occur, for example, in translation process research.

Any results that can pass the high bar set by the Bonferroni correction are quite convincing. However, most applied research will use more recently developed techniques to control the familywise error rate following a significant ANOVA. The Bonferroni correction does remain relevant in contexts where more sophisticated procedures are unavailable. Such is the case for some nonparametric tests, so even though it has been mostly supplanted in the setting of one-way ANOVA, the Bonferroni correction is still employed in other settings.

The most common post hoc procedure is *Tukey's HSD test* (1949), because it both controls the familywise error rate and provides simultaneous confidence intervals for the differences between the group means. Tukey's HSD involves calculating the differences in means for every group and comparing them to a calculated cutoff value. If the difference exceeds the critical cutoff value, then the two groups are different in a statistically significant sense.[10]

126 *Analyzing differences*

The mathematics of Tukey's HSD test rely on the distribution of the *Studentized range statistic* (q). A full discussion of the Studentized range statistic lies outside the scope of this discussion,[11] but q provides a critical value for a 5% Type I error, based on the number of groups being compared and the degrees of freedom for the residual error in the one-way ANOVA. In the case of our elevation example, there are 5 groups and a total sample size of 140, so a statistical table could be used to find the 5% critical value for 5 groups and 135 degrees of freedom. The resulting critical value for those figures is approximately $q = 3.9$. Most software packages do not provide the actual q statistic, because it contains no inherent meaning in relation to the units of the sample data. Its calculation is only an intermediate step to a final determination of statistical significance.

The critical value (q) is used to calculate the minimum difference that would be considered statistically significant. This minimum difference is sometimes referred to as the honestly significant difference, and it provides a cutoff in the same units of measurement as the original sample data. The formula is $HSD = q\sqrt{MS_E / m}$, in which MS_E comes from the one-way ANOVA table, and m is the number of observations in each group.[12] For the elevation example, $HSD = 3.9\sqrt{547,589 / 28} = 545.4$, which is expressed in the original measurement units (in this case meters).

The final step in Tukey's HSD test is to calculate the differences in the sample means for all possible pairs. Any of the differences that exceed the HSD (in absolute value) are statistically different at the 5% level. For example, the difference in sample means for Nepal and Ethiopia is $2,862.3 - 1,221.3 = 1,641$ meters. Because this exceeds the HSD of 545.4 meters, we can conclude at the 5% level that there is evidence of a statistically significant difference in the average elevations of Nepal and Ethiopia. Conversely, for Switzerland and Ethiopia the observed difference in the sample means is just 155.7 meters, which is less than the HSD statistic and therefore not statistically significant. All pairwise comparisons can be easily requested from computer software, but output will generally not report the HSD itself, just whether the difference of each pair exceeds the level necessary for statistical significance.

As mentioned at the beginning of the discussion of Tukey's HSD, the test provides not just a decision rule but also a confidence interval. A full interpretation of study results requires more than the basic determination of statistical significance. The researcher will also want to provide a confidence interval to help contextualize the results for the reader. For example, the mean difference between the elevation in Ethiopia and Canada lies in a 95% CI [62.5, 1,156.2]. Interpretation of the size and significance of this effect is idiosyncratic to the study, based on costs and benefits, relative importance, theoretical implications, and any number of other factors specific to the study.

Output from a statistical software program will usually obviate any need for calculating the HSD statistic itself. Instead, the output typically provides the mean difference, a confidence interval for the mean difference, and an adjusted *p*-value. In that case, the rules for inference follow the expected pattern that any adjusted *p*-value less than .05 represents a statistically significant difference.

Table 8.5 Example data adapted from Köpke and Nespoulous (2006)

Group	Task 1	Task 2
Novices	9.200	4.539
Experts	8.488	3.910
Bilinguals	8.198	3.510
Students	7.175	3.445

Köpke and Nespoulous (2006) employ Tukey's follow-up tests to determine statistically significant differences among four types of participants. A simplified portion of their results (from Tables 2 and 3 in their paper) appear in Table 8.5. In Task 1, novices outperformed the other groups, and Tukey's HSD tests confirm that the difference is statistically significant. In Task 2, however, novices outperformed only the groups of bilinguals and students to a statistically significant degree. There is not enough evidence to conclude that experts and novices differ in their performance on Task 2, because Tukey's HSD test is not significant. Appropriate post hoc tests provide stronger evidence for study results than commentary on observed differences in means.

By using Tukey's HSD, the familywise Type I error is limited to 5%, and the multiplicity of pairwise comparisons does not inflate the risk of false conclusions. While more conservative than necessary for all cases, the test usefully provides both a decision rule and confidence intervals when a study compares all of the group means to each other. By contrast, the final post hoc test discussed here is *Dunnett's test* (1955, 1964), which should be utilized only in the case of a study that makes multiple comparisons to a control group.

Dunnett's procedure follows a similar structure to Tukey's HSD by calculating a cutoff value for the difference between two means, with the formula given by $t_d \sqrt{2MS_E / m}$, in which m and MS_E are the same sample size and mean squared error as in Tukey, and t_d is a critical value that depends on the number of groups and the sample size. Once again, statistical software will usually suppress the cutoff value itself and provide only the corresponding *p*-value for the comparisons of the means. Dunnett's test is useful in the case of comparisons to a control group because it possesses greater power than Tukey's HSD by exploiting the smaller number of comparisons. A study of nine treatment groups would involve 36 pairwise comparisons with Tukey's HSD but only 8 comparisons of each group to the control with Dunnett.

Examples of Dunnett's test in T&I studies are relatively rare, because typically researchers are interested in all pairwise comparisons, not just the comparisons of each group to a control. Maney et al. (2012) provide one example in the context of MT when they compare comprehension of MTs across eight different types of errors to a control group of subject-verb-object (SVO) word order. For example, some of the sentence types they investigate exhibit a deleted verb or adjective, a modified preposition, or a modified word order. The purpose of the study is not to compare the effect of these sentence types to one another (as with Tukey's HSD). Indeed, such a comparison would be relatively meaningless because the groups are not equivalent. The effects of word deletion and a modified word order cannot be directly compared to each other. However, they can each be compared to a baseline sentence with no deletions and SVO word order. Comparing multiple groups to a common baseline calls for Dunnett's test.

Effect size

Reporting of effect size is important in order to communicate the practical relevance of a statistical relationship. While the *p*-value and *F*-statistic provide evidence that a relationship exists, the effect size provides a measure of the magnitude of the effect. For a one-way ANOVA, the goal when estimating effect size is to explain what percent of the variation in the dependent variable is explained by the independent variable. For instance, an effect size of 20% would imply that the independent factor explains[13] one-fifth of the observed variation, while the remaining 80% is due to unknown factors and residual error.

In many cases, effect size is more interesting than statistical significance because it informs the reader about the practical relevance of the relationship. Yudes, Macizo, and Bajo (2011) examine several research questions using ANOVA and report the associated effect size for each test. To give just two examples without context, they report effect sizes of 18% and 57% in two different cases. While both are statistically significant, surely the latter reveals a stronger and more interesting relationship for future research. Without a reported effect size, this important distinction would be lost.

While the goal is rather easily stated, measuring the effect size is not a trivial mathematical problem. A number of competing estimates of effect size exist for the one-way ANOVA. While traditionally the most common in past reporting, the use of eta squared (η^2) can no longer be recommended without qualification, particularly in the case of small sample sizes. Several recently published statistical simulation studies challenge the traditional reporting practice in favor of omega squared (ω^2) or epsilon squared (ε^2). Although the three effect size estimates all converge to the same value as sample sizes grow toward infinity (Maxwell, Camp, and Arvey 1981), in small samples the difference between the estimates can be substantial. This section will describe the computation of these three measures and summarize the current usage recommendations from the statistics literature.

The most commonly reported measure of ANOVA effect size is eta squared (η^2), which is calculated by dividing the sum of squared deviations due to the model by the total sum of squared deviations: $\eta^2 = SS_M / SS_T$. The estimate can range from zero to one and can be interpreted as the percentage of variance explained by the independent variable. For the elevation study, η^2 is approximately 55%, so the country in which an observation is made can be said to account for 55% of the variation. A common rule of thumb suggests that η^2 values of .01, .06, and .14 correspond to small, medium, and large effect sizes (Cohen 1988).

Most statistical software packages automatically report this statistic.[14] However, η^2 overestimates the effect size (Keselman 1975; Grissom and Kim 2004), and the situation is exacerbated for small sample sizes even up to one hundred observations

(Okada 2013). Consequently, applied researchers should employ one of the better alternative estimates. The ubiquity of η^2 in previously published literature necessitates its coverage here, but we urge authors and researchers to employ the demonstrably superior methods discussed in the remainder of this section.

A second measure of effect size for a one-way ANOVA is omega squared (Hays 1963), which is calculated by the following formula: $\omega^2 = \dfrac{SS_M - df_M MS_E}{SS_T + MS_E}$.

The formula is sometimes described as an adjustment to η^2 because the numerator and denominator still contain SS_M and SS_T, respectively. All of the numbers needed for this formula are provided in an ANOVA table, which is important because ω^2 is not often provided by existing software programs and will generally need to be calculated by hand. The resulting calculation will always be less than η^2. For the elevation example, ω^2 is 53.4%.

As an estimate of effect size, ω^2 is similar in interpretation to η^2 as the percentage of variability in the dependent variable that is explained by the independent factor. When the ANOVA F-statistic is less than one, ω^2 will be negative, but the null hypothesis will be rejected only for $F > 1$ so that this problem is unlikely to occur in situations of practical interest. If the situation does occur that ω^2 is negative, the value is often reported as zero (Olejnik and Algina 2000). Omega squared has been shown to provide a more accurate estimate of effect size than eta squared (Keselman 1975).

A third measure of effect size is epsilon squared (Kelley 1935). The formula to calculate this statistic is almost identical to that of omega squared, with one less term in the denominator: $\varepsilon^2 = \dfrac{SS_M - df_M MS_E}{SS_T}$. Once again, hand calculation will likely be necessary, and the resulting figure carries the same interpretation as the previous two measures. Typically, omega squared and epsilon squared will only differ slightly (Carroll and Nordholm 1975), but epsilon squared will always be larger than omega squared (Okada 2013).[15] Of the three measures discussed here, epsilon squared seems to appear with the least frequency in publications.

Confronted with three competing measures of effect size, the non-statistician might become frustrated in deciding what to report. Simulation studies have demonstrated that η^2 is the worst of the three measures, and quotes from recent studies are unequivocal in their recommendations: "Therefore, although it is the most frequently reported index, we do not recommend using η^2 for inferential purposes, especially when the sample size is small" (Okada 2013: 143). Skidmore and Thompson (2013: 536) are similarly strong in their conclusion: "Our results corroborate the limited previous related research and suggest that η^2 should *not* be used as an ANOVA effect size estimator" (emphasis original). Therefore, despite its widespread use, we advise against reporting η^2 as a measure of overall ANOVA effect size.

The difference between ω^2 and ε^2 is typically small. Statistical research is still ongoing in this area, since each simulation study can examine only a fraction of the practical situations a researcher might face. Skidmore and Thompson (2013) make no strong recommendation in selecting between the two measures in their simulation study results. Okada (2013: 143) presents simulation results showing that ε^2 has the least bias of the three measures and refers to the statistic as "a promising effect size index." Our recommendation is to use ω^2 because it has received more attention in statistics literature and textbooks. Therefore, it will potentially be more meaningful to a reader.[16] The debate reinforces the importance for researchers to seek information on the latest best practices and advice from statistical literature. Additionally, the controversy around η^2 reveals the problem with heavy reliance on statistical software; Kirk (1996) suggests that the ubiquity of η^2 and rarity of ω^2 arise at least in part from the former's inclusion as the default measure in some popular programs.

Power and sample size determination

Although presented here as the final sub-topic of Fisher's F-test, power considerations should actually be part of the planning process of a study. Though power is sometimes mistakenly calculated after data have been collected, this *retrospective power* (also sometimes called *observed power*) is essentially meaningless and statistically flawed (Hoenig and Heisey 2001).

For applied research, the most useful calculation is the sample size requirement to attain a given level of power. For ANOVA, there is a fundamental relationship among the sample size, the number of groups, the effect size, the significance level, and power. Specifying any four of these allows for calculation of the fifth.

Specification of the effect size is the most challenging aspect of prospective power analysis. Lenth (2001) provides extensive commentary on the necessary practical considerations. Researchers should predict in advance the kind of effect size they anticipate seeing, as well as consider the minimum effect size that would be of practical interest.

The remaining figures are generally more straightforward. The number of groups is determined by the experimental design. The significance level is traditionally set at 5%, and a common choice for power is 0.80. If desired, the power level can be varied to estimate the sample size that is required for each case.[17] Of course, larger samples will always have greater power, meaning that a larger sample allows for the analysis of more groups and/or for the detection of smaller effect sizes.

Power must always be considered in the context of a particular study, but for four groups in a one-way ANOVA sample size of less than 30 will almost surely result in power below 0.80. In a given situation, increasing sample size may be prohibitively expensive in terms of time or resources. If participants with specific skillsets are required, it may be impossible to increase the sample size. In such a case, it may not be possible to test for small effect sizes, or the research design may need to limit the number of levels of the independent factor.

Finally, power can be increased by selection of the statistical test with the best performance. Violations of a test's assumptions can severely weaken its power to detect differences. Because the assumptions of Fisher's F-test are so often violated, alternative testing procedures are often preferable. The two main alternatives for one-way ANOVA are Welch's F-test and the Kruskal-Wallis test.

Welch's F-test

When the assumption of equal variances is violated, Fisher's F-test can be unreliable, due to an inflated probability of a Type I error and diminished power. Statisticians have recognized these significant flaws and are quite blunt in their recommendation to abandon the basic test in most settings: "If the goal is to avoid low power, the worst method is the ANOVA F-test." (Wilcox 1998: 313). Welch's F-test is one alternative that corrects for these problems.[18] Welch (1951) follows a similar logic to Fisher's F-test, but the calculation is more complicated. The idea behind the modification is to calculate a weighted grand mean, with the weights based on the sample size and variance within each group. This weighted grand mean results in a modified measure of SS_M. We suppress further details of the calculations since they are easily carried out in SPSS and other software.

The interpretation of Welch's test is still based on an F-statistic. The numerator degrees of freedom are still one less than the number of groups, but the denominator degrees of freedom are adjusted as part of the accommodation for the unequal variances among the groups. This adjustment results in a non-integer number of degrees of freedom. For instance, in the elevation example, the denominator degrees of freedom are 65.093, considerably fewer than the 135 degrees of freedom for Fisher's F-test with the same data. As with Welch's t-test, the degrees of freedom are sometimes rounded down to the nearest integer, although this is not necessary for computer calculations or reporting.

One difference between the two ANOVA tests discussed here is that Welch's F-test often does not include an ANOVA table because it is calculated differently. Statistical software will report the statistic, its degrees of freedom, and the p-value. Explicit references to Welch are sometimes omitted from reporting because the non-integer degrees of freedom imply the type of test; for example, analysis of the elevation data would be reported as $F(4, 65.09) = 28.55, p < .001$). A thorough research report might choose to include the name of the test for completeness.

When two competing tests are available, a researcher should decide prior to analysis which test is proper. For one-way ANOVA, Welch's F-test should be the almost universally preferred procedure. The assumption of homogeneous variances will generally be violated, which invalidates the use of Fisher's F-test. Furthermore, it is inappropriate to run a pre-test on the variances and then select between Fisher and Welch based on the results.

Statistical research consistently upholds the superiority of Welch's F-test. When groups have unequal variances but are approximately normal, Welch's F-test has been shown to outperform other common ANOVA tests by demonstrating improved statistical power and an appropriate Type I error rate in simulation studies (Tomarken and Serlin 1986). In a meta-analysis, Lix, Keselman, and Keselman (1996) reported Welch's F-test to be among the best performing tests for situations of heterogeneous variance. In another meta-analysis survey of simulation studies, Harwell, Rubinstein, Hayes, and Olds (1992) report that

Welch's *F*-test is insensitive to heterogeneous variances when the underlying population is normally distributed. Finally, for balanced design and heterogeneous variances, Welch's *F*-test is the only statistic that Wilcox, Charlin, and Thompson (1986) find satisfactory in a simulation study.

Despite its acknowledged superiority by statisticians, Welch's *F*-test often does not receive enough attention in introductory statistics classes and appears infrequently in applied research literature in T&I. Dewaard (2012), in her examination of perceptions of Russian pronoun usage, is an example of the more robust test being employed. We hope that growing awareness of the appropriateness of the Welch test for ANOVA will increase its usage.

Though Welch's *F*-test is in almost all cases preferable to Fisher's *F*-test, that is not to say that it is flawless or universally appropriate. The alternative test was developed to counteract the effect of heterogeneous variances. However, it remains sensitive to violations of the normality assumption (Lix, Keselman, and Keselman 1996). When the data are demonstrably non-normal, the preferred test is the Kruskal-Wallis test.

Post hoc tests

Rejection of the null hypothesis of Welch's *F*-test only determines that a minimum of one of the group means is different from the others. As before, follow-up testing is required to determine the relationship among the means of the various groups. When equal variance cannot be assumed, changes are necessary for the follow-up testing procedure.

Tukey's HSD, the preferred procedure for Fisher's *F*-test, employs MS_E in its calculation, but that choice implicitly assumes that pooling all of the data will result in one universally appropriate estimate of variance. When the group variances are not, in fact, equal, the Type I error of the pairwise tests can greatly exceed 5% in simulation studies (e.g., Dunnett 1980; Korhonen 1982). Therefore, modifications can be made to the HSD formula to control the total familywise error. This subsection describes three related extensions of that procedure to samples with heterogeneous variances.

One such adjustment is the Games-Howell procedure (1976), which adjusts the degrees of freedom for the Studentized range statistic (q) and combines separate sample variance estimates from each group when making the pairwise comparisons. Two other comparison methods developed by Dunnett are also in common use: Dunnett's T3 and Dunnett's C (1980).[19] These three procedures are available in popular statistical processing packages. Of the three, the Games-Howell test has the highest power but can occasionally exceed the 5% Type I error level because it results in the smallest confidence intervals. This problematic situation is most likely to occur when the ratio of variance to sample size $\left(\dfrac{s_i^2}{n_i}\right)$ is approximately equal for all groups. Between the T3 and C tests, the T3 is preferable for small samples while the C procedure outperforms in larger samples.

Comparing multiple groups

Any of the three procedures would be appropriate in most cases, and the guidelines above can help in selecting the best test, based on considerations of sample size and estimates of the variance of each group. In most cases, Games-Howell should be preferred for its superior power.

Effect size

Given the extended discussion on effect size above, we recommend omega squared as the preferable measure of effect size for Welch's F-test. Few computer programs will provide this figure, so it will need to be calculated by hand. The computation is straightforward, and the necessary inputs are the F-statistic, the sample size (n), and the number of groups (k):

$$\omega^2 = \frac{(k-1)(F-1)}{(k-1)(F-1)+n}$$

The interpretation of effect size remains the percentage of the total variance in the dependent variable that is accounted for by the independent variable. A research report should always include the appropriate measure of effect size to accompany ANOVA results.

Kruskal-Wallis test

For cases when the assumptions of a parametric one-way ANOVA are not satisfied, the Kruskal-Wallis test is the most common nonparametric alternative.[20] Like all nonparametric procedures, the test requires fewer assumptions about the underlying population. In the same way that the Mann-Whitney U-test provides an alternative rank-based procedure to the independent t-test, the Kruskal-Wallis test can substitute for the parametric one-way ANOVA because its overall structure is identical: one continuous dependent variable is measured for one independent factor with three or more levels.

As noted above, the primary difference from the parametric test is a less restrictive set of assumptions. Two of the three assumptions of the one-way ANOVA remain the same for the Kruskal-Wallis test—namely, the variance or measure of spread for each group should be the same and the observations must be independent (Hollander and Wolfe 1999). However, the Kruskal-Wallis test does not require an assumption that the residual errors be normally distributed. Instead of a requirement of normality, the test requires only that the dependent variable be similarly distributed within each group. A second important point of departure from the parametric one-way ANOVA occurs in the hypotheses being tested. The null hypothesis is that the median of each group is identical, while the alternative hypothesis is that at least one of the medians is different.

The Kruskal-Wallis test utilizes the ranks of the data points to compare the medians of each group. The first step in calculating the test statistic is to rank all of the observations in the entire sample, regardless of group, assigning a value of one to the smallest observation and so on up to a value of n for the largest observation.

134 *Analyzing differences*

Table 8.6 Kruskal–Wallis example data

Raw data				Ranks of data		
Group A	Group B	Group C		Group A	Group B	Group C
8.15	6.39	6.78		6	2	3
7.51	9.11	9.38		5	8	9
8.23	4.39	7.29		7	1	4
			Sum	18	11	16

Ties should be assigned the average of the ranks that would have been assigned without ties. For example, if the third, fourth, and fifth smallest observations were identical, all would receive a rank of four. Then the ranks within each group are summed. The ranks are assigned with all of the observations pooled as if they were one group, but the ranks are summed within each group defined by the independent variable.

The small example presented in Table 8.6 is meant to clarify the process. On the left are the raw data for a one-way ANOVA with three levels and nine participants. On the right are the associated ranks and the group sums that would be calculated in the first step of computing the Kruskal-Wallis test statistic.

Deciding whether to reject the null hypothesis is equivalent to a formal test of whether the sum of the ranks in each group are approximately equal to each other or if they differ to a statistically significant degree. If the null hypothesis were true and the medians of each group were identical, then the ranks would be randomly assigned across the entire set of sample data. In that case, the sum of the ranks in each group would be equal (or nearly equal due to random experimental error). One might suspect that this is likely the case in the example provided; the sums of the ranks are quite similar across the three groups. By contrast, if the alternative hypothesis were true, the sums of the ranks would be noticeably different from one another. The test statistic and its distribution provide a formal way to evaluate the difference.

The Kruskal-Wallis test statistic is referred to as H. The formula for the test statistic is formidable, but the computation is more tedious than difficult:

$$H = \frac{12}{n(n+1)} \sum_{i=1}^{k} \frac{R_i^2}{n_i} - 3(n+1)$$

In this formula, R_i stands for the sum of the ranks within each group, which is squared and divided by the size of the group. The resulting figures for the groups are then summed. The remainder of the formula consists of numerical adjustments related to the sample size. The calculation for the example data should clarify the calculations involved:

$$H = \frac{12}{9(9+1)} \left(\frac{18^2}{3} + \frac{11^2}{3} + \frac{16^2}{3} \right) - 3(9+1) = 1.156$$

For relatively small samples, calculating the H-statistic manually with a computer spreadsheet is not too difficult. Simulation studies have provided exact p-values for the Kruskal-Wallis test, and the best practice would be to report the H-statistic and the corresponding p-value from available statistical tables.[21] The manual calculations may be necessary in some cases, because the most popular computer programs for statistical processing do not calculate the H-statistic. The alternative that software packages generally report is an approximate chi-squared (χ^2) statistic with $k-1$ degrees of freedom. This alternative is appropriate for larger samples,[22] and the software will calculate both the test statistic and its associated p-value. Whether the H- or χ^2-statistic is utilized, the typical decision rules apply. If the p-value is less than .05, the null hypothesis is rejected in favor of the alternative. In other words, for small enough p-values, the sample data provide evidence that the medians differ to a statistically significant extent.

The Kruskal-Wallis test is designed for data that violate the assumption of normally distributed residual errors, but there is little evidence that the test provides substantial benefits beyond other available statistics. Specifically, Adams, Gayawan, and Garba (2009) demonstrate that for sample sizes greater than 15 Fisher's F-test and the Kruskal-Wallis test have approximately equal power. Similarly, Harwell, Rubinstein, Hayes, and Olds (1992) suggest that the F-test is quite robust to violations of the normality assumption so that using the Kruskal-Wallis test provides relatively little benefit except in the case of small sample sizes.

The Kruskal-Wallis test is also closely related to the process of transforming the data to ranks and performing a one-way ANOVA on the ranks. Given an experiment with sample size n, an independent variable with k groups, and the Kruskal-Wallis H, this so-called rank-transformed F-statistic is equivalent to this formulation: $F_R = \dfrac{(n-k)H}{(n-1-H)(k-1)}$ (Conover and Iman 1981). When comparing the Kruskal-Wallis test, the rank-transformed F-test, and Fisher's F-test, Zimmerman (2012) concluded that in very few cases would the decision of a hypothesis test be altered due solely to the choice of test. Overall, the Kruskal-Wallis test should be used with caution and only when the primary concern is a violation of the normality assumption. In many cases, Welch's F-test would perform equally well, if not better, than the Kruskal-Wallis test (Lix, Keselman, and Keselman 1996).

Post hoc tests

The reason for selecting the Kruskal-Wallis test was a belief that the residuals were not normally distributed. Therefore, the appropriate post hoc test should also be a nonparametric procedure. The most logical choice in making all pairwise comparisons is to use the Mann-Whitney U-test, which was described in Chapter 7.

Just as with the parametric post hoc tests discussed earlier, multiple pairwise testing raises the probability of a Type I error beyond the nominal 5% level. Consequently, the Bonferroni correction must be employed. Unlike the case for parametric tests, other modifications to correct for the problem are not widely

136 *Analyzing differences*

known or employed. In other words, there is no standard nonparametric counterpart to Tukey's HSD test or the Games-Howell test. The Dunn-Nemenyi (Dunn 1964) and Steel (1961) tests are sometimes proffered (van der Laan and Verdoren 1987; Elliott and Hynan 2011), but these alternative tests seem to receive scant use in applied research. Therefore, the Mann-Whitney U-test with Bonferroni correction to the p-value cutoff is an appropriate choice to make pairwise comparisons following a statistically significant Kruskal-Wallis test.

Effect size

Given the approximate χ^2-statistic from the Kruskal-Wallis test, a measure of effect size is given by $\eta^2 = \frac{\chi^2}{(n-1)}$, in which n is the total sample size. If the H-statistic is available, then the following formula for effect size can alternatively be calculated: $\varepsilon^2 = \frac{H}{(n-1)}$. As with the extended discussion regarding effect size for the one-way ANOVA, ε^2 is less biased and preferable whenever possible. For either effect size measure, the interpretation is identical to the case of the parametric one-way ANOVA; the effect size represents the percent of variation in the dependent variable that is explained by the independent variable. Because post hoc tests employ the Mann-Whitney U-test, the appropriate measure of effect size for the pairwise tests would be r, as described in Chapter 7.

Repeated measures ANOVA

As we have described so far in this chapter, the one-way ANOVA model can be conceived as an extension of the t-test. In both cases, a measurement is made on different groups (two groups for the t-test and three or more groups for the one-way ANOVA). The groups are independent from each other, with data collected from different people or different corpora, for example. However, in some cases it is preferable to collect data from the same participants multiple times. This experimental design is called a *repeated measures ANOVA* (rANOVA) and can also be referred to as a *within-subjects design*.[23] A one-way ANOVA is an extension of the independent samples t-test, and rANOVA is the analogous extension of the paired t-test.

There are two primary benefits to rANOVA. First, because participants in a study are measured multiple times, their individual variation can be eliminated as a source of variation between the groups. Sometimes this is described by saying that each individual serves as his or her own control. From a statistical perspective, the error term will be reduced and the power of statistical tests will be increased. Second, the experimental design of rANOVA requires fewer participants, so it is particularly attractive when participant pools are limited in size, difficult to access, or expensive to obtain. This situation is common to T&I research; finding volunteers who meet study criteria can be difficult, time-consuming, or costly.

Therefore, it is important to maximize data collection and inference.[24] Repeated measures ANOVA contributes to those goals by using the same participants in multiple rounds of data collection.

The design of a repeated measures ANOVA can be recognized from the fact that each participant is measured on the dependent variable three or more times. There are two main ways to implement repeated measurements. First, the participants could be observed at multiple points in time. For example, in Fraser's (1999) study of lexical processing strategies, eight participants were assessed at four different points in time. Measurements included their rate of use of three lexical processing strategies (consult, ignore, and infer), as well as vocabulary retention. The independent variable in this study is time, and we will refer to this kind of model as a time-based rANOVA.

A second model that utilizes rANOVA involves measuring a response variable for participants in three or more different treatment conditions. Folse (2006) employs this experimental design by having students practice vocabulary exercises in three different conditions. The first learning strategy was a fill-in-the-blank exercise; the second consisted of three fill-in-the-blank exercises; and the third strategy required original sentence writing. Each participant completed a vocabulary quiz following each of the three instructional methods. The levels of the independent factor in this type of model are the different conditions under which the measurements are made (the three learning strategies in this case), and we will refer to this as a treatment-based rANOVA.

Assumptions

The one-way ANOVA required three assumptions: independence of the observations, normality of the sample data, and equality of variance. Each of these is modified in rANOVA. A repeated measures design purposely involves dependence between the observations because the same participants are measured multiple times; therefore, we do not need to consider independence for any particular subject in the study. However, the participants must still be measured independently from one another. The second assumption of normality of the sample data is still required. As before, the residuals should be examined graphically and possibly with a formal test such as the Shapiro-Wilk test.

The third assumption of equal variance must be altered to account for the dependence among the observations. Instead of an assumption of equal variance, rANOVA requires an assumption of a statistical property called *sphericity*. The formal definition of sphericity is that the variances of the differences of all possible pairs are equal. The property is difficult to understand in the abstract, so an example of the testing procedure for the property will help to clarify it. To test for sphericity, the differences between the levels of the between-subject factor are calculated. For example, for each one of the participants the differences would be calculated between time 1 and time 2, between time 1 and time 3, and between time 2 and time 3.

Consider an adapted and simplified version of Folse (2006) as an example by assuming that five students are given three different strategies for learning

138 *Analyzing differences*

Table 8.7 Repeated measures ANOVA example data

Subj.	Tr1	Tr2	Tr3	Tr1 – Tr2	Tr1 – Tr3	Tr2 – Tr3
P1	7	11	15	–4	–8	–4
P2	6	13	18	–7	–12	–5
P3	8	9	19	–1	–11	–10
P4	5	12	13	–7	–8	–1
P5	10	15	19	–5	–9	–4
Variance				6.2	3.3	10.7

new words in a foreign language. Each student is assigned 20 new words and is given an hour to practice with a strategy and then complete a quiz. The same five students then go on to repeat the process with 20 new words for each of the second and third strategies. This is a treatment-based rANOVA, and each student participates in all three of the experimental conditions. Example data appear in Table 8.7.

There is one row for each student in the study and one column for each measurement. The last three columns of the table show the paired differences between the treatments. Once those differences have been computed, the variance is calculated for each of the sets of differences, as shown in the table. Sphericity describes a situation in which these three variances are approximately equal.

Mauchly (1940) developed a statistical test for the equality of these variances, and in many computer programs it is automatically included in rANOVA output. Therefore, explicit calculation of the differences and their variances is not necessary. The null hypothesis of Mauchly's test is that all of the variances of the differences are equal, and the alternative hypothesis is that at least one of the variances is different. Therefore, as with Levene's test, the preferred outcome of Mauchly's test is a nonsignificant result, defined as a p-value greater than .05. In that case, the assumption of sphericity is adequately met. By contrast, if Mauchly's test rejects the null hypothesis, modifications must be made to the usual significance tests of the rANOVA.[25] The two most common modification procedures are the Greenhouse-Geisser (1959) and Huynh-Feldt (1976) corrections to the degrees of freedom. The correction procedures do not affect the calculation of the rANOVA F-statistic described below; they only alter the degrees of freedom for finding the critical value and p-value of the test. We will describe their application at the end of our description of the F-test.

Also like Levene's test and other tests for the equality of variances, Mauchly's test is not robust to departures from normality in the data (Keselman, Rogan, Mendoza, and Breen 1980). If the underlying population is not normally distributed, Mauchly's test is more likely to make an incorrect conclusion. Additionally, Mauchly's test has rather low power in general. Consequently, sphericity should also be assessed by examining the descriptive statistics. Using the Greenhouse-Geisser correction for all applications of rANOVA, regardless of the results of Mauchly's test, is a recommended practice.

rANOVA F-test

The underlying mathematical logic of rANOVA is again based on partitioning of variability based on various sources. In this case, the total variability is divided into between-subject and within-subject categories: $SS_T = SS_{Subj} + SS_W$. In this equation, SS_{Subj} stands for the between-subject variability and SS_W for the within-subject variability. Total variability (SS_T) can be found by calculating the variance of the entire sample and multiplying it by the degrees of freedom for the variance, $n-1$. Symbolically, $SS_T = s^2(n-1)$. For the example data given above, the sample variance of all 15 observations considered as one pooled sample is 21, so the total sum of squares is $SS_T = 21(15-1) = 294$.

Between-subject variability is caused by the personal characteristics of the particular individuals in the sample. In our vocabulary learning example, the between-subject variability could be described as the different levels of language aptitude, motivation, or intelligence. Many factors could cause one person to learn new vocabulary more easily than another person. In the data presented in Table 8.7, Participant 5 always outperformed Participant 4, no matter what learning strategy was employed. The between-subject effect is the differential performance across participants, or vertical comparisons in the table. This effect is not due to anything directly related to the experimental conditions or to the particular learning strategy; it is caused by the different abilities of the two subjects in the study. Therefore, in rANOVA, the between-subject effect is rarely of interest.

The within-subject effect, by contrast, was caused partly by the experimental manipulation of the three different treatments. In terms of the study, the participants' performance in the three treatment effects differs due to the various strategies they are asked to use. This effect is the differential performance across treatments (or across time). The sample data shows much better performance for nearly all students when the third strategy is used and the worst performance when the first strategy is used. A research project would certainly hope to demonstrate a significant effect in this dimension because it demonstrates an influence of the manipulated independent variable.

Contained in the within-subject effect, there also remains the residual, unexplained variation that occurs in the various quiz scores. Consequently, rANOVA extends the one-way ANOVA model by further partitioning the within-subject variability into two parts due to the treatment or time condition and the residual error: $SS_W = SS_{Cond} + SS_E$. As with one-way ANOVA, SS_E is the sum of squares associated with error. SS_{Cond} is the sum of squares associated with the condition of the measurement, either due to different treatments or different timing of the measurements.

To summarize the overall logic of rANOVA, the total variability is measured by the total sum of squared deviations. That total variability is considered to be comprised of three different sources. One of the sources is variability between the participants (SS_{Subj}), which is not usually an interesting variable in a study. The second source is due to the different levels of the treatment or different times when measurements are taken (SS_{Cond}), which is almost always the main focus of

140 *Analyzing differences*

Table 8.8 Repeated measures ANOVA table

Source	SS	df	MS	F	Sig.
Condition	SS_{Cond}	$k-1$	$SS_{Cond}/k-1$	MS_{Cond}/MS_E	p
Subjects	SS_{Subj}	$m-1$	$SS_{Subj}/m-1$	MS_M/MS_E	p
Error	SS_E	$(k-1)(m-1)$	$SS_E/n-k$		
Total	$\Sigma(x_i - \bar{x}_{grand})^2$	$n-1$			

the statistical inference. Finally, the third source is residual error. Putting all of this together, $SS_T = SS_{Subj} + SS_{Cond} + SS_E$.

Each of these sums of squares has an associated number of degrees of freedom. Let k represent the number of treatments, meaning either the number of observations in a time-based rANOVA or the number of different conditions in a treatment-based rANOVA. Additionally, let m stand for the number of subjects in the study. Finally, n stands for the total number of observations, which can be calculated from the number of groups and subjects in each group: $n = k*m$. With this notation, the degrees of freedom for each sum of squares term can be found in Table 8.8. The table also shows that when the SS terms are divided by their associated degrees of freedom, the results are mean square figures, just as in one-way ANOVA.

There are two *F*-statistics for rANOVA, one for the within-subject condition (either treatment or time) and one for the between-subject effect. Each of these statistics is computed as a ratio of mean square terms. The last column of a complete rANOVA table gives the appropriate *p*-values for the statistical significance of the *F*-statistics. One reason to understand the structure of the complete rANOVA table is that some additional statistics, such as effect size, will need to be calculated by hand.

The test for the between-subjects factor is often not of interest to the researcher. One motivation to conduct repeated measures analysis is to eliminate the inherent variability that exists between the individuals in the study because it is expected that people will vary in their performance. In other words, the between-subjects effect is quite often significant, but the only interpretation of this statistical significance is that people, rather unsurprisingly, differ in their performance. In Folse (2006) and Fraser (1999) the implication of a significant between-subjects effect would be that students differ in their vocabulary retention. In another application of rANOVA, Klonowicz (1994) measured blood pressure and heart rate of 16 professional interpreters at nine different times during their work day at a conference. A between-subjects effect in this case would mean that simultaneous interpreters differ in their baseline cardiovascular measures. The finding that people exhibit variation in variables such as vocabulary retention or cardiovascular measures is

Table 8.9 Between-subjects repeated measures ANOVA

Source	SS	df	MS	F	Sig.
Condition	SS_{Cond}	$k-1$	$SS_{Cond}/k-1$	MS_{Cond}/MS_{Err}	p
Error	SS_E	$(k-1)(m-1)$	$SS_E/n-k$		

neither surprising nor meaningful in terms of the research goals. None of these three studies even report the F-statistic for the between-subjects factor, because it is of no interest in the study.

Because the between-subject effect is rarely of interest, computer packages often will not present a complete rANOVA table. Instead, a table will be presented only for the within-subjects factor (either the different treatment conditions or time) and the error,[26] an example of which is provided in Table 8.9.

The sole F-statistic in this table is for the variable of interest to the researcher: the effect of the treatment or time in the study. The numerator degrees of freedom are $k-1$, and the denominator degrees of freedom are $(k-1)(m-1)$.

The complete rANOVA table for our sample data appears in Table 8.10. Based on the discussion of the reduced form table, the most interesting line of the results is the first row and the inferential statistics related to the treatment condition. From these results, we can state that there is a statistically significant effect due to the learning strategy employed ($F[2,8] = 34.22, p < .001$).

Finally, we return to the issue of sphericity and potential violations of this assumption of rANOVA. When the variances of the paired differences are significantly different from one another, the standard F-ratio that was computed above cannot be compared to the typical F-distribution without a loss of both power and control of Type I error. A correction factor should be applied to the degrees of freedom of the test before finding the critical value or calculating the p-value. The calculation of the F-statistic itself does not change, but the critical value is different due to a change in the degrees of freedom. The alteration to the degrees of freedom is based on an estimate of how seriously the sphericity assumption is violated.

Table 8.10 Repeated measures ANOVA table of example data

Source	SS	df	MS	F	p
Condition	230.40	2	115.20	34.22	<.001
Subjects	36.67	4	9.17	2.72	.107
Error	26.93	8	3.37		
Total	294	14			

142 *Analyzing differences*

Table 8.11 Repeated measures ANOVA with corrections for sphericity

Method	df	F	p
Sphericity assumed	3.00, 58	3.2	.0298
Greenhouse-Geisser	1.76, 58	3.2	.0541
Huynh-Feldt	1.81, 58	3.2	.0528

The two most common correction procedures are the Greenhouse-Geisser and the Huynh-Feldt corrections, both of which estimate a statistic called ε, which describes the severity of the violation of sphericity in the sample data. If $\varepsilon = 1$, then there is no violation of sphericity, and the closer the estimate gets to zero, the more serious the violation. The worst case result for the statistic can be calculated as $1/(k-1)$, so for three treatment effects, .5 is the lowest possible value. The two correction methods have different procedures for calculating ε, with Greenhouse-Geisser generally considered to be a conservative estimate and Huynh-Feldt to be more liberal in its estimation. For this reason, a commonly referenced standard is to use the Huynh-Feldt correction for $\varepsilon > .75$ and the Greenhouse-Geisser correction in all other cases.

The application of the correction factor ε is made to the degrees of freedom of the rANOVA's F-test. Neither the calculations for the sums of squares nor the F-statistic itself are affected by the correction. The degrees of freedom and the p-value, however, are changed. This fact is made clear by some computer output that calculates and presents multiple correction factors side-by-side. In each case, the F-statistic is identical, but the appropriate correction factor and its p-value should be used and the rest ignored in such output. An example appears in Table 8.11.

The F-statistic in the table does not change from one method to another. The adjustment takes place in the numerator degrees of freedom, which in turn alters the p-value of the test. According to the table, the test is significant at the 5% level if sphericity is assumed, but it is not significant when either correction factor is applied. This kind of situation is possible in practice, and it shows the importance of examining the test's assumptions before drawing conclusions.

Post hoc tests

As with a one-way ANOVA, a statistically significant rANOVA only reveals that at least one of the conditions differs from the others. Descriptive statistics and pairwise follow-up tests are necessary to determine the specific pattern and statistical significance of the relationships among the conditions. The case is simpler than one-way ANOVA, because all of the pairwise tests are computed as paired t-tests. In other words, there are no analogous methods to Tukey's HSD or the Games-Howell procedure.

The need for controlling familywise Type I error still remains. Therefore, a Bonferroni correction should be applied to the p-value criterion for the multiple comparisons. SPSS provides an option to adjust *p*-values appropriately for the post hoc tests, as well as confidence intervals for the differences between all paired levels of the independent factor.

Trend analysis

When the levels of the rANOVA's independent variable are ordered, the pairwise comparisons are not usually as interesting as the overall trend. This is almost always the case for time-based rANOVA. When Klonowicz (1994) collects cardiovascular data from conference interpreters at nine different points in time, for example, none of the possible paired comparisons are intrinsically meaningful. There is no clear interpretation for why the measures should differ from time two to time eight, for example. However, the overall trend in the course of a workday might be interesting. Trend analysis can identify linear trends, such as a steady increase over the course of the day, as well as higher order trends that allow for curvature, such as quadratic or cubic trends.

Plotting the estimated marginal means also aids interpretation of trend analysis. Consider a much-simplified set of results for a study similar to Klonowicz (1994). Heart rate of interpreters is measured on four occasions, with results of 60, 84, 90, and 92 beats per minute. Graphing these results shows that the trend is increasing at a decreasing rate. Therefore, we would expect a significant linear and quadratic effect, due to the curvature of the graph.

Conducting trend analysis tests overcomes the objection of running all pairwise tests and inflating the overall Type I error of the research. Trend analysis focuses only on the change over time, which can be more interesting and of practical use. Furthermore, it allows more flexibility in modeling the relationship between the variables by considering quadratic and cubic curvature. A final benefit is the graphical output that can aid interpretation of the data.

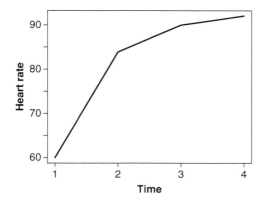

Figure 8.6 Trend analysis example

144 *Analyzing differences*

Effect size

The effect size for repeated measures ANOVA should also be measured with ω^2 (Olejnik and Algina 2003). The formula for the effect size typically needs to be calculated by hand, because software does not provide it:

$$\omega^2 = \frac{\left(SS_{Cond} - (k-1)*MS_E\right)}{(m*k)MS_E + m*\left(MS_{Subj} - MS_E\right) + \left(SS_{Cond} - (k-1)*MS_E\right)}$$

While the formula looks intimidating, all of the terms can be found in a complete rANOVA table or calculated by hand from the reduced table, if necessary. Referring back to the example in Table 8.10, we can calculate the effect size of the research:

$$\omega^2 = \frac{(230.4 - (2)3.37)}{(3*5)3.37 + 5(9.17 - 3.37) + (230.4 - (2)3.37)} = .74$$

As we mentioned previously, some computer software presents only a reduced form of the rANOVA table. The only term that does not appear in the reduced table is the between-subjects mean square, which can be found with the following formula:

$$MS_{Subj} = \frac{SS_T - SS_{Cond} - SS_E}{m - 1}$$

When necessary, total sum of squares can be found by taking the variance of the pooled observations multiplied by the total degrees of freedom: $SS_T = (n-1)\,s^2$.

An alternative and simpler measure of effect size is partial-eta squared:

$$\eta_P^2 = \frac{SS_{Cond}}{SS_{Cond} + SS_E}$$

All of the numbers necessary for this calculation are available in the reduced form rANOVA table, and it can be found commonly in past publications. However, this measure of effect size is biased upward (Keselman 1975). For our example data, $\eta_P^2 = .895$, which is considerably larger than the effect size calculated by ω^2. An improvement of the partial-eta squared statistic is the generalized eta squared statistic (Olejnik and Algina 2003; Bakeman 2005):

$$\eta_G^2 = \frac{SS_{Cond}}{SS_{Cond} + SS_E + SS_{Subj}}$$

Like the formula for ω^2 the calculation of η_G^2 requires either the complete rANOVA table or hand calculation of the total sum of squares. The generalized version will always be smaller in magnitude, and for the example data, $\eta_G^2 = .784$. We prefer the unbiased measure ω^2, though a contradictory view is expressed by Bakeman (2005), who argues that the upward bias of η_G^2 shrinks as the sample size grows.

Limitations

While there are several benefits of rANOVA designs, particularly the ability to use a smaller sample and the increase in statistical power that comes from repeated measurements, there are several drawbacks that must be considered. First, the measurements could be adulterated by order effects, which occur when participants perform differently due to the repetition inherent in the data collection process for rANOVA. The simplest example of an order effect is boredom and consequent deterioration of performance as an experiment continues. Therefore, researchers should respect the time of participants not only for ethical reasons but also because it limits any influence on their performance in an experiment. O'Brien (2009) notes that eye tracking studies often limit texts to fewer than 300 words in order to prevent boredom and a drop in motivation. Boredom effects can be combatted by limiting the length of time spent completing tasks or responding to surveys, as well as by providing appropriate breaks during the data collection process.

Order effects can manifest in at least two other ways in addition to boredom. First, repetition of a task can lead to learning effects, leading to an improvement in performance over time. Participants might remember questions on a survey taken multiple times, or they might develop strategies for improving their performance, particularly if the task is interesting or useful to them. Second, responses might exhibit a carryover effect, which occurs when experience on a previous task alters the performance on a subsequent task. For example, when post-editing translation output, a particularly grievous error in an early segment might cause a participant to over-edit later segments that have adequate translations. The impression created by the early task carries over and affects the response to later task.

The influence of learning and carryover order effects can be limited by randomized blocking, which means assigning participants to complete the tasks in a different order. For example, Chang (2009) asked 121 students to listen to four professional interpreters and then rate their perceived professionalism on a 7-point Likert-type scale. To limit order effects, the various renderings were presented in random order to different groups of participants.

Another challenge of rANOVA is the need to create or procure additional experimental materials that are as identical as possible in each treatment. Folse (2006) describes in some detail the creation of word lists for his vocabulary learning exercises. He considers nine factors, including part of speech and length of the word, in order to ensure that the word list for each condition is as similar as possible. Whenever repeated measures are used in an experiment, the research report should similarly describe the efforts made to ensure similar conditions for each of the observations.

Strategies to avoid or mitigate the shortcomings of rANOVA require careful planning. Materials and procedures must be well-prepared to avoid the influence of order effects, interaction effects, and confounding factors from different materials. This should serve as a reminder that no amount of expertise in statistical analysis can salvage poor research design and implementation.

146 *Analyzing differences*

Table 8.12 Friedman's test example

Subj.	Tr. 1	Tr. 2	Tr. 3	Rank 1	Rank 2	Rank 3
P1	7	11	15	1	2	3
P2	6	18	13	1	3	2
P3	10	9	19	2	1	3
P4	5	12	12	1	2.5	2.5
P5	10	15	19	1	2	3
Sum				6	10.5	13.5

Friedman's test

When the data suggest that the underlying population is not normally distributed, an important assumption of rANOVA is violated. In that case, a nonparametric procedure that does not require the assumption of normality can provide greater power and control over Type I error. The most commonly cited nonparametric counterpart to the one-way repeated measures ANOVA is Friedman's Test (1937, 1939, 1940). Like most of the nonparametric procedures described in this book, the test is based on the ranks of the sample data. As with the parametric rANOVA, Friedman's test assumes that each participant is measured multiple times, whether that be in different treatment conditions or at different times, and the measurements of each subject are independent from the performance of every other subject. The variable of interest needs to be at least ordinal and capable of being ranked.

The computation of Friedman's test involves finding the ranks within each subject and then summing the ranks within each treatment. A modified set of results from our earlier experiment appear in Table 8.12. The columns on the left display the raw data, while the rank columns on the right give the ranks within each participant. Ties are assigned the average of the appropriate ranks.

The sums within each treatment are used in calculating a statistic with an approximate distribution of a chi-squared variable with k–1 degrees of freedom:

$$\chi^2 = \frac{12}{m*k(k+1)} \Sigma R_j^2 - 3*m(k+1)$$

The summation term requires squaring each of the sums in the table and then adding them. The computation for the example appears below:

$$\frac{12}{5*3(3+1)}(6^2 + 10.5^2 + 13.5^2) - 3*5(3+1) = 5.7$$

The *p*-value for this statistic is .058, so it would not be statistically significant at the traditional 5% level.

Friedman's test is useful for small samples but has several shortcomings. The procedure often suffers from low power, especially in the case of small samples or few repeated measures (Zimmerman and Zumbo 1993). The problem is that Friedman's test only ranks the data within each subject. The result is that the test is not an extension of the Wilcoxon signed-ranks test in the same way that rANOVA is an extension of the paired t-test. Instead, Friedman's test is an extension of the sign test, which is a simpler variant of the Wilcoxon signed-ranks test (see Chapter 6).

An alternative nonparametric procedure is based on the application of parametric procedures on rank-transformed data. First, the data are converted to ranks and then rANOVA is conducted on the ranks, as if they were continuous data. Whether the ranking is done across all observations or within subjects only, this approach compares well to the performance of Friedman's test (Conover and Iman 1981). In the case of repeated measures ANOVA design, nonparametric statistics provide relatively little advantage.[27]

Post hoc tests

Because the data represent paired observations and because the nonparametric Friedman test was selected for the overall analysis, the appropriate post hoc testing procedure is to use the Wilcoxon signed-ranks test. To control the Type I error for the multiple comparisons made, a Bonferroni correction should be applied to the p-value cutoff. Remember that the Bonferroni correction is conservative so that it is possible that a significant overall test (Friedman) may yield no statistically significant pairwise comparisons (Wilcoxon).

Effect size

There is no universally acknowledged measure of effect size for Friedman's test, but a statistic called Kendall's W, also referred to as Kendall's coefficient of concordance, is sometimes used. The procedure for calculating the statistic begins, like Friedman's test, by ranking each subject's performance in different treatments. Kendall's W is equal to 1 when there is perfect agreement in the ranking; for instance, if one participant performed the best in every treatment, another performed the worst in every treatment, and so on. The statistic is zero when there is a total lack of agreement in the rankings. Therefore, the statistic provides a measure of association. The appropriate measure of effect size for the Wilcoxon signed-ranks post hoc tests is r, as described in Chapter 7.

Reporting

This final section of this chapter is intended to provide guidance in writing a research report. The fictional results of a one-way ANOVA with three levels of the independent factor are reported in Figure 8.7. The three levels of the independent group are simply referred to as A, B, and C, while the dependent variable is called "scores." The reporting of any one-way or repeated measures ANOVA would follow a similar structure. Following the example, we comment on some of its features.

These results provide the reader with all of the necessary information to understand the study. First, for the overall ANOVA results, the F-statistic, its degrees

One-way ANOVA showed a statistically significant difference in scores for the three groups in the study ($F[2,27] = 3.43$, $p = .047$). The effect size was large with approximately 14% of the variation in scores due to Group ($\omega^2 = .139$). ANOVA model assumptions were adequately met for the sample. Visual inspection showed no serious deviations from homogeneity of variance, and a QQ plot of the ANOVA residuals displayed no noteworthy departure from normality. Testing revealed that the residuals were approximately normal according to the Shapiro-Wilk test ($p = .178$), and the group variances were approximately equal according to Levene's test ($p = .533$). Thus, the assumptions of the ANOVA were adequately satisfied.

Table 1 Participant scores by group

Group	n	Mean	SD
A	10	33.95	10.85
B	10	30.32	7.88
C	10	23.61	7.85

Descriptive statistics are provided in Table 1. Post hoc analysis was conducted with Tukey's Honestly Significant Difference test (HSD). The scores for Group A were higher than Group C at a statistically significant level ($p = .04$, 95% CI [−20.30, −.40]), and Cohen's d implied a large effect size ($d = 1.09$). There was not a statistically significant difference between the mean scores of Groups A and B ($p = .64$, 95% CI [−13.58, 6.31], $d = .383$) nor between Groups B and C ($p = .23$, 95% CI [−16.66, 3.23], $d = .854$).

Figure 8.7 Example of complete reporting of ANOVA results

of freedom, and the corresponding p-value are provided. It is inappropriate to provide only the relative level of the p-value (for instance, "$p < .05$" or "statistically significant at the 5% level"). The practice of reporting less exact p-values is an anachronism from a time before computers readily provided them, and the reporting of exact p-values to two or three decimal places has been advocated by many style guides and professional associations, including the *Publication Guide of the American Psychological Association* since its fourth edition, published in 1994. Exact reporting also helps avoid thinking of a statistical test as a dichotomous decision rule (Rosnow and Rosenthal 1989). Interpretation of results and guidance for future research are aided by knowing the exact p-value.

Second, a measure of effect size for the ANOVA is reported, along with an interpretation of its magnitude. This discussion should be extended for understanding the relative size and importance of the difference in the context of the particular study. Reporting of exact p-values and a measure of effect size are both useful in guiding future studies and in carrying out meta-analyses (Finch, Cumming, and Thomason 2001).

Third, critical analyses of the assumptions of the statistical test are reported; this provides confidence for the reader that the appropriate test was selected for the sample. Of all the information provided in this example, these tests are the least vital for reporting results of the study. The report could state that the assumptions were met from an examination of the data. However, they do suggest that the inferential statistics were chosen carefully and for good reasons, which allows the main results to speak more confidently. Minimal information is provided about these tests, with just the *p*-values necessary for interpretation. This further demonstrates the minor emphasis on these results.

In the second paragraph, follow-up analysis is presented in the form of post hoc pairwise tests to help distinguish the relationships among the groups. The paragraph itself does not report numerical means or standard deviations, because they are presented in the accompanying table. With such a small study, it would also be possible to report these results in the text, but an author should select either a table or in-text reporting of the descriptive statistics, not both. The selection of post hoc test is given, along with the results of all comparisons, including specific *p*-values, confidence intervals, and effect sizes.

The goals of reporting results are to be both concise and correct. These two paragraphs present all of the relevant statistics and accompanying descriptions and conclusions. A full interpretation of the meaning and implications of those results would appear elsewhere in the paper's discussion.

Notes

1 This discussion is based on naïve use of the standard *t*-test to make multiple comparisons. Wilcox (1987) is one author to note that modern statistical techniques do, in some cases, allow valid use of multiple comparison tests, provided that the sample data can meet the assumptions and the appropriate testing procedure is employed. We hesitate to endorse this view for broad application, precisely because the assumptions are rarely met and selection of the correct test would require significant expertise in statistics.
2 Not every text makes explicit reference to Fisher as the originator of the test. We do so in order to distinguish it from other ANOVA tests.
3 For example, Wilcox (1998, 2005) is a prominent advocate for the use of medians, trimmed means, and *M*-estimation (e.g., Huber 1981).
4 It is always incorrect to suggest using the nonparametric Kruskal-Wallis test in the case of unequal variances, and this fact should serve as a reminder that nonparametric tests do not provide an assumption-free panacea.
5 QQ plots are introduced in Chapter 4's discussion of descriptive statistics.
6 Unfortunately, the language and notation surrounding the various sums of squared deviations are not standardized across textbooks or authors. Exercise caution when encountering any SS abbreviation with a subscript to ensure that you understand if it is a reference to the total variance, the model variance, or the residual error.
7 The actual error rate for *m* tests each conducted with a Type I error rate of .05 is given by the formula $1-(.95)^m$. So for just six pairwise tests, the actual Type I error rate is .265!
8 Given the many available procedures and in light of space limitations, a number of other tests have been omitted from this discussion. Two of the omitted tests, Fisher's Least Significant Difference and Scheffé's test, are available in most statistical software packages. However, statistical simulation studies generally find Tukey's HSD procedure to be the superior methodology in general settings (e.g., Stoline 1981; Jaccard, Becker, and Wood 1984), and as a result we have focused on this particular test while consciously omitting a range of other possible tests. For those interested, a more comprehensive treatment is provided by Hancock and Klockars (1996) as well as in a very thorough and technical volume by Hochberg and Tamhane (1987).
9 Thanks to modern statistical software, the Bonferroni correction is implemented in the simple manner described here. This was not the case when the test was first developed; tables of critical values were provided by Dunn (1961).
10 The Newman-Keuls test is another post hoc test with a very similar methodology to Tukey's HSD.

11 One of earliest descriptions of the statistic is in Tippett (1925), while Tukey (1949) and Keuls (1952) developed its use in the setting of ANOVA's multiple pairwise comparisons. An approachable description can be found in Howell (2009).
12 When the sample size of each group in the ANOVA is not identical, a slight modification is necessary in the calculations of HSD. The changes were first proposed by Kramer (1956), so the test is sometimes referred to by the name Tukey-Kramer. However, this nomenclature is uncommon.
13 In casual parlance, one might be tempted to use the word "causes," but as statisticians are so fond of saying, correlation is not causation!
14 Many of them label it partial-eta squared or η_p^2, which is appropriate terminology only for more complicated ANOVA models, not the one-way model.
15 For the elevation example, ε^2 is approximately 54%, demonstrating the universal relationship $\omega^2 < \varepsilon^2 < \eta^2$.
16 While statistical textbooks including Howell (2009) and Tabachnik and Fidell (2012) are rather favorably disposed toward ω^2, Fritz, Morris, and Richler (2012) could find only one instance of it in a review of more than 450 articles published in the *Journal of Experimental Psychology*. Therefore, use of ω^2 will necessitate some description and citation for the reader for the foreseeable future.
17 A number of useful power calculators are available on the Internet, e.g., http://www.cs.uiowa.edu/~rlenth/Power.
18 Other available tests include the Yuen-Welch test, the Brown-Forsythe test, and Wilcox's Z-test. Moder (2007) also suggests Hotelling's T^2 test. Coombs, Algina, and Oltman (1996) provide a relatively comprehensive overview of the available tests, but for the most commonly encountered situations Welch's F-test will suffice.
19 We omit the technical details of these tests and direct the interested reader to Hochberg and Tamhane (1987) for their development.
20 Alternatives such as the Jonckheere-Terpstra test (Jonckheere 1954), and Agresti-Pendergast test (1986) may have greater power in specific situations but lie outside the scope of this general discussion.
21 Among the most recent simulation papers, Meyer and Seaman (2013) provide the exact probability distribution for up to 105 observations in 3 groups and up to 40 observations in 4 groups.
22 The χ^2 approximation is known to be overly conservative (e.g., Spurrier 2003; Meyer and Seaman 2013), but its use is standard across most software packages. Some programs, such as R, have extension code that provides the exact statistic. Still, most research using the Kruskal-Wallis statistic results in the reporting of a χ^2-statistic unless the researchers calculate the *H*-statistic by hand or through purposive coding.
23 We will often utilize the abbreviation rANOVA, which is common in methodological papers, but research reports of empirical results should prefer the full name of repeated measures ANOVA.
24 One potential way to avoid this challenge is by collecting process data online. Mellinger (2015) describes the challenges inherent to this means of data collection and ways to mitigate for these issues. He demonstrates the use of rANOVA methods in conjunction with more targeted population sampling to increase statistical power in Mellinger (2014). For more on sampling, see Chapter 2.
25 Serious violations of the sphericity assumption may call for a completely different analysis from rANOVA. The most common alternative would be a multivariate ANOVA (MANOVA).
26 SPSS gives this table the title "Tests of Within-Subjects Effects."
27 A different approach that extends the Wilcoxon signed-ranks test was proposed by Fidler and Nagelkerke (1986), but it has received little attention in the literature.

9 Comparing groups on multiple factors

This chapter extends the applications of ANOVA presented in Chapter 8 to more complex experimental designs. The statistical procedures of ANOVA can encompass more complicated situations, primarily by including more independent variables in a factorial ANOVA. Every ANOVA model represents a unique way to divide the total variability of the dependent variable. This conceptual framework provides flexibility in broad applications of the tools of ANOVA; however, these gains also entail potential challenges in interpreting the results.

To maximize this volume's usefulness for applied research, we omit many of the mathematical details of the models in this chapter.[1] Instead, we provide examples and discussion of possible applications of simpler versions in lieu of the mathematically more complex tests. As with all of the inferential statistics presented thus far, a word of caution is in order—more complex models do not preclude the need to meet assumptions. Situations involving multiple variables or complicated relationships will require more sophisticated models. However, increases in complexity are accompanied by increases in the likelihood that an assumption is violated. Therefore, the simplest model capable of answering the research question should be preferred.

Independent factorial ANOVA

The simplest expansion of ANOVA is the inclusion of additional independent factors. Rather than only one categorical variable being used to define groups, two or more categorical variables can be employed to create multiple combinations of the categories. When all of the possible combinations of levels from multiple variables are tested, the experimental design is a *factorial ANOVA*. When none of the participants are measured more than once (i.e., there are no repeated measures), then the model is also an independent ANOVA. We focus on independent observations in this section, postponing the inclusion of repeated measures until later in the chapter.

There are two ways to name factorial ANOVA designs. The first is to provide the number of independent variables included in the model. In Chapter 8 we presented the one-way ANOVA, which considers a single independent variable. When two independent variables are included, the model is a two-way ANOVA, and so on. While there is no mathematical constraint on the number of variables, models should usually be constrained to three or four independent variables at the very most. Otherwise, the interpretation of the results becomes unwieldy. More complicated analysis requires stricter adherence to the assumptions in order to yield correct decisions. Therefore, too many variables in a quasi-experimental or observational setting can diminish the value of the statistical analysis.

The second way to describe a factorial ANOVA is to enumerate the number of levels of each independent variable. For example, a three-by-four ANOVA has two independent variables—one variable has three levels while the other has four. This same experiment could be described as a two-way independent ANOVA, but explicitly listing the number of levels provides more information about the independent variables.

Each combination of levels from the independent factors creates a cell in the factorial ANOVA structure. For example, a simple study might have novice and experienced translators perform a task in different environmental conditions related to background noise—its four levels might be silence, background conversations in the source language, background conversations in the target language, and instrumental music. Some dependent measure of performance could then be studied. The design of this experiment is a two-by-four ANOVA because there are two levels of experience and four levels of background noise.[2] In total, eight combinations of the two variables exist.

The experiment must have multiple observations, called *replications*, at each level in order to estimate variability. For instance, for each of the eight cells to have five replications, a total of 40 people are needed for the study. A diagram of the study's design appears in Table 9.1. Each cell represents a combination of experience level and background noise, and the table emphasizes the fact that five different participants would complete the experiment for each of these conditions (sample size of each cell, $j = 5$). Maintaining equal sample size within each cell is called a *balanced design*. This equality improves statistical power.

Whenever possible, participants should be randomly allocated into the various treatment combinations. This is not always possible; for instance, in this study natural variation in the experience variable can be observed. However, the background noise condition can and should be randomly assigned.

As a reminder from Chapter 8, a one-way ANOVA divides total variability into two parts: between-group and within-group variation. Mathematically, that

Table 9.1 Independent factorial ANOVA study design

Background noise	Experience level	
	Novice	Experienced
None	$j = 5$	$j = 5$
Target	$j = 5$	$j = 5$
Source	$j = 5$	$j = 5$
Music	$j = 5$	$j = 5$

division is represented by the model sum of squares and the error sum of squares, respectively. The *F*-test is the ratio of explained (between-group) variability and unexplained (within-group) variability. Statistical significance of ANOVA implies that differences in the independent factor explain a substantial portion of the variability in the dependent variable.

A factorial ANOVA follows this same general design, but the between-group variability is partitioned into further subcategories. In the example study, some of the between-group variability is due to background noise, some of it is due to the translator's experience, and the remainder is attributable to the interaction between background noise and experience level. Each of these three components has an associated sum of squares, and when they are added together, the resulting figure represents the model sum of squares.

The test statistic follows analogously from Fisher's *F*-test for one-way ANOVA. In that model, the *F*-statistic is the mean square of the model divided by the mean square of the error. Put another way, the test divides the explained variance by the unexplained variance: $F = MS_M / MS_E$. We can denote generic groups of a two-way ANOVA as simply A and B, with their interaction symbolized as AB. There are three test statistics, each based on the portion of variance explained by these sources, divided by the mean squared error. For example, to test the effect of the independent variable A, the test statistic is $F = MS_A / MS_E$.

The degrees of freedom for these *F*-tests also come from sub-dividing the model. Each group has degrees of freedom equal to the number of levels minus one. The interaction degrees of freedom are given by the product of the degrees of freedom from the two groups. For our fictitious example, there are four levels of background noise, so the variable would have three degrees of freedom. Similarly, there are two levels of experience and consequently just one degree of freedom. The interaction term would have three degrees of freedom (the result of one times three in this situation). The total degrees of freedom remain, as usual, one less than the sample size; the remaining degrees of freedom are attributed to the error term.

All of the previous description of the sums of squares, mean squares, and *F*-statistics are summarized in Table 9.2. In the degrees of freedom formulas, *a* and *b* stand for the number of levels in Factor A and B, respectively.

Table 9.2 Sums of squares, mean squares, and *F*-statistics

Source	SS	df	MS	F
Factor A	SS_A	$a-1$	MS_A	MS_A / MS_E
Factor B	SS_B	$b-1$	MS_B	MS_B / MS_E
Interaction	SS_{AB}	$(a-1)(b-1)$	MS_{AB}	MS_{AB} / MS_E
Error	SS_E	$n-ab$	MS_E	
Total	SS_T	$n-1$		

Interpreting a factorial ANOVA requires examining each of the F-statistics or its associated p-value. The null hypothesis being tested in each case is that the means do not differ across the levels of the independent variable or the interaction. In slightly more accessible, but less statistically precise, language, the test asks whether the factor (or interaction) explains a statistically significant portion of the variability in the dependent variable.

Interaction effects

When interpreting the results of a factorial ANOVA's hypothesis tests, the interaction effect should be considered the first priority. Some authors adopt the draconian position that in the presence of a significant interaction effects, other effects should not be interpreted at all. While this position is extreme, large interaction effects can complicate the interpretation of factorial ANOVA results. If interaction effects are not statistically significant, then interpretation should focus on the main effects, which are described in the next section.

Statistically significant interaction effects imply that the effect of one variable is different based on the level of another variable. In some cases, that difference is inherently interesting. In our example study, interaction between noise level and experience would mean that novices and experts react differently to background noise. This result is more nuanced than a simple finding that background noise matters. An interaction effect would suggest not only that noise does matter, but also that it matters in a different way based on the level of experience.

For a two-way ANOVA, interaction effects can usually be understood and described. Furthermore, independent variables with a limited number of ordered levels can help in understanding any observed interaction. If in the example study the number of levels for experience were to be expanded to include three categories—e.g., students, novices, and experts—the interaction would not be overly complicated given the natural ordering of the levels. However, a similar study that used English-German and French-Russian translators as the two groups would have a more difficult time explaining any interaction effect. Furthermore, if the model included all three variables (i.e., language pair, level of experience, and background noise) then interpreting significant interactions in a meaningful way is ostensibly impossible.

Main effects

Any difference observed when considering one factor at a time, across all levels of the other variables, is called a *main effect*, so a factorial ANOVA has one main effect for each independent variable. In most factorial ANOVA designs, the main effects are of primary interest because the independent variables are chosen for their likely association with the dependent variable. Furthermore, main effects are easy to interpret and generalize to other situations. Each main effect is tested for statistical significance in a separate F-test.

The interpretation of a main effect is the average effect of one factor across all levels of the other study variables. For our example study, testing the main effect due to level of experience determines whether there is a statistically significant difference between the performance of novices and experts. Similarly, testing the main effect due to noise level determines if noise level exerts a statistically significant influence on performance, regardless of experience level. These examples demonstrate that main effects ignore the other factor(s) in the model.

If a model has a statistically significant interaction effect, then describing only the main effects does not truly reflect the data. In some cases, main effects can still be significant and useful to understand even when there is a significant interaction. However, the interpretation is more limited because the main effect is not the same for all levels of the other variables. Generalizations to the population about the observed main effect, therefore, ought to be restricted when interaction effects are present.

Simple effects

Another way to examine the effects of independent variables is to consider the effect of one variable while holding the other variable constant. Examining the model in this way is referred to as a test for a *simple effect*. Typically, simple effects are of most interest when there is a significant interaction between the variables and the main effects are not significant. In such a situation, simple effects can demonstrate that some combinations of the effects do represent statistically significant differences.

Simple effects can be a good way to bolster arguments based on observed cell means when the relationships among the variables is complex. However, main effects always represent a stronger finding for a study. Because main effects and interaction effects are both more common and preferable from an interpretation point of view, we omit further description of simple effects. For a description of the testing and interpretation of simple effects, see Howell (2012).

Effect size

When discussing the effect size of one-way ANOVA, we noted that the most commonly reported measure is eta squared but that omega squared (ω^2) is a less-biased estimate. The same holds true for factorial ANOVA. Though most statistical software will automatically report partial-eta squared (η_p^2), it is better to calculate the less-biased effect size measure using the ANOVA table, which provides all of the numbers needed to calculate the formula:

$$\omega_A^2 = \frac{SS_A - (a-1)MS_E}{SS_T + MS_E}$$

This formula calculates the effect size for the main effect due to the independent factor A. Analogous formulas can be calculated for main effects or interaction effects by replacing the particular sum of squares in the numerator and the correct degrees of freedom. We encourage calculation of omega squared as the preferred effect size. However, it is possible to convert from one measure to the other, so it is better to report partial-eta squared than to omit a measure of effect size altogether.

Post hoc tests

If an F-test is significant for a factor that has only two levels, no follow-up testing is necessary because the difference obviously exists between the two levels. However, an independent factor with more than two levels could be further tested to determine the source of the difference. Pairwise comparisons can be made between the means of all levels of the independent variable. As with the one-way ANOVA, the pairwise comparisons must be adjusted to control for the familywise Type I error.

The same general recommendations from Chapter 8 apply to the post hoc procedures for a factorial ANOVA. Tukey's HSD generally has the best power when the assumptions of independence, normality, and homogeneity of variance are met. The Bonferroni correction is a conservative way to control the Type I error. Finally, the Games-Howell procedure offers the best performance when the variances are not equal in each cell. Because the variance assumption is often the most tenuous, we recommend the Games-Howell procedure for most post hoc comparisons. The decision about which pairwise test method to employ should be guided by the situation, but in no case should the decision be made after the fact by estimating them all and picking the procedure that gives the best statistical significance.

Summary

Factorial designs offer four benefits. First, a single experiment can investigate multiple independent variables. Limited participant pools and potentially time-consuming research protocols are challenges regularly faced by applied researchers. Therefore, the ability to collect sample data once and contribute to an understanding of multiple variables is a valuable attribute of factorial ANOVA.

Second, experimental control is extended to multiple factors, known as *blocking*. Controlling the amount of error in the model is an important goal of experimental design. The ANOVA F-test has the unexplained variability as its denominator. Therefore, anything that decreases the unexplained variability will increase the likelihood of a statistically significant result. In other words, statistical power increases in models with several variables that are related to the dependent variable.

Third, an effect observed across multiple groups can be more widely generalized. One way to diminish error and increase statistical power is to test a relatively homogeneous sample. For instance, a study that limits the sample to novice translators will likely observe similar performance levels compared with a study that includes people with various years of experience. The gained statistical power of this design is not without a tradeoff; generalizations can only be made to the relevant population from which the sample was drawn. In this case, the results would only apply to novice translators. A second study would be necessary to understand if the conclusions were valid for experienced translators. By contrast, factorial ANOVA with multiple levels of experience allows findings about background noise to be generalized to a larger population of the two groups.

Fourth, the interaction term can be investigated. Sometimes a researcher hopes to show that a factor exerts a different influence in various circumstances. In the example study, novice translators might need silence to focus on their work and perform much worse with background noise of any kind. Meanwhile, experienced translators might be able to tolerate more noise and still perform well. In that case, the conclusion regarding background noise would depend on the level of experience. A significant interaction effect can demonstrate that two groups perform differently under different conditions.

The principal drawback of factorial ANOVA is that a statistically significant interaction term can complicate the interpretation of the results. In some cases, a researcher specifically seeks to model an interaction term, but in most cases, interaction effects only muddle the main effects. When interaction effects are not statistically significant, then each main effect operates independently and knowing the level of one variable does not change the predicted effect of another variable. However, when interaction effects are significant, then the response to one independent variable depends on the level of another independent variable. For small models, such as a two-by-two ANOVA, the effects might still be interpretable. For larger models, especially for three or more independent factors, significant interaction effects can cloud the relationships among the variables to the point where the experimental data become nearly meaningless. In that case, follow-up studies that consider fewer variables are often necessary.

Two-way ANOVA example

To help clarify the interpretation of factorial ANOVA results, this section presents another fictitious example. Graphs are also shown that depict all possible outcomes of the model's estimation. The model is the most basic factorial ANOVA, a two-by-two independent design.

To understand interpreter performance in different settings, a study is conducted to compare the performance of remote and on-site interpretation among novice and experienced interpreters. This example is not a repeated measures design; each participant is measured just one time. A sample of 40 conference interpreters, 20 of whom are experienced and 20 of whom are novices, is split randomly between the on-site and remote conditions. The resulting design has four groups of 10, who are then measured on some dependent variable of interest, in this case the number of omissions that occur when interpreting a 15-minute speech.

The three F-tests for this two-by-two design are associated with the two main effects and the one interaction effect. Given this experimental design, eight possible outcomes could occur. The results of a factorial ANOVA can be presented

158 *Analyzing differences*

Table 9.3 Factorial ANOVA with no significant effects

Location	Level of experience	
	Novice	Experienced
On-site	15	15
Remote	15	15

in a table or plot of the cell means. The simplest possible outcome is that there is no significant difference in performance for either main effect; the same number of omissions are observed for both novice and experienced interpreters, whether they are working on-site or at a remote location. Table 9.3 displays the mean number of omissions observed for each cell; this extreme case of equality among all cells also represents the null hypothesis of no difference between any of the levels.

The second and third cases involve only one significant main effect. The results could indicate that the location has a statistically significant effect, and both groups increase the number of omissions when working remotely. Table 9.4 displays the possible cell means for this situation. The other possibility is that only the level of experience matters, but the location does not have a statistically significant effect on the number of omissions.

A fourth possible outcome is that both effects are significant. Rather than produce a table of marginal means, a research report can display the results in a plot. Figure 9.1 provides a sketch of the four outcomes we have described so far. The dependent variable (number of omissions) is measured on the vertical axis. The independent variable of location appears on the horizontal axis, and two lines are drawn on the plot. The solid line represents the average performance of novices, while the dashed line represents the average performance of experienced interpreters.

Which independent variable appears on the axis and which receives multiple lines is a matter of choice, and the presentation can emphasize whichever variable is more interesting to communicate the study's main results. When a study involves a factor with two levels and another factor with more than two levels, it often makes sense to draw a line for the two-level factor and let the multi-level factor be represented on the x-axis. This design simplifies the graph by requiring just two lines, and any trend in the multi-level factor can be easily spotted.

Table 9.4 Factorial ANOVA with significant main effect

Location	Level of experience	
	Novice	Experienced
On-site	12	12
Remote	15	15

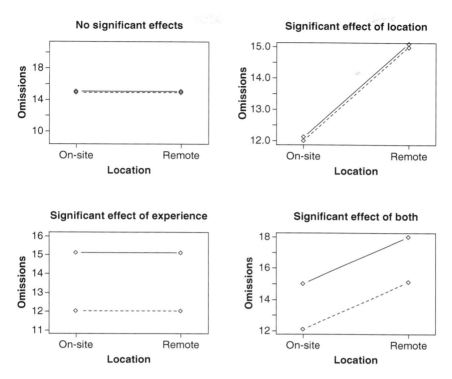

Figure 9.1 Factorial ANOVA outcomes—no interaction

Interpreting the plots is a matter of examining the slope of the lines and the distance between the lines. When the location is significant (as in the upper right plot), the lines are sloped, representing the change in level of the independent variable that is plotted on the horizontal axis. When the experience level is significant (as in the lower left plot), the lines are separated from one another with a vertical shift. The solid line for the novice interpreters is higher, reflecting a larger mean number of omissions. When both effects are significant, the lines are both sloped and separated (as in the lower right plot).

The plots can also display a boxplot or bar chart for each level of the independent variable that is presented on the horizontal axis. Doing so would draw more attention to that independent variable and also give a sense of the effect size or meaningful difference between the groups. Furthermore, boxplots and bar charts are more appropriate when a multi-level factor is not inherently ordered. The previous example involving noise level, for instance, would be better presented with a box plot because the ordering of the noise level on the x-axis would be arbitrary. All of the information from the tables above can be seen in the plots, so a research report should favor one form or the other, whichever communicates the study's main results clearly.

160 *Analyzing differences*

The other four possible results are analogous in terms of the main effects, but an interaction effect is also significant in each case. As discussed previously, these results can be harder to interpret. Plots are often more useful than tables when interaction effects are present, and the interaction is portrayed by the different slopes of the two lines. The remaining four possible outcomes from the study are displayed in Figure 9.2.

In some of these cases, the interaction term leads to interesting results for prediction and practical application. For instance, the upper left plot suggests that experienced interpreters work better in a remote location, while novices perform better on-site. This result could influence working conditions and assignments, or it could suggest changes in training or practice. The problem with interaction effects, though, is that it can be difficult to generalize or theorize about the results. The fictitious example here is an extreme and unusual case, but the idea that the location and level of experience have differential effects would make a general theory about either variable impossible. Therefore, even when interaction effects can be interpreted and applied, they can provide a challenge for advancing the body of theoretical knowledge in the discipline.

Even the simplest factorial designs can have a rather large number of possible outcomes. Conducting the appropriate F-tests is only the first step in understanding the relationships among the variables. Cell means should be calculated, and a table or plot should be reported to show the main effects and interaction effects.

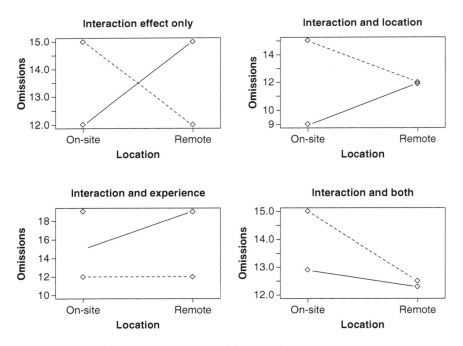

Figure 9.2 Factorial ANOVA outcomes—with interaction

We end our description of independent factorial ANOVA with an example from the translation and interpreting (T&I) literature. Kepner (1991) conducted a two-by-two ANOVA to determine the influence of feedback on the quality of writing in an intermediate Spanish class. One of the variables was the verbal ability of the 60 students in the study; this variable was determined based on GPA and grades in previous English classes. The second variable was the type of feedback provided for regular journal writing assignments. The feedback emphasized either error correction or message-related comments, which were written in Spanish and responded to the content of the students' writing. One dependent variable in the study was the level of the students' writing, operationalized by the author as a count of higher-level propositions. The main effect of each independent variable was statistically significant. Greater verbal ability and message-related feedback were both associated with better writing outcomes for the students. The primary conclusion of Kepner (1991) is that message-related feedback is more effective at improving students' writing abilities. The independent variable of verbal ability is not of primary interest in the study; however, its inclusion increases statistical power and allows generalization to students with diverse levels of verbal ability.

Factorial repeated measures design

Repeated measure designs can also be extended to include multiple independent variables. There are two complications that need to be considered. First, the assumption of sphericity must be satisfied. Mauchly's test is typically provided by computer output, but as we discussed in Chapter 8, there are statistical problems with using a pre-test to determine the appropriate model. The Greenhouse-Geisser or Huynh-Feldt corrections can be made to the degrees of freedom to account for violations of the sphericity assumption.

The second issue with a factorial repeated measures design comes from considering the effect of each subject as a variable. In that case, there is only one observation per cell and no way to estimate a within-cell variance. This problem is overcome by using the interaction mean squares for each variable as the denominator in the F-statistic. What this solution means in practical terms is that the subject variable cannot be tested. As we mentioned in Chapter 8, though, this test is rarely of interest because it only tests whether the subjects are different from each other. Additionally, the degrees of freedom for the test of each within-subjects variable will often be quite low, which attenuates some of the power advantage of the repeated measures design.

As in the one-way repeated measures design, the participants in a factorial repeated measures experiment act as their own controls. Statistical power is increased because the same people are measured in every condition. This power advantage is traded off against the fewer degrees of freedom in the hypothesis tests, but repeated measures designs generally result in improved power by removing some of the variability due to the subjects and the related sampling error.

Another advantage of repeated measures design is the need for fewer participants. The related drawback is that the number of conditions needs to be limited

162 *Analyzing differences*

to prevent fatigue effects and to treat the participants in an ethical manner by respecting their time and willingness to participate. Furthermore, the order of the measurements should vary according to a blocking scheme to avoid any confounds due to order effects.

The mathematical details of repeated measures designs are omitted here, but the resulting F-statistics and p-values can be interpreted in the same way as any ANOVA model results. Each main effect and interaction effect will have a separate hypothesis test. The Greenhouse-Geisser adjustment should be used to control for sphericity violations. When the p-value is below 5%, the variable has a significant effect on the dependent variable.

Perhaps more than any other ANOVA test, the factorial repeated measures design is best understood by examining the cell means and confidence intervals. Computer software will provide the descriptive statistics along with confidence intervals that allow for pairwise comparisons. The Bonferroni correction is typically employed to control for familywise Type I error. These results create confidence intervals and p-values to understand the relationships among the levels of each independent variable.

An example from the T&I literature provides a good example of the utility of descriptive statistics to understand the result of estimating a factorial repeated measures ANOVA. Christoffels and de Groot (2004) employed a two-by-three repeated measures design to investigate the cognitive challenges of interpreting. A sample of 24 university students who were fluent in both Dutch and English completed tasks of shadowing, paraphrasing, and interpreting sentences presented to them in Dutch. Additionally, they performed these three versions simultaneously and with a delay. The participants' performance was rated by two judges, and their scores were the dependent variable. Table 9.5 displays a simplified summary of the cell means in the study.

The results of Christoffels and de Groot (2004) are an excellent example of significant main effects and interaction. The main effect of task-type was statistically significant; the participants performed best at shadowing and worst at paraphrasing, with average performance at interpreting between these two. The main effect of timing was also statistically significant; simultaneous work was rated lower in all cases than the delayed condition. However, the interaction term was also significant and the simple effect of shadowing was not significant. The paper provides a comprehensive summary of these results, which involves reporting the results of 12 different F-tests.

Table 9.5 Adapted from Christoffels and de Groot (2004: 234, Table 1)

Task	Timing	
	Simultaneous	*Delayed*
Shadowing	88.63	89.65
Interpreting	69.35	84.44
Paraphrasing	65.26	81.72

The presentation of the paper's results also serves as a testament to the utility of a table of means. With only a cursory look at Table 9.5, the patterns are evident. The unusually high score for the shadowing task with simultaneous timing is the source of the interaction. Formal hypothesis testing (and statistical methods generally) should always support and clarify observed differences and intuitions regarding a study's results in this way.

Another example of a factorial repeated measures design is Seeber and Kerzel (2012), who estimate a three-way repeated measures ANOVA. The study examines pupil dilation as a measure of cognitive load in the context of simultaneous interpreting German into English. The three independent variables were time (four periods of interest were examined), syntax of the sentences (verb-final or verb-initial), and whether the sentences were presented within a larger discourse or in a cluster of three sentences. Therefore, the design was four-by-two-by-two; all of the conditions were within-subjects variables. The author's primary result was that a verb-final construction led to larger pupil dilation, suggesting greater cognitive load.

The final consideration of this section is effect size. Omega squared can be calculated for the overall model; Olejnik and Algina (2003) supply the necessary formulas to compute the effect size by hand. The resulting figure is less biased than the eta squared that is typically provided by computer software. Some authors advocate an effect size from the r family to describe the effect size of each independent variable separately (e.g., Field 2013). Rather than examining the overall model, these effect sizes describe the usefulness of each variable in understanding the dependent variable. Since the model can be complicated to understand, this information might ease interpretation by considering only one variable at a time.

Mixed ANOVA

When a model includes both within-subject and between-subject variables, the design is described as a *mixed ANOVA*.[3] The total variability of a mixed ANOVA is divided first into between- and within-group portions. If there are multiple between-subject variables, then the between-group variability is further subdivided into one piece for each variable as well as their interactions. The within-group variability is divided between treatment effects and residual errors. The overall idea of partitioning measurement error remains at the model's core, even as the sub-divisions become more complicated and difficult to envision.

The interpretation of a mixed ANOVA is not substantially different from any of the previous models. The test results in F-statistics for each main effect and interaction. The between-subjects factors should be analyzed with the Games-Howell follow-up comparisons, while the within-subjects factors can be compared using confidence intervals with a Bonferroni correction. The omega squared effect size for the overall model needs to be calculated by hand (see Olejnik and Algina 2003), while the individual variable effects can be reported with r family effect size measures.

164 *Analyzing differences*

Mixed effects models are useful because they provide the increased power that comes from repeated measurements while also allowing the comparison of different groups of participants. Liu and Chiu (2009) provide an example of this model in their comparison of undergraduate and graduate interpreting students. Each participant interpreted three passages, and judges rated their overall performance. The study represents a two-by-three mixed ANOVA with the two groups as a between-subjects factor and the three passages as a within-subjects factor. As in all advanced ANOVA models, statistical testing and the pattern of the reported cell means provide an understanding of how the independent variables affect the dependent measure.

Fixed and random effects

In estimating ANOVA models, an important distinction is whether a given variable should be considered a *fixed effect* or a *random effect*. A fixed effect is an independent variable for which all of the relevant levels are tested. The goal of the research is to understand only the particular groups or treatments that are represented in the ANOVA model. This chapter has repeatedly used the groups of novices and experts as a variable, for example. If these are the only two categories of interest, then the variable is a fixed effect. As another example, Christoffels and de Groot (2004) compared simultaneous and delayed methods in their interpreting study. Treating this variable as a fixed effect assumes that these are the only interesting levels to understand.

By contrast, a random effect assumes that the levels of a variable are drawn from a larger population. The background noise variable earlier in the chapter might be an example of a random effect, because there are many more types of distractors that could be used in the experiment. The four chosen levels are particular instances of the larger concept of background noise. Typically, however, the most important random effect comes from repeated measures designs, in which each subject is assumed to be a part of a larger population. In all of the models we have discussed so far, we have assumed that experimental treatments are fixed effects and that repeated measures are treated as random effects.

The mathematical difference between fixed and random effects models comes from considering the cell means to be random variables. If a variable is assumed to be a fixed effect, then the relevant question is whether the means of the cells differ from one another. Testing a random effect, by contrast, is a question of whether the variances of each cell differ.

The practical difference between the effects is in the level of generalization from the tests. A fixed effect is relevant only to the levels that were tested. Random effects generalize to the entire population from which the random effects were collected. This generalization assumes that the sample was randomly selected.

The distinction between fixed and random effects model is vital for proper estimation of more complicated ANOVA designs. Most research in T&I will utilize fixed effects treatment variables because all of the levels of interest are tested. Researchers generally employ random effects only when estimating repeated measures designs because the goal is to generalize the findings to a broader population of people.

Analysis of covariance

All of the ANOVA models we have considered so far have involved categorical independent variables. When a continuous variable is added to the estimation, the model is referred to as *analysis of covariance (ANCOVA)*. The continuous variable that is added to the model is referred to as a *covariate*.

In estimating an ANCOVA model, the effect of the categorical variable(s) remains the primary interest of the estimation. In an experimental setting, the research design still involves controlling or manipulating the levels of the categorical variables in order to understand their effect. By contrast, a covariate typically lies outside the researcher's control. Therefore, a covariate is distinct from the typical independent–dependent dichotomy. The covariate is not manipulated, so it is not an independent variable, but it is also not the measurement of interest. Instead, the covariate is a potentially confounding or nuisance variable, and ANCOVA allows its effect on the dependent variable to be removed from the main analysis of the categorical variable(s).

The most common reason to include a covariate in a model is to control statistically for a variable that a researcher cannot control experimentally. As a simple example, a researcher might compare three basic language learning techniques: written flash cards, spaced repetition oral practice, and a computer program with pictures. A group of students are randomly assigned to different groups, practice a set of vocabulary words with the technique, and are tested the next day for retention. The researcher might suspect that other variables would affect vocabulary acquisition. One possible variable would be the students' GPA; students with better grades might be smarter and/or more likely to enjoy the learning process. Some of the variation in individual performance is plausibly due to GPA and not to the learning technique. An ANCOVA model would include the continuous measure of GPA as a covariate, thereby removing its effect on the dependent variable.

Inclusion of a covariate adds another explanatory source of the total variation. The main idea behind ANOVA modeling and the F-test is the comparison of the amount of explained variance to the unexplained variance. The inclusion of a covariate potentially decreases the amount of unexplained variance, which improves the test's statistical power in most cases. The reason ANCOVA does not automatically increase power is that the covariate also reduces the degrees of freedom in the F-test. Therefore, it is important to select a covariate that is associated with the dependent variable.

The assumptions of ANCOVA include the same three assumptions as ANOVA (i.e., independence, normality, and homogeneity of variance). Two additional assumptions must also be met. First, the effect of the covariate should be independent of the treatment effect. Second, the linear relationship between the dependent variable and the covariate should be the same in both groups.[4] The assumptions are best met when participants are randomly assigned to treatment groups. In the example above, GPA and learning method are independent due to the design of the study; therefore, the relationship between GPA and learning should be the same in each group.

Without random assignment, ANCOVA models can be problematic (see Miller and Chapman 2001). Any naturally occurring groups that would be used in a quasi-experimental or observational study might differ on the covariate. For instance, a T&I study might want to compare monolinguals, bilinguals, and interpreters as three groups, but participants cannot be randomly assigned to these groups. Any covariates to be used in a model must be independent of the group assignment.

Robust test procedures

While several nonparametric tests have been proposed and developed for more complicated ANOVA designs, their statistical properties rarely hold up to scrutiny in simulation studies (e.g., Toothaker and Newman 1994). One useful method is to apply a rank transformation to the data and conduct the typical parametric procedure on the ranks (Conover and Iman 1981). This procedure can be appropriate in 2-by-2 designs (Blair, Sawilowsky, and Higgins 1987). Other robust estimation methods are described in Wilcox (2012). The relative complexity of these techniques and their lack of availability in most statistical software programs have prevented their wide adoption so far. The F-test is certainly the most common form of estimation, but significant violations of the test's assumptions might motivate a researcher to consult a statistician who is familiar with robust procedures.

Notes

1 Howell (2012) provides a thorough treatment of the computation and mathematics of advanced ANOVA models.
2 The model could also be described as 4-by-2. The ordering of the independent factors makes no difference.
3 More generally, a mixed effects model is one that includes both fixed and random effects. In most cases, a T&I study will only use within-subjects factors as random effects.
4 In the language of the general linear model, this assumption can be referred to as an assumption of homogeneous regression slopes.

10 Testing categorical data

Data that are collected by counting frequencies or classifying observations are measured at the categorical level. Equivalently, these measurements represent discrete data, and frequency tables are among the best methods to summarize and display such data succinctly. Many of the test statistics for analyzing this kind of data utilize the χ^2-distribution, which was described briefly in Chapter 5.

The various χ^2-tests are grouped together in this chapter based upon their mathematical similarities. One of the more interesting questions for translation and interpreting (T&I) research is whether a variable is distributed differently in distinct populations. For instance, do novice and expert interpreters and translators behave similarly on a given variable? A χ^2-test may also be employed to test if two variables are independent and whether sample data were drawn from a population with a certain distribution. All of these applications are described in the chapter.

Testing categorical data: overview

χ^2-test for homogeneity

Purpose: To determine if two or more groups differ in the relative frequency of occurrence of a variable

Null hypothesis: The variable of interest is distributed identically for all groups

Alternative hypothesis: The variable of interest exhibits a different distribution in at least one group

χ^2-test for independence

Purpose: To determine if two categorical variables are independent of each other

Null hypothesis: The two variables are independently distributed

Alternative hypothesis: The two variables are dependent

Goodness-of-fit test

Purpose: To determine if observed data match an expected distribution

Null hypothesis: The observations are drawn from a population with the expected distribution

Alternative hypothesis: The observations do not match the frequencies of the expected distribution

168 *Analyzing differences*

Table 10.1 Testing categorical data: Examples from T&I literature

1 Timarová and Salaets (2011: Table 5) compare frequencies of four different learning styles between two different groups. The groups are described as interpreters and a control group, and the full table is 4-by-2. They report a non-significant result and conclude that there is not enough evidence of a difference in distribution between the two groups. This example could formally be described as a test of homogeneity.
2 Oakes (2012) compares the frequency of word usage in two different translations of a text. Over 3,000 2-by-2 chi-squared tests are run, each comparing the relative frequency of a specific word in the two texts. Due to the large number of tests, a Bonferroni correction is used for the p-value cutoff, and the use of six words is found to differ between the two translations at a statistically significant level.
3 Ji and Oakes (2012) compare the number of phrases that are two, three, or four words in length in two different translations. The data are presented in a 2-by-3 table, but the differences between the two texts is not statistically significant in this case.

The distribution of the sample variance also follows the χ^2-distribution. When the population is assumed to be normally distributed, a one-sample test may be conducted to determine whether the sample variance is equal to a given value. However, this test is rarely employed in practical research, because an estimation of the variance of a population is not often interesting. Therefore, we omit any further discussion of the one-sample test for the variance, instead focusing our attention on tests of categorical data in this chapter. Three examples from the literature are listed in Table 10.1.

To demonstrate the steps in a χ^2-test, we consider a fictional experiment involving discrete count data. A random sample of 77 books is collected from all of the books translated from European languages into English in a given year. The books are then all categorized along two dimensions: source language and fiction versus non-fiction. The results appear in Table 10.2.

There are potential complications with this classification of source language, including the number of categories to be considered. Furthermore, some classification decisions (also known as coding decisions) can prove more difficult. For instance, should a book in Italian be classified into a category of its own or be added to the generic "Other" category? We gloss over these complications for the purposes of this example; however, this chapter will describe the particular challenges in the context of the chi-squared-test, and Chapter 11 discusses issues of reliability in coding decisions.

Table 10.2 Chi-squared example data

	Fiction	Non-fiction	Total
French	6	10	16
German	15	7	22
Spanish	12	5	17
Other	8	14	22
Total	41	36	77

One potential research question is whether the two variables are independent from each other. Independence would imply that source language and fiction versus non-fiction do not influence each other. A violation of independence would mean, for example, that English translations of French books were predominantly non-fiction while English translations of German books were mostly fiction. The χ^2-test of independence provides a statistical test for examining the null hypothesis of independence versus the alternative hypothesis that the categories are not independent.

Visual inspection of Table 10.2 suggests that the null hypothesis is not true. Translations from French and "Other" are largely non-fiction, while English translations of German and Spanish tend to be of fictional works, according to these data. This intuition is supported by the χ^2-test of independence ($\chi^2[3] = 8.14$, $p = .043$, $V = .325$). The remainder of this chapter will describe the testing procedure and interpretation of these results.

Tests for independence and homogeneity

The chi-squared tests for homogeneity and for independence are two different tests that use exactly the same computation formula. The computational relationship has led to terminological confusion and application of the tests without a clear understanding of the null and alternative hypotheses. We aim to clarify the distinction between the two tests, with the primary goal of assisting the interpretation of the results of each test.

For both tests, a two-dimensional table similar to Table 10.2 can be useful for displaying the raw data. The table is called a *contingency table*, and each number occupies one *cell* of the table. The use of the row and column totals of the table also result in the chi-squared test being referred to as *cross tabulation*. We will denote the number of rows with the letter m and the number of columns with k. The resulting table will be referred to as an m-by-k contingency table.

Test for independence

The chi-squared test for independence examines whether two variables are related. The null hypothesis is that the variables are independent, which means that the value of one variable has no bearing on the other. For instance, a random sample of people could be asked two questions: Do you own a pet? Do you like sushi?[1] There is no reason to expect these variables to be related. Whether someone owns a pet is rather unlikely to affect whether they like the taste of sushi. Therefore, these variables are independent, and the null hypothesis would not be rejected. By contrast, we could collect a random sample of people and ask two different questions: Do you have a valid passport? Have you traveled outside of your home country in the past year? The answers to these two questions are clearly related and not independent. Not everyone with a valid passport has traveled in the past year, but the likelihood is much higher.

In both of these examples, the research question is whether two different random variables are related to each other. Only one sample is collected, and the participants are measured on two different categorical variables. Crucially, the researcher does not control either variable. This research design is common in content analysis, which uses frequency data to draw inferences about texts, images, films, or other cultural artifacts. A researcher might examine advertisements for tourist destinations that appeared in China and ask whether they used non-Chinese words and whether the images were of city skylines, specific destinations inside cities, or landscapes. One sample of advertisements would be collected in order to determine if these two variables were independent from each other.

In summary, the test for independence requires one random sample and two variables that are outside a researcher's control. The null hypothesis is that the two variables are independent. The alternative hypothesis is that the variables are related.

Test for homogeneity

The chi-squared test for homogeneity should be used to test whether a particular variable is distributed differently across different groups. The groups are predefined by the researcher, and a different sample is recruited from each group. Most of the examples of chi-squared tests in the T&I research literature would be properly described as tests for homogeneity.

By way of example, a researcher could randomly sample fifty professional translators and fifty members of the general public to ask them one question: Did you read works of fiction in more than one language in the past twelve months? Because the researcher controlled the groups and collected two samples, the research question of interest is whether the distribution of the two groups are different. The null hypothesis is that the two groups have the same underlying distribution (are homogeneous), and the alternative hypothesis is that the two groups differ in the distribution of the response variable.

This simple version is a binary response variable. The variable could provide multiple response categories, but they must be mutually exclusive categories in order to conduct chi-squared tests. Ribas (2012) provides an example in which novice and advanced interpreters are asked to describe problems they encounter in various aspects of interpreting. They are allowed to provide more than one answer, so the paper does not include any chi-squared tests, though it has several examples of frequency tables. However, the same survey could be conducted with the slight adaptation that respondents were instructed to pick the category that they feel is the most difficult problem, thereby limiting each person to one answer and allowing for further statistical analysis.

To summarize the test for homogeneity, multiple random samples are collected and data are collected regarding one variable of interest. The null hypothesis is that the different samples (representing different groups) have the same pattern of responses. The alternative hypothesis states that the groups respond differently.

Test statistic calculation

Carefully distinguishing between the tests for independence and homogeneity is useful for clarifying the purpose of a research study, ensuring proper sampling and data collection methodology, and assisting with the final interpretation and contextualization of results. However, the mathematical implementation of the tests is identical. Consequently, most software packages have only one command or procedure for calculating the χ^2-statistic, often using the terms "cross tabulation" or "contingency table" in the analysis. The indistinguishable test procedure has likely led to the lax distinction of the motivation, description, and explanation of the test and its results.

The structure of the χ^2-statistic is the comparison of the observed frequency table to frequencies that would be expected if the null hypothesis were true. The differences between the observed and expected values for each cell are squared and divided by the expected value. The resulting figures for each cell are added together, so the summation occurs across all rows and columns of the table. In rough mathematical notation:

$$\chi^2 = \sum_{Rows} \sum_{Cols} \frac{(Obs - Exp)^2}{Exp}$$

The only remaining question is how to calculate the expected frequencies. We will use the example data from the beginning of this chapter to demonstrate the computation.

Calculation of the expected frequencies is based on the idea that the total observations within each category represent the probabilities of observing those categories.[2] For instance, the probability of observing an English translation of any French book (fiction or non-fiction) can be computed as 16/77 = 20.8%, because sixteen of the seventy-seven books sampled were originally in French. Similarly, the probability that a book in the sample was a work of fiction is 41/77 = 53.2%. Under the null hypothesis, the probability that a book was originally a French work of fiction is the product of these two probabilities: 20.8% * 53.2% = 11.1%. The expected frequency is the sample size multiplied by this probability. Since the sample contains seventy-seven books, the actual number of books that are expected to fall into this category is 11.1% of 77 = 8.5 books.

The mathematical formula can be simplified a bit. The mechanics of generating the expected frequency for each cell follow the same simple procedure: multiply the row total by the column total and divide by the sample size (or grand total, which is the same thing). Therefore, the expected number of German non-fiction books is the total number of German books in the sample (the row total, which is 22) multiplied by the total number of non-fiction books (the column total, which is 36), divided by the sample size (77). In equation form: 22*36 / 77 = 7.5 books. The results for our example are shown in Table 10.3.

The expected values do not have to be, and generally will not be, whole numbers. We have chosen to round the numbers in the table to one decimal place,

172 Analyzing differences

Table 10.3 Chi-squared example data—expected vs. observed values

	Observed			Expected	
	Fiction	Non-fiction	Total	Fiction	Non-fiction
French	6	10	16	8.5	7.5
German	15	7	22	11.7	10.3
Spanish	12	5	17	9.1	7.9
Other	8	14	22	11.7	10.3
Total	41	36	77	41	36

though computer calculations will conduct the intermediate calculations without such dramatic truncation of the decimals. While half of a book or .3 of a book has no meaning in the context of the original research project, the decimals pose no problem for computing the test statistic. The *Yates correction* is a correction for this mismatch between the continuous expected values and the discrete observed values. However, statistical evidence suggests that the correction factor is too conservative and diminishes the statistical power of the test (see, for example, Camilli and Hopkins 1978; Delucchi 1983). When the sample size is large enough that none of the cells have fewer than 5 observations, the correction factor is not needed. Meanwhile, for limited sample sizes, a better testing procedure is *Fisher's exact test* (1922), which is described in a later section.

Finding the test statistic requires calculating the expected frequency for every cell and then applying the chi-squared formula. The difference between each of the expected and observed frequencies is squared and divided by the expected frequency. The results are added for all cells. To give one example, for Spanish fiction, the calculation would be $\frac{(12-9.1)^2}{9.1} = .924$. Repeating this process for all eight cells and adding them results in the final statistic of 8.14.

The degrees of freedom for the test are calculated as one less than the number of rows multiplied by one less than the number of columns: $(m-1)*(k-1)$. For our example data, the degrees of freedom are $(4-1)*(2-1) = 3$. The χ^2-test is a one-tailed test, meaning that large values result in rejection of the null hypothesis. For three degrees of freedom and a 5% level of significance, the critical value is approximately 7.81. Since the test statistic of 8.14 exceeds the critical value, we can reject the null hypothesis. Additionally, statistical software reports that the *p*-value for a χ^2-statistic of 8.14 and three degrees of freedom is .043. A *p*-value below 5% also implies rejection. Remember that the critical value and *p*-value approaches are identical. Thanks to modern computing, basing a decision on the *p*-value is more common.

Effect size

For the χ^2-test of homogeneity, the effect size can be measured with Cramér's *V* (1946). The formula requires the χ^2-statistic, the sample size, and the smaller of the number of rows and columns. In the formula, the notation $\min[m,k]$ stands for the smaller of the number of rows and the number of columns. For instance, $\min[6,4]$ would be 4 and $\min[5,2]$ would be 2.

$$V = \sqrt{\frac{\chi^2}{n*(\min[m,k]-1)}}$$

The resulting figure will range from zero to one, with zero implying no association between the variables. A common guideline for interpretation is that effect sizes of .1, .3, and .5 are considered small, medium, and large, respectively (Ellis 2010). For the example of the English translations of European books (Table 10.2), the moderate effect size of .325 comes from the calculation of this formula:

$$V = \sqrt{\frac{8.14}{77*(\min[4,2]-1)}} = \sqrt{\frac{8.14}{77*(2-1)}} = .325$$

Cramér's V is closely related to the phi coefficient (φ), which can be used only for 2-by-2 tables. Other competing measures of effect size for contingency tables exist, but Cramér's V provides an adequate and widely used measure of effect size for frequency data.

Unfortunately, the power of the χ^2-test is quite low when the expected frequencies are small (Overall 1980). Large sample sizes are one method to combat the low power. However, detecting a difference of 10% between groups can require hundreds of observations (Holt, Kennedy, and Peacock 1967). When further data collection is impossible, Fisher's exact test provides an alternative methodology. Larger samples yield improvements in the statistical power; however, in the case of chi-squared tests, extremely large samples inflate the likelihood of rejecting the null hypothesis. Therefore, care must be taken in interpreting the importance of statistically significant results for very large samples (Mosteller 1968). Reporting of effect size is one way to improve the analysis.

Extensions

Frequency tables are typically straightforward presentations of two variables, such that the basic χ^2-test is adequate for most analysis. The process assumes, however, that the number of categories is appropriate for each of the variables. Whenever possible, the definition of each variable's categories should be grounded in theory or derived from a pilot study to determine a valid and reliable scheme. If data collection results in a large portion of the data being classified into a miscellaneous category, a more nuanced categorization scheme should be developed. The number of categories may also be combined after data collection. If categories appear to be redundant, they should be combined. The need for simplification can be tested with Marascuilo's procedure (1966). Due to its relatively infrequent application, we omit a description of this technique; see

174 *Analyzing differences*

Table 10.4 Goodness-of-fit example data

	German	French	Italian	Romansh	Other	Total
Frequency	42	15	10	2	6	75

Gries (2014) for the basics and an example of this procedure. Rather than letting the mathematics drive the classification scheme, it would be preferable to rely on theory and previous research.

If a large contingency table is assembled, a researcher might want to examine a subset of the data. The testing of a subset is referred to as partitioning the dataset. We again omit the details because adequately large datasets for partitioning are rare. For mathematical details of the process, see Bresnahan and Shapiro (1966) or Shaffer (1973); for an example of the procedure, see Gries (2014).

Test for goodness-of-fit

A χ^2-test can also be used to make any comparison between observed and expected frequencies. There are two situations in which such a test is referred to as a *goodness-of-fit test*. The first is a one-dimensional contingency table. A very simple example would be the collection of data on the L1 of 75 people living in Zurich, Switzerland (see Table 10.4).

The research question is whether the observed distribution differs from the expected frequencies. The issue is determining the expected values for comparison. In exploring new datasets or for cases in which there is no theory or previous studies for guidance, the null hypothesis will state that the expected frequency in each category will be identical. In this case, a sample of 75 people would be evenly split into five groups of 15 each. The test statistic would be calculated using the same chi-squared formula. For the first cell (German), the computation would be $\frac{(42-15)^2}{15} = 48.6$. The calculation would be completed for all five cells, and the sum is 66.93.

The critical value for comparison comes from a chi-squared distribution with $(k-1)$ degrees of freedom, where k is the number of categories. In this case, the 5% critical value is 9.49, so the null hypothesis is clearly rejected. The data do not match the expectation of equal division among the categories.

This example draws attention to the importance of defining a relevant null hypothesis. The argument that L1 would be equally divided among these five categories is a straw man argument, because the overall language distribution in the whole country is already known from previous data collection. Therefore, a better null hypothesis would be that a random sample in Zurich would align with the known distribution for the country. Rejection of this null hypothesis would be meaningful because it would imply that the language pattern in Zurich differed from the rest of the country. Table 10.5 gives an approximate percent distribution

Table 10.5 Goodness-of-fit example data—expected values

	German	French	Italian	Romansh	Other	Total
Expected %	63	23	8	1	5	100
Expected #	47.25	17.25	6	0.75	3.75	75

of the languages across Switzerland,[3] and the corresponding expected values, which are obtained by multiplying the percent by the sample size of 75.

The actual figures can be compared to these more appropriate expected values. The calculation for the German cell in this scenario is $\frac{(42-47.25)^2}{47.25} = .583$. The sum for all five cells is 6.98, which does not exceed the critical value. Not only do these example data show the use of the chi-squared goodness-of-fit test, but they also serve as a reminder of the importance of defining an appropriate research question and null hypothesis.

The second use of the goodness-of-fit test is to compare observed data to a probability distribution. The same generic comparison of observed and expected frequencies is utilized, but the categories must be defined as subdivision of a continuum. This definition of bins is qualitatively similar to the creation of a histogram. Therefore, it is possible to compare an observed histogram to the expected histogram of a normal distribution. We do not delve into further detail here, because alternative methods are generally superior, such as the Shapiro-Welk test for normality testing, which we described in Chapter 5.

Other tests for categorical data

When a research project results in categorical data, the χ^2-test is almost always a useful procedure for analysis. However, automatic application of the test without consideration of its assumptions and limitations can yield incorrect or meaningless results (Lewis and Burke 1949; Delucchi 1983). This brief section provides an overview of three alternative tests.

The most common alternative to the χ^2-test is a likelihood ratio test referred to as a G-test (Wilks 1935). For basic applications, including goodness-of-fit tests, the advantages of the G-test are slight (Gart 1966; Delucchi 1983). One advantage of the procedure is better performance in partitioning a larger contingency table (Delucchi 1983). Another motivation for using a G-test is that χ^2-tests do not perform well for rare events that result in cells of a frequency table with small expected frequencies (Larntz 1978). A guideline for judging when the χ^2-test is inadequate is that no single cell of a contingency table should have an expected frequency less than five. In those cases, the G-test provides a better testing procedure. Therefore, G-tests might be useful for corpus studies (e.g., Dunning 1993).

For small sample sizes, another alternative procedure is Fisher's exact test. The test simulates all possible outcomes for a given simple size, so the procedure is computationally intensive. The test is only preferable for very small sample sizes, which might occur in a pilot study or for an expensive or difficult to obtain sample. Daniel (1990) provides significance tables for samples as small as six and as large as 40.

In a situation with paired observations, the chi-squared test should be replaced with McNemar's test (1947). The variable of interest in McNemar's test must be binary and the observations must be paired. The same respondent could be examined before and after some intervention, treatment, or training. Otherwise, respondents could be paired naturally (siblings or married couples) or matched by the researcher on any traits of interest (two students in a class of the same gender, L1, and similar average grades).

Of the three tests covered in this concluding section, the G-test is the most widely used. Some statisticians recommend its use in place of the χ^2-test for most applications. Fisher's exact test and McNemar's test are useful for the case of very small sample sizes and paired data, respectively. For general application, the χ^2-test performs adequately.

Notes

1 In this simple example, the variables have only two possible responses, but the number of categories could be increased and the question and method would remain the same. For example, rather than asking if a person owns a pet, a survey could ask if they own a dog, a cat, a hamster, or some other pet.
2 The derivation of the formula here presents the conceptually easier perspective of the test of independence. However, the final calculation is identical whether one approaches it from the perspective of homogeneity or independence. The difference between the two tests lies in the sampling and interpretation, not in the mathematics of the test itself.
3 These data are adapted from information provided in the 2013 Federal Population Census: Structural Survey, available at http://www.bfs.admin.ch/bfs/portal/en/index/themen/01/05/blank/key/sprachen.html (accessed January 1, 2016).

Part IV
Analyzing relationships

The chapters in Part IV present statistical tools for analyzing relationships between variables, in contrast to the prior chapters that tested for differences between groups. The distinction between these two types of tests is common when describing applied statistics because it aligns with research designs. However, from a mathematical point of view nearly all of the parametric statistics in this book use the same underlying linear model. Therefore, similarities and overlapping terminology will begin to occur more frequently in Part IV.

Once again, we stress that the statistical tests of this part rely on adequate preparation and data collection. As each test is described, we provide details of hypothesis testing, confidence intervals, and effect size. Simple examples are given for purposes of illustration, along with numerous citations to translation and interpreting studies that employ the various tests.

There are three chapters in Part IV. The first is dedicated to correlation and reliability; the second discusses simple linear regression; and the final chapter provides a brief introduction to more advanced regression models.

11 Correlation and reliability

This chapter presents two related sets of statistics: measures of correlation and measures of reliability. Correlation is useful for describing and establishing the statistical significance of the comovement of two variables. For example, a research question might ask if students with higher math grades also perform well in language classes, or explore the relationship between a personality trait like extraversion and a conference interpreter's performance. The parametric statistic for describing this relationship is Pearson's r. We describe two nonparametric alternatives and explain several reasons Kendall's τ should be the preferred statistic.

The second measure, reliability, is a distinct topic from correlation, though the mathematics is identical or similar in some cases. The primary uses of reliability analysis are for survey and assessment instruments. The statistics included in this section include Cronbach's α, Cohen's κ, and Krippendorff's α.

Correlation: Overview

Purpose: To measure the strength of the linear relationship between two variables

Null hypothesis: No linear relationship exists, $H_0: r = 0$

Alternative hypothesis: The two variables are linearly related, either directly or inversely, $H_1: r \neq 0$

Experimental designs:

1. Two continuous variables are measured and tested for linear relationship (Pearson's r)
2. Three (or more) variables are measured, but the relationship between two of them is tested (partial correlation)

Parametric tests: Pearson's r

Nonparametric tests: Spearman's ρ, Kendall's τ

Effect size: Not applicable

---

180 *Analyzing relationships*

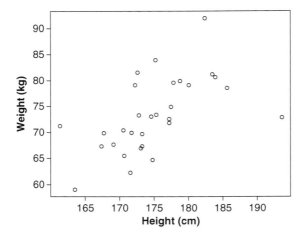

Figure 11.1 Correlation example

Once again, we use a simple example to illustrate the general idea of the statistical concept. In this case, we analyze the correlation between a person's weight (in kilograms) and height (in centimeters). Fictitious data with a sample size of 30 were generated and plotted in Figure 11.1.

A correlation coefficient quantifies the strength of the linear relationship between the variables. The plot is suggestive of an approximately linear relationship between weight and height. The statistics in this chapter are tools to describe and test the existence of such a relationship. Three examples from the literature are listed in Table 11.1.

Pearson's *r*

The classic parametric statistic to measure correlation is Pearson's product-moment correlation, which is sometimes shortened to just Pearson's correlation or Pearson's *r*. The statistic is used to quantify the amount of linear association between two continuous variables.

Correlations are calculated for paired observations. In our example, measurements of height and weight are both collected from each of the 30 participants in the study. Therefore, the sample size is 30, with a total of 60 measurements (two for each participant).

Assumptions

To calculate Pearson's *r* as a measure of the linear relationship between two continuous variables, the only necessary assumption is that both variables are measured at the interval or ratio level. For valid confidence intervals and statistical

Table 11.1 Correlation: Examples from T&I literature

1. Lawson and Hogben (1996) asked 15 participants in a lab setting to learn new vocabulary words in Italian and to describe aloud the learning strategies they employed during their study time. Correlation analysis provided an understanding of the relationship between learning strategies and word recall. Two elaborative strategies and one repetition-based strategy were correlated with performance on a recall exam at the end of the session.
2. Gómez, Molina, Benítez, and de Torres (2007) attempted to identify factors that predict success in learning a signed language and developing signed language interpreting skills. Because their goal was explicitly to predict a dependent variable, their primary analysis was linear regression (which we discuss in Chapter 12). However, correlation and regression analyses are closely related, and they calculate a large number of correlations as one preliminary step in their regression analysis.
3. Sun and Shreve (2014) developed a formula for measuring the translation difficulty of a text. In the process, they examined the correlation of translation difficulty score with a number of candidate predictive variables. For instance, they report a weak, negative correlation between translation difficulty and translation quality. They further report a weak, positive correlation between translation difficulty and time spent on a translation. These results imply that more difficult translations are associated with lower quality scores and more time spent on the translation.

tests, though, five additional assumptions are necessary. We will discuss them briefly and then turn our attention to analyzing plots of the data as a means to check the assumptions.

First, the data should follow a bivariate normal distribution. This is a stringent requirement, and even in the best of circumstances one can only hope for approximate normality. Often, this assumption is met through reference to the Central Limit Theorem (CLT) for larger sets of data or from graphical analysis.

The second, related assumption is that the data do not exhibit any significant outliers. As discussed in Part II, outliers should be examined for data entry errors and considered for possible trimming or winsorizing. Outliers have the potential to affect the data, skew the observed distribution, and significantly affect inferences. Therefore, they should always be removed if they represent errors. If the data have many outliers, correlation analysis may not be appropriate. The example data of height and weight arguably exhibit one outlier on the far right side of the graph. One individual is recorded with a height of 193.6 cm and a weight of 72.8 kg. These measurements are implausible, though not impossible. As a result, one must double check the data to identify possible errors in the dataset. The analysis could also be repeated to test the significance the outlier has on the results. Figure 11.2 depicts the stronger linear relationship with the outlier removed.

Third, the data should be homoscedastic, meaning that the variance of one variable does not change based on the level of the other variable. Fourth, there must be a linear relationship between the two variables, which means the rate of change is constant across the sample. The scatterplot should not show any evidence of a curvilinear relationship. Many relationships are linear over at least some common range of the independent variable.

182 *Analyzing relationships*

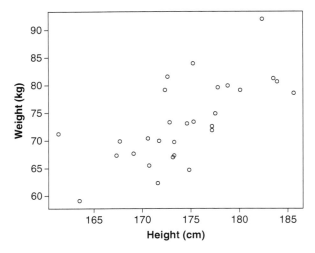

Figure 11.2 Correlation example—outlier removed

Finally, the fifth assumption is that the data are independent. Each observation must be collected in a manner that is unaffected by other observations. Furthermore, the two variables that are collected should be independent of each other. The assumptions are best examined by creating a scatterplot of the data. Recall the Anscombe Quartet (1973) that was discussed in Chapter 5. The four scatterplots of the data are repeated here for reference.

Only the upper left graph displays data that fully meets the assumptions of Pearson's r, yet all four of these sets of data result in the same Pearson correlation ($r = .816$). However, when the assumptions are not met, the calculated statistic is incorrect to the point of being meaningless. The bottom two graphs have obvious outliers. When those offending points are appropriately corrected or removed, the graph on the lower left will exhibit perfect correlation ($r = 1$). Meanwhile, the graph on the right reveals that the variable on the x-axis is not, in fact, a variable; it is a constant and not suitable for correlation analysis. Finally, the graph on the upper right implies a curvilinear relationship between the two variables. Correlation analysis would not be appropriate in this situation either. These extreme examples are important reminders of examining plots of the raw data, considering the distributional assumptions of tests, and dealing appropriately with outliers.

Calculation

Pearson's correlation coefficient is the ratio of the covariance of two variables to the product of their individual standard deviations. Covariance is positive if two variables are directly related and negative if two variables are inversely related. However, covariance depends on the measurement scale. If length were measured in centimeters or inches, the resulting covariance would differ. Furthermore, the

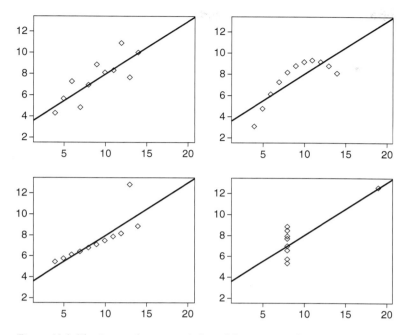

Figure 11.3 The Anscombe quartet (adapted from Anscombe 1973)

size of the covariance is not useful in understanding the strength of the relationship between the two variables.

Pearson's *r* overcomes the shortcomings of covariance by dividing by the product of the standard deviation of each variable:

$$r = \frac{\sum_{i=1}^{n}(x_i - \bar{x})(y_i - \bar{y})}{(n-1)s_x s_y}$$

The purpose of this rescaling of the covariance is to generate a statistic that ranges from −1 to +1 to allow for easy interpretation. A perfect correlation of positive one (+1) implies that all of the data lie on a straight line with an upward slope, while a perfect correlation of negative one implies that the line has a downward slope. The correlation between weight and height is .56 for the example data. With the potential outlier removed, the correlation is .67, and the large difference between these estimates is a reminder of the need to check the outlier carefully.

Significance testing and confidence intervals

The Pearson product-moment correlation coefficient can be tested for statistical significance by considering the null hypothesis that *r* is zero versus the two-tailed alternative hypothesis that *r* is nonzero: $H_0: r = 0$; $H_A: r \neq 0$. The appropriate test statistic follows a *t*-distribution and is calculated using the following formula, in which *n* represents the sample size:

$$t_{(n-2)} = r\sqrt{\frac{n-2}{1-r^2}}$$

The critical values come from a *t*-distribution with $(n-2)$ degrees of freedom, and a critical value can be found in the appropriate table of the *t*-distribution. Alternatively, most statistical software output will automatically include a *p*-value for this statistical test. The example data (with the outlier removed in this section only) resulted in $r = .67$, which yields the following test statistic:

$$t_{(28)} = .67\sqrt{\frac{30-2}{1-.67^2}} = 4.78$$

Such a large *t*-statistic is statistically significant with a *p*-value less than 1%. Whenever a research report includes a correlation matrix, the statistical significance of every coefficient should be provided.

Calculating a confidence interval for the correlation coefficient aids interpretation and should also be reported, even if it necessitates hand calculation because some software packages do not automatically give the confidence interval in test results. The calculation requires the use of Fisher's *z*-transformation of *r* (Fisher 1921). We first present the required formulas with general comments and then give an example that shows the relative ease with which these computations can be done:

$$z_r = \frac{1}{2}\ln\left(\frac{1+r}{1-r}\right)$$

The purpose of the transformation is to enable the use of the normal distribution in calculating the confidence interval. The resulting numerical value for z_r is not meaningful, just a step in this larger process. The transformed variable has a standard error of $\frac{1}{\sqrt{n-3}}$. A 95% confidence interval for the transformed variable is then given by the following expression:

$$z_r \pm 1.96 * \frac{1}{\sqrt{n-3}}$$

This confidence interval is expressed in terms of the transformed variable. Therefore, as a final step the endpoints are converted back into the original scale of the correlation coefficient by using the inverse *z*-transformation. This conversion will be done twice, once for each endpoint of the confidence interval, and the process converts the numbers back into the same −1 to 1 scale of the original *r* coefficient. The formula for the inverse *z*-transformation is as follows:

$$\frac{e^{2z_r}-1}{e^{2z_r}+1}$$

We will use the example data for weight and height to demonstrate the calculations. Recall that the correlation coefficient was earlier calculated to be .67 based on a sample of 30 participants. We can use the formulas in this section to demonstrate the calculation of the confidence interval for this statistic. First, the correlation coefficient is transformed into its associated z-score.

$$z_r = \frac{1}{2}\ln\left(\frac{1+.67}{1-.67}\right) = 0.8107$$

A 95% confidence interval is then calculated for this transformed statistic.

$$0.8107 \pm 1.96 * \frac{1}{\sqrt{30-3}} = (0.4335, 1.1879)$$

Finally, the two endpoints are transformed back into the original scale.

$$\left(\frac{e^{2*.4335}-1}{e^{2*.4335}+1}, \frac{e^{2*1.1879}-1}{e^{2*1.1879}+1}\right) = (.41, .83)$$

Thus, we can state with 95% confidence that the correlation coefficient lies between .41 and .83 for the example data. Confidence intervals provide an important piece of information for interpreting the correlation coefficient, because they describe the potential range of the underlying parameter. While software often provides *p*-values, programs all too rarely provide confidence intervals for *r* by default. Consequently, far too few research reports include confidence intervals, and some studies make mistaken claims about the difference between two correlation coefficients. It would be incorrect, for example, to argue that one pair of variables with a correlation of .73 has a demonstrably stronger linear relationship than another pair with a correlation of .64. While the correlation is indeed numerically larger, the 95% confidence intervals would quite possibly have a great degree of overlap. If the confidence intervals for this simple example were [.62, .84] and [.53, .75], then the argument that one is significantly larger becomes tenuous at best.

The only experimental factor that affects the width of the confidence interval for Pearson's *r* is the sample size. Therefore, narrower 95% confidence intervals can be obtained only by increasing the number of observations. The confidence interval also depends on the underlying correlation parameter, but that lies outside the control of the researcher, of course. Bonett and Wright (2000) provide useful guidelines for planning appropriate sample sizes for a desired confidence interval width. For example, a confidence interval with a width less than .3 requires sample sizes of approximately 13, 28, or 49 observations for variables that have an expected correlation of .9, .8, or .7, respectively. The lower the expected correlation and the narrower the confidence interval required, the larger the sample needs to be.

Testing the difference between two correlation coefficients is a rarely employed research design. Researchers must remember an important caveat when using correlation coefficients—the coefficient is scale-free. This means that an observed correlation of .40 is in no meaningful way double the correlation of .20. If researchers want to make comparisons between correlation coefficients, tests specific to this type of comparison must be used. Three different situations can arise when trying to make this type of comparison, each with its own test. We will describe each situation and associated tests but omit the computational details for considerations of space. The first situation compares the same pair of variables for two different groups. For instance, the correlation between weight and height could be calculated separately for men and women, and the resulting correlations could be compared. The appropriate procedure is based on the same z-transformation used to create the confidence interval (Fisher 1921).

The second situation compares the correlation of overlapping pairs of variables. All of the measurements would be collected from one sample, which introduces dependence in the structure of the data. For instance, the correlation between weight and height could be compared to the correlation between height and shoe size. To give a practical example, Lawson and Hogben (1996) calculated correlations between vocabulary learning strategies and recall performance. In their study, one learning strategy that the researchers call "Appearance Similarity" exhibited a correlation of .46 with the students' ability to recall vocabulary. Another strategy, "Sentence Translation," had a correlation of .27. These strategies are different for vocabulary learning, but the researchers employed the same assessment method. Therefore, these two correlations would be considered overlapping pairs, since one of the variables (i.e., the assessment) is the same, while the level of the other variable (i.e., the vocabulary learning strategy) is different. Several statistics have been developed for cases such as these, and comparisons suggest that Steiger's z-test performs the best (Steiger 1980; Meng, Rosenthal, and Rubin 1992).

The third and final situation involves comparison of non-overlapping correlations. In presenting the statistical test for this situation, Raghunathan, Rosenthal, and Rubin (1996) give the example of comparing the correlation between vocabulary and verbal comprehension. The authors suggest that perhaps researchers would be interested in comparing the correlation of these two variables in a given sample, and to do so in both their first and their second languages. In this case, the researchers would be interested in whether vocabulary and verbal comprehension are intrinsically linked or if this relationship differs between the person's L1 or L2. The comparison of these two correlations are considered to be non-overlapping, since none of these four measures (i.e., vocabulary and verbal comprehension in L1 and in L2) are used in the calculation of two different correlation coefficients.

As mentioned earlier, all three of these experimental designs involving the comparison of correlation coefficients are only occasionally appropriate. In many cases, the data would be better analyzed in a linear regression model. The sources provided will supply the formulas for conducting comparisons, but careful thought should be given to the purpose of the analysis before conducting any tests. In the majority of cases, the only statistical test conducted for Pearson's r is whether it differs significantly from zero, as described above.

Interpretation

There is no more important cliché in statistics than the caution that correlation does not imply causation. The trope may seem overused, but that does not diminish its relevance. A statistically significant correlation coefficient implies only that a linear relationship exists between two variables. When examining the relationship that is implied by the correlation, there are several possible scenarios: the first variable causes the second, the second variable causes the first, or both are affected by an unknown third variable. The last of these scenarios is sometimes referred to as a *spurious correlation* because the two variables may only be related through their relationship to the unspecified third variable. Another possibility is a Type I error; the coincidental relationship is true only for the particular sample but does not imply any underlying relationship.

The correlation coefficient measures the *strength* of the relationship between two variables, but it does not provide information on the *magnitude* of that relationship. In other words, if one variable increases by 10% then a variable with which it is positively correlated will also increase, but there is no way of knowing how much it will increase. More, less, or the same as 10% are all possible; correlation does not measure this relationship. Linear regression would be needed for such a relationship to be estimated and predicted.

Positive correlation coefficients imply a direct relationship between two variables: high values of one are associated with high values of the other. Conversely, negative correlation coefficients imply an inverse relationship: high values of one are generally observed with low values of the other.

Interpretation of the size of a correlation coefficient depends on the situation. In social science research, effect sizes of .10, .30, and .50 are often considered small, medium, and large, following Cohen's (1992) recommendation. Hemphill (2003) examined meta-analytic studies of 380 papers in the psychological literature to determine an approximate distribution of reported correlation coefficients. He reports that the lower third consists of correlations below .20, the middle third between .20 and .30, and the upper third greater than .30 with .78 the strongest correlation reported in the reviewed literature. These suggestions can be compared to Asuero, Sayago, and González (2006), who suggest anything above .9 is very high, above .7 is high, above .5 is moderate, and above .3 is low. No one-size-fits-all approach will work for interpreting the coefficient, though Cohen's guidelines provide a useful starting point. The coefficient needs to be interpreted in the context of the study, with consideration given to the accuracy of the measurement scale, previous results in the literature, and the importance of the relationship. As always, the distinction between statistical significance and practical significance must be kept in mind when interpreting correlations.

Though correlations consider only two variables at a time, they are often calculated for all of the possible pairs within a set of variables. The resulting correlation

188 Analyzing relationships

Table 11.2 Correlation matrix example

	Weight (kg)	Shoe size
Height (cm)	0.56 (.001)	0.5 (.005)
Weight (kg)		0.05 (.792)

coefficients are then displayed in a correlation matrix that shows all of the possible paired relationships. In order to have a correlation matrix for our sample data, another variable, shoe size, is added to the example dataset. The matrix shows both the correlation coefficient and their associated *p*-values in parentheses. In the data, shoe size is significantly associated with height but not with weight.

Correlation matrices are often displayed incorrectly. Because every variable is perfectly correlated with itself, there is no need to display the name of every variable in both the columns and rows of the matrix. One row and one column should be omitted. Additionally, a correlation matrix is symmetric across the main diagonal, so only the upper right or lower left triangle needs to be completed. Compare a well formatted table (Table 11.2) to an incorrectly oversized and repetitive correlation matrix of the same data (Table 11.3).

Not only does the table now take up more room in the finished research report, but it is also larger due solely to repetition and unnecessary information. The correlations are all presented twice, which is redundant, and the main diagonal simply reports that each variable is perfectly correlated with itself, which does not need to be reported. Because there are three variables in our example data, the proper dimensionality of the correlation matrix is two rows by two columns.

Coefficient of determination

Squaring Pearson's *r* results in a statistic that measures the amount of shared variance between the two variables. Called the *coefficient of determination* and denoted R^2, it is a percentage measure of the variability accounted for. For the weight and height comparison, $R^2 = 31.36\%$. Therefore, the results suggest that 31.36% of a person's height is accounted for by weight. However, these results

Table 11.3 Correlation matrix example—incorrect reporting

	Height (cm)	Weight (kg)	Shoe size
Height (cm)	1	0.56 (.001)	0.5 (.005)
Weight (kg)	0.56 (.001)	1	0.05 (.792)
Shoe size	0.5 (.005)	0.05 (.792)	1

could be stated the other way—that 31.36% of a person's weight is accounted for by his or her height. Among the correlation coefficients reported by López Gómez, Bajo, Padilla, and Santiago de Torres (2007) was .92 for the relationship between rating of an interpreter's technique in signed language interpreting and rating for skill with Spanish sign language (LSE). The shared variance is 85%, so the results provide evidence that 85% of interpreting technique is associated with LSE skills. The coefficient of determination cannot be used to infer causality any more than Pearson's r, but it does quantify the strength of the relationship.

Limitations

Like all statistics, r depends on the nature of the sample data. The range of the observations can have a large influence on the calculation and interpretation of the correlation coefficient. If one of the variables can only be observed over a limited range, any possible relationship can be obscured. If, for instance, the weight and height study included only participants whose height was between 174 and 182 cm, then the data would be appear as in Figure 11.4.

This is a subset of the original data, but the linear relationship is not at all clear. In fact, the correlation in this case is just .42, which shows the importance of good sampling procedures, as well as the need to interpret statistics in terms of the available sample. To give a simple example in T&I studies, if a sample consisted entirely of seasoned conference interpreters, then it would be inappropriate to utilize second language vocabulary as a variable in a correlation with their ability to interpret simultaneously into their L1. The size of an interpreter's L2 vocabulary might be of interest in a study, but when the dataset is limited to experienced conference interpreters who ostensibly have near-perfect command of the language from which they interpret, the variation may be limited and the relationship might not be readily apparent.

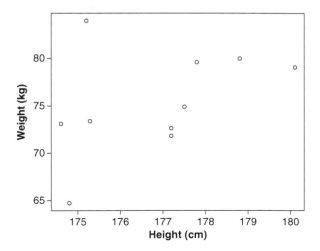

Figure 11.4 Correlation example—restricted range

A second problem with correlation coefficients is that the relationship can lack predictive ability. This is particularly problematic for studies that do not select their variables based on a theory. Theory-free correlations are tenuous and unlikely to hold for new samples or across time. To give an extreme example, in a small sample it might turn out that brown hair is correlated with translation skill. However, this relationship is obviously not based in theory and would not likely be observed in new samples if the study were replicated.

Similarly, correlations should not be extrapolated beyond the range of the variables. To continue a fictitious example from earlier, any relationship that might be established between L2 vocabulary and interpreting performance among experienced conference interpreters is not suggestive of the same relationship in interpreting students. A correlation established with the large vocabularies of seasoned interpreters may not hold for students with more limited vocabulary. Furthermore, these samples are different far beyond their vocabulary size and do not take into consideration many other factors such as domain expertise, professional experience, L1 proficiency, or training. If predictions or causality are of interest, the correct analysis tool is linear regression.

Kendall's τ

Hypothesis tests of the Pearson product-moment correlation coefficient are only appropriate when the sample data approximately follow a bivariate normal distribution or when the sample is large enough to appeal to the CLT for approximate normality (Kowalski 1972). An alternative nonparametric statistic called Kendall's τ (Kendall 1938) is available as a measure of the linear association between two variables when this assumption cannot be met. Kendall's τ is more robust to outliers and nonlinearity than Pearson's r (Newsom 2002). The statistic ranges between -1 and 1 with the same general interpretation.

The only necessary assumptions for Kendall's τ are that the observations are independent and capable of being ranked, which means the variables are ordinal, interval, or ratio. Kendall's τ is calculated based on the idea of concordant ranks. If correlation were perfect in a positive direction, then the lowest ranked x-variable would be observed in a pair with the lowest ranked y-variable, and then then next highest, and so on. The computation involves counting the number of times this happens. We omit the full details of this process and formula here, since the calculation is relatively complex, but the statistic itself is readily obtainable from most software packages.

Testing for statistical significance and constructing a 95% confidence interval for Kendall's τ is beyond the scope of this volume, given its mathematical complexity. Interested readers can refer to Long and Cliff (1997) for details. Usually, software capable of producing the statistic will provide a p-value and confidence interval.[1] As with Pearson's r, sample size is the primary influence on the width of the confidence interval. Bonett and Wright (2000) report that for a confidence interval to have a width less than .3 requires sample sizes of approximately 8, 15, or 24 for variables that have an expected correlation of .9, .8, or .7, respectively.

Alternative nonparametric procedures are available, notably Spearman's ρ, which is discussed later in the chapter. However, there are a number of papers, stretching as far back as Fieller, Hartley, and Pearson (1957) and Kruskal (1958), suggesting that Kendall's τ is the superior nonparametric measure. The statistic possesses a number of desirable statistical qualities, including the ability to handle tied ranks[2] and a relatively more rapid approximation to the normal distribution as the sample size increases (Gilpin 1993). Confidence intervals are generally smaller, bias is minimized, and the statistic is more easily interpreted in applied work (Arndt, Turvey, and Andreasen 1999). Kendall's τ is slightly more robust and efficient than Spearman's ρ (Croux and Dehon 2010).

Kendall's τ generally results in an estimate closer to zero than Pearson's r or Spearman's ρ (e.g., Winner 2006). For instance, reanalyzing the weight and height data depicted in Figure 11.1 with Kendall's τ results in a correlation of .45, compared to .56 for Pearson's r. However, hypothesis testing will almost always yield identical results regarding statistical significance (Daniel 1990). The more difficult computational problem of calculating the statistic is likely one reason that it did not obtain wide usage before the advent of affordable computing power. Pearson's r and Kendall's τ may both be reported to show that the measures yield qualitatively similar outcomes.

Partial correlation

As presented so far in this chapter, correlation is a measure of association between two variables. However, it is possible to calculate a *partial correlation coefficient*, which measures the relationship between two variables while holding a third variable constant. The mathematics of calculating a partial correlation remove the effect of the third variable, which is referred to as a *covariate*. The purpose of the partial correlation coefficient is to remove the influence of confounding variables from the relationship of interest.

In some cases, partial correlation is useful for demonstrating spurious correlations by demonstrating that the two variables are not actually correlated but only appear to be so because of their correlation with a third variable. For instance, monthly sales of ice cream cones and monthly sales of swimsuits in a town might be highly correlated over the course of the year. However, that correlation would be much lower after controlling for average monthly temperature because sales of both ice cream cones and swimsuits will be higher in the hotter weather.

The partial correlation can be calculated from a combination of the three pairwise correlations. We omit the formula here to focus on the interpretation, in part because most interesting research questions related to partial correlation could be investigated instead with regression analysis. Return to the example above; assume that sales of ice cream cones and swimsuits have a correlation of .90, while each of them individually has a correlation of .80 with the average monthly temperature. The partial correlation coefficient would calculate the unique correlation between sales of the two goods, after controlling for the temperature. In this example, the measured correlation would be reduced to .72, a significant reduction that implies the relationship is still strong, but weaker than was implied by the initial correlation.

A fictitious example from translation studies would consider language proficiency (reading in the subject language and writing in the target language) to be plausibly correlated with passage of a certification exam in translation. One interesting question would be the potential influence of years of education in translation studies on the relationship. If the correlation between passing the exam and language proficiency were weakened after controlling for years of education in translation studies, it would provide evidence of the importance of translation pedagogy for the purpose of passing the exam. Of course, one correlation coefficient can never prove causal relationships, but it can provide motivation for further investigation of the interrelationship among variables.

Partial correlations are quite rare in the published literature. One example can be found in Timarová et al. (2014: Table 3, 157), who explore the relationship between working memory capability and simultaneous interpreting skill. The authors present the correlation between work experience (measured separately in years and days) and a range of other variables related to working memory and simultaneous interpreting tasks, after controlling for the age of the 28 participants in their sample. Because age and years of experience are highly correlated, the correlation coefficients in the table are lower than they would be without controlling for age.

All of the information found from partial correlations can also be found through multiple linear regression, which is generally the preferred technique, since the regression model can both include additional variables and result in a broader understanding of the relationship among the variables. Therefore, partial correlation should rarely be used on its own, but it may be reported occasionally in the context of a larger model. More information on multiple linear regression can be found in Chapter 12.

Other correlation coefficients

For most applied research, either Pearson's r or Kendall's τ will be adequate when analyzing correlations. However, alternative measures of correlation are available for use in specific situations (Bishara and Hittner 2012). We review just two of the more common statistics in this section. They are relegated to this brief mention because more effective modern methods exist. Osborne (2010) is among the most emphatic voices on this subject. He argues that both of these correlation measures are archaic, and he says that their use should be taken as a signal of outdated training in quantitative methods. We mention them primarily because they can be found in the existing literature and are worth recognizing.

Spearman's ρ

A nonparametric procedure called Spearman's ρ (Spearman 1904) was often recommended in the past. As with Kendall's τ, the statistic does not require the data to be normally distributed and better handles outliers and skewness. Furthermore, because the test is based on ranks, it can be used with ordinal level data.

The statistic has been popular, in part, because its calculation is conceptually easy. The data need to be converted to ranks (if they are not already ordinal). Then Pearson's r can be computed for the ranked data. This is equivalent to the alternative methodology originally described by Spearman (Roberts and Kunst 1990). The interpretation of Spearman's ρ is identical to other correlation coefficients, ranging from −1 to +1, and computer software will typically provide the statistic quite easily. Based on the comparison studies described previously, though, we advocate the use of Kendall's τ whenever a nonparametric correlation coefficient is desired.

Binary correlations

All of the correlation coefficients discussed so far have required ratio, interval, or ordinal data. Two measures of association are available for binary categorical data: the point biserial and biserial correlation coefficients. Both of them require that one of the variables has just two levels. The difference between them is in the underlying assumption about those levels. The point biserial coefficient is appropriate if the two choices are the only possible outcomes, for instance the categories of pregnant and non-pregnant. The biserial is appropriate if the two categories represent an underlying continuous variable. An example of this would be pass-fail for an exam based on a cutoff score, as for many certification exams. The candidate receives a score, but that score is converted into the binary decision of pass or fail.

The computational details of both the biserial and point biserial coefficients can be found in Terrell (1982a, 1982b). However, we agree with Osborne (2010) that such coefficients are outdated. Research designs that involve binary variables are often better modeled with logistic regression.

Reliability

As discussed in Chapter 3, the fundamental concept of reliability is consistency.[3] For T&I studies, reliability is most commonly discussed for surveys and assessments. In this section, we discuss various reliability coefficients that attempt to quantify the consistency of a measurement. These measures are all rooted in the philosophy that a reliable instrument should yield nearly identical results in repeated uses. The challenge of calculating a reliability statistic is that any measurement is inevitably subject to random uncertainty. This uncertainty extends across several dimensions, which results in three primary ways to measure reliability.

Think-aloud protocols (TAP) are one example from translation process research in which consideration of reliability is a vital part of the analysis. Jääskeläinen (2000) issued a general call for methodological improvements in terms of validity and reliability in TAP studies. In a comprehensive survey of methodological issues related to TAP, Li (2004) also draws attention to issues of reliability. When analyzing 15 published studies, Li finds that 86.7% of them failed to report intercoder reliability. The validity and reliability of these studies would be enhanced if multiple coders were used and appropriate statistics reported so that the coding process could include analysis of reliability.

The origin of reliability theory is an assumption that no phenomenon can ever be measured perfectly in empirical work. Thus, any observed score is considered to be the sum of two parts: the true measurement and a random error.[4] Less variability in a measure is taken as a sign of precision in assessing the true, unknown measurement. Therefore, the statistical basis for all reliability measures is the idea of replication in order to assess the degree of variability.

As an analogy to the physical sciences, consider a scientific instrument that is used to determine the weight of an object. In order for us to compare the weight of two or more objects, reliable measurements are necessary from the scale. Weighing an object should be consistent when repeated, even if a different person reads the scale. To give a specific example, a bathroom scale that can only measure a person's weight with a random error of up to 10 kg in either direction would produce results that were useless for comparison or inference. Repeated measurements of the same person might vary widely due solely to the unreliability of the scale. The same holds true for a survey instrument. An unreliable measurement tool is misleading and nearly useless.

Measurement error is rather self-evidently problematic when applied research cannot accurately measure one of the variables of interest. All descriptive and inferential statistics consider the collected data to be an accurate measurement of the phenomenon being studied. Therefore, any mismeasurements will degrade the quality of the results, the associated inferences, and the ability to generalize from a given sample (Onwuegbuzie and Daniel 2002).

The formal statistical problem is called *attenuation*. Observed correlations and effect sizes will be calculated to be less than the true underlying correlations (Hoyt and Melby 1999; Schmidt and Hunter 1996). These changes can result in incorrect statistical inference. Specifically, measurement error can obscure effects by increasing standard errors, resulting in a greater likelihood of Type II error.

To describe the same effect in positive terms, strong reliability improves statistical power through more precise measurements of the underlying phenomenon (Henson 2001). Similarly, greater reliability allows for the detection of smaller effect sizes (Reinhardt 1996). Therefore, smaller sample sizes can still yield useful results when reliable measurements are utilized in a study. Adequate reliability and validity are necessary components of a quality research report. Consequently, a reliability coefficient should be provided for any data gleaned from a survey or assessment instrument (Wilkinson 1999; Thompson 1994; Thompson and Vacha-Haase 2000).

A participant's score on a survey or assessment will fluctuate randomly due to a number of factors. Experimental and environmental factors that can affect reliability are discussed by Angelelli (2009), based on the structure set forth by Bachman and Palmer (1996). Threats to reliability exist both in the instrument itself and in the broader experimental setting. Some of these potential problems are discussed briefly below.

First, the survey itself may have vaguely worded questions or inadequate directions. This issue can be compounded in the context of T&I research when surveys are administered in multiple languages. Researchers may be tempted to translate surveys that have been originally developed in one language for use with a different population. Without proper validation of the translated version, these surveys could potentially result in mismeasurement as a result of the translation process. For example, the translated version of the survey might employ locale-specific terminology or have an inconsistent register or tone, which could influence any results obtained using this instrument. To combat these challenges, survey design must include careful consideration of item writing and conduct pilot studies to improve reliability. Pilot studies can also be qualitative in nature to allow for feedback and interaction with respondents. A well-run pilot study with a few participants can ensure that useful data are generated in the actual data collection that follows.[5]

Second, in the broader setting of a study, the research protocol must be carefully planned. Participants may answer questions differently if they are asked to complete a survey individually or in a group setting, in their homes or in a public place, in person or through a communication medium such as phone, email, or a website. Responses can also be influenced by any number of the test administrator's personal traits, including gender, race, personal appearance, and affect. Impression management research has described various reactions and decisions made based on these factors.[6] Consideration of these potential influences, careful training of survey administrators, a thorough literature review, and the Institutional Review Board (IRB) review process can all help minimize these confounding factors.

Variation in scores can arise from a number of different sources. Three main sources of variability will guide the structure of our presentation of reliability statistics across three dimensions. First, error may stem from observations that are taken at different times. This source of variability is an issue of *test-retest reliability*, which is measured by a correlation coefficient. Second, error may exist because a measurement tool consists of a survey or questionnaire in which not all questions are related to the same construct. This variability is a problem of *internal reliability*, and it can be measured by Cronbach's α and other internal consistency measures. Third, error may come from inconsistencies among coders who are tasked with assigning a rating or category to data. This variability is a matter of *intercoder reliability*, which can be measured using a number of statistical tools, including Cohen's κ and Krippendorff's α. Random response error is the final source of error, which cannot be controlled or measured directly (Lakes and Hoyt 2009; Schmidt, Le, and Ilies 2003). The various statistics are designed to measure only one dimension of reliability and should not be used for alternate purposes. The unfortunate use of Cronbach's α to measure intercoder reliability, for instance, is inappropriate.

The three-part structure of reliability presented here is our summary of the existing state of the art in the statistical literature.[7] The ongoing evolution of measures of reliability are evident in the statistical literature, with Guttman (1945) listing just two dimensions of error across trials and items (similar to test-retest

196 *Analyzing relationships*

and internal reliability). Alternative terminology also exists for the various types of error. One scheme refers to the sources of error as transient error, specific factor error, and rater bias. These are equivalent to issues of test-retest, internal, and intercoder reliability, respectively. Another similar scheme is outlined by Vermeiren, Van Gucht, and De Bontridder (2009), who use the terms intra-rater reliability, form reliability, and interrater reliability. In an applied setting, ISO 9000 refer to the repeatability and reproducibility of a system, which are analogous with internal reliability and intercoder reliability.

In the remainder of this section, we outline the statistical tools of reliability. In addition to the three categories presented here, alternative methods for reliability analysis exist that are capable of simultaneously recognizing the multi-dimensionality of the error term and the various ways that replication can be conducted. This more complex modeling is called Generalizability Theory (Cronbach et al. 1972).[8] Generalizability Theory uses ANOVA to segregate the error into its various sources (Hoyt and Melby 1999). The complexity of this analysis is omitted for concerns of space and practicality. Most applied research will examine reliability only in some dimensions, because the nature of the project's hypotheses and measurement tools will suggest an appropriate focus on just one or two of the three dimensions.

Reliability: Overview

Purpose: To quantify the consistency of measurements across three different dimensions

Type of reliability	Appropriate statistic
Test-retest	Pearson's r, Kendall's τ
Internal	Cronbach's α
Intercoder	Krippendorff's α, Cohen's κ

Test-retest reliability

The purpose of calculating test-retest reliability is to demonstrate that a measure is repeatable over time. A reliable measurement instrument should plausibly produce similar measurements for the same person or object of analysis at different points in time. This differs from a pre- and post-test experimental design, which would measure each participant twice with some kind of treatment or intervention between measurements. In test-retest reliability, all factors should be held constant (to the extent this is possible) between measurements. Computationally, test-retest reliability is measured by calculating a correlation coefficient. Higher correlation coefficients are preferred because they represent consistency and stability in the measurement.

Two measurements taken at different points in time cannot be expected to be identical, but major changes could be a sign of instability in the measurement tool.[9] For instance, a person's weight should not change too much when measured on two consecutive days. If a difference of 10 kilograms were observed, the scale would be suspected of inaccuracy. Personal traits such as IQ are often thought to be quite stable over time, and even translation or interpreting skill should not vary substantially within a short time span. Therefore, all of these measurements should exhibit high levels of test-retest reliability.

The computation for test-retest reliability is straightforward: a correlation coefficient is computed for the data collected at two different times. Pearson's correlation coefficient is acceptable if the assumptions of the test can be met, and Kendall's τ is an appropriate nonparametric alternative.[10] Table 11.4 provides a simple example. Imagine a survey with five questions on a 5-point Likert-type scale so that total scores for any respondent could range from 5 to 25. Eight participants completed the survey at two different times, and their total scores were computed. The scores varied slightly in all directions, some increasing (e.g., P1), some decreasing (e.g., P2), and some remaining constant for the second score (e.g., P7). The Pearson correlation between the two scores is approximately .92 (Kendall's $\tau = .91$) for the data presented in the table.

Recall that the square of the correlation coefficient provides the percent of variability explained by the relationship. Therefore, in this case approximately 85% of the variability is explained by the duplication of the test ($R^2 = .92^2 = .846$). The remaining 15% is due to experimental or random error. There is no strict cutoff for an appropriate level of test-retest reliability, but a correlation coefficient below .80 would bear further investigation for potential problems.

The same participants need to complete the test both times. The conception of reliability as a set of multi-dimensional measures can only be upheld if other factors are held constant. Since test-retest reliability attempts to measure stability over time, the participants and the survey should remain identical. One potential problem is that attrition in a study can lead to missing data. If the attrition is random, it is likely not problematic for analysis. However, missing data that is due to some commonality among the missing observations results in biased analysis. Studies that use two different groups of participants to assess test-retest reliability must rely on a very strong assumption that the samples are truly random and representative of the population. This is a poor practice, and test-retest correlations calculated on different samples provide little in the way of useful information.

Table 11.4 Test-retest reliability example data

Participant	Time 1	Time 2
P1	18	22
P2	8	7
P3	12	14
P4	16	15
P5	17	16
P6	17	18
P7	10	10
P8	6	9

198 *Analyzing relationships*

One of the main challenges of conducting test-retest reliability is determining the appropriate length of time between measurements. The analogy of measuring a person's weight suggests one side of the problem. While a person's weight will not vary dramatically from one day to the next, measurements taken a month apart will reflect the effects of diet and exercise (or lack thereof). In such a setting, it would be unclear if the different measurements were due to the quality and properties of the scale or changes in the subject being measured. Too much time between measurements will admit extraneous factors to confound the test-retest reliability calculation.

The other side of the timing problem is that measurements too close together are subject to learning, memory, or carryover effects. For instance, one trait that the Myers-Briggs test purports to measure is a person's level of introversion. If the test were administered twice with only an hour break, the respondent would likely recall some of the questions and answers from the first test while completing the questionnaire the second time. The reliability coefficient would be affected by this carryover effect, particularly if results or feedback were provided to the respondent between administrations of the test. To give another example, optometrists will ask patients to read a row of letters from a screen. If one eye is tested first and then the other, the patient might remember the letters, skewing the results of the second test.

There is no ideal time lag between measurements for calculating test-retest reliability. The researcher must take into account the complexity and length of the measurement tool, the characteristics of the respondents, and the likelihood of a change in the status of the underlying variable. A time period that is too short is problematic due to carryover effects, while a time period that is too long allows for many extraneous factors to confound the results.

Time lags can vary a great deal depending on the measurement and the purpose of the study. Marx et al. (2003) examined the influence of lag time on test-retest reliability by comparing the correlation coefficients for groups measured with a two-day and a two-week time interval between administrations of various tests related to knee health. The results showed no substantial difference between the calculated test-retest reliability, which they interpret to mean that when measuring generally stable phenomenon any time period between two and fourteen days is likely acceptable. In a study of foreign language anxiety and its effect on language learning, Horwitz (1986) asked participants to complete the Foreign Language Classroom Anxiety Scale twice with an eight-week time lag and found adequate test-retest reliability. In the context of a questionnaire for participant-oriented research, Saldanha and O'Brien (2014: 160) suggest that three months might be required to prevent memory and carryover effects. No universally relevant standard can be applied haphazardly to all studies. The lag time between measurements must be evaluated in the context of a particular study.

Internal reliability

Every study that collects data through a survey or multi-question assessment needs to report a measure of internal reliability. Such measures describe the variance among multiple items on a survey or assessment. For example, the Myers-Briggs test asks multiple questions on the topic of introversion, and each question attempts to capture one aspect of the underlying construct of introversion. A respondent should respond similarly to each of these items if they are all truly measuring the same construct. In other words, answers to questions that attempt to measure the same construct should have a high degree of correlation.

A given survey instrument or assessment is capable of measuring multiple constructs. The Myers-Briggs test measures four different personality traits, for instance. Internal reliability needs to be calculated separately for each subsection in such cases. A good example from the communication studies literature is a scale for rituals in committed romantic relationships (RCRR; Pearson, Child, and Carmon 2010). Based on prior research, the authors expected that rituals could be described in five categories: couple-time rituals, everyday talk rituals, idiosyncratic rituals, daily routines and tasks, and intimacy rituals. The researchers drafted ten questions in each category and conducted a pilot test. For the resulting data, measures of internal reliability were used to identify the most useful subset of questions to include in the final scale. For example, the Likert-type scale includes the following two items in the category of daily routines and tasks (Pearson, Child, and Carmon 2010: 475):

> As a couple, we share certain meals during the day.
>
> [. . .]
>
> We have routines geared toward accomplishing everyday tasks.

The expectation is that these two questions are related to the same underlying topic of rituals related to daily routines and tasks, so respondents would be likely to answer similarly on both questions. However, they still measure slightly different aspects of the underlying construct so that some variability can be expected. Overall, the paper demonstrates the use of reliability in creating a survey instrument. We will occasionally refer back to this study as an example in our discussion of internal reliability.

Cronbach's α

The most widely used measure of internal reliability is Cronbach's α. The statistic is built upon the idea of correlation between answers on a survey. If a participant sample answered the two questions above from the RCRR, the correlation between answers for the two questions would likely be quite high. Couples with rituals around meals are more likely to have routines for everyday tasks, and vice versa. Internal reliability involves the correlation across multiple survey items. This differs from test-retest reliability in which the same respondent is measured at two different times. Here, the same respondent is measured on different survey items.

The calculation of Cronbach's α is a generalization of the practice of split-half reliability, in which a survey is split in half (e.g., a 30-item survey is divided into two shorter surveys consisting of the first 15 and last 15 questions) and the correlation of the scores is calculated.[11] Mathematically, the two challenges of split-half reliability involve the shortening of the survey, which causes an underestimation of reliability, and the myriad number of ways it is possible to split a larger survey into two halves.[12] Kuder and Richardson (1937) provided the first generalization of split-half estimation in the case of binary choice questions, and Cronbach (1951) extended this measure to his eponymous α measure, which has the following formula:

$$\alpha = \frac{k}{k-1}\left(1 - \frac{\sum_{i=1}^{k} \sigma_i^2}{\sigma_{Total}^2}\right)$$

The formula is a function of the length of the survey and the variance of the responses. In the formula, k stands for the number of items in the survey, σ_{Total}^2 represents the variance of the total scores, and σ_i^2 is the variance of each item. Before further discussion, an example will help clarify the formula. Consider a five-item survey on a 5-point Likert-type scale that is administered to four participants. Possible results appear in Table 11.5 with each row representing the survey responses of one participant.

At a glance, the five questions appear to be internally consistent. Participants one and two exhibit generally high scores on each question, participant number four tends to have low scores, and participant number three falls in the middle.[13] Therefore, we expect a high measurement of reliability because responses to the five items are internally consistent in these data. The computation of Cronbach's α compares the variance of the total score (in this case, 34.25) with the sum of the variance from each item in the survey (in this case, $2.00 + 4.25 + 3.58 + 1.67 + 0.25 = 11.75$). Including the consideration for the number of survey items yields the following:

$$\alpha = \frac{5}{5-1}\left(1 - \frac{11.75}{34.25}\right) = .82$$

When Cronbach's α is calculated with a statistical computing package, the resulting output will often include analysis of the change that would occur in α if each item were deleted from the survey. If the α coefficient increases greatly upon deletion of an item, then that survey item should be examined more closely for

Table 11.5 Internal reliability example data

	Q1	Q2	Q3	Q4	Q5	Total score
P1	5	5	5	5	3	23
P2	2	5	5	3	3	18
P3	2	2	4	4	3	15
P4	3	1	1	2	2	9
Column variance	2.00	4.25	3.58	1.67	0.25	34.25

potential problems and possibly be deleted from the survey. As a general guideline, deviations from the overall α should not differ more than .05 in either direction.

One of the benefits of Cronbach's α is that its calculation demands only one administration of a survey for its calculation. It should be stressed, however, that the resulting reliability coefficient is a function of the data, not the survey instrument (Streiner 2003). No matter how carefully a researcher develops a test in terms of reliability and validity, the resulting survey can never be definitively declared reliable in all circumstances. Consequently, even when a researcher is utilizing a previously developed scale that has exhibited adequate reliability in one setting, Cronbach's α must be calculated and reported for the new sample (Thompson and Vacha-Haase 2000).[14]

Cronbach's α is a statistic, so a confidence interval can be constructed around the point estimate. It is exceedingly rare to see such a confidence interval reported in the literature, and to our knowledge no statistical computing programs provide this capability easily. However, reporting a confidence interval improves interpretation and might help eliminate blind adherence to a cutoff value by drawing attention to the potential range of the sample's reliability. Calculation of an appropriate confidence interval is a difficult statistical problem, and several methods have been developed in the statistical literature.[15] One relatively simple and adequate method due to Feldt (1965) requires an F-distribution; the 95% confidence interval is given by the following bounds (Charter 1997):

$$\left[1-(1-\alpha)F_{.975}, 1-(1-\alpha)F_{.025}\right]$$

In this expression, α stands for Cronbach's α, not the confidence level. The 2.5% and 97.5% levels are found from an F-distribution with numerator and denominator degrees of freedom given by $(n-1)$ and $(n-1)(k-1)$, respectively, where n is the sample size and k the number of items in the survey.

We demonstrate these calculations by continuing the example. The appropriate degrees of freedom are calculated first: $(n-1) = 4 - 1 = 3$ for the numerator and $(n-1)(k-1) = (4-1)(5-1) = 12$ for the denominator of the F-distribution. Using a table or statistical program, the 2.5% and 97.5% levels of the F-distribution are found to be 0.0698 and 4.4742, respectively. Recall that α was calculated to be .82 earlier. Therefore, the 95% confidence interval is $\left[1-(1-.82)4.4742, 1-(1-.82).0698\right] = [.19, .99]$. Reporting only the point estimate for α would obscure this wide range of possible values.

This discussion demonstrates the importance of interpreting statistics in terms of their confidence intervals and not simply point estimates. Based on an α of .82, the survey scores have a high degree of reliability. However, the 95% confidence interval is quite wide due to the small number of items and the small sample size. Increasing either of these numbers would decrease the width of the confidence interval. Charter (1999) provides an example of the seriousness of this problem by advising minimum sample sizes of 400. We mention this figure not because it can be readily implemented in many T&I studies but because it highlights the tentative nature of statistical conclusions based on small samples.

202 *Analyzing relationships*

Empirical work in T&I requires careful interpretation, cautious generalization, and frequent replication to compensate for some of the challenges inherent to the specific research setting.

Some statisticians have argued that Cronbach's α is biased downward, meaning that the resulting figure is an underestimate of the true reliability, and the statistic represents a lower bound for the true measure (e.g., Cortina 1993; Tavakol and Dennick 2011). This problem is worse for tests with fewer items (Graham 2006), and the bias is likely negligible for sample sizes larger than 50 (Feldt, Woodruff, and Salih 1987). When smaller samples are necessary, an unbiased estimate of Cronbach's α corrected for sample size is potentially useful:

$$\alpha_{unbaised} = \frac{(n-3)\alpha}{n-1} + \frac{2}{n-1}$$

In most cases, reporting the standard computation of α in a larger discussion of the reliability and validity of a given measure will be adequate, but awareness of the potential bias and computation problems can aid interpretation.

Interpretation and application of Cronbach's α

Because Cronbach's α involves a ratio of two variance measures and the numerator represents sub-components of the denominator, the resulting coefficient will generally range from zero to one. A larger figure implies a more internally consistent measure.

It is mathematically possible for Cronbach's α to be negative. This result can occur when there is negative correlation between items in the scale. One possible source of such a problem is a failure to adjust items whose responses were reverse-coded. Putting aside this data handling error, the other possible source of a negative Cronbach's α is that the survey's questions are measuring multiple constructs (Henson 2001). This would necessitate a reconceptualization of the survey to align better with the underlying constructs being measured. A well-developed and valid scale should never result in a negative value for Cronbach's α, so any such calculations demand a careful check of the data entry process or a redesign of the survey instrument to cover multiple dimensions. This situation emphasizes the importance of proper instrument development; if data are collected from an instrument in which this occurs, the researcher may be forced to discard this work and start over.

Given a theoretically maximum value of one for Cronbach's α, the question arises of an adequate level for applied research. Many researchers across the social sciences consider .70 to be a minimum acceptable value for Cronbach's α, with numerous papers citing the textbook by Nunnaly (1978) as the source of this standard. Like all strict cutoff values, this general rule is too simplistic. Furthermore, even the purported source of this rule is more nuanced in its guidance. Lance, Butts, and Michels (2006) describe the widespread repetition of this standard as an urban legend with a kernel of truth. Nunnaly does, indeed, mention .70 for areas of new research but in the same paragraph comments that .80 may be inadequate in many applied settings. In their monograph on reliability and validity, Carmines and Zeller (1979) offer .80 as an appropriate general rule. Because the length of a survey and the sample size can both influence the estimate of Cronbach's α, Ponterotto and Ruckdeschel (2007) and Ponterotto and Charter (2009) propose a more complex scheme for evaluation. They argue that .75 is an excellent reliability value and that .70 is good for any scale with fewer than seven items administered to fewer than 100 subjects. Peterson (1994) conducts a meta-analysis of published work in marketing and psychology journals and reports that 75% of reported coefficients exceeded .70.

While most discussions of Cronbach's α focus on the minimum acceptable level, levels that are too high can also represent a problem with the survey design. A primary concern in this area is redundancy in the survey (Boyle 1991). If substantially similar questions appear on a survey, then respondents will naturally answer them in the same manner, which will result in the calculated statistic being quite high. Such a result is due not to homogeneity in responses but to redundancy of the questions. Streiner (2003) suggests that α above .90 could be considered symptomatic of this issue. Careful examination of a survey instrument for validity and alignment with theory are important to prevent this problem.

The issue of excessively high consistency measures is discussed by Angelelli (2004) in the construction of the Interpreter's Interpersonal Role Inventory (IPRI). An initial version of the instrument consisted of 62 items, which were used in a pilot study. Levels of internal consistency that were too high were considered redundant, while those that were too low were considered not to be aligned with the underlying construct of interest. These criteria (and others) are used to trim the number of items to the survey's final form.

Surveys can also yield deceptively high levels of Cronbach's α solely due to the number of items included. For example, Cortina (1993) demonstrated that even with low levels of correlation between individual survey items, a questionnaire with 14 items would result in .70 as a measure of Cronbach's α. The ability to inflate reliability measures solely by lengthening a survey with additional items should highlight the importance of thoughtful, parsimonious design. We urge researchers to refrain from survey development without adequate expertise and to evaluate and employ previously developed surveys with some of these cautions in mind.[16]

A final issue with interpreting Cronbach's α stems from variability among respondents. Because the variability of the sample's total scores appears in the calculation, a more diverse sample will yield a higher result. A targeted sample can be expected to yield lower reliability measures than the same survey would produce when a sample was drawn from the general population (Caruso 2000). For example, targeted samples for a T&I study might require translators who can work with a specific language pair or interpreters with a certain number of years of experience. As always, careful sampling and planning are vital steps to ensure the usefulness of the statistical analysis.

We recommend that a reliability coefficient of .70 is considered the baseline point of comparison in a broader analysis that takes into account the confidence interval of Cronbach's α, the sample size, the length of the survey, and previously published studies that use the same scale. Previous work has emphasized that small, homogeneous samples can yield artificially imprecise estimates of Cronbach's α. Therefore, a confidence interval for the statistic should also be provided. Developing a more nuanced understanding requires wider analysis of the study and a deeper engagement of the researcher with the underlying statistics. However, the effort avoids simplistic application of blind adherence to a so-called standard and will improve the quality of the research.

The translation of surveys is widely studied to ensure that the resulting survey instruments are still reliably measuring the same underlying construct. Consequently, Cronbach's α has been employed as a way to ensure consistency among surveys conducted in more than one language. Previously validated surveys and assessments often serve as the starting point for new research projects and can be translated for use in other languages. Once a survey has been translated, administration of it to similar samples in different languages should result in similar levels of Cronbach's α. This evaluation technique is often used in the setting of health surveys. For example, Hilton and Skrutkowski (2002) discuss at length the practice of translating health surveys into multiple languages. One criterion they suggest is to compute Cronbach's α for each version of a questionnaire as evidence that the translated survey still adequately measures the same underlying construct.

Because it is important that medical questionnaires should be of high quality, there have been a large number of studies that examine similar translation challenges. Schoppink et al. (1996), for example, discuss the translation of a pain and disability scale into Dutch. The researchers explicitly ask whether it is better to translate medical scales than it is to create new instruments for each language or culture. The high reliability of their results suggest that translation is appropriate because participants completing the survey in different languages yield similar results. One might consider, however, that these results are generalizable only to similar patient populations. Patient groups that differ significantly in discoursal preferences and cultural beliefs may require a different instrument to be developed.

Despite the importance of creating linguistically and culturally appropriate versions of research instruments, most inquiry into how these target language versions should be prepared has come from outside of T&I studies. The health sciences, in particular, recognize the importance of multilingual versions of research instruments, and researchers in these fields have reflected on the challenges of creating and administering them (e.g., Simmons et al. 2011). Hendricson et al. (1989) also describe these issues and include a thorough discussion of reliability as it relates to multiple language versions of research instruments. The authors calculate and interpret Cronbach's α in the administration of a Spanish-language translation of a questionnaire for rheumatoid arthritis patients. Another approach is to create a new version that is linguistically and culturally appropriate in the target language by means of *transcreation*.[17] The idea of creating locale-specific research instruments naturally aligns with functionalist approaches to translation, yet as noted previously, relatively little attention has been paid to its use within the T&I research community. Given the complexities of the translation task, T&I scholars have much to contribute to this discussion and are in a prime position to help those outside of the discipline develop reliable instruments.

Reliability measures are also important for research with a focus on individuals rather than on survey development. For instance, Baker, Hayes, and Fortier (1998) measured patient satisfaction with interpreting services for Spanish-speaking patients in a medical setting and reported .86 for Cronbach's α as proof of reliability before advancing to further analysis. Complex constructs related to human thought, mood, or behavior such as motivation and anxiety are necessarily measured with multi-item surveys. Inferential statistics and conclusions drawn from these studies rely on adequate reliability statistics of their surveys.

To capture more than one aspect of reliability, many studies measure both Cronbach's α and test-retest reliability of a survey. For example, Walker, Kerr, Pender, and Sechrist (1990) provide both statistics (among others) in their thorough examination of a Spanish-language version of the Health-Promoting Lifestyle Profile. Lee et al. (2006) similarly provide a number of reliability measures in describing the translation of four neck pain surveys into Korean. It is vital to embed reliability statistics in a broader discussion of survey adequacy so that the numbers support and confirm the overall argument.

Other measures of internal reliability

Cronbach's α is the most common measure of internal reliability, but it is one among many. For instance, Hattie (1985) describes more than thirty candidate measures in five categories. Nor is Cronbach's α without detractors. Schmitt (1996) describes limitations of Cronbach's α and encourages reporting of intercorrelations to accompany estimations of Cronbach's α, and Schmidt, Le, and Ilies (2003) criticize the statistic for failing to capture all of the relevant error in a measurement. Meanwhile, Sijtsma (2009) discusses the greatest lower bound (glb) estimate of reliability and the possibly limited utility of Cronbach's α. Revelle and Zinbarg (2009) review a number of candidate measures and prefer an alternative measure named omega. Both glb and omega are offered as alternatives to Cronbach's α by Peters (2014), who suggests a comprehensive approach of a correlation matrix and multiple reliability measures with their associated confidence intervals as a means of assessing reliability.

To date, no alternative measure of reliability can compete with Cronbach's α for ease of interpretation as well as wide acceptance and application in the empirical literature of the social sciences. Searching for one ideal statistical measure might actually miss the larger issues of appropriate unidimensionality, consistency, and alignment with theoretical constructs. Hattie (1985: 159) mentions an "act of judgment" on the part of an investigator. It is vital to remember that estimation of Cronbach's α is only one step of the larger process of considering a survey's reliability and validity.

Intercoder reliability

The third type of reliability measures the consistency of decisions made by multiple evaluators. We will refer to this type of reliability as *intercoder reliability*, though it is sometimes referred to as interrater reliability, interrater agreement, interannotator agreement, or interobserver reliability.[18] Intercoder reliability can be thought of as a measure of consensus among the coders or as a measure of the possible reproducibility of the research by a different group of coders with access to the same categorical definitions (Krippendorff 2004b). High agreement among a number of coders indicates less measurement error and stronger reliability (Bayerl and Paul 2011). Because human judgment is involved, the data are more prone to variability or errors than other types of measurement. Therefore, the triangulation of multiple coders and a measure of their consistency is an important part of justifying the analysis of such data.

Coders working with translated materials pose significant challenges for intercoder reliability because the coders are not measuring identical objects, because of the translation. Additionally, training coders in multiple languages or with varying degrees of fluency in the training language could result in misunderstandings that lead to coding errors. Peter and Lauf (2002) discuss some of the possible confounding factors of cross-national analysis. Their data show that self-reported language skills influence measures of reliability.

Agreement among multiple coders is more likely when a thorough rubric is prepared. All coders should be trained by the lead author, preferably in simultaneous sessions so that all coders hear the same information and have opportunities to ask clarifying questions. Coders should also have an opportunity to practice on their own with a subset of the data or pilot study. Disagreements can be discussed, and any necessary additions can be made to the rubric. The statistical analysis of intercoder reliability is the final step in this longer process.

Russell and Malcolm (2009) describe the extensive process of training coders to ensure reliable assessment of ASL-English interpreters. The training takes place over three days, and each session includes a review of the standard, examination of previous ratings, and practice ratings until agreement is reached 95% of the time. They also mention ongoing monitoring of consistency. This level of detail builds great confidence in the reliability of the assessment.

A meta-analysis of intercoder reliability practices in communication studies was conducted by Lombard, Snyder-Duch, and Bracken (2002). They conclude with ten recommendations for best practices regarding intercoder reliability. The recommendations include proper selection, calculation, interpretation, and reporting of a measure of intercoder reliability. Furthermore, they stress the importance of assessing reliability during the training of coders and using pilot studies to ensure adequacy of definitions and agreement in judgments.[19]

Percent agreement

The simplest measure of intercoder reliability is percent agreement. For example, two coders could be independently tasked with assigning 50 observations into four discrete categories. The total number of identical decisions is divided by the total sample size to give the percent of agreement between the coders. In this example, the denominator would be the 50 observations. If the coders agreed on the ranking for 16 of them (and disagreed on the remaining 34), then the percent agreement would be 16/50 = 32%. Ease of calculation and conceptual simplicity are two factors in favor of percent agreement. However, the statistic has inherent problems such that Lombard, Snyder-Duch, and Bracken (2002) emphatically state that it is incorrect to use only percent agreement as a measure of intercoder reliability.

Unfortunately, percent agreement calculations have an inherent upward bias, because a score of zero implies that the raters never agreed. However, the worst-case scenario for a measurement is not total disagreement among the coders but complete randomness in the scores. If coders were assigning scores independently and randomly, the measurement would be inherently meaningless, but their scores would agree at times due to chance. Therefore, measures of intercoder reliability must account for these chance agreements. All of the subsequent measures in this section properly adjust for this.

Cohen's κ

A correction for chance agreement is part of the calculation for the most widely cited statistic for intercoder reliability, Cohen's κ (1960). The statistic measures agreement between two coders who classify observations into any number of categories. Cohen makes three assumptions in his seminal paper: (1) the units of analysis are independent; (2) the nominal scale possesses independent, mutually exclusive, and exhaustive categories; and (3) the coders make their decisions independently. The last condition is violated whenever coders are able to consult in their decisions. Consulting during the definition and training phases of a research project is important to build reliability, but the final coding should always be completed independently. Consensus building through consulting violates the assumptions of the statistical analysis and could even be considered an unethical misrepresentation of research results. Therefore, researchers are advised to consider their methodology carefully before calculating and reporting Cohen's κ.

One application of Cohen's κ is verifying that human raters agree in their identification of items in a text. Specia, Cancedda, and Dymetman (2010), for example, present a manually annotated dataset to allow for future inquiry on human evaluation of machine translation (MT) output and automated quality metrics. To create this resource, professional translators were tasked with reading the MT output and identifying segments that require post-editing. The raters categorized each segment into one of four categories: requires complete retranslation, a lot of post-editing needed, a little post-editing needed, or fit for purpose. Cohen's κ was calculated as a reliability measure that could demonstrate adequate agreement among the coding decisions. Hamon et al. (2009) use a similar methodology to establish reliability of ratings of the output of an automatic simultaneous translation system. Multiple judges examined the output of the computer system's translation and ranked it in terms of fluency and correctness. Another example is He (2000), who asked Chinese and English bilinguals to examine translations of the titles of articles in medical journals and rank them on a five-point scale regarding their equivalence. The reliability of the coder's decisions was demonstrated by calculating Cohen's κ.

In many cases, the statistic will be calculated at least twice in the course of a study, because the coders need training and practice to build agreement in their categorizations. First, the coders would work with a training sample that consists of a random selection of the data. Often 20% of the data is recommended as an appropriate size for a pilot test of this kind. If the calculated reliability is inadequate, further refinement of definitions and additional training takes place. After coding the entire sample, Cohen's κ would be calculated again for reporting. If coding requires a long time span, intercoder reliability might be calculated at several different times to ensure that changes are not occurring in coders' decisions. Reporting of the preliminary coefficients is not necessary, but the process should be fully described in the research report. For instance, Angelelli (2004) reports reliability of the IPRI in a pilot study before proceeding to the main analysis.

The formula for Cohen's κ can be defined in terms of either proportions or frequencies; we could state the results of the previous example as either two coders agreeing on 16 decisions or on 32% of the decisions. Frequencies generally makes for easier hand computation and conceptual understanding of the statistic, as will be seen in the subsequent example here. The formulation of the statistic in terms of frequencies is given by the following expression:

$$\kappa = \frac{f_o - f_c}{n - f_c}$$

The notation follows Cohen's original, in which f_o represents the observed frequency of agreement, n is the sample size, and f_c represents the expected frequency due to chance. Using this notation, percent agreement would be calculated as f_o / n, so the correction for chance agreement is conducted by subtracting an expected frequency from both the numerator and denominator. Cohen's κ is one of several measures for intercoder reliability that utilize this same general form but differ slightly in their definitions of f_c. The most well-known alternative in the case of two coders is *Scott's π* (Scott 1955). Extensions to broader situations are described below, but we provide examples of Cohen's κ because it is relatively easy to calculate by hand and demonstrates the general principles that all measures of intercoder reliability follow.

As a numerical example of calculating Cohen's κ, consider a model of interpreter assessment. Two coders listen to a rendering of a brief passage, judge the result against some well-defined standard, and assign one of three scores to the performance: exceeds the standard, meets the standard, or lies below the standard. Possible results for a sample of 100 interpreters appear in Table 11.6.

Table 11.6 Cohen's κ example data

	Coder 1			
Coder 2	Exceeds	Meets	Below	Total
Exceeds	29	5	7	41
Meets	9	22	3	34
Below	2	4	19	25
Total	40	31	29	100

In the opinion of Coder 1, 40 of the interpreters exceeded the standard, 31 met the standard, and 29 failed to meet the standard. Of those 100 rankings, Coder 1 was in agreement with Coder 2 for a total of 70 of the observations (29 exceeding, 22 meeting, and 19 below the standard). However, the implied percent agreement of 70% is too high, because some of those agreements could be solely due to chance.

Cohen's κ computes the number of chance agreements through the use of the row and column totals (known collectively as the marginal totals). To calculate the expected number of times that both coders would rate someone as exceeding the standard, multiply the row total for Coder 2 by the column total for Coder 1 and divide by the total number of participants[20]: 41*40 / 100 = 16.4. Therefore, of the 29 apparent agreements, 16.4 of them could be expected due solely to chance. Similarly, for the other two categories: the number of expected agreements for participants who meet the standard is 34*31 / 100 = 10.54, and for those whose performance does not meet the standard it is 25*29 / 100 = 7.25. Therefore, the total expected agreement is 16.4 + 10.54 + 7.25 = 34.19, and Cohen's κ can be calculated:

$$\kappa = \frac{70 - 34.19}{100 - 34.19} = .54$$

The maximum observed value for Cohen's κ is one, which occurs only when there is complete agreement between the two coders. Cohen's κ is zero when the number of observed agreements is equal to the number of expected agreements. Such a situation is different from saying that the coders disagree in all cases. Table 11.7 provides an example of data that would result in Cohen's κ of zero, even though percent agreement between the coders is 36%.[21]

At the other extreme, it is possible for κ to be negative, and Cohen (1960) describes lower bounds for the statistic. In practice, however, any observed value below .2 would certainly be inadequate, so the precise value becomes a moot point. As a general benchmark, Landis and Koch (1977) suggest that values from .41 to .60 are moderate, .61 to .80 are substantial, and values above .81 are almost perfect. These should not be taken as absolutes, but κ values below .60 would be considered problematic in many settings.

Output from statistical packages will usually provide a measure of the standard error, which can be used to calculate a 95% confidence interval by the formula

Table 11.7 Cohen's κ example data, κ = 0

	Coder 1			
Coder 2	Exceeds	Meets	Below	Total
Exceeds	4	5	11	20
Meets	9	12	9	30
Below	7	23	20	50
Total	20	40	40	100

$\kappa \pm 1.96 * SE_\kappa$. The formula for the correct standard error requires a large number of calculations, but an approximate 95% confidence interval can be calculated from a relatively simple formula for the standard error:

$$\sigma_\kappa = \frac{\sqrt{f_o(1 - f_o/n)}}{n - f_c}$$

This formula is only an approximation, but it has been shown to be generally conservative by Fleiss, Cohen, and Everitt (1969), who also provide the correct formula for the standard error. If a particular computer program does not provide an estimate of the standard error, little is lost by using the approximation formula above. For the example data, the standard error is approximately 0.0696, which results in a 95% confidence interval of (.41, .68).

So far, the discussion of intercoder reliability has been limited to the case of categorizing sample data without any regard for the relationship between the categories. However, a ranked categorization may be of particular interest to a researcher. In the example provided, the categories are inherently ordered: failure to meet the standard is the worst case, and exceeding the standard is the best case performance. When the degree of disagreement is important, intercoder reliability can be measured by a weighted version of Cohen's κ (Cohen 1968). This statistic is rarely used, in part because the weights must be specified by the researcher, and this judgment has a strong influence on the final statistic.

The popularity of Cohen's κ is undisputed. However, the statistic is not without critics. For a given set of data, it is not always mathematically possible for the measure to reach the maximum value of one. Furthermore, it does not account for individual biases among the coders, who might preference one category over others. Among the more vehement critics is Krippendorff (2004b, 2008), who argues that Cohen's κ is unsuitable for measuring reliability. His particular focus is on content analysis in the field of communication (Krippendorff and Bock 2008), but his mathematical concerns are broad enough that caution must be advised in the use of Cohen's κ.

Fleiss's κ

When more than two coders are used to differentiate data into discrete categories, an appropriate statistic for measuring intercoder reliability is Fleiss's κ (Fleiss

1971).²² The statistic allows more flexibility not only by allowing more than two coders but also by allowing the possibility for each subject to be evaluated by different coders. The only requirement is that each subject should be categorized by the same total number of coders. For example, if 80 subjects were each evaluated three times by five judges, it would be permissible for subject one to be evaluated by judges A, B, and C; subject two by judges B, D, and, E; and so on. Evaluating Fleiss's κ uses the same rough numerical categories as Cohen's κ. While it is a useful extension to multiple coders, it has been largely supplanted by the next measure of intercoder reliability.

Krippendorff's α

The reliability measures discussed above for measuring intercoder reliability (Cohen's κ, Scott's π, and Fleiss's κ) share a number of undesirable traits. They are influenced by sample size, the number of coders, the number of categories, prevalence of the categories, and any bias the researchers have in favor of one category over another (Sim and Wright 2005). These problems are overcome by one of the most general measures of intercoder reliability, Krippendorff's α (1970). In contrast to the measurements discussed so far in this subsection, which measure agreement among coders, Krippendorff's α measures disagreement. The overall form of the statistic is $\alpha = 1 - \frac{D_o}{D_c}$, in which D_o is the observed amount of disagreement and D_c is the disagreement that would be expected due to chance. The particular calculations of disagreement depend on the experimental setting.

Krippendorff's α incorporates other reliability indices into a more general model. It is a flexible statistic, able to accommodate multiple coders and categories, which means it can be used in all situations for which Fleiss's κ would be used. Furthermore, Krippendorff's α can be used on measurements at any level, beyond categorical and ordinal to interval and ratio. The statistic can also still be calculated with missing data. These are among the positive traits of the statistic outlined by Hayes and Krippendorff (2007). The statistic is also comparable across different numbers of coders, sample sizes, or measurements.

Another good aspect of the statistic is that it can be interpreted similarly to other reliability measures, with a coefficient of one representing perfect agreement. Krippendorff (2004a) argues that .667 is the lowest acceptable figure for intercoder reliability while noting that .80 is a traditional benchmark for adequacy. Krippendorff's α has been employed widely in the field of communication studies, particularly for content analysis.

The primary drawback of Krippendorff's α is its unavailability in the basic version of many statistical computing programs. However, free resources to calculate the statistic are widely available. These include extensions and scripts for popular statistical packages and software, as well as online calculators. We heartily endorse further adoption of Krippendorff's α as a measure of intercoder reliability, particularly since it addresses many of the concerns that regularly arise in T&I research designs.

Intraclass correlation coefficient

A final measure for intercoder reliability, called the intraclass correlation coefficient (ICC; Tinsley and Weiss 1975), is available in the case when the measurement of interest is interval or ratio scaled.[23] Rather than assigning objects to categories, coders would be providing a numerical rating. This situation would be common in assessment situations such as some certification exams. Judges might use a rubric to assign a continuous score from 0 to 100 based on their evaluation of a candidate's performance, for example.

The ICC statistic is built on an ANOVA framework, in which the variance is partitioned between various sources. The coefficient is the ratio of the variance attributable to coders by the sum of the variance attributable to the coders and the residual error. It ranges from 0 to 1 and, as with all other reliability coefficients, higher scores represent greater consistency in the ratings.

Shrout and Fleiss (1979) outline three situations in which ICC can be used, depending on the number of coders, how many units they each measure (all units or a random sample), and whether the coders are considered a random sample from a larger population. They also consider an additional dimension based on whether the reliability of the mean rating may be the actual value of interest, rather than the reliability of individual coders. This results in three additional models based on the reliability of the mean, for a total of six different ICC models in common usage. The notation and nomenclature of Shrout and Fleiss are now considered standard and continue to guide ICC usage.

The selection of an appropriate measure of intercoder reliability is sometimes mentioned explicitly in research reports. Porro et al. (2014) task three coders with comparing raw MT and automatic post-editing output, selecting whether one is better than the other or if they are equal. Given the highly skewed data, they eschew Cohen's κ in favor of a two-way ICC, which exhibits adequate reliability for their sample.

One drawback of ICC is that it depends on the relationship between variance measurements, which means that it is susceptible to different results if the judges or the sample are particularly homogeneous. In particular, if the sample exhibits low variance, the computed ICC will be low. This might be the case in T&I studies because the purposive samples often have a high degree of similarity.

Another challenge of employing ICC as a measure of intercoder reliability is that it requires specification of a proper ANOVA model. An excellent flowchart for selecting the best model is provided by McGraw and Wong (1996a, 1996b). Their work supplies the necessary formulas for the ICCs and their exact confidence intervals. We omit them here for considerations of space.

Additionally, notice that Krippendorff's α already allows for the analysis of continuous data (though this fact is perhaps not widely known). Therefore, the more easily estimated and interpreted statistic can be used in place of ICC. Meanwhile, generalizability theory extends the ICC's ANOVA framework in a more complex direction to account for multiple sources of variability. Therefore, while the ICC is sometimes employed in applied research, it could be argued that it should be supplanted by either of these methodologies, depending on the context.

Summary

Intercoder reliability is of vital importance to the conclusions of a research study that involves multiple coders making independent decisions. Of the three categories of reliability coefficients discussed here, it is likely the most controversial in terms of selecting the best statistic. We endorse Krippendorff's α as likely the best available statistic due to its flexibility, statistical properties, and ease of interpretation.

Statistical complexities aside, it is important to remember that reliability is an important foundational step for applied research. Analysis of the data is secondary to good design and procedures. Intercoder reliability can be improved through training and careful operationalization. To begin with, all coders should agree on the precise meanings of the phenomena being analyzed. For instance, if multiple coders were listening to a conference interpreter for speech disfluencies, the concept of disfluency must be precisely defined and operationalized. It could refer to pauses or filler words or false starts, for example. Whenever possible, the lead author of an article should be responsible for training coders but not actually participate in the coding process because they may struggle to maintain objectivity, knowing the hypotheses and goals of the research (van Someren, Barnard, and Sandberg 1994). In all cases that involve coding decisions, best practices dictate that more than one coder should be involved. Bayerl and Paul (2011) also recommend using relatively few categories and coders with similar levels of expertise. All of these procedures, coupled with an adequate measure of intercoder reliability, provide confirmation for the reader that the research project is potentially reproducible.

Notes

1 Relative ease in conducting computationally intensive procedures such as finding the 95% confidence interval for Kendall's τ is a substantial point in favor of the R language and its dedicated software environment. The freely-available open source code and contributed packages that extend the R language offer greater functionality than that of some off-the-shelf programs, which offer more limited capabilities and less ability to alter or extend the programming.
2 Technically, in the presence of tied ranks, the appropriate statistic is referred to as τ_b.
3 For a thorough history of the evolution in thinking about reliability, see Brennan (2001).
4 In statistical parlance, this sum is referred to as the *linear error model*.
5 Angelelli (2004) gives an example of the value of preliminary studies. In constructing the Interpreter's Interpersonal Role Inventory, she administered a draft survey to four people, followed by a small-scale try-out with 10 respondents and finally a pilot study with 29 participants. This careful evolution should serve as an example for building reliable (and valid) survey instruments.
6 Many examples of such effects exist in various social science disciplines. The popular book *You Are What You Wear: The Key to Business Success* (Thourlby 1978), for example, lists ten broad categories of decisions people make based on a person's attire. Medical studies have demonstrated a so-called *white coat effect* on blood pressure (e.g., Ayman and Goldshine 1940) as well as the effect of attire on patient perceptions of professionalism and competence (e.g., Gjerdingen, Simpson, and Titus 1987).

214 *Analyzing relationships*

    Studies of educators have found effects of attire (e.g., Morris, Gorham, Cohen, and Huffman 1996) and humor (e.g., Wanzer and Frymier 1999) on students' perceptions of professors. In politics, the controversial *Bradley effect* considers the influence of race on survey response and voting behavior (Payne 2010). As a final example, the juror selection process has been accused of bias based on race and gender (e.g., Rose 1999).

7 Another approachable overview of the literature on reliability is provided by Thye (2000), who explicitly sets out to provide a nontechnical summary of reliability in the discipline of sociology.
8 Brennan (1997) outlines the history of Generalizability Theory.
9 The issue of the time interval between measurements is discussed later in this section.
10 Quite a few studies have used Spearman's ρ, but as discussed previously in this chapter Kendall's τ has been shown to be the preferred nonparametric statistic.
11 This design presumes that the survey is measuring only one underlying construct. If a survey attempts to measure multiple dimensions, then the division of the survey and the correlation must be conducted separately for each dimension. For instance, Pearson, Child, and Carmon (2010) calculated five different reliability coefficients, one for each sub-dimension of the RCRR scale.
12 To give one example, for a 10-item survey there are $\binom{10}{5} = 252$ ways to split the sample into two equal halves.
13 Note that we are assuming any reverse-coded survey items have been adjusted before conducting this calculation. Again referring to Pearson, Child, and Carmon (2010: 475), one item in the category of daily routines and tasks stated "We do not have a routine, as a couple, for tasks related to the end of the day." Respondents who strongly agree with this are actually strongly disagreeing with the underlying construct of the existence of rituals in the category. Recoding appropriately, if necessary, will ensure that higher scores indicate more presence of the construct and lower scores indicating less.
14 The APA Task Force on Statistical Inference (Wilkinson 1999) has expressed this distinction between *test reliability* and *test score reliability* as important for reporting research results.
15 A mathematical comparison of the various methods is provided by Romano, Kromrey, Owens, and Scott (2011).
16 For an overview of the use of survey-based studies in T&I studies, see Sun (2016). Book-length treatments of survey design and methodology are provided by Fowler (2013) and Groves et al. (2009).
17 Within translation studies, this term most regularly appears in the context of localization or advertising.
18 Some authors also use these terms in their hyphenated form.
19 Krippendorff (2004b) takes issue with some of the mathematical details of the article and misconceptions regarding intercoder reliability, though his rejoinder does not affect the general recommendations.
20 This calculation is the same procedure as the chi-squared test of independence, as described in Chapter 10.
21 The calculations to demonstrate that Cohen's κ is zero are summarized here as a reference and another example of calculating the statistic:

$$f_c = \frac{20*20}{100} + \frac{30*40}{100} + \frac{50*40}{100} = 36; \; \kappa = \frac{36-36}{100-36} = 0$$

22 The name of this statistic has caused some confusion, because it is actually a generalization of Scott's π rather than Cohen's κ (Conger 1980).
23 Rousson, Gasser, and Seifert (2002) discuss some of the broader issues of reliability when dealing with continuous measures.

12 Linear regression

Linear regression is the statistical procedure to find the equation of a line that best fits a set of data. There are two possible goals when conducting regression analysis. First, regression analysis can assess whether or not a dependent variable is linearly related to one or more independent variables. In other words, linear regression determines the strength of the relationships between the independent and dependent variables. Second, the regression model can be used for predicting the dependent variable, based on available data of the independent variable. The mathematical model is identical, and we will present examples of both uses.

A strong similarity exists between correlation analysis and linear regression, particularly in the case of simple linear regression. Both statistical tools examine the strength of the relationship between two variables, but there are three main differences. First, the response variable is generally thought to be the result of the changes in the explanatory variable. In an experimental design, the researcher's control or manipulation of the independent variable strengthens the case for causation (Asuero, Sayago, and González 2006). In an observational design, the tentative argument for causation can be based on theories, reference to the larger body of work on the variables of interest, or because the dependent variable occurs later in time than the independent variable.

A second difference from correlation is that linear regression can model the dependent variable as the result of the collective influence of multiple independent variables. Therefore, the linear regression model is more flexible and powerful in describing the relationships among several constructs included in one model. A third difference is that correlation analysis only measures the strength of the relationship between variables; linear regression additionally provides an estimate of the numerical relationship between variables. The estimated regression equation can be used for prediction and generalization beyond the sample.

The regression model encompasses a set of techniques to examine the relationship between a dependent variable and one or more independent variables. The dependent variable can be referred to as the *target variable*, the *response variable*, or the *regressand*. Meanwhile, the independent variables are sometimes called *explanatory variables*, *predictors*, or *regressors*.

> **Linear Regression: Overview**
>
> *Purpose:* To determine whether there is a statistically significant, linear relationship between one or more independent variables and a continuous dependent variable.
>
> *Null hypothesis:* There is no linear relationship between the independent and dependent variables.
>
> *Alternative hypothesis:* A linear relationships exists between the independent and dependent variables.
>
> *Experimental designs:*
>
> 1. One or more independent variables are manipulated by the researcher and a resulting dependent variable is measured;
> 2. Some independent variables are manipulated by the researcher while other blocking variables are outside of the researcher's control, and a resulting dependent variable is measured;
> 3. Independent and dependent variables are measured in an observational study.
>
> *Parametric tests:* F-test, t-test
>
> *Effect size:* R^2

A simple, fictitious experiment will help to illustrate linear regression estimation and testing: a sample of fifteen participants are tasked with translating a 250-word passage, and the time required to complete the task is measured as the dependent variable. A number of variables would plausibly influence the outcome of this very basic experiment. Some factors would be inherent to the translator (participant variables), such as years of practical experience, degrees or certifications earned, or even typing speed. Other variables would relate to the working environment, such as the temperature, lighting, or distractions in the room. Finally, the availability of tools such as a translation memory, machine translation, or term base would also affect the length of time spent on the translation.

The variables described above represent a variety of different kinds of variables and measurements. Some of them, including years of experience and typing speed, are continuous variables that can take on a range of numerical values. Others, such as degrees earned or the availability of tools, are categorical, taking on only a few possible values. The researcher can control some of the variables, including the environmental factors and availability of tools, while participant variables are observable but uncontrollable by the researcher. Choosing independent variables to include in a regression equation is called *model selection*. The selection of an appropriate set of independent variables is driven not only by statistical considerations but also by previous studies and underlying theories that suggest the existence of relationships. Two examples of studies using regression in the field of T&I are given in Table 12.1.

Table 12.1 Linear regression: Examples from T&I literature

---

1 López Gómez, Bajo, Padilla, and Santiago de Torres (2007) estimate two regression models for the purpose of predicting success in signed language acquisition and interpreting. The participants were university-level students enrolled in a signed language interpreting program. An instructor in the program provided evaluations of the students' skills with Spanish Sign Language (LSE) and signed language interpreting (SLI). These two variables were the dependent variables, while personality traits, perceptual-motor skills, and cognitive factors served as independent variables.
2 Setton and Motta (2007) collect data from recordings of 47 different sessions of simultaneous interpreting with text. They estimate a regression model to determine the effects that errors, elaboration, and paraphrases have on the overall quality of the interpretations, as determined by three expert judges.

In this chapter, we will use this elementary experiment to illustrate several concepts. To begin, we will consider time on task as a function only of the years of experience of the translator. The model is extended to include other variables, and our discussion of multiple linear regression includes years of experience, typing speed, and temperature of the room as three predictor variables. Finally, we use the various translation tools to illustrate the use of discrete predictor variables. This simple model is meant only for illustrative purposes, and we do not suggest that it would match real-world results nor that years of experience is a sole or primary determinant of the time it takes a translator to complete his or her work.

Simple linear regression

When a research project has only one independent variable, the analysis can be referred to as *simple linear regression*. A regression model finds the line of best fit by specifying the slope and intercept of a straight line that, in a precisely defined mathematical sense, comes closest to describing the data. The resulting equation can then be used for prediction or for hypothesis testing about the relationship between the variables.

When a model employs multiple independent variables, the procedure can be called *multiple linear regression*.[1] The distinction between simple and multiple linear regression is convenient for pedagogical purposes but is generally not necessary. Since both methods use the same statistical methods, the term linear regression adequately encompasses both models. Because it includes only one independent variable, simple linear regression can be easier to visualize and understand. Multiple regression is introduced later in the chapter as a generalization of the methodology.

Regression modeling involves estimating the straight line that best summarizes the relationships between the variables. The equation of a straight line contains two variables as well as two parameters, the slope and the intercept. As always, parameters represent traits of a population. In this case, the intercept provides the expected value of the dependent variable when the independent variable is zero, and the slope provides the expected change in the dependent variable for a unit

218 *Analyzing relationships*

increase in the independent variable. We will discuss the interpretation of these parameters further in a later section.

The independent (predictor) variable is typically labeled x, and the dependent variable is labeled y. Because there are multiple values for the variables, one for each participant or observation, they are subscripted in formal equations. The parameters of the equation are the slope and the intercept of the line. In regression equations, the slope is denoted β_1 and the intercept β_0. This results in the following equation:

$$y_i = \beta_0 + \beta_1 x_i + \varepsilon_i$$

This simple linear model shows that the dependent variable can be predicted from the value of the independent variable by multiplying by β_1 and adding β_0. Unexplained variation (i.e., the difference between the model's prediction and the actual value of the dependent variable) is captured by the residual error, ε_i. As in previous chapters, we first discuss the assumptions of this model; then we proceed to estimate and test the statistical significance of the model and its parameters.

Assumptions

Simple linear regression requires four assumptions:

1 The true relationship between x and y is linear.
2 The variance of the residuals is constant (homoscedasticity).
3 The residuals are independent.
4 The residuals are normally distributed.

As with all inferential statistics, the assumptions are necessary for valid hypothesis testing and construction of confidence intervals. Because most of the assumptions of linear regression are assessed by examining the residuals, the model must be estimated prior to any formal testing of the assumptions. Therefore, the visual check and conceptual model of linearity should not be taken lightly. Also, checking of the assumptions following estimation of the model is similar to the advice provided in Chapter 8.

The first assumption of linearity can be checked by creating a scatterplot of the data as a preliminary step in estimating any regression model. Visual inspection also aids in recognizing obvious outliers, which may represent data collection or entry errors. Figure 12.1 depicts data that were simulated for our fictitious experiment in which the time required to translate a 250-word passage is modeled as a function of the translators' experience, measured in years. The scatterplot includes no obvious outliers. A more formal test for outliers will be discussed later in the chapter, but this screening is still useful to spot data errors or serious violations of the model's assumptions. Additionally, the plot depicts a downward trend that is approximately linear. More years of experience appear to be associated with less time on task, and the relationship does not exhibit any visually obvious curvature.

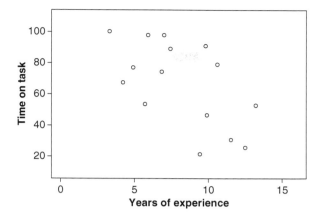

Figure 12.1 Simple linear regression raw data—scatterplot

Estimating a linear regression model for a nonlinear relationship is always incorrect. In some cases, a data transformation can be applied to the variables that will make the relationship linear, as described in a later section. The other possible solution to a nonlinear relationship is to estimate the relationship for only a certain portion of the independent variable. A simple example is the relationship between height and age. The relationship over a lifetime is clearly nonlinear, but from age four to fourteen it might be approximately linear. Similarly, language acquisition ebbs and flows, but over certain subsets or for a given treatment, it might be possible to model a linear relationship.

Once the researcher determines that a linear model is appropriate, the model itself can be estimated. The appropriateness of a straight line model will be further assessed by examining the residuals after estimating the regression equation. Therefore, the remaining three assumptions in this section are all described in terms of the residuals.

If the data cannot meet the equal variance assumption, hypothesis tests will be incorrect due to bias in the variance estimate. Additionally, homoscedasticity prevents any particular subset of the independent variable from exercising an unusually large influence on the coefficient estimates. The most typical way to assess the variance is through graphing the residuals.[2] The residuals are plotted on the vertical axis, and they are checked for a pattern or relationship against three other variables: the independent variable, the predicted values from the regression, and time. The last of these is generally referred to as a runs plot, as we described in Chapter 8. The residuals should not show any obvious pattern in their vertical spread for any of these plots. Figure 12.2 shows the results of our example data, and the residuals are appropriately random.

By way of contrast, Figure 12.3 displays problematic patterns of heteroscedasticity. The plots show two different, particularly exaggerated patterns to stress the effect, but residuals should never change dramatically in their variance. They should appear randomly in a horizontal band.

220 *Analyzing relationships*

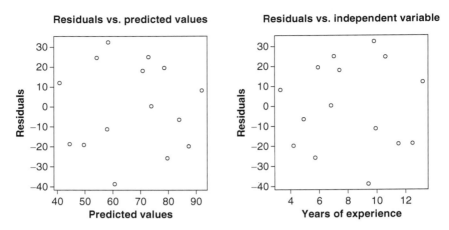

Figure 12.2 Residuals vs. predicted values and independent variable—scatterplot

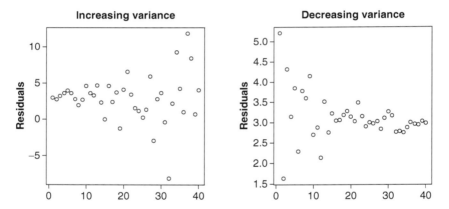

Figure 12.3 Scatterplots exhibiting heteroscedasticity—increasing and decreasing variance

In some cases, an alternative estimation technique called *weighted least squares* can correct for the problem of homoscedasticity. A formal derivation of weighted least squares is a specialized topic beyond the introduction to regression in this chapter, but the output and interpretation of the model are similar.

Independence of the residuals can be assessed from a plot of the *autocorrelation* of the residuals. Autocorrelation is the correlation of a series with its own lagged values, and for independent data, these values should all be near zero. Statistical software often generates such a plot automatically. The first autocorrelation can also be tested with a formal statistical procedure called the *Durbin-Watson test* (1950, 1951). The Durbin-Watson test statistic can range from zero to four and should be approximately equal to two when the residuals are independent. Values between 1.5 and 2.5 are generally acceptable, but the formal test should be consulted for borderline cases.

Finally, the normality of the residuals can be checked by reference to a QQ plot. Note that it is not necessary for the raw data itself to be normally distributed. However, the residuals should follow a normal distribution.[3] Linear regression is robust to mild departures from normality, and severe departures are typically noticeable in the preliminary plot of the data or from outlier detection procedures, which are covered in a later section of this chapter. Sample data that exhibit substantial departures from normality may preclude regression analysis, or at the very least require alternative methods such as robust or nonparametric regression.

Omnibus F-test

The output of a linear regression model comes in several parts. The first step is to test the statistical significance of the overall model. The mathematics of this step involve comparing sums of squared deviations and are equivalent to the calculations involved in ANOVA. For that reason, the highest level of results from a linear regression are presented in an ANOVA table (see Table 12.2).

There are only two noticeable differences from the ANOVA tables presented in Chapter 8. First and most importantly, the mean squared error (MS_E) is also known as variance of the regression (s^2). The square root of this number is the *standard error of the regression*, and it is used in the hypothesis tests for the individual coefficients. Second, the source of variation due to the model is often called the regression sum of squares instead of the model sum of squares. We label the source "Regression" in the table but retain the notation SS_M as a reminder that the calculation is identical to the ANOVA equations.

The F-statistic in this table tests the null hypothesis that the regression model is not useful in predicting the dependent variable. The goal of linear regression is to reject this null in favor of the alternative that consideration of the independent variable leads to a better prediction. For our data, the null hypothesis is that there is no relationship or predictive value of years of experience for the dependent measure of time on task. The ANOVA table for the example dataset appears in Table 12.3.

Because the p-value is less than 5%, the null hypothesis is rejected. The overall regression model is statistically significant, and we can conclude that years of

Table 12.2 ANOVA table—linear regression

Source	df	SS	MS	F	Sig.
Regression	1	SS_M	$MS_M = SS_M / 1$	$F = MS_M / MS_E$	p
Residual	$n-2$	SS_E	$MS_E = s^2 = SS_E / (n-2)$		
Total	$n-1$	SS_T			

Table 12.3 ANOVA table for regression example

Source	df	SS	MS	F	Sig.
Model	1	3556.5	3556.5	6.95	.021
Residual	13	6655.4	512.0		
Total	14				

experience have an effect on the speed of a translator. The ANOVA table of a regression model is not typically included in a final report but simply summarized in terms of the F-statistic and its significance.

Estimates for intercept and slope parameters

Estimating the regression parameters involves finding the beta coefficients (β_0 and β_1) that minimize the sum of the squared deviations between the data and the fitted regression line. The goal is to find the straight-line model that is closest to the observed data. The regression line can be thought of as a set of predictions, and solving for the best model can be thought of as selecting the intercept and slope that provide the best fit to the data.

Figure 12.4 illustrates this idea in four plots of the example data, with the x-axis representing the reported years of work experience (in years) and the y-axis as the length of time (in minutes) to complete the 250-word translation task. The top left plot depicts the raw data from the experiment. The top right plot shows a candidate regression line that is purposely drawn too low, with the majority of the data points clearly above the line. The lower left plot displays a line that has the wrong slope to match the data. Finally, the lower right plot provides the line of best fit. The graphs depict what the statistical analysis is trying to accomplish, namely to find the straight-line model that best aligns with the sample data. The line of best fit suggests that more experienced translators are generally able to complete the task more quickly because it slopes downward. More years of work experience appear to lead to less time-on-task.

Mathematically, regression is conducted by means of *ordinary least squares* estimation. The objective is to minimize the squared residuals, which are the vertical distance from the raw data to the regression line. One example residual has been drawn and labeled on the lower right graph of Figure 12.4.[4] The residual is the vertical distance between the actual data point and the prediction value of the regression line. Recall from earlier that the regression equation is $y_i = \beta_0 + \beta_1 x_i + \varepsilon_i$. For our example, β_1 explains the relationship between the independent variable of years of experience and the time needed to translate the passage. The equation can be rewritten to show that any individual residual is the difference between the observed value of the dependent variable and the predicted value of the dependent variable: $\varepsilon_i = y_i - \beta_0 - \beta_1 x_i$. Residuals can be found for each data point, squared, and then summed, resulting in the following expression for the sum of squared deviations:

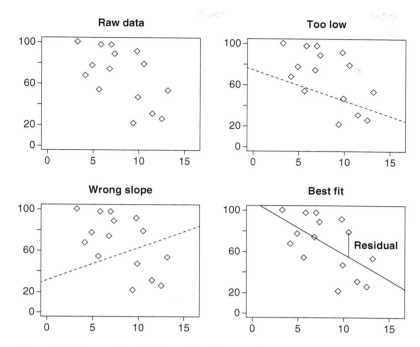

Figure 12.4 Scatterplot with line of best fit examples

$$\sum_{i=1}^{n}\left(y_i - \beta_0 - \beta_1 x_i\right)^2$$

The residuals represent the errors that the regression equation makes in predicting the dependent variable. Graphically, residuals are the vertical distance between the observed points and the straight-line model. Because they represent errors, the goal of estimating a linear regression model is to minimize the (squared) residuals. Specific to our example, we want to use years of experience to predict time on task with the minimum amount of error in our prediction. The final step is to find the beta coefficients that yield the minimum value for the sum of squared deviations. The solutions are given by the following formulas:

$$\beta_1 = \frac{\sum_{i=1}^{n}(x_i - \bar{x})(y_i - \bar{y})}{\sum_{i=1}^{n}(x_i - \bar{x})^2}$$

$$\beta_0 = \bar{y} - \beta_1 \bar{x}$$

The slope coefficient β_1 equals the covariance of the independent and dependent variables divided by the variance of the independent variable. The slope represents the relationship between the two variables. For every one unit increase in the independent variable, the dependent variable changes by β_1 units. For example, if the slope coefficient is −5.2 then each year of added experience is associated with 5.2 fewer minutes spent on the translation. The formula for the intercept estimate is provided, but in most cases the intercept is not of interest and should not be interpreted in a study's results. If the assumptions of the linear regression model are met, then these formulas provide the best possible regression line a statistical sense of being unbiased and with the lowest variance of any possible linear estimate.[5]

The standard error for each of the coefficients can also be calculated. The formulas involve the standard error of the regression. The resulting values can be used for hypothesis testing and for constructing a confidence interval around each of the point estimates. The coefficients can be tested individually for statistical significance using a t-test. The null hypothesis is that the parameter is equal to zero, while the alternative hypothesis states that the parameter is not equal to zero. These significance tests follow the overall F-test for the significance of the regression. Results of the parameter coefficient estimates will generally appear in a table that appears something like Table 12.4. The estimate for β_0 is referred to as the intercept, while β_1 is labeled by its variable name.

From this table, we can see that both the intercept and the slope coefficient are significant at the 5% level. Notice that the p-value of the t-test is identical to the p-value from the F-test; this will always be true in a simple linear regression because there is only one independent variable. More important for the applied researcher is an understanding of what these estimated coefficients represent in terms of a study's hypotheses and variables. The intercept represents the predicted outcome of the dependent variable if the independent variable were equal to zero. For the example data, this means that a translator with zero years of experience would take 109.1 minutes to translate the 250 words. The intercept should not be literally interpreted if a zero value of the independent variable is not possible or if data were not collected for values near zero. The second condition is certainly true in this case; the participant with the least amount of experience had just under four years of experience. In many cases, the intercept is not of interest to the researcher because the zero point is arbitrary or unlikely to be observed.

The interpretation of the slope coefficient is the predicted change in the dependent variable for a one unit increase in the value of the independent variable. In this case, one additional year of experience is expected to produce a 5.2 minute drop in the time needed to translate the 250 words.

Table 12.4 Parameter coefficient estimates

Coefficients	Estimate	SE	t-stat	Sig.
Intercept	109.1	16.98	6.42	<.0001
Experience	−5.2	1.96	−2.64	.021

The standard error of the coefficients can be used to create 95% confidence intervals for the parameters. The formula involves critical values from a t-distribution with $(n-2)$ degrees of freedom (one less for each of the two estimated parameters):

$$\beta_1 \pm t * SE$$

Therefore, the confidence interval for the slope coefficient is $-5.2 \pm 2.16 * 1.96 = [-9.39, -0.93]$. Full reporting of a regression model's estimates should include, at a minimum, the estimated parameter value, a 95% confidence interval, and the p-value.

Effect size and diagnostics

The measure of effect size for a regression model is the coefficient of determination (R^2), which was introduced in Chapter 11. In the previous discussion, we described it as the percentage of the variability accounted for due to the correlation between two variables. The interpretation in the regression setting is similar; R^2 measures the percentage of variability in the dependent variable that is explained by changes in the independent variable. The directionality of the relationship is one distinguishing feature between correlation and linear regression.

The R^2 value is calculated by dividing the model sum of squares by the total sum of squares. Therefore, hand calculation from the ANOVA table is quite simple, though computer output usually includes the R^2 measure separately. For our example data, the coefficient of determination is 34.8%, which can be interpreted as the amount of variability in time-on-task that can be explained by a translator's years of experience. The remaining variability is due to other factors outside the model.

One guideline for interpreting the magnitude of R^2 is provided by Cohen (1988), who suggests .02, .13, and .26 represent small, medium, and large effect sizes, respectively. Of all the effect sizes in this volume, the interpretation of the coefficient of determination should be least restrained by guidelines. Researchers clearly hope to explain a large portion of the variability, but this can be difficult in the social sciences. Rather than comparing to a particular number, a research report should be descriptive about the utility of the model for explaining and predicting outcomes. Comparisons should be made to other studies involving similar variables, and the discipline as a whole should always be striving to surpass previous understandings and increase the amount of variation that can be explained by ever-improving models.

Prediction

The first steps in the regression model involved estimation and hypothesis testing to demonstrate that the model could describe the particular sample. If the model is statistically significant, both at the overall level of the F-test and at the individual coefficient level of the *t*-tests, then it can also be used to predict outcomes. Retesting a regression model with new participants can powerfully demonstrate its utility.

Making a prediction of the dependent variable involves inputting values for the independent variables and calculating the expected value of the dependent variable. While the equation can be calculated for inputs of any size, a regression model has only been properly fitted to the input values that were present in the original estimation. The values of the independent variable for the dataset used in this chapter ranged from approximately 4 to 13 years of experience. Using any input value between those endpoints is an example of *interpolation*. A good regression model with a large coefficient of determination should supply useful predictions for interpolated values.

By contrast, *extrapolation* is the process of making predictions for independent variables outside of the original data. Such inference can be quite inaccurate if the linear relationship of the variables does not extend beyond the sampled data. A regression model is not designed for extrapolation or to make claims beyond the particular values that were used in the original estimation. If a different set of inputs is required, a follow-up study should be conducted with a new sample that can lead to estimation of the range of interest.

Data transformations

Estimating a linear regression model requires that the relationship between the independent and dependent variables is linear and constant over the relevant range of the independent variable. However, some nonlinear relationships between variables can still be modeled with linear regression after the application of appropriate data transformations. A transformation can be applied to the dependent variable, or all of the independent variables can be transformed using the same mathematical formula. Whenever possible, the transformations should be suggested by theories about the relationships among the variables. However, trial-and-error is a common and acceptable method of exploring possible transformations of the data.

The process of finding the best model is iterative, involving the estimation of several linear regression models in order to find the transformation that provides the best fitting model for the sample data. However, the purpose is not to search for the model with the best *F*-statistic but to find the model that has the best linear relationship. Transformations change the hypothesis being tested and complicate interpretation of output, so they should be employed only when necessary due to nonlinearities.

In the case of simple linear regression, the need for a data transformation should be evident from examining a scatterplot of the raw data, because the data will exhibit a curvilinear relationship. For multiple regression, a linear model can be conducted as a first step to assess the fit based on the residuals. If the residuals are approximately normal with homogeneous variance, then a transformation of the independent variables can sometimes improve the linearity of the sample data.

The three most common adjustments to the independent variables are the logarithmic, square root, and reciprocal transformations. The logarithmic and square root transformations refer to performing the stated calculation on every value of the independent variable. The reciprocal transformation calculates the number one divided by each of the observed values of the independent variable; this transformation will reverse the order of the data. All three of these transformations eliminate positive skew and can improve linearity. They can be applied to situations in which the scatterplot of a simple linear model exhibits a concave relationship. The left side of Figure 12.5 displays a concave relationship, in which the growth rate of the dependent variable tapers as the independent variable increases.

The opposite situation from concavity is convexity, which is presented on the right side of Figure 12.5. For this nonlinearity, a *polynomial transformation* can be employed. A polynomial model involves squaring the raw values of the independent variable, or even raising it to a higher power in some cases. A polynomial regression typically includes all lower powers of the variable as well, so the data in the scatterplot could be modeled with a regression equation that included both a linear and quadratic term.

If an initial estimation of the raw data results in residuals that exhibit heterogeneous variance or unequal variances, taking the logarithm of the dependent variable may also improve the fit of the linear model. Transformations of the dependent variable should be avoided when the residuals exhibit homogeneous variances and are approximately normal because the transformation will alter both of these traits.

Selecting the proper data transformation requires exploring the data and estimating several different models to find the one that provides the best fit. The goal is to uncover the regression model that results in appropriately random, normally distributed residuals with approximately equal variance.

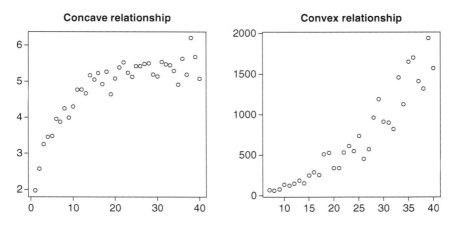

Figure 12.5 Scatterplots implying a need for transformation

Multiple linear regression

The simple linear regression model considers only one explanatory or independent variable. In many cases, however, a researcher will want to consider several explanatory variables simultaneously. In our example, time on task could be a function of not only years of experience but also typing speed and completion of a university degree program. For this situation, the regression model is expanded to accommodate k multiple predictor variables and is referred to as multiple linear regression.

Assumption of no multicollinearity

For a multiple linear regression, all four of the previously discussed assumptions of linear regression must be met. Additionally, the independent variables must not exhibit *multicollinearity*. This term describes variables that are linearly related to each other, meaning that some relationship exists between the variables. Either they increase together or decrease together and therefore exhibit a high degree of correlation.

Violations of this assumption do not affect the F-test for the overall regression model. However, violations do alter the estimation of coefficients for the independent variables that are correlated with each other. Estimates may change dramatically due to small changes in the data, which causes large errors in predictions and makes the model useless for extrapolation or application to new data sets. Additionally, the standard errors of the coefficients will be inflated, which means t-tests will be less likely to reject the null hypothesis of no relationship between the affected independent variables and the dependent variable (a Type II error). In fact, one indicator of possible multicollinearity is a significant F-test for the overall regression model but no significant t-tests for individual coefficients in the same model.

In the extreme case, two variables could exhibit a perfect linear relationship and estimation of the regression equation would be impossible. An example would be to include two variables that measure the same phenomenon on different scales, such as including the temperature in Fahrenheit and Celsius as if they were two different variables. Because these variables represent exactly the same underlying data, they should not both be included as predictor variables. Including just one of these measures will improve the model, but including both will destroy it. Multicollinearity can also occur for inversely-related variables. For example, the number of questions answered correctly on some test and the number of questions answered incorrectly on the same test would exhibit perfect (negative) collinearity: every unit increase in one measure would lead to a unit decrease in the other. Perfect multicollinearity can also occur in the case of dummy variables, which will be discussed more fully in a subsequent section. These three extreme cases are easily fixed by removing one or more variables from the model.

In less extreme cases, variables might exhibit strong but less than perfect correlation. For example, age and years of work experience will have a relatively high correlation within any given sample. Some individuals may be outliers, perhaps by starting to work in a given field at a very young age, by changing careers, or by delaying entry into the work force, but in the general population there will be a high degree of correlation between these two variables. A participant in a study with many years of work experience will likely be older than a participant with fewer years of work experience. Therefore, the two variables are highly correlated and should not both be included in the study. The research question, theories, and previous research literature can guide which variable truly influences the dependent measure. In cases where the correlation is quite high, the best solution is again often to omit one of the variables from the analysis, due to their high degree of overlap.

One method for identifying collinear variables is to calculate all of the pairwise correlations among the independent variables. Ideally, the calculated correlation coefficients would all be close to zero, or at least not statistically significant. One common standard is to consider any correlation greater than .4 as potentially problematic. Computing a correlation matrix can help to prevent estimation of poor regression models. Furthermore, including the correlation matrix in a research report is generally a good idea to convince the reader that the regression assumptions are adequately met.

While the correlation matrix is quite effective at identifying problematic pairs of variables, other statistical tools are also available for general cases. One common detection tool is the *variance inflation factor* (VIF). The VIF of a given variable is found by using it as the dependent variable in a separate regression that considers all of the other original independent variables as regressors. The R^2 of that preliminary regression is then used to calculate VIF with the following equation: $VIF_i = \frac{1}{1-R_i^2}$. As the fit of this regression model approaches 100%, the VIF increases; higher levels of R^2 imply a larger VIF, which suggests a high degree of linear relationship among the independent variables. Therefore, large VIFs are a sign of a multicollinearity and a poor regression model. Any VIF larger than 10 bears further examination and is very likely problematic. Some texts suggest that a VIF greater than 5 indicates significant multicollinearity. As with any general numerical guideline, these levels should not be used as exact cutoffs (R. O'Brien 2007), but they do help suggest situations that bear further investigation.

Multicollinearity is most commonly remedied by omission of one or more variables. If the omitted variable was truly redundant, then nothing is lost from this alteration. However, if the variable is an important factor in predicting the dependent variable, its omission will result in biased estimation. Another possible solution is collecting a larger sample, which could improve the power of the coefficient estimates. *Ridge regression* is an advanced statistical method that can also be used in the case of multicollinearity. Finally, the independent variables can be standardized by calculating their z-scores and using those transformed variables as regressors in the linear regression model.

Hypothesis testing

The first hypothesis test for a multiple regression is an F-test. The null hypothesis is that the independent variables collectively are not associated with the dependent variable. Put another way, the null hypothesis asserts that the independent variables are not useful for prediction. Because the F-test considers all of the coefficients simultaneously, the numerator degrees of freedom are the number of explanatory variables.

To provide an example of multiple regression, the example of this chapter is now expanded to consider additional variables. The typing speed of the participants (measured in words per minute) and whether or not the participant has earned a college degree are included as additional predictor variables. The variable for completion of the degree is assigned the value one if the participant reports earning a degree and zero otherwise. For simplicity, we do not consider the possibility of graduate degrees or other training in this example. This is an example of a dummy variable, a type of variable that is discussed in a later section.

The results of the ANOVA are statistically significant ($F[3, 11] = 11.48$, $p = .001$). The results of the overall significance of the regression can be presented in this way in the text of a research report, simply as the result of the F-test and corresponding p-value. However, this result does not guarantee that every one of the independent variables is a statistically significant predictor variable. Therefore, the second step is to conduct a t-test for each of the individual coefficients. The results are displayed in Table 12.5.

The independent measure of years of experience is still statistically significant, as is the completion of a degree program. Words-per-minute (WPM), however, is not significantly related to the time needed to complete the translation task. The p-value of the t-test implies that the data do not present enough evidence to conclude that the coefficient is different from zero.

The values of the coefficients can be interpreted in the same manner as for simple linear regression. A one unit increase in experience leads to a decrease of 4.68 minutes in time, while participants who have completed a degree program take 36.39 fewer minutes, on average. Because the variable WPM is not statistically significant, the magnitude of the coefficient should not be interpreted.

Statistical software will also provide 95% confidence intervals around these point estimates. The reporting section at the end of this chapter shows the table that would typically appear in a research report. The format is similar to Table 12.5 but includes confidence intervals to aid interpretation.

Table 12.5 Individual coefficient t-test example data

Coefficient	Estimate	SE	t–stat	Sig.
Intercept	205.27	86.42	2.375	.037
Experience	−4.68	1.36	−3.437	.006
WPM	−1.01	1.08	−0.929	.373
Degree	−36.39	8.72	−4.17	.002

Effect size

In multiple regression, the value of R^2 is inflated by the inclusion of additional independent variables. With each new variable added to a regression model, the R^2 cannot get smaller and may get larger. Therefore, the effect size measure would be biased in favor of larger models. To account for this bias, the usual formula is corrected and the resulting figure is referred to as the *adjusted R^2*:

$$R^2_{Adj} = 1 - \left(1 - R^2\right)\left(\frac{n-1}{n-k-1}\right)$$

The original formulation of the coefficient of determination is used in the formula, along with the sample size and the number of independent variables. When reporting the results of a multiple linear regression, the adjusted value should always be used. The resulting figure can be interpreted in the usual manner.

Model selection

In exploratory research, the variables to include in a regression model may not be evident from an existing theory. Alternatively, a number of competing theories and models might exist, all proposing variables that should be considered influential on some dependent variable. One useful tool in these cases is *stepwise regression*, which aids in selecting the set of variables that are most useful in predicting the value of the dependent variable. Related techniques for model selection include *forward selection* and *backward elimination*.

A preliminary step in stepwise regression is specifying an acceptable level of Type I error. Because the model selection process is often conducted in an environment of greater uncertainty, 10% is a common and acceptable choice in place of the usual 5% (Draper and Smith 1998). Once the significance level is specified, the first step of the procedure is to estimate all of the possible models with one independent variable and select the independent variable with the smallest p-value (provided that it is below the specified level of significance).

The subsequent step considers all of the available variables for possible addition to create a two-variable regression model. The one with the smallest p-value is added to the model, and the variable included from the first step is checked again for its statistical significance. Its p-value will change when the second variable is added, and if it is no longer statistically significant it is removed from the model. This process is repeated algorithmically, considering all possible candidates for inclusion and double checking previously added variables for possible removal if their p-values exceed the threshold. Eventually, the stepwise procedure will result in a regression model with the largest possible number of statistically significant independent variables.

Forward selection is a nearly identical procedure to stepwise selection. The only difference is that once a variable is included in the model it is never removed. Stepwise regression, with its more stringent requirement for inclusion, generally produces a superior model. Backward elimination takes a philosophically opposite approach to model selection by estimating the model first with all of the candidate variables. The variable with the largest nonsignificant *p*-value is eliminated, and the new model is estimated. The process is repeated until all of the variables are significant.

Stepwise selection, forward selection, and backward elimination are all informative tools in the process of model selection. However, the statistical algorithm is completely data driven and atheoretical. They are completely dependent upon the candidate independent variables that are included in the dataset. The responsibility of selecting likely causal variables rests with the researcher and should be based on previous literature and theories to the greatest extent possible.

Dummy variables

Sometimes a linear regression model will include categorical independent variables; an example in the chapter's fictional dataset is completion of a college degree. Demographic variables are often included in this way, such as including a participant's biological sex as one factor in a larger regression model. Annual salary can be turned into a categorical variable by defining several response ranges. Other simple binary variables could include whether a respondent has completed a college degree. Sometimes these variables are interesting in their own right, and other times they are included as control variables to allow for a regression model to focus on other relationships.

Categorical variables are included in a regression model through the use of *dummy variables*, which are defined as independent variables that are either valued as zero or one. Estimation with these variables implies different parallel lines in the regression model. Categorical variables with more than two possible values can also be included with dummy variables by using one less dummy variable than the number of categories. For instance, if an income variable was defined to have four categories, then there would be three dummy variables.

Outliers

The inclusion of outliers in a dataset can substantially alter the estimation of a regression model. A point sufficiently far away from the bulk of the observations can cause significant mis-estimation of the slope coefficient. This problem is exacerbated by outliers in the independent variable. Figure 12.6 demonstrates this problem by showing a random set of data on the left that should not even be modeled by linear regression because no apparent linear relationship exists. The scatterplot on the right includes one significant outlier along with an estimated regression line that is statistically significant ($F[1, 49] = 4.2, p = .046$). A researcher who estimated the model without checking for outliers would make a significant error in drawing conclusions. Any predictions made from this model would be meaningless.

As the discussion of outliers so far implies, graphical analysis can be one tool for spotting outliers. Two statistical techniques are also widely recommended.

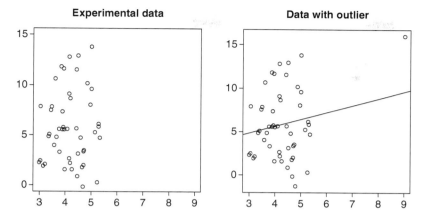

Figure 12.6 Scatterplot example with outlier

First, *studentized residuals* can be calculated by dividing each of the residuals by a measure of its standard deviation. The term refers to the structure of Student's *t*-test, in which a point estimate of the mean is divided by a measure of standard deviation. Any studentized residuals with values greater than three can be considered outliers. A second tool for identifying influential points is *Cook's distance*, which considers the change in the regression model's estimation when each point is removed from the dataset. The distance is measured for every point in the dataset, usually resulting in a graph of the results. Any strict cutoff would be controversial and ill-advised when it comes to assessing the magnitude of Cook's distance. However, values that are much larger than the rest of the observations would be considered outliers, and some authors recommend that any value larger than one is an outlier.

The problems of outlier detection and handling are challenging and complex.[6] Points that have been identified as outliers should be inspected for possible data handling errors. If a large number of outliers are present in the model, a data transformation might be necessary, possibly to include truncation or winsorization. Nonparametric or other robust estimation might also be explored as possible alternatives. Any dataset that is suspected of problems with outliers may need attention from a skilled statistician.

Advanced regression techniques

The model of linear regression can be extended in at least three different ways. First, linear regression can be viewed as one particular instance of the more broadly applicable *generalized linear model* (Nelder and Wedderburn 1972). The advantage of the model is its ability to predict discrete dependent variables, including binary decisions and frequencies. Second, mixed effects models allow for the incorporation of random effects and repeated measures; these regression models are capable of estimating more complicated ANOVA models. Third, non-parametric regression techniques require fewer assumptions than the standard linear regression model. All three of these extensions are thoroughly described by Faraway (2006). For translation and interpreting (T&I) studies, the three most likely applicable methods are mixed effects models, binary logistic regression, and Poisson regression, which are outlined in this final section.

Mixed effects models

In various places, we have mentioned that underlying all of the parametric tests in this volume is the general linear model of statistics. What this means in practical terms is that the distinction between ANOVA and regression is arbitrary. We have described a few places where the border is blurry: dummy variables allow comparison of groups in a regression model and ANCOVA permits inclusion of continuous covariates in ANOVA models.

A mixed effects regression model, also known as a multi-level linear model, is a powerful model for estimating complex relationships. The estimation is mixed because it includes both fixed and random effects in predicting the dependent variable. The influence of a fixed effect variable on the dependent variable is modeled as systematic; the relationship is assumed to hold across all observations in the dataset. Random effects have an idiosyncratic effect on the dependent variable. The most common example of a random effect is a participant variable; each subject in a study is assumed to have a unique response relationship to the treatment variables. Furthermore, a different sample would yield a different model for that relationship.

Another way of describing a fixed effect is that the variable includes an exhaustive list of the levels of the variable; if the research project were repeated, the same levels of the variable would be used. Random effects are variables whose levels are drawn randomly from a larger population of possibilities. The levels of the variable would differ if the experiment were repeated.

The assumptions necessary for linear regression (i.e., linearity, homoscedasticity, independence, and normality) all apply to mixed effects models as well. Furthermore, the independent variables must not be collinear. For random effects, the independence of observations is violated because multiple observations at each level is a necessary part of the model. Independence among levels of fixed effects variables is still an important assumption, however.

In a mixed effects model, the random effects can be modeled as having a random intercept, a random slope, or both. In a random intercept model, each level of the random effect variable has a different baseline of the dependent variable for comparison. At the same time, the influence of the fixed effects is assumed to be the same. In practical terms, every unit change in the fixed effect variable produces the same reaction for each subject. The model can be expanded to include a random slope coefficient. In that case, every level of the random effect can have a different reaction to changes in the fixed effect treatments. In most cases, a random effect due to the subjects in a study should be modeled with both a random intercept and slope. After all, each person will have an idiosyncratic baseline level of the dependent measure as well as a unique reaction to the fixed effect variables. Furthermore, mixed effects models without random slopes have a higher propensity for Type I errors.

Significance testing in a mixed effects model is conducted by a *likelihood ratio test*, which results in the reporting of a χ^2-statistic. A likelihood ratio test compares two models, one with a particular variable and one without it. The test concludes whether including the variable improves the fit to the data. If a greater portion of variability in the dependent variable is explained in the model with the variable, then it is significant.

Mixed effects regression models have several advantages over repeated measures ANOVA designs. Random intercept and slope coefficients allow for a more precise fit of the model to the data. Regression models allow the incorporation of more variables and are more powerful than factorial ANOVA designs in most cases. Mixed effects models can also be estimated even with missing data for some measurements and for unbalanced designs. The flexibility to include a variety of variable types in the regression equation simultaneously aids understanding of more complex relationships.

The drawback of mixed effects regression models is their complexity. The problem is partly the inherent challenge of understanding the model and interpreting results. Additionally, a large sample size is preferred, and the assumptions of the regression model must be met. Any violations only compound the errors and problems of interpretation in the results. The most likely applications of these models is in corpus-based or eye tracking studies because both produce large sets of data (e.g., Baayen, Feldman, and Schreuder 2006; Balling, Hvelplund, and Sjørup 2014). This volume emphasizes the most basic and widely applicable statistical tools, and advanced topics like mixed effects models can be afforded only a brief overview. Balling (2008) provides a further introduction to the topic.

Binary logistic regression

In some cases, the goal of research is to predict a binary outcome, such as whether a candidate passes or fails a certification exam, whether an admitted student enrolls in a university program, or whether a person votes in an election. Gries and Wulff (2012) suggest several examples of binary choice in the translation process, including synonym choice and word order in various optional situations. In any of these cases, the dependent variable takes only the values zero and one. Modeling a dichotomous dependent variable can be accomplished with *binary logistic regression*. The goals of the regression model remain estimation and prediction, and multiple predictors can still be examined for their relationship to the dependent variable.

However, there are five ways in which binary logistic regression differs from ordinary least squares regression. First, the residuals will not be normally distributed, so the estimation and interpretation of the model's results need to be adjusted. Second, the model does not make specific predictions about the outcome of the dependent variable. Instead, the logistic regression model uses a *logit transformation* so that the predicted value is the probability of the outcome. The regression model's parameters can be utilized to make predictions outside of the sample in terms of the probability of observing either possible outcome.

While the first two differences lay in the model's mathematics; the remaining three differences are consequences of this changed structure. The third difference from multiple regression is that the model must be estimated by a process called *maximum likelihood estimation*; in practical terms this just means that no formulas exist for the beta coefficients. The model must be estimated by a computer algorithm. Fourth, the overall model's F-test and the individual coefficient t-tests are both typically replaced with χ^2-statistics. Decisions about statistical significance can be made from the p-values of these tests. Fifth, the typical R^2 formula needs to be replaced by a different measure of effect size. A number of competing measures exist, and they are all referred to as pseudo-R^2. When reporting results, an author should be specific about the mathematical choices made in estimating a binary logistic regression model, because so many competing methods exist.

Anyone familiar with multiple linear regression will be able to interpret the output of a binary logistic regression model when presented in a research report. For those researchers interested in designing and estimating such a model, some further discussion of the mathematics of binary logistic regression is provided by Gries and Wulff (2012). They also demonstrate the estimation of a binary logistic regression model with various types of predictor variables. Collett (2002) provides complete coverage of binary models.

Poisson regression

Frequencies or count variables are a versatile and widely used type of measurement in T&I studies. Corpus studies count word occurrences, translation studies can count errors or pauses, and interpreting studies can count disfluencies, to give just a few examples. These variables pose no issues as independent variables in a multiple regression; Balling (2008) presents several models with the logarithm of frequency as a predictor variable of reaction time, for example. *Poisson regression* is a technique that uses a frequency variable as the dependent variable.

A Poisson regression model is also known as a log-linear model, because the independent variables are used to predict the logarithm of the frequency. Like binary logistic regression model, Poisson regression is an instance of the generalized linear model. Formulas for estimating the beta coefficients cannot be provided, and it is only thanks to modern statistical software that the model can be used with ease. Hypothesis testing and the statistical significance of the overall model are tested with χ^2-statistics, and the goodness-of-fit is measured by either the Pearson χ^2-statistic or a deviance statistic, both of which are computations involving the model's residuals.

Poisson regression has received little attention in the T&I literature to date. One recent example is Guerberof (2014), who employs Poisson regression in a study of post-editing behavior in various conditions. The dependent variable is the number of errors, and the regression compares the error count for translators who worked with a translation memory, machine translation, or human translation conditions. The model also includes the text length as an offset, which is an independent variable whose coefficient is constrained to equal one. This controls for the influence of text length on the number of errors.

A significant advantage of using Poisson regression is the ability to use the actual frequency of occurrence in the model, rather than artificially creating categories of high and low usage. This shift also improves the utility of the model for prediction purposes. The ability to include multiple independent variables is a further benefit of modeling count data in a regression model rather than with a χ^2-test. As the quantitative rigor of T&I studies continues to increase, we anticipate Poisson regression will receive considerably more attention. See Cameron

---

A sample of fifteen participants translated a 250-word passage. The time required to complete the task was measured in minutes. It was anticipated that completion time would be a function of the translators' years of experience and typing speed (measured in words-per-minute). Additionally, completion of a university-level degree program was expected to influence the time necessary to complete the task. A multiple linear regression model was estimated to test the significance of these three independent variables.

Estimation of the model showed a statistically significant relationship between the independent variables and completion time ($F[3, 11] = 11.48, p = .001$). The model accounted for approximately 69% of the variation in the number of minutes spent completing the translation, which represents a substantial effect size. Graphical analysis of the residuals revealed no significant departures from normality or concerns for heteroscedasticity. Furthermore, estimation of Cook's distance did not suggest any outlying observations with undue influence, and none of the studentized residuals exceeded 2.5 in absolute value.

Table A provides estimates for the predictor variables. More years of experience and degree completion were statistically significant, and both led to declines in time on task. Typing speed was not a statistically significant predictor.

Table A

		95% CI		
	Estimate	Lower	Upper	p
Intercept	205.27	15.05	395.49	.037
Experience	−4.68	−7.68	−1.68	.006
WPM	−1.01	−3.37	1.37	.373
Degree	−36.39	−55.58	−17.19	.002

The magnitude of the effect of degree completion is large, with an average decline of more than 36 minutes for translators who had completed a degree. With less than a 5 minute reduction for each year of experience, degree completion has an effect comparable to more than 7 years of professional experience.

Figure 12.7 Example of complete reporting of study results including regression results

and Trivedi (2013) for a comprehensive treatment of regression with frequency data or Tang, He, and Tu (2012) for a general view of categorical data analysis.

Reporting

This section provides an example of how the results of the example study could be reported. Regression results can be presented in various formats, and the overall goal is clarity in communicating the main statistical results of a study. As usual, point estimates, confidence intervals, exact p-values, and effect size estimates constitute a minimum set of statistics to be included.

The description here is brief, and further interpretation would be provided in the discussion section of the paper. Descriptive statistics, including correlation measures and possibly even a correlation matrix of all the independent variables, would also be provided prior to estimation of the regression model.

Notes

1 Because the terms are so similar, multiple linear regression is sometimes confused with *multivariate linear regression*. The latter term describes a model with more than one dependent variable and receives very little application in social science research. The difference is stark: terminologically, mathematically, and logically. We do not discuss multivariate regression; the interested reader can consult Tabachnik and Fidell (2012).
2 A formal test called the *Goldfeld-Quandt test* is recommended by some sources, but a visual check of the residuals is often adequate.
3 Technically, the dependent variable needs to exhibit a normal distribution conditional on a given level of the independent variable. However, that jargon-heavy distinction is more easily summarized and checked by examining the distribution of the residuals.
4 This line would not be drawn when reporting data, but is included here to illustrate this concept.
5 This is proved in the Gauss-Markov theorem.
6 Aguinis, Gottfredson, and Joo (2013) list 39 different identification techniques and 20 different ways to handle outliers.

Part V
Interpreting results

13 Interpreting results

Once data collection and analysis are complete, researchers will inevitably desire to share the results of a research project with the greater academic community. Conference presentations and posters, articles, manuscripts, book chapters, and monographs are all potential venues to disseminate research. Each outlet has its own specific academic standards and requirements, but most require evaluation by experts, peer reviewers, editors, publishers, or some combination thereof. This process is the same regardless of the research methodology used; however, clear communication of quantitative research is imperative so that the analytical work can be critically evaluated based on its merits. Research that is improperly reported can make interpreting the results difficult. Furthermore, unclear or muddled descriptions may raise questions related to ethics and research integrity.

In this final chapter, we discuss research integrity, particularly as it relates to research reporting. Specifically, we address research misconduct, conflicts of interest, and questions related to authorship. We also revisit the concepts of effect size and statistical significance, emphasizing that the interpretation of study results must consider both to reach appropriate conclusions. We end the volume with a discussion of the limitations of quantitative analysis and generalization, noting especially that researchers must exercise caution when interpreting results and attempting to generalize to the larger population. While a powerful tool, statistical analysis is not the only approach to research, and researchers must recognize the limits to its use.

Research integrity

As discussed in the broader coverage of ethics in Chapter 2, research integrity is often associated with the later stages of a research project, usually discussed most explicitly in relation to the reporting and dissemination of research. Professional associations and research institutions provide guidance for researchers about ethical practices in the form of codes of conduct. However, the ethical principles related to *research misconduct* are often provided as prohibitions rather than best practices. The Federal Research Misconduct Policy of the United States Office of Science and Technology Policy lists and defines the following three types of research misconduct:

- *Fabrication* is making up data or results and recording or reporting them.
- *Falsification* is manipulating research materials, equipment, or processes, or changing or omitting data or results such that the research is not accurately represented in the research record.
- *Plagiarism* is the appropriation of another person's ideas, processes, results, or words without giving appropriate credit.
- Research misconduct does not include honest error or differences of opinion.

(2000: 76262, emphasis added)

Many professional organizations and research institutions rely on these definitions to investigate and classify fraudulent research. Some entities use this list to constrain specific types of behavior and also expand the list to cover specific, additional situations. For example, the American Medical Association in its *AMA Manual of Style* describes this U.S. standard as:

> [applying] to US government-funded research, and academic and research institutions that accept government funding must comply with the definition and associated regulations. However, this definition and associated regulations have become de facto rules for US academic and other research institutions and are applied to any work done by their employees or under their aegis regardless of the source of funding.
>
> (Iverson et al. 2007: 157)

While these three types of misconduct are defined specifically in the U.S. context, Israel (2015) notes that such misconduct forms part of various codes of conduct throughout the world. Researchers should familiarize themselves with their respective national level and institutional classifications of research misconduct to ensure compliance.

Allegations of scientific fraud must be substantiated with evidence, and the researcher must demonstrate willful negligence of ethical principles, as implied by the last bullet point of the Federal Register definition. To illustrate the wide range of behavior that can constitute research misconduct, Levin (2011) provides five case studies drawn from his editorial experience with various APA publications, including potential cases of data fabrication, uncomfortably close paraphrases, unattributed translations of previous works, and inadvertent and blatant plagiarism. These examples illustrate the varying gravity of the offense as well as some of the consequences or sanctions that can be imposed. Scholars should be intrinsically motivated to conduct ethical research; however, sanctions might provide additional extrinsic impetus to behave appropriately. Unethical behavior can be sanctioned in a variety of ways depending on each specific case, but penalties could include the following: corrections or retractions of articles; university-imposed sanctions; required oversight by university officials of all research activities; preclusion from grant-funding opportunities on a temporary or permanent basis; dismissal from research or academic positions; or even imprisonment.[1]

In quantitative research *fabrication* constitutes the creation of fictitious datasets or analyses that were never collected or conducted. For example, a researcher who conducts a research study with a relatively small sample and then manufactures fictitious participants to make the study appear larger would be committing fabrication. *Falsification*, in contrast, describes a situation in which a researcher changes data that were obtained in a study in order to support his or her hypothesis. To illustrate this idea, suppose a researcher has collected data and run the appropriate statistical analysis and found nonsignificant results. If the researcher were to change, trim, or omit data for the purpose of obtaining a significant result, then he or she would be conducting falsification.

The last example should not be read as a blanket prohibition on the practice of trimming data. Some statistical procedures, such as the trimmed mean, are scientifically sound methods for improving estimation, and removing outliers can be conducted in an ethical and appropriate manner. As Hubert and Wainer (2011) describe, researchers must be honest in reporting how they have handled outliers in sample data. McArdle (2011: 334) further attests that the impact of their removal from the data should be reported. See Chapter 5 in this volume for more information on statistical methods for trimming and methods by which this practice should be reported.

Sterba (2006) describes several ways that misconduct can be classified. The author states that *overt* misconduct is detectable by methodological reviewers, who can often spot this type of activity when reading the results section of an article. Peer reviewers or referees are used as a safeguard against this type of scientific fraud; however, *covert* misconduct, as the name implies, is often difficult to spot in the reported results. The review process is an important part of research dissemination to help detect and deter scientific missteps. Should an editor or reviewer suspect that either type of misconduct has been committed, many journals include in their submission policies the right of the journal to request the study's data for examination. This practice is particularly common in the hard sciences to verify statistical results; however, there is an increasing call for transparency in related disciplines. Consequently, researchers should strive for ethical practice throughout the research process to avoid any missteps.

The third type of research misconduct listed in the Federal Register is *plagiarism*. In addition to detecting methodological and conceptual issues, peer reviewers also may note passages in a manuscript that are inappropriately cited or unattributed. Software packages are available to check manuscripts automatically for passages that are similar to previously published work. These tools provide a quick reference for editors and can corroborate suspected cases of unattributed use of previous research. While these tools cannot redress plagiarism of ideas or processes since they focus solely on previously published work, they do help serve as an initial safeguard to blatant cases of plagiarism. As a general rule, manuscript authors should cite any research that has informed their work, including papers written by the authors themselves.

The concept of *self-plagiarism* is the subject of considerable discussion with regard to publishing practices. Researchers are subject matter experts and often publish on similar topics. Consequently, their research may rely on their own previous description or development of constructs, concepts, instruments, etc. On the one hand, authors may claim to be the originator of the work and should be able to reuse previously authored material. On the other hand, non-attribution of this work may result in significant overlap in published work, which could border on a duplicate publication or infringe on copyright. To give two examples, the editors of *ACS Nano* and *Research Policy* have written editorials on the dangers of self-plagiarism and the challenges of upholding research integrity in their editorial capacities. Both outline the pressures of academic publishing in tension with "an already overloaded peer-review and editorial system" (*ACS Nano* 2012: 1) and the impact that questionable publishing practices can have on research quality (Martin 2013). In short, authors are advised to carefully tailor their publishing practices in line with current publishing standards and consult with publishing venues should questions arise.

Conflicts of interest

The three previously cited types of research misconduct are not the only reporting missteps with which authors should concern themselves; authors must also consider and divulge any conflicts of interest that may impact their study. Broadly speaking, a *conflict of interest* "occurs when an individual's objectivity is potentially, but not necessarily, comprised by a desire for prominence, professional advancement, financial gain, or successful outcome" (Iverson et al. 2007: 168). Researchers have two duties related to conflict of interest: to separate themselves from any position in which they cannot remain unbiased and to disclose the existence of any potential conflicts of interest when reporting.

As noted in the introduction to the volume, translation and interpreting (T&I) studies are increasingly collaborative in their investigations. Researchers working in areas that have commercial implications for quality, product, and process improvement may attract the attention of industry stakeholders. This increased attention is not inherently bad; in fact, it may lead to research partnerships in which scholars gain access to participants, tools, resources, or information that was previously out of reach. However, researchers must remain cognizant of possible conflicts that could yield biased results. Gile (2000: 311) notes the potential conflicts of interest from practicing conference interpreters conducting research in the field when remuneration of these two professions is often skewed in favor of the professional interpreter.

Institutional and granting agencies all have specific requirements related to disclosure, management, and mitigation of conflicts of interest. Israel (2015: 168–174) provides an overview of ethical considerations that must be accounted for when conflicts of interests arise. Collaborative research with colleagues, who do not have a conflict of interest, can help prevent ethical lapses and provide further assurance to the research community that the research was conducted in an ethical manner.

Authorship

As noted in previous sections, collaborative research is increasingly common in T&I studies. When multiple people lend their expertise to the same study, the need arises to attribute their individual contributions to the research project appropriately. Many organizations and journals have adopted the definition provided by the International Committee of Medical Journal Editors (ICMJE) on what constitutes authorship. Their recommendation is based on four criteria:

- Substantial contributions to the conception or design of the work; or the acquisition, analysis, or interpretation of data for the work; AND
- drafting the work or revising it critically for important intellectual content; AND
- final approval of the version to be published; AND
- agreement to be accountable for all aspects of the work in ensuring that questions related to the accuracy or integrity of any part of the work are appropriately investigated and resolved.

(ICMJE 2016)

In addition to these four criteria, the guidelines state the importance of the author's ability to identify contributions of co-authors in the work and to attest to their integrity. The ICMJE stresses that these criteria should not be used to preclude people from the opportunity to take part in the drafting or final approval of the manuscript; however, individuals who are listed as authors ought to meet these four criteria. The guidelines provide further guidance on how other individuals may be acknowledged for providing support despite not being an author of the manuscript. Overall, the guidelines provide a framework within which authors can discuss the contributions of research team members or colleagues.

Such editorial guidance, however, is not how authors always behave (Albert and Wager 2003: 32). Flouting of these guidelines can prove problematic, and may lead to two additional concerns related to research integrity: *ghost authorship* and *gift authorship*. These practices arguably constitute deception or a potential conflict of interest. In the case of ghost authorship, someone who wrote part of the manuscript is not attributed in the author list. Gift or *honorary authorship*, in contrast, is the attribution of authorship to someone who did not take substantial part in the conception or drafting of the research. This situation may arise in an attempt to garner favor from publishers by including a particular scholar; likewise, publication lists may become inflated if researchers agree to include each other on articles that the other has written. Both practices degrade the integrity of authorship and obfuscate the contributions of scholars to the field. Baskin and Gross's editorial (2011) describes attempts by the journal of *Neurology* to strengthen the ICMJE recommendations to maintain the integrity of authorship in research publications. Their straightforward ethical suggestion is to give proper credit when it is due. This advice would be well heeded by all researchers.[2]

Statistical significance, confidence intervals, and effect sizes

Throughout this volume, we have placed considerable emphasis on sound research design and appropriate statistical analysis. The presentation has focused on the dominant model of quantitative analysis in applied research: null hypothesis statistical testing (NHST). This analytical method has been strongly criticized at times for its misapplications and theoretical problems as well as for the misunderstandings of practitioners. Nickerson (2000) comprehensively reviews both sides of this argument and concludes that despite potential pitfalls NHST can effectively improve the inferences drawn from data.

A *p*-value of less than 5% is usually deemed statistically significant. The meaning of such a finding is that under the assumption of the null hypothesis, the probability of observing the test statistic or a more extreme result is less than 5%. No additional interpretation of the results should be made based on a hypothesis test. Furthermore, the validity of this conclusion rests on the satisfaction of the test's assumptions.

For example, in a regression analysis design (see Chapter 12), the results might indicate that years of experience is associated with speed of translation with a *p*-value of .04, while difficulty of the text is not associated with speed due to a *p*-value of .07. However, these *p*-values cannot be directly compared, and due to experimental error, they represent nearly identical levels of statistical significance. Moreover, it might very well be the case that text difficulty has a stronger practical effect than years of experience, based on the observed effect size. Relying solely on *p*-values to make decisions and attempting to make direct comparisons between *p*-values are both serious mistakes to be avoided.

Hypothesis testing should be supplemented to provide a more complete interpretation of results. The binary decision on whether to reject the null hypothesis should be made perfunctorily using the pre-specified level of significance, and then the analysis should continue to examine other important aspects of the sample and to interpret the results in practical language. Armstrong (2007) argues in favor of effect sizes, confidence intervals, meta-analyses, and replication and extensions of hypotheses. To these, we would add power analysis for sample size determination. Along with the description of each test statistic in this volume, we have provided information on calculating and interpreting both confidence intervals and effect sizes.

The rationale for our insistence on the inclusion of effect sizes when reporting results is precisely to aid the readers of published research in interpreting and contextualizing results of statistical analysis. Complete reporting provides a well-rounded look at the results of a quantitative study to improve understanding of the constructs, processes, and phenomenon being studied. A fictitious, concrete example will help illustrate this point.

Imagine a researcher who was investigating whether public speaking coaching affects consecutive interpreting performance. To investigate this research question, he develops a 50-hour teaching protocol that will specifically incorporate public speaking into a consecutive interpreting course. As a control, he will incorporate this into one section of the class, while the other section will be taught as usual. At the end of the semester, the students' exam scores are compared. The researcher finds a statistically significant result with a small effect size. The difference in average exam scores indicate that the scores can be increased several points by the coaching.

The description of these results from this made-up study show the importance of indicating both statistical significance and effect size. The researcher was able to demonstrate that the 50-hour teaching protocol improved the students' performance in consecutive interpreting at a statistically significant level; however, the implications of the study may not necessarily be that every course should incorporate this treatment. For instance, questions can be raised about the limited size of the effect that the treatment had on the student's performance. Also, cost–benefit analysis of this result could indicate that the small increase in scores does not warrant the necessary expense to implement the 50 hours of education. When interpreting results, we must take into account more than the detected difference; we must also weigh the potential effects.

In addition, reporting of effect sizes allows researchers to conduct meta-analyses of published literature on a specific topic or area. These summaries of the body of the literature are useful in guiding the direction of the discipline. For instance, in communication studies, there was a period of time in which gender differences were examined for a number of variables including self-disclosure. Dindia and Allen (1992) described that the results obtained from many studies seemed to be in conflict with each other—the relative importance of sex differences varied widely from study to study. Based on a literature review alone, it was impossible to determine whether the significant findings in some studies were in conflict with those found in others. Consequently, Dindia and Allen conducted a meta-analysis of published works and found that the average effect size across a wide sample was small ($d = .18$). The effect of sex differences on self-disclosure seemed to be affected by other variables (called *moderator variables*). The authors asserted that the magnitude of the difference may not be sufficient to impact self-disclosure in a way that would affect relationships between men and women.

This example is illustrative of the dangers of relying solely on statistical significance to interpret and generalize results of a study. Without information related to a standardized effect size (e.g., Cohen's d, Hedges' g), researchers cannot effectively compare their results with related literature or communicate the practical effect to the greater academic community. Moreover, the statistical significance of a difference does not indicate its magnitude. Complete analysis of all inferences demands reporting of effect sizes, which allow for a better understanding of the results.

In addition to effect sizes, confidence intervals should be reported for all parameter estimates. Proper interpretation of a confidence interval can improve statistical inference by providing an interval estimate of the parameter (Miller and Ulrich 2015; Coulson, Healey, Fidler, and Cumming 2010). A number of fallacies exist in the interpretation of confidence intervals. We will not list them here for fear of only reinforcing them; see Morey et al. (2014) for an approachable discussion of the most common mistakes of interpretation. In Chapter 6 we described the interpretation of a confidence interval. The best interpretation of a confidence interval is an interval estimate of the population parameter. If the study's protocol were repeated a very large number of times (technically approaching infinity), then the parameter would likely be inside the confidence interval 95% of the time.

Confidence intervals provide a better understanding of a study's results than point estimates alone.

Some statisticians favor a fundamentally different approach to the process of statistical testing. The most developed of these is Bayesian inference, in which prior beliefs are tested and revised based on data. Bayesian statistics is not discussed in this volume, as we wish to focus on providing the basic NHST skills. While NHST has shortcomings, the best remedy is good human judgment, based on an understanding of both the statistical tests employed and the nature of the sample data, theories, and previous findings in the discipline. As Nickerson (2000: 291) describes, "[s]tatistical methods should facilitate good thinking, and only to the degree that they do so are they being used well."

Finally, we note that improvements in statistical practice and interpretation can also be made through collaborative, cross-disciplinary research. Mathematically inclined T&I scholars working in collaboration with language-oriented statisticians have the ability to advance the discipline in terms of rigor.

Conclusion

The previous discussion of statistical significance, effect sizes, and confidence intervals highlights some of the limitations encountered when conducting quantitative research. As researchers, we must be mindful that the results obtained in each study need to be considered in relationship to the literature in the field. While novel differences or relationships may uncover new lines of research, a solitary study is not and cannot be definitive in its conclusions. Replication of research studies and triangulation with additional quantitative and qualitative data points are of utmost importance to advance the discipline.

With this volume, we hope to enhance the methodological rigor of the discipline by outlining the application of quantitative research methods to questions that arise in T&I studies. The combination of sound research design principles with appropriate statistical analyses complements many of the qualitative methods used in the field. Discussions of sampling, measurement, and ethics provide guidance on research design employing quantitative methods. The growing number of examples of statistical analysis in the T&I studies literature illustrate the importance of these tools for quantifying effects, testing theories, and expanding the field of inquiry.

Notes

1 In a *New York Times* article, Interlandi (2006) documents the legal action taken against Eric Poehlman, a formerly-tenured professor, who became the "first researcher sentenced to prison for scientific misconduct."
2 Albert and Wager (2003) provide guidance to new researchers on authorship and suggest ways that authors can negotiate the authorship process. Their work is included as part of *The COPE Report*, issued by the Committee on Publication Ethics. Its website (http://publicationethics.org/) provides a wealth of information and serves as a "forum for editors and publishers of peer reviewed journals to discuss all aspects of publication ethics."

References

Adams, Samuel O., Ezra Gayawan, and Mohammed K. Garba. 2009. "Empirical comparison of the Kruskal Wallis statistics and its parametric counterpart." *Journal of Modern Mathematics and Statistics* 3(2): 38–42.
Aggarwal, Charu C. 2013. *Outlier Analysis*. New York: Springer.
Agresti, Alan, and Jane Pendergast. 1986. "Comparing mean ranks for repeated measures data." *Communications in Statistics—Theory and Methods* 15(5): 1417–1433.
Aguinis, Herman, Ryan K. Gottfredson, and Harry Joo. 2013. "Best-practice recommendations for defining, identifying, and handling outliers." *Organizational Research Methods* 16(2): 270–301.
Albers, Willem, Pieta C. Boon, and Wilbert C.M. Kallenberg. 2000. "The asymptotic behavior of tests for normal means based on a variance pre-test." *Journal of Statistical Planning and Inference* 88(1): 47–57.
Albert, Tim, and Elizabeth Wager. 2003. "How to handle authorship disputes: A guide for new researchers." *The COPE Report*. 32–34.
Algina, James, and H.J. Keselman. 2003. "Approximate confidence intervals for effect sizes." *Educational and Psychological Measurement* 63(4): 537–553.
Allen, Mary J., and Wendy M. Yen. 2001. *Introduction to Measurement Theory*. Long Grove, IL: Waveland Press.
American Psychological Association. 2009. *Publication Manual of the American Psychological Association*, 6th Edition. Washington, DC: APA.
American Psychological Association. 2010. *Ethical Principles for Psychologists and Code of Conduct*. Washington, DC: APA.
Angelelli, Claudia V. 2004. *Revisiting the Interpreter's Role: A Study of Conference, Court, and Medical Interpreters in Canada, Mexico, and the United States*. Amsterdam: John Benjamins.
Angelelli, Claudia V. 2009. "Using a rubric to assess translation ability: Defining the construct." In *Testing and Assessment in Translation and Interpreting Studies*, edited by Claudia V. Angelelli and Holly E. Johnson, 13–47. Amsterdam: John Benjamins.
Anscombe, Frank J. 1960. "Rejection of outliers." *Technometrics* 2(2): 123–147.
Anscombe, Frank J. 1973. "Graphs in statistical analysis." *American Statistician* 27(1): 17–21.
Armstrong, J. Scott. 2007. "Significance tests harm progress in forecasting." *International Journal of Forecasting* 23(2): 321–327.
Arndt, Stephan, Carolyn Turvey, and Nancy C. Andreasen. 1999. "Correlating and predicting psychiatric symptom ratings: Spearman's r versus Kendall's tau correlation." *Journal of Psychiatric Research* 33(2): 97–104.

Arnold, Barry C. 1970. "Hypothesis testing incorporating a preliminary test of significance." *Journal of the American Statistical Association* 65(332): 1590–1596.

ASTM International. ASTM F2089: 2007. *Standard Guide for Language Interpretation Services*. West Conshohocken, PA: ASTM, 2007.

Asuero, A.G., A. Sayago, and A.G. González. 2006. "The correlation coefficient: An overview." *Critical Reviews in Analytical Chemistry* 36(1): 41–59.

Ayman, David, and Archie D. Goldshine. 1940. "Blood pressure determinations by patients with essential hypertension." *American Journal of the Medical Sciences* 200(4): 465–474.

Baayen, R. Harald. 2001. *Word Frequency Distributions*. Dordrecht, Netherlands: Kluwer Academic Publishers.

Baayen, R. Harald, L.B. Feldman, and R. Schreuder. 2006. "Morphological influences on the recognition of monosyllabic monomorphemic words." *Journal of Memory and Language* 55(2): 290–313.

Bachman, Lyle, and Adrian Palmer. 1996. *Language Testing in Practice*. Oxford: Oxford University Press.

Baessler, Judith, and Ralf Schwartzer. 1996. "Evaluación de la autoeficacia: adaptación española de la Escala de Autoeficacia general." *Ansiedad y estrés* 2(1): 1–8.

Bakeman, Roger. 2005. "Recommended effect size statistics for repeated measures designs." *Behavior Research Methods* 37(3): 379–384.

Baker, David W., Risa Hayes, and Julia Puebla Fortier. 1998. "Interpreter use and satisfaction with interpersonal aspects of care for Spanish-speaking patients." *Medical Care* 36(10): 1461–1470.

Balling, Laura Winther. 2008. "A brief introduction to regression designs and mixed-effects modelling by a recent convert." *Copenhagen Studies in Language* 36: 175–192.

Balling, Laura Winther, and Kristian Tangsgaard Hvelplund. 2015. "Design and statistics in quantitative translation (process) research." *Translation Spaces* 4(1): 169–186.

Balling, Laura Winther, Kristian Tangsgaard Hvelplund, and Annette C. Sjørup. 2014. "Evidence of parallel processing during translation." *Meta* 59(2): 234–259.

Baraldi, Claudio, and Christopher D. Mellinger. 2016. "Observations." In *Researching Translation and Interpreting*, edited by Claudia V. Angelelli and Brian James Baer, 257–268. New York: Routledge.

Bartlett, M.S. 1937. "Properties of sufficiency and statistical tests." *Proceedings of the Royal Society of London, Series A* 160(901): 268–282.

Baskin, Patricia K., and Robert A. Gross. 2011. "Honorary and ghost authorship." *BMJ* 343: d6223.

Bayerl, Petra Saskia, and Karsten Ingmar Paul. 2011. "What determines inter-coder agreement in manual annotations? A meta-analytic investigation." *Computational Linguistics* 37(4): 699–725.

Beecher, Henry K. 1966. "Ethics and clinical research." *The New England Journal of Medicine* 274(24): 367–372.

Bergmann, Richard, John Ludbrook, and Will P.J.M. Spooren. 2000. "Different outcomes of the Wilcoxon-Mann-Whitney test from different statistics packages." *American Statistician* 54(1): 72–77.

Biber, Douglas. 1993. "Representativeness in corpus design." *Literary and Linguistic Computing* 8(4): 243–257.

Bird, Kevin D. 2002. "Confidence intervals for effect sizes in analysis of variance." *Educational and Psychological Measurements* 62(2): 197–226.

Bishara, Anthony J., and James B. Hittner. 2012. "Testing the significance of a correlation with nonnormal data: Comparison of Pearson, Spearman, transformation, and resampling approaches." *Psychological Methods* 17(3): 399–417.

Blair, R. Clifford, James J. Higgins, and William D.S. Smitley. 1980. "On the relative power of the U and t tests." *British Journal of Mathematical and Statistical Psychology* 33(1): 114–120.

Blair, R. Clifford, Shlomo S. Sawilowsky, and James J. Higgins. 1987. "Limitations of the rank transform statistic in tests for interactions." *Communications in Statistics: Simulation and Computation* 16(4): 1133–1145.

Blair, R. Clifford. 1981. "A reaction to 'Consequences of failure to meet assumptions underlying the fixed effects analysis of variance and covariance.'" *Review of Educational Research* 51(4): 499–507.

Bolaños-Medina, Alicia. 2014. "Self-efficacy in translation." *Translation and Interpreting Studies* 9(2): 197–218.

Bonett, Douglas G., and Thomas A. Wright. 2000. "Sample size requirements for estimating Pearson, Kendall, and Spearman correlations." *Psychometrika* 65(1): 23–28.

Bowker, Lynne, and Jairo Buitrago Ciro. 2015. "Investigating the usefulness of machine translation for newcomers at the public library." *Translation and Interpreting Studies* 10(2): 165–186.

Boyle, Gregory J. 1991. "Does item homogeneity indicate internal consistency or item redundancy in psychometric scales?" *Personality and Individual Differences* 12(3): 291–294.

Bradburn, Norman M., Seymour Sudman, Brian Wansink. 2004. *Asking Questions: The Definitive Guide to Questionnaire Design*. San Francisco: Jossey-Bass.

Braun, Sabine. 2013. "Keep your distance? Remote interpreting in legal proceedings: A critical assessment of a growing practice." *Interpreting* 15(2): 200–228.

Brennan, Robert L. 1997. "A perspective on the history of generalizability theory." *Educational Measurement: Issues and Practice* 16(4): 14–20.

Brennan, Robert L. 2001. "An essay on the history and future of reliability from the perspective of replication." *Journal of Educational Measurement* 38(4): 195–317.

Bresnahan, Jean L. and Martin M. Shapiro. 1966. "A general equation and technique for the exact partitioning of chi-square contingency tables." *Psychological Bulletin* 66(4): 252–262.

Brewer, Marilynn B., and William D. Crano. 2014. "Research design and issues of validity." In *Handbook of Research Methods in Social and Personality Psychology*, 2nd edition, edited by Harry T. Reis and Charles M. Judd, 11–26. Cambridge: Cambridge University Press.

Bridge, Patrick, and Shlomo Sawilowsky. 1999. "Increasing physicians' awareness of the impact of statistics on research outcomes: Comparative power of the t-test and Wilcoxon rank-sum test in small samples applied research." *Journal of Clinical Epidemiology* 52(3): 229–235.

Brown, Morton B., and Alan B. Forsythe. 1974. "Robust tests for the equality of variances." *Journal of the American Statistical Association* 69(346): 364–367.

Brown, Timothy A. 2015. *Confirmatory Factor Analysis for Applied Research*, 2nd edition. New York: Guilford Press.

Brunner, Edgar, and Ullrich Munzel. 2000. "The nonparametric Behrens-Fisher problem: Asymptotic theory and a small-sample approximation." *Biometrical Journal* 42(1): 17–25.

Cameron, A. Colin, and Pravin K. Trivedi. 2013. *Regression Analysis of Count Data*. 2nd Edition. New York: Cambridge University Press.

Camilli, Gregory, and Kenneth D. Hopkins. 1978. "Applicability of chi square to 2x2 contingency tables with small expected cell frequencies." *Psychological Bulletin* 85(1): 163–167.

Carifio, James, and Rocco J. Perla. 2007. "Ten common misunderstandings, misconceptions, persistent myths and urban legends about Liker scales and Likert response formats and their antidotes." *Journal of Social Sciences* 3(3): 106–116.

Carl, Michael, and Arnt Lykke Jakobsen. 2009. "Toward statistical modelling of translators' activity data." *International Journal of Speech Technology* 12(4): 125–138.

Carl, Michael, Barbara Dragsted, Jakob Elming, Daniel Hardt, and Arnt Lykke Jakobsen. 2011. "The process of post-editing: A pilot study." In *Human-Machine Interaction in Translation: Proceedings of the 8th International NLPCS Workshop*, edited by Bernadette Sharp, Michael Zock, Michael Carl, and Arnt Lykke Jakobsen, 131–142. Frederiksberg: Samfundslitteratur.

Carmines, Edward G., and Richard A. Zeller. 1979. *Reliability and Validity Assessment*. Thousand Oaks, CA: SAGE Publications.

Carroll, Robert M., and Lena A. Nordholm. 1975. "Sampling characteristics of Kelley's ε and Hays' ω." *Educational and Psychological Measurement* 35(3): 541–554.

Caruso, John C. 2000. "Reliability generalization of the NEO personality scales." *Educational and Psychological Measurement* 60(2): 236–254.

Caudill, Steven B. 1988. "Type I errors after preliminary tests for heteroscedasticity." *Journal of the Royal Statistical Society. Series D (The Statistician)* 37(1): 65–68.

Chang, Feng-lan. 2009. "Do interpreters need to sound like broadcasters?" *Compilation and Translation Review* 2(1): 101–150.

Charter, Richard A. 1997. "Confidence interval procedures for retest, alternate-form, validity, and alpha coefficients." *Perceptual and Motor Skills* 84(3C): 1488–1490.

Charter, Richard A. 1999. "Sample size requirements for precise estimates of reliability, generalizability, and validity coefficients." *Journal of Clinical and Experimental Neuropsychology* 21(4): 559–566.

Cheung, Shirmaine. 2010. "Translation of short texts: A case study of street names in Hong Kong." Unpublished thesis, University of Queensland, Australia. Retrieved from: http://espace.library.uq.edu.au/view/UQ:210155. Last accessed 7 January 2016.

Christoffels, Ingrid K., and Annette M.B. De Groot. 2004. "Components of simultaneous interpreting: Comparing interpreting with shadowing and paraphrasing." *Bilingualism: Language and Cognition* 7(3): 227–240.

Cico, Stephen John, Eva Vogeley, and William J. Doyle. 2011. "Informed consent language and parents' willingness to enroll their children in research." *IRB: Ethics & Human Research* 33(2): 6–13.

Clifford, Andrew. 2005. "Healthcare interpreting and informed consent: What is the interpreter's role in treatment decision-making?" *TTR* 18(2): 225–247.

Clinch, Jennifer J., and H.J. Keselman. 1982. "Parametric alternatives to the analysis of variance." *Journal of Educational Statistics* 7(3): 207–214.

Cochran, William G. 1965. "The planning of observational studies of human populations." *Journal of the Royal Statistical Society. Series A* 128(2): 234–266.

Cochran, William G. 1977. *Sampling Techniques*. 3rd edition. New York: John Wiley and Sons.

Cohen, Jacob. 1960. "A coefficient of agreement for nominal scales." *Educational and Psychological Measurement* 20(1): 37–46.

Cohen, Jacob. 1962. "The statistical power of abnormal-social psychological research: A review." *Journal of Abnormal and Social Psychology* 65(3): 145–153.

Cohen, Jacob. 1968. "Weighted kappa: Nominal scale agreement provision for scaled disagreement or partial credit." *Psychological Bulletin* 70(4): 213–220.

Cohen, Jacob. 1988. *Statistical Power Analysis for the Behavioral Sciences*. 2nd edition. Hillsdale, NJ: Lawrence Erlbaum Associates.
Cohen, Jacob. 1992. "A power primer." *Quantitative Methods in Psychology* 112(1): 155–159.
Colegrave, Nick, and Graeme D. Ruxton. 2003. "Confidence intervals are a more useful complement to nonsignificant tests than are power calculations." *Behavioral Ecology* 14(3): 446–447.
Coleman, James A., Árpád Galaczi, and Lluïsa Astruc. 2007. "Motivation of UK school pupils towards foreign languages: A large-scale survey at Key Stage 3." *Language Learning Journal* 35(2): 245–280.
Collett, David. 2002. *Modelling Binary Data*. 2nd edition. Boca Raton: CRC Press.
Conger, Anthony J. 1980. "Integration and generalization of kappas for multiple raters." *Psychological Bulletin* 88(2): 322–328.
Conover, W.J., and Ronald L. Iman. 1981. "Rank transform as a bridge between parametric and nonparametric statistics." *The American Statistician* 35(3): 124–133.
Conover, W.J., Mark E. Johnson, and Myrle M. Johnson. 1981. "A comparative study of tests for homogeneity of variances, with applications to the outer continental shelf bidding data." *Technometrics* 23(4): 351–361.
Cook, R. Dennis. 1977. "Detection of influential observations in linear regression." *Technometrics* 19(1): 15–18.
Coombs, William T., James Algina, and Debra Olson Oltman. 1996. "Univariate and multivariate omnibus hypothesis tests selected to control Type I error rates when population variances are not necessarily equal." *Review of Educational Research* 66(2): 137–179.
Cortina, Jose M. 1993. "What is coefficient alpha? An examination of theory and applications." *Journal of Applied Psychology* 78(1): 98–104.
Coulson, Melissa, Michelle Healey, Fiona Fidler, and Geoff Cumming. 2010. "Confidence intervals permit, but do not guarantee, better inference than statistical significance testing." *Frontiers in Psychology* 1: 26.
Cramér, Harald. 1946. *Mathematical Methods of Statistics*. Princeton, NJ: Princeton University Press.
Cronbach, Lee J. 1951. "Coefficient alpha and the internal structure of tests." *Psychometrika* 16(3): 297–334.
Cronbach, Lee J., Goldine C. Gleser, Harinder Nanda, and Nageswari Rajaratnam. 1972. *The Dependability of Behavioral Measurements: Theory of Generalizability for Scores and Profiles*. New York: Wiley.
Croux, Christophe, and Catherine Dehon. 2010. "Influence functions of the Spearman and Kendall correlation measures." *Statistical Methods and Applications* 19(4): 497–515.
Cumming, Geoff, and Sue Finch. 2001. "A primer on the understanding, use, and calculation of confidence intervals that are based on central and noncentral distributions." *Educational and Psychological Measurement* 61(4): 532–574.
Daniel, Wayne. 1990. *Applied Nonparametric Statistics*. Pacific Grove, CA: Duxbury.
Delaney, Harold, and Andras Vargha. 2000. "The effect of non-normality on Student's two-sample t test." Paper presented at the 81st Annual Meeting of the American Research Association, New Orleans, April.
Delucchi, Kevin L. 1983. "The use and misuse of chi-square: Lewis and Burke revisited." *Psychological Bulletin* 94(1): 166–176.
DeMars, Christine. 2010. *Item Response Theory*. New York: Oxford University Press.
Denkowski, Michael, and Alan Lavie. 2012. "TransCenter: Web-based translation research suite." *AMTA 2012 Workshop on Post-Editing Technology and Practice Demo Session*.

Dewaard, Lisa. 2012. "Learner perception of formal and informal pronouns in Russian." *Modern Language Journal* 96(3): 400–418.

Dillinger, Mike. 1994. "Comprehension during interpreting: What do interpreters know that bilinguals don't." In *Bridging the Gap: Empirical Research in Simultaneous Interpretation*, edited by Barbara Moser-Mercer and Sylvie Lambert, 155–189. Amsterdam: John Benjamins.

Dindia, Kathryn, and Mike Allen. 1992. "Sex differences in self-disclosure: A meta-analysis." *Psychological Bulletin* 112(1): 106–124.

Doherty, Stephen, Sharon O'Brien, and Michael Carl. 2010. "Eye tracking as an MT evaluation technique." *Machine Translation* 24(1): 1–13.

Draper, Norman R., and Harry Smith. 1998. *Applied Regression Analysis*. 3rd Edition. New York: Wiley.

Dunn, Olive Jean. 1961. "Multiple comparisons among means." *Journal of the American Statistical Association* 56(293): 52–64.

Dunn, Olive Jean. 1964. "Multiple comparisons using rank sums." *Technometrics* 6(3): 241–252.

Dunnett, Charles W. 1955. "A multiple comparison procedure for comparing several treatments with a control." *Journal of the American Statistical Association* 50(272): 1096–1121.

Dunnett, Charles W. 1964. "New tables for multiple comparisons with a control." *Biometrics* 20(3): 482–491.

Dunnett, Charles W. 1980. "Pairwise multiple comparisons in the unequal variance case." *Journal of the American Statistical Association* 75(372): 796–800.

Dunning, Ted. 1993. "Accurate methods for the statistics of surprise and coincidence." *Association for Computational Linguistics* 19(1): 61–74.

Dupont, William D., and Walton D. Plummer, Jr. 1990. "Power and sample size calculation: A review and computer program." *Controlled Clinical Trials* 11(2): 116–128.

Durbin, J., and G.S. Watson. 1950. "Testing for serial correlation in least squares regression. I." *Biometrika* 37(3/4): 409–428.

Durbin, J., and G.S. Watson. 1951. "Testing for serial correlation in least squares regression. II." *Biometrika* 38(1/2): 159–177.

Editorial Board, ACS Nano. 2012. "Recycling is not always good: The dangers of self-plagiarism." *ACS Nano* 6(1): 1–4.

Elliott, Alan C., and Linda S. Hynan. 2011. "A SAS® macro implementation of a multiple comparison post hoc test for a Kruskal-Wallis analysis." *Computer Methods and Programs in Biomedicine* 102(1): 75–80.

Ellis, Paul D. 2010. *The Essential Guide to Effect Sizes: Statistical Power, Meta-Analysis, and the Interpretation of Research Results*. Cambridge: Cambridge University Press.

Evans, Jonathan St. B. T. 2013. *The Psychology of Reasoning*. London: Psychology Press.

Eyde, Lorraine D. 2000. "Other responsibilities to participants." In *Ethics in Research with Human Participants*, edited by Bruce D. Sales and Susan Folkman, 61–74. Washington, DC: APA.

Faden, Ruth R., Tom L. Beauchamp, and Nancy M.P. King. 1986. *A History and Theory of Informed Consent*. Oxford: Oxford University Press.

Fagerland, Morten W., and Leiv Sandvik. 2009. "The Wilcoxon-Mann-Whitney test under scrutiny." *Statistics in Medicine* 28: 1487–1497.

Faraway, Julian J. 2006. *Extending the Linear Model with R: Generalized Linear, Mixed Effects, and Nonparametric Regression Models*. Boca Raton, FL: Chapman & Hall/CRC.

Feinauer, Ilse, and Harold M. Lesch. 2013. "Health workers: Idealistic expectations versus interpreters' competence." *Perspectives: Studies in Translatology* 21(1): 117–132.

Feldt, Leonard S. 1965. "The approximate sampling distribution of Kuder-Richardson reliability coefficient twenty." *Psychometrika* 30(3): 357–370.
Feldt, Leonard S., David J. Woodruff, and Fathi A. Salih. 1987. "Statistical inference for coefficient alpha." *Applied Psychological Measurement* 11(1): 93–103.
Feltovich, Nick. 2003. "Nonparametric tests of differences in medians: Comparison of the Wilcoxon-Mann-Whitney and robust rank-order tests." *Experimental Economics* 6(3): 273–297.
Ferguson, Christopher J. 2009. "An effect size primer: A guide for clinicians and researchers." *Professional Psychology: Research and Practice* 40(5): 532–538.
Few, Stephen. 2012. *Show Me the Numbers: Designing Tables and Graphs to Enlighten*. 2nd edition. Burlingame, CA: Analytics Press.
Fidler, V. and N.J.D. Nagelkerke. 1986. "A generalized signed-rank test for comparison of P treatments." *Statistica Neerlandica* 40(3): 145–155.
Field, Andy. 2013. *Discovering Statistics using IBM SPSS Statistics*. 4th edition. London: SAGE Publications.
Fieller, E.C., H.O. Hartley, and E.S. Pearson. 1957. "Tests for rank correlation coefficients. I." *Biometrika* 44(3/4): 470–481.
Finch, Sue, Geoff Cumming, and Neil Thomason. 2001. "Reporting of statistical inference in the *Journal of Applied Psychology*: Little evidence of reform." *Educational and Psychological Measurement* 61(2): 181–210.
Fisher, Ronald Aylmer. 1921. "On the 'Probable error' of a coefficient of correlation deduced from a small sample." *Metron* 1: 3–32.
Fisher, Ronald Aylmer. 1922. "On the interpretation of χ^2 from contingency tables, and the calculation of P." *Journal of the Royal Statistical Society* 85(1): 87–94.
Fleiss, Joseph L. 1971. "Measuring nominal scale agreement among many raters." *Psychological Bulletin* 76(5): 378–382.
Fleiss, Joseph L., Jacob Cohen, and B.S. Everitt. 1969. "Large sample standard errors of kappa and weighted kappa." *Psychological Bulletin* 72(5): 323–327.
Fligner, Michael A., and George E. Policello. 1981. "Robust rank procedures for the Behrens-Fisher problem." *Journal of the American Statistical Association* 76(373): 162–168.
Folse, Keith S. 2006. "The effect of type of written exercise on L2 vocabulary retention." *TESOL Quarterly* 40(2): 273–293.
Fowler Jr., Floyd J. 1995. *Improving Survey Questions*. 1st edition. Washington, DC: SAGE.
Fowler Jr., Floyd J. 2013. *Survey Research Methods*. 5th edition. Washington, DC: SAGE.
Fraser, Carol A. 1999. "Lexical processing strategy use and vocabulary learning through reading." *Studies in Second Language Acquisition* 21(2): 225–241.
Friedman, Milton. 1937. "The use of ranks to avoid the assumption of normality implicit in the analysis of variance." *Journal of the American Statistical Association* 32(200): 675–701.
Friedman, Milton. 1939. "A correction: The use of ranks to avoid the assumption of normality implicit in the analysis of variance." *Journal of the American Statistical Association* 34(205): 109.
Friedman, Milton. 1940. "A comparison of alternative tests of significance for the problem of m rankings." *Annals of Mathematical Statistics* 11(1): 86–92.
Fritz, Catherine O., Peter E. Morris, and Jennifer J. Richler. 2012. "Effect size estimates: Current use, calculations, and interpretation." *Journal of Experimental Psychology: General* 141(1): 2–18.
Gaito, John. 1980. "Measurement scale and statistics: Resurgence of an old misconception." *Psychological Bulletin* 87(3): 564–567.

Games, Paul A., and John F. Howell. 1976. "Pairwise multiple comparison procedures with unequal N's and/or variances: A Monte Carlo study." *Journal of Educational Statistics* 1(2): 113–125.

Gart, John J. 1966. "Alternative analyses of contingency tables." *Journal of the Royal Statistical Society. Series B: Methodological* 28(1): 164–179.

Gelman, Andrew, and Hal Stern. 2006. "The difference between 'Significant' and 'Not Significant' is not itself statistically significant." *American Statistician* 60(4): 328–331.

Gile, Daniel. 1998. "Observational studies and experimental studies in the investigation of conference interpreting." *Target* 10(1): 69–93.

Gile, Daniel. 2000. "The History of research into conference interpreting: A scientometric approach." *Target* 12(2): 291–321.

Gile, Daniel. 2016. "Experimental research." In *Researching Translation and Interpreting*, edited by Claudia V. Angelelli and Brian James Baer, 220–228. New York: Routledge.

Gilpin, Andrew R. 1993. "Table for conversion of Kendall's tau to Spearman's rho within the context of measures of magnitude of effect for meta-analysis." *Educational and Psychological Measurement* 53(1): 87–92.

Gjerdingen, Dwenda K., Deborah E. Simpson, and Sandra L. Titus 1987. "Patients' and physicians' attitudes regarding the physician's professional appearance." *Archives of Internal Medicine* 147(7): 1209–1212.

Gosling, Samuel D., and Winter Mason. 2015. "Internet research in psychology." *Annual Review of Psychology* 66: 877–902.

Gosset, William [Student]. 1908. "The probable error of a mean." *Biometrika* 6(1): 1–25.

Graham, James M. 2006. "Congeneric and (essentially) tau-equivalent estimates of score reliability: What they are and how to use them." *Educational Psychological Measurement* 66(6): 930–944.

Greenhouse, S.W., and S. Geisser. 1959. "On methods in the analysis of profile data." *Psychometrika* 24: 95–112.

Gries, Stefan Th. 2009. *Quantitative Corpus Linguistics with R: A Practical Introduction*. New York: Routledge.

Gries, Stefan Th. 2010. "Useful statistics for corpus linguistics." In *A Mosaic of Corpus Linguistics: Selected Approaches*, edited by Aquilino Sánchez and Moisés Almela, 269–291. Frankfurt: Peter Lang.

Gries, Stefan Th. 2013. *Statistics for Linguistics with R: A Practical Introduction*. 2nd edition. Boston: De Gruyter Mouton.

Gries, Stefan Th. 2014. "Frequency tables: Tests, effect sizes, and exploration." In *Corpus Methods for Semantics: Quantitative Studies in Polysemy and Synonymy*, edited by Dylan Glynn and Justyna A. Robinson, 365–389. Philadelphia: John Benjamins.

Gries, Stefan Th., and Stefanie Wulff. 2012. "Regression analysis in translation studies." In *Quantitative Methods in Corpus-Based Translation Studies*, edited by Michael P. Oakes and Meng Ji, 35–52. Amsterdam: John Benjamins.

Grissom, Robert J., and John J. Kim. 2004. *Effect Sizes for Research: A Broad Practical Approach*. New York: Springer.

Groves, Robert M. et al. 2013. *Survey Methodology*. 2nd edition. Hoboken, NJ: Wiley.

Guerberof Arenas, Ana. 2008. "Productivity and quality in the post-editing of outputs from translation memories and machine translation." *The International Journal of Localisation* 7(1): 11–21.

Guerberof Arenas, Ana. 2014. "Correlations between productivity and quality when post-editing in a professional context." *Machine Translation* 28(3/4): 165–186.

Guttman, Louis. 1945. "A basis for analyzing test-retest reliability." *Psychometrika* 10(4): 255–282.

Halverson, Sandra. 1998. "Translation studies and representative corpora: Establishing links between translation corpora, theoretical/descriptive categories and a conception of the object of study." *Meta* 43(4): 494–514.

Hamon, Olivier et al. 2009. "End-to-end evaluation in simultaneous translation." *Proceedings of the 12th Conference of the European Chapter of the Association for Computational Linguistics.* Athens, Greece.

Hancock, Gregory R., and Alan J. Klockars. 1996. "The quest for α: Developments in multiple comparison procedures in the quarter century since Games (1971)." *Review of Educational Research* 66(3): 269–306.

Harwell, Michael R., Elaine N. Rubinstein, William S. Hayes, and Corley C. Olds. 1992. "Summarizing Monte Carlo results in methodological research: The one- and two-factor fixed effects ANOVA cases." *Journal of Educational Statistics* 17(4): 315–339.

Hattie, John. 1985. "Methodology review: Assessing unidimensionality of tests and items." *American Psychological Measurement* 9(2): 139–164.

Hayes, Andrew F., and Klaus Krippendorff. 2007. "Answering the call for a standard reliability measure for coding data." *Communication Methods and Measures* 1(1): 77–89.

Hays, William L. 1963. *Statistics for Psychologists.* New York: Holt, Rinehart, and Winston.

He, Shaoyi. 2000. "Translingual alteration of conceptual information in medical translation: A crosslanguage analysis between English and Chinese." *Journal of the American Society for Information Science* 51(11): 1047–1060.

Hedges, Larry V. 1981. "Distribution theory for Glass's estimator of effect size and related estimators." *Journal of Educational Statistics* 6(2): 106–128.

Hemphill, James F. 2003. "Interpreting the magnitudes of correlation coefficients." *American Psychologist* 58(1): 78–79.

Hendricson, William D., I. Jon Russell, Thomas J. Prihoda, James M. Jacobson, Alice Rogan, and George D. Bishop. 1989. "An approach to developing a valid Spanish language translation of a health-status questionnaire." *Medical Care* 27(10): 959–966.

Henrich, Joseph, Steven J. Heine, and Ara Norenzayan. 2010. "The weirdest people in the world?" *Behavioral and Brain Sciences* 33(2-3): 61–83.

Henson, Robin K. 2001. "Understanding internal consistency reliability estimates: A conceptual primer on coefficient alpha." *Measurement and Evaluation in Counseling and Development* 34(3): 177–189.

Hertwig, Ralph, and Andreas Ortmann. 2008. "Deception in experiments: Revisiting the arguments in its defense." *Ethics & Behavior* 18(1): 59–82.

Hilton, Ann, and Myriam Skrutkowski. 2002. "Translating instruments into other languages: Development and testing processes." *Cancer Nursing* 25(1): 1–7.

Hochberg, Yosef, and Ajit C. Tamhane. 1987. *Multiple Comparison Procedures.* New York: Wiley.

Hodges, J.L., Jr., and E.L. Lehmann. 1963. "Estimates of location based on rank tests." *Annals of Mathematical Statistics* 34(2): 598–611.

Hoenig, John M., and Dennis M. Heisey. 2001. "The abuse of power: The pervasive fallacy of power calculations for data analysis." *American Statistician* 55(1): 19–24.

Hollander, Myles, and Douglas A. Wolfe. 1999. *Nonparametric Statistical Methods.* 2nd Edition. New York: Wiley.

Holt, W.R., B.H. Kennedy, and J.W. Peacock. 1967. "Formulae for estimating sample size for chi-square test." *Journal of Economic Entomology* 60(1): 286–288.

Horwitz, Elaine K. 1986. "Preliminary evidence for the reliability and validity of a foreign language anxiety scale." *TESOL Quarterly* 20(3): 559–562.

Howell, David C. 2009. *Statistical Methods for Psychology*. 7th edition. Belmont, CA: Wadsworth Publishing.

Howell, David C. 2012. *Statistical Methods for Psychology*. 8th edition. Belmont, CA: Wadsworth Publishing.

Hoyt, William T., and Janet N. Melby. 1999. "Dependability of measurement in counseling psychology: An introduction to generalizability theory." *The Counseling Psychologist* 27(3): 325–352.

Huber, Peter J. 1981. *Robust Statistics*. New York: Wiley.

Hubert, Lawrence, and Howard Wainer. 2011. "A statistical guide for the ethically perplexed." In *Handbook of Ethics in Quantitative Methodology*, edited by A.T. Panter and Sonya K. Sterba, 61–124. New York: Routledge.

Hurtado Albir, Amparo, Fabio Alves, Birgitta Englund Dimitrova, and Isabel Lacruz. 2015. "A retrospective and prospective view of translation research from an empirical, experimental, and cognitive perspective: the TREC Network." *Translation & Interpreting* 7(1): 5–25.

Huynh, H., and L.S. Feldt. 1976. "Estimation of the Box correction for degrees of freedom from sample data in randomised block and split-plot designs." *Journal of Educational Statistics* 1(1): 69–82.

Hyslop, Terry, and Paul J. Lupinacci. 2003. "A nonparametric fitted test for the Behrens-Fisher problem." *Journal of Modern Applied Statistical Methods* 2(2): 414–424.

Interlandi, Jeneen. 2006. "An unwelcome discovery." *New York Times* 22 October.

International Committee of Medical Journal Editors (ICMJE). 2006. "Defining the role of authors and contributors." Last accessed 3 January 2016. http://www.icmje.org/recommendations/browse/roles-and-responsibilities/defining-the-role-of-authors-and-contributors.html

Israel, Mark, and Ian Hay. 2006. *Research Ethics for Social Scientists: Between Ethical Conduct and Regulatory Compliance*. Thousand Oaks, CA: SAGE Publications.

Israel, Mark. 2015. *Research Ethics and Integrity for Social Scientists*. 2nd ed. Thousand Oaks, CA: SAGE Publications.

Iverson, Cheryl et al. 2007. *AMA Manual of Style: A Guide for Authors and Editors*. New York: Oxford University Press.

Jääskeläinen, Riitta. 2000. "Focus on methodology in think-aloud studies on translating." In *Tapping and Mapping the Process of Translation and Interpreting: Outlooks on Empirical Research*, edited by Sonja Tirkkonen-Condit and Riitta Jääskeläinen, 71–83. Amsterdam: John Benjamins.

Jääskeläinen, Riitta. 2011. "Back to basics: Designing a study to determine the validity and reliability of verbal report data on translation processes." In *Cognitive Explorations of Translation*, edited by Sharon O'Brien, 15–29. New York: Continuum.

Jaccard, James, Michael A. Becker, and Gregory Wood. 1984. "Pairwise multiple comparisons procedures: A review." *Psychological Bulletin* 96(3): 589–596.

Jakobsen, Arnt Lykke. 1999. "Logging target text production with Translog." In *Probing the Process in Translation: Methods and Results*, edited by Gyde Hansen, 9–20. Copenhagen: Samfundslitteratur.

Ji, Meng, and Michael P. Oakes. 2012. "A corpus study of early English translations of Cao Xueqin's *Hongloumeng*." In *Quantitative Methods in Corpus-Based Translation Studies*, edited by Michael P. Oakes and Meng Ji, 177–208. Philadelphia: John Benjamins.

Johnson, Keith. 2008. *Quantitative Methods in Linguistics*. Malden, MA: Blackwell.
Jonckheere, A.R. 1954. "A distribution-free k-sample test against ordered alternatives." *Biometrika* 41(1/2): 467–471.
Kelley, Truman L. 1935. "An unbiased correlation ratio measure." *Proceedings of the National Academy of Sciences* 21(9): 554–559.
Kendall, Maurice G. 1938. "A new measure of rank correlation." *Biometrika* 30(1/2): 81–93.
Kepner, Christine Goring. 1991. "An experiment in the relationship of types of written feedback to the development of second-language writing skills." *Modern Language Journal* 75(3): 305–313.
Kerby, Dave S. 2014. "The simple difference formula: An approach to teaching nonparametric correlation." *Innovative Teaching* 3(1): 1–9.
Keselman, H.J. 1975. "A Monte Carlo investigation of three estimates of treatment magnitude: Epsilon squared, eta squared, and omega squared." *Canadian Psychological Review* 16: 44–48.
Keselman, H.J. et al. 1998. "Statistical practices of educational researchers: An analysis of their ANOVA, MANOVA, and ANCOVA analyses." *Review of Educational Research* 68(3): 350–386.
Keselman, H.J., Joanne C. Rogan, Jorge L. Mendoza, Lawrence J. Breen. 1980. "Testing the validity conditions of repeated measures F tests." *Psychological Bulletin* 87(3): 479–481.
Keuls, M. 1952. "The use of the 'Studentized Range' in connection with an analysis of variance." *Euphytica* 1(2): 112–122.
Keyton, Joann. 2014. *Communication Research: Asking Questions, Finding Answers*. 4th edition. New York: McGraw-Hill.
Kirk, Roger E. 1996. "Practical significance: A concept whose time has come." *Educational and Psychological Measurement* 56(5): 746–759.
Kithinji, Caroline, and Nancy E. Kass. 2010. "Assessing the readability of non-English-language consent forms: The case of Kiswahili for research conducted in Kenya." *IRB: Ethics & Human Research* 32(4): 10–15.
Klonowicz, Tatiana. 1994. "Putting one's heart into simultaneous interpretation." In *Bridging the Gap: Empirical Research in Simultaneous Interpretation*, edited by Barbara Moser-Mercer and Sylvie Lambert, 213–224. Amsterdam: John Benjamins.
Köpke, Barbara, and Jean-Luc Nespoulous. 2006. "Working memory performance in expert and novice interpreters." *Interpreting* 8(1): 1–23.
Korhonen, M. 1982. "On the performance of some multiple comparison procedures with unequal variances." *Scandinavian Journal of Statistics* 9(4): 241–247.
Kowalski, Charles J. 1972. "On the effects of non-normality on the distribution of the sample product-moment correlation coefficient." *Journal of the Royal Statistical Society. Series C (Applied Statistics)* 21(1): 1–12.
Kramer, Clyde Young. 1956. "Extension of multiple range tests to group means with unequal numbers of replications." *Biometrics* 12(3): 307–310.
Kreuter, Frauke, Stanley Presser, and Roger Tourangeau. 2008. "Social desirability bias in CATI, IVR, and web surveys." *Public Opinion Quarterly* 72(5): 847–865.
Krippendorff, Klaus, and Mary Angela Bock. 2008. *The Content Analysis Reader*. Thousand Oaks, CA: SAGE Publications.
Krippendorff, Klaus. 1970. "Estimating the reliability, systematic error, and random error of interval data." *Educational and Psychological Measurement* 30(1): 61–70.
Krippendorff, Klaus. 2004a. *Content Analysis: An Introduction to Its Methodology*. Thousand Oaks, CA: SAGE Publications.

Krippendorff, Klaus. 2004b. "Reliability in content analysis: Some common misconceptions and recommendations." *Human Communication Research* 30(3): 411–433.
Krippendorff, Klaus. 2008. "Systematic and random disagreement and the reliability of nominal data." *Communication Methods and Measures* 2(4): 323–338.
Kruger, Haidee. 2012. "A corpus-based study of the mediation effect in translated and edited language." *Target* 24(2): 355–388.
Kruskal, William H. 1958. "Ordinal measures of association." *Journal of the American Statistical Association* 53(284): 814–861.
Kuder, G.F. and M.W. Richardson. 1937. "The theory of the estimation of test reliability." *Psychometrika* 2(3): 151–160.
Läärä, Esa. 2009. "Statistics: Reasoning on uncertainty, and the insignificance of testing null." *Annales Zoologici Fennici* 46(2): 138–157.
Lakens, Daniël. 2013. "Calculating and reporting effect sizes to facilitate cumulative science: A practical primer for *t*-tests and ANOVAs." *Frontiers in Psychology* 4: 863.
Lakes, Kimberley D., and William T. Hoyt. 2009. "Applications of generalizability theory to clinical child and adolescent psychology research." *Journal of Clinical Child & Adolescent Psychology* 38(1): 144–165.
Lance, Charles E., Marcus M. Butts, and Lawrence C. Michels. 2006. "The sources of four commonly reported cutoff criteria: What did they really say?" *Organizational Research Methods* 9(2): 202–220.
Landis, J. Richard and Gary G. Koch. 1977. "The measurement of observer agreement for categorical data." *Biometrics* 33(1): 159–174.
Larntz, Kinley. 1978. "Small-sample comparisons of exact levels for chi-squared goodness-of-fit statistics." *Journal of the American Statistical Association* 73(362): 253–263.
Lawson, Michael J., and Donald Hogben. 1996. "The vocabulary-learning strategies of foreign-language students." *Language Learning* 46(1): 101–135.
Lederer, Susan E. 1997. *Subjected to Science: Human Experimentation in America Before the Second World War*. Baltimore, MD: Johns Hopkins University Press.
Lee, Haejung, Leslie L. Nicholson, Roger D. Adams, Chris G. Maher, Mark Halaki, and Sung-Soo Bae. 2006. "Development and psychometric testing of Korean language versions of 4 neck pain and disability questionnaires." *SPINE* 31(16): 1841–1845.
Lee, San-Bin. 2014. "An interpreting self-efficacy (ISE) scale for undergraduate students majoring in consecutive interpreting: Construction and preliminary validation." *The Interpreter and Translator Trainer* 8(2): 183–203.
Leijten, Mariëlle, Luuk Van Waes, and Sarah Ransdell. 2010. "Correcting text production errors: Isolating the effects of writing mode from error span, input mode, and lexicality." *Written Communication* 27(2): 189–227.
Lenth, Russell V. 2001. "Some practical guidelines for effective sample size determination." *The American Statistician* 55(3): 187–193.
Levene, Howard. 1960. "Robust tests for equality of variances." In *Contributions to Probability and Statistics. Essays in Honor of Harold Hotelling*, edited by Ingram Olkin and Harold Hotelling, 278–292. Stanford: Stanford University Press.
Levin, Joel R. 2011. "Ethical issues in professional research, writing, and publishing." In *Handbook of Ethics in Quantitative Methodology*, edited by A.T. Panter and Sonya K. Sterba, 463–492. New York: Routledge.
Lewis, Don, and C.J. Burke. 1949. "The use and misuse of the chi-square test." *Psychological Bulletin* 46(6): 433–489.
Li, Defeng. 2004. "Trustworthiness of think-aloud protocols in the study of translation processes." *International Journal of Applied Linguistics* 14(3): 301–313.

Likert, Rensis. 1932. "A technique for the measurement of attitudes." *Archives of Psychology* 22(140): 5–55.
Liu, Minhua, and Yu-Hsien Chiu. 2009. "Assessing source material difficulty for consecutive interpreting: Quantifiable measures and holistic judgment." *Interpreting* 11(2): 244–266.
Lix, Lisa M., Joanne C. Keselman, and H.J. Keselman. 1996. "Consequences of assumption violations revisited: A quantitative review of alternatives to the one-way analysis of variance 'F' test." *Review of Educational Research* 66(4): 579–619.
Lombard, Matthew, Jennifer Snyder-Duch, and Cheryl Campanella Bracken. 2002. "Content analysis in mass communication: Assessment and reporting of intercoder reliability." *Human Communication Research* 28(4): 587–604.
Long, Jeffrey D., and Norman Cliff. 1997. "Confidence intervals for Kendall's tau." *British Journal of Mathematical and Statistical Psychology* 50(1): 31–41.
López Gómez, María José, Teresa Bajo Molina, Presentación Padilla Benitez, and Julio Santiago de Torres. 2007. "Predicting proficiency in signed language interpreting: A preliminary study." *Interpreting* 9(1): 71–93.
Lord, Frederic M. 1953. "On the statistical treatment of football numbers." *American Psychologist* 8: 750–751.
Mahalanobis, Prasanta Chandra. 1936. "On the generalised distance in statistics." *Proceedings of the National Institute of Sciences of India* 2(1): 49–55.
Maney, Tuker, Linda Sibert, Dennis Perzanowski, Kalyan Gupta, and Astride Schmidt-Nielsen. 2012. "Toward determining the comprehensibility of machine translations." In *Proceedings of the First Workshop on Predicting and Improving Text Readability for Target Reader Populations*, 1–7. Madison, WI: Omnipress.
Mann, Henry B., and Donald R. Whitney. 1947. "On a test of whether one of two random variables is stochastically larger than the other." *Annals of Mathematical Statistics* 18(1): 50–60.
Marascuilo, Leonard A. 1966. "Large-sample multiple comparisons." *Psychological Bulletin* 65(5): 280–290.
Marcus-Roberts, Helen M., and Fred S. Roberts. 1987. "Meaningless statistics." *Journal of Educational Statistics* 12(4): 383–394.
Mark, Melvin M., and Aurora L. Lenz-Watson. 2011. "Ethics and the conduct of randomized experiments and quasi-experiments in field settings." In *Handbook of Ethics in Quantitative Methodology*, edited by A.T. Panter and Sonya K. Sterba, 185–210. New York: Routledge.
Marlow, Jennifer, Paul Clough, Juan Cigarrán Recuero, and Javier Artiles. 2008. "Exploring the effects of language skills on multilingual web searches." In *Advances in Information Retrieval: 30th European Conference on IR Research, ECIR 2008*, edited by Craig Macdonald, Iadh Ounis, Vassilis Plachouras, Ian Ruthven, and Ryan W. White, 126–137. Berlin: Springer-Verlag.
Martin, Ben R. 2013. "Whither research integrity? Plagiarism, self-plagiarism, and coercive citation in an age of research assessment." *Research Policy* 42(5): 1005–1014.
Marx, Robert G., Alia Menezes, Lois Horovitz, Edward C. Jones, and Russell F. Warren. 2003. "A comparison of two time intervals for test-retest reliability of health status instruments." *Journal of Clinical Epidemiology* 56(8): 730–735.
Mauchly, J. W. 1940. "Significance tests for sphericity of a normal n-variate distribution." *Annals of Mathematical Statistics* 11(2): 204–209.
Maxwell, Scott E., Cameron J. Camp, and Richard D. Arvey. 1981. "Measures of strength of association: A comparative examination." *Journal of Applied Psychology* 66(5): 525–534.

McArdle, John J. 2011. "Some ethical issues in factor analysis." In *Handbook of Ethics in Quantitative Methodology*, edited by A.T. Panter and Sonya K. Sterba, 313–339. New York: Routledge.

McGill, Robert, John W. Tukey, and Wayne A. Larsen. 1978. "Variation of box plots." *American Statistician* 32(1): 12–16.

McGraw, Kenneth O. and S.P. Wong. 1996a. "Forming inferences about some intraclass correlation coefficients." *Psychological Methods* 1(1): 30–46.

McGraw, Kenneth O. and S.P. Wong. 1996b. "Forming inferences about some intraclass correlation coefficients: Correction." *Psychological Methods* 1(4): 390.

McGuinness, Keith A. 2008. "Of rowing boats, ocean liners and tests of the ANOVA homogeneity of variance assumption." *Austral Ecology* 27(6): 681–688.

McNemar, Quinn. 1946. "Opinion-attitude methodology." *Psychological Bulletin* 43(4): 289–374.

McNemar, Quinn. 1947. "Note on the sampling error of the difference between correlated proportions or percentages." *Psychometrika* 12(2): 153–157.

Mellinger, Christopher D. 2014. "Computer-assisted translation: An empirical investigation of cognitive effort." Unpublished Ph.D. dissertation, Kent State University: Kent, OH. Retrieved from http://bit.ly/1ybBY7W

Mellinger, Christopher D. 2015. "On the applicability of Internet-mediated research methods to investigate translators' cognitive behavior." *Translation & Interpreting* 7(1): 59–71.

Meng, Xiao-Li, Robert Rosenthal, and Donald B. Rubin. 1992. "Comparing correlated correlation coefficients." *Psychological Bulletin* 111(1): 172–175.

Meyer, J. Patrick and Michael A. Seaman. 2013. "A comparison of the exact Kruskal-Wallis distribution to asymptotic approximations for all sample sizes up to 105." *The Journal of Experimental Education* 81(2): 139–156.

Micceri, Theodore. 1989. "The unicorn, the normal curve, and other improbably creatures." *Psychological Bulletin* 105(1): 156–166.

Miller, Gregory A., and Jean P. Chapman. 2001. "Misunderstanding analysis of covariance." *Journal of Abnormal Psychology* 110(1): 40–48.

Miller, Jeff, and Rolf Ulrich. 2015. "Interpreting confidence intervals: A comment on Hoekstra, Morey, Rouder, and Wagenmakers (2014)." *Psychonomic Bulletin and Review* 1–7.

Moder, Karl. 2007. "How to keep the Type I error rate in ANOVA if variances are heteroscedastic." *Austrian Journal of Statistics* 36(3): 179–188.

Morey, Richard D., Eric-Jan Wagenmakers, Rink Hoekstra, Jeffrey N. Rouder, and Michael D. Lee. 2014. "The fallacy of placing confidence in confidence intervals." Presentation at the annual meeting of the Psychonomic Society, Long Beach, CA.

Morris, Tracy L., Joan Gorham, Stanley H. Cohen, and Drew Huffman. 1996. "Fashion in the classroom: Effects of attire on student perceptions of instructors in college classes." *Communication Education* 45(2): 135–148.

Moser, Barry K., and Gary R. Stevens. 1992. "Homogeneity of variance in the two-sample means test." *American Statistician* 46(1): 19–21.

Moser, Barry K., Gary R. Stevens, and Christian L. Watts. 1989. "The two-sample t test versus Satterthwaite's approximate f test." *Communications in Statistics, Theory and Methods* 18(11): 3963–3975.

Mosteller, Frederick. 1968. "Association and estimation in contingency tables." *Journal of the American Statistical Association* 321(63): 1–28.

National Council on Interpreting in Health Care. 2009. *Sight Translation and Written Translation: Guidelines for Healthcare Interpreters.* Working Paper Series.

Neel, John H., and William M. Stallings. 1974. "A Monte Carlo study of Levene's test of homogeneity of variance: Empirical frequencies of Type I error in normal distributions." Paper presented at the Annual Meeting of the American Educational Research Association Convention, Chicago, April 1974.

Nelder, J.A., and R.W.M. Wedderburn. 1972. "Generalized linear models. *Journal of the Royal Statistical Society, Series A* 135(3): 370–384.

Newsom, Roger. 2002. "Parameters behind 'nonparametric' statistics: Kendall's tau, Somers' D, and median differences." *Stata Journal* 2(1): 45–64.

Newton, Paul E., and Stuart D. Shaw. 2014. *Validity in Educational & Psychological Assessment.* Washington, DC: SAGE.

Ng, Marie, and Rand R. Wilcox. 2011. "A comparison of two-stage procedures for testing least-squares coefficients under heteroscedasticity." *British Journal of Mathematical and Statistical Psychology* 64(2): 244–258.

Nickerson, Raymond S. 2000. "Null hypothesis significance testing: A review of an old and continuing controversy." *Psychological Methods* 5(2): 241–301.

Nishimura, Adam et al. 2013. "Improving understanding in the research informed consent process: A systematic review of 54 interventions tested in randomized control trials." *BMC Medical Ethics* 14(1): 28.

Nunnaly, Jum C. 1978. *Psychometric Theory.* New York: McGraw-Hill.

O'Boyle Jr., Ernest, and Herman Aguinis. 2012. "The best and the rest: Revisiting the norm of normality of individual performance." *Personnel Psychology* 65: 79–119.

O'Brien, Robert M. 2007. "A caution regarding rules of thumb for variance inflation factors." *Quality & Quantity* 41(5): 673–690.

O'Brien, Sharon. 2007. "An empirical investigation of temporal and technical post-editing effort." *Translation and Interpreting Studies* 2(1): 83–136.

O'Brien, Sharon. 2008. "Processing fuzzy matches in translation memory tools: An eye-tracking analysis." *Copenhagen Studies in Language* 36: 79–102.

O'Brien, Sharon. 2009. "Eye tracking in translation process research: methodological challenges and solutions." *Copenhagen Studies in Language* 38: 251–266.

Oakes, Michael P. 2012. "Describing a translational corpus." In *Quantitative Methods in Corpus-Based Translation Studies*, edited by Michael P. Oakes and Meng Ji, 115–147. Amsterdam: John Benjamins.

Oakes, Michael P., and Meng Ji (eds). 2012. *Quantitative Methods in Corpus-Based Translation Studies.* Philadelphia: John Benjamins.

Oehlert, Gary W. 1990. *A First Course in Design and Analysis of Experiments.* New York: W.H. Freeman.

Office of Science and Technology Policy, United States Federal Research Misconduct Policy. 2000. *Federal Register* 65(235): 76260–76264.

Okada, Kensuke. 2013. "Is omega squared less biased? A comparison of three major effect size indices in one-way ANOVA." *Behaviormetrika* 40(2): 129–147.

Olejnik, Stephen, and James Algina. 2000. "Measures of effect size for comparative studies: Applications, interpretations, and limitations." *Contemporary Educational Psychology* 25: 241–286.

Olejnik, Stephen, and James Algina. 2003. "Generalized eta and omega squared statistics: Measures of effect size for some common research designs." *Psychological Methods* 8(4): 434–447.

Olejnik, Stephen. 1987. "Conditional ANOVA for mean differences when population variances are unknown." *Journal of Experimental Education* 55(3): 141–148.

Onwuegbuzie, Anthony J. and Larry G. Daniel 2002. "A framework for reporting and interpreting internal consistency reliability estimates." *Measurement and Evaluation in Counseling and Development* 35(2): 89–103.

Osborne, Jason W. 2002. "Notes on the use of data transformation." *Practical Assessment, Research, & Evaluation* 8(6): np.

Osborne, Jason W. 2010. "Correlation and other measures of association." In *The Reviewer's Guide to Quantitative Methods in the Social Sciences*, edited by Gregory R. Hancock and Ralph O. Mueller, 55–69. New York: Routledge.

Osborne, Jason W. 2014. *Best Practices in Exploratory Factor Analysis*. CreateSpace.

Osborne, Jason W., and Amy Overbay. 2004. "The power of outliers (and why researchers should always check for them." *Practical Assessment, Research, & Evaluation* 9(6): np.

Overall, John E. 1980. "Power of chi-square tests for 2x2 contingency tables with small expected frequencies." *Psychological Bulletin* 87(1): 132–135.

Panter, A.T., and Sonya K. Sterba (eds). 2011. *Handbook of Ethics in Quantitative Methodology*. New York: Routledge.

Parra-Frutos, Isabel. 2009. "The behaviour of the modified Levene's test when data are not normally distributed." *Computational Statistics* 24(4): 671–693.

Patton, Jon M. and Fazli Can. 2012. "Determining translation invariance characteristics of James Joyce's *Dubliners*." In *Quantitative Methods in Corpus-Based Translation Studies*, edited by Michael P. Oakes and Meng Ji, 209–229. Amsterdam: John Benjamins.

Payne, J. Gregory. 2010. "The Bradley effect: Mediated reality of race and politics in the 2008 U.S. presidential election." *American Behavioral Scientist* 54(4): 417–435.

Pearson, Judy C., Jeffrey T. Child, and Anna F. Carmon. 2010. "Rituals in committed romantic relationships: The creation and validation of an instrument." *Communication Studies* 61(4): 464–483.

Penfield, Douglas. 1994. "Choosing a two-sample location test." *Journal of Experimental Education* 62(4): 343–360.

Peter, Jochen, and Edmund Lauf. 2002. "Reliability in cross-national content analysis." *Journalism & Mass Communication Quarterly* 79(4): 815–832.

Peters, Gjalt-Jorn Y. 2014. "The alpha and the omega of scale reliability and validity: Why and how to abandon Cronbach's alpha and the route towards more comprehensive assessment of scale quality." *Bulletin of the European Health Psychology Society* 16(2): 56–69.

Peterson, Robert A. 1994. "A meta-analysis of Cronbach's coefficient alpha." *Journal of Consumer Research* 21(2): 381–391.

Pöchhacker, Franz. 2009. "Conference interpreting: Surveying the profession." *Translation and Interpreting Studies* 4(2): 172–186.

Ponterotto, Joseph G., and Daniel E. Ruckdeschel. 2007. "An overview of coefficient alpha and a reliability matrix for estimating adequacy of internal consistency coefficients with psychological research measures." *Perceptual and Motor Skills* 105(3): 997–1014.

Ponterotto, Joseph G., and Richard A. Charter. 2009. "Statistical extensions of Ponterotto and Ruckdeschel's (2007) reliability matrix for estimating the adequacy of internal consistency coefficients." *Perceptual and Motor Skills* 108(3): 878–886.

Porro, Victoria, Johanna Gerlach, Pierrette Bouillon, and Violeta Seretan. 2014. "Rule-based automatic post-processing of SMT output to reduce human post-editing effort." In *Translating and the Computer*. 66–76.

R Core Team. 2015. *R: A Language and Environment for Statistical Computing*. Vienna: R Foundation for Statistical Computing.
Raghunathan, T.E., Robert Rosenthal, and Donald B. Rubin. 1996. "Comparing correlated but nonoverlapping correlations." *Psychological Methods* 1(2): 178–183.
Rao, C.V. and K.P. Saxena. 1981. "On approximation of power of a test procedure based on preliminary tests of significance." *Communications in Statistics, Theory and Methods* 10(13): 1305–1321.
Rasch, Dieter, Klaus D. Kubinger, and Karl Moder. 2011. "The two sample t test: Pretesting its assumptions does not pay off." *Statistical Papers* 52(1): 219–231.
Rasch, Dieter, Klaus D. Kubinger, Jörg Schmidtke, and Joachim Häusler. 2004. "The misuse of asterisks in hypothesis testing." *Psychology Science* 46(2): 227–242.
Rasinger, Sebastian M. 2008. *Quantitative Research in Linguistics*. New York: Continuum.
Redelinghuys, Karien, and Haidee Kruger. 2015. "Using the features of translated language to investigate translation expertise." *International Journal of Corpus Linguistics* 20(3): 293–325.
Reinhardt, Brian. 1996. "Factors affecting coefficient alpha: A mini Monte Carlo study." In *Advances in Social Science Methodology: Vol. 4*, edited by Bruce Thompson, 3–20. Greenwich, CT: JAI Press.
Revelle, William, and Richard E. Zinbarg. 2009. "Coefficients alpha, beta, omega, and the GLB: Comments on Sijtsma." *Psychometrika* 74(1): 145–154.
Ribas, Marta Arumí. 2012. "Problems and strategies in consecutive interpreting: A pilot study at two different stages of interpreter training." *Meta* 57(3): 812–835.
Roberts, Dennis M., and Ruthe E. Kunst. 1990. "A case against continuing use of the Spearman formula for rank-order correlation." *Psychological Reports* 66(1): 339–349.
Rochon, Justine, and Meinhard Kieser. 2011. "A closer look at the effect of preliminary goodness-of-fit testing for normality for the one sample t-test." *British Journal of Mathematical and Statistical Psychology* 64(3): 410–426.
Romano, Jeanine L., Jeffrey D. Kromrey, Corina M. Owens, and Heather M. Scott. 2011. "Confidence interval methods for coefficient alpha on the basis of discrete, ordinal response items: Which one, if any, is the best?" *Journal of Experimental Education* 79(4): 382–403.
Rose, Mary R. 1999. "The peremptory challenge accused of race or gender discrimination? Some data from one county." *Law and Human Behavior* 23(6): 695–702.
Rosiers, Alexandra, June Eyckmans, and Daniel Bauwens. 2011. "A story of attitudes and aptitudes? Investigating individual difference variables within the context of interpreting." *Interpreting* 13(1): 53–69.
Rosnow, Ralph L., and Robert Rosenthal. 1989. "Statistical procedures and the justification of knowledge in psychological science." *American Psychologist* 44(10): 1276–1284.
Rosnow, Ralph L., and Robert Rosenthal. 2011. "Ethical Principles in Data Analysis: An Overview." In *Handbook of Ethics in Quantitative Methodology*, edited by A.T. Panter and Sonya K. Sterba, 37–59. New York: Routledge.
Rousson, Valentin, Theo Gasser, and Burkhardt Seifert. 2002. "Assessing intrarater, interrater, and test-retest reliability of continuous measurements." *Statistics in Medicine* 21(22): 3431–3446.
Royston, Patrick. 1992. "Approximating the Shapiro-Wilk W-test for non-normality." *Statistics and Computing* 2(3): 117–119.
Roziner, Ilan, and Miriam Shlesinger. 2010. "Much ado about something remote: Stress and performance in remote interpreting." *Interpreting* 12(2): 214–247.

Russell, Debra, and Karen Malcolm. 2009. "Assessing ASL-English interpreters." In *Testing and Assessment in Translation and Interpreting Studies*, edited by Claudia V. Angelelli and Holly E. Jacobson, 331–376. Amsterdam: John Benjamins.

Ruxton, Graeme D., David M. Wilkinson, and Markus Neuhäuser. 2015. "Advice on testing the null hypothesis that a sample is drawn from a normal distribution." *Animal Behaviour* 107: 249–252.

Ruxton, Graeme. 2006. "The unequal variance *t*-test is an underused alternative to Student's *t*-test and the Mann-Whitney *U* test." *Behavioral Ecology* 17(4): 688–690.

Saldanha, Gabriela, and Sharon O'Brien. 2014. *Research Methodologies in Translation Studies*. New York: Routledge.

Sawilowsky, Shlomo S., and R. Clifford Blair. 1992. "A more realistic look at the robustness and Type II error properties of the t test to departures from population normality." *Psychological Bulletin* 111(2): 352–360.

Sawyer, David B. 2004. *Fundamental Aspects of Interpreter Education*. Philadelphia: John Benjamins.

Schmidt, Frank L., and John E. Hunter. 1996. "Measurement error in psychological research: Lessons from 26 research scenarios." *Psychological Methods* 1(2): 199–223.

Schmidt, Frank L., Huy Le, and Remus Ilies. 2003. "Beyond alpha: An empirical examination of the effects of different sources of measurement error on reliability estimates for measures of individual differences constructs." *Psychological Methods* 8(2): 206–224.

Schmitt, Neal. 1996. "Uses and abuses of coefficient alpha." *Psychological Assessment* 8(4): 350–353.

Schoppink, Liesbeth E.M., Maurits W. van Tulder, Bart W. Koes, Sandra AJHM Beurskens, Rob A. de Bie. 1996. "Reliability and validity of the Dutch adaptation of the Quebec Back Pain Disability Scale." *Physical Therapy* 76(3): 268–275.

Schrag, Zachary M. 2010. *Ethical Imperialism: Institutional Review Boards and the Social Sciences, 1965–2009*. Baltimore: John Hopkins University Press.

Schucany, William R., and Hon Keung Tony Ng. 2006. "Preliminary goodness-of-fit tests for normality do not validate the one-sample student *t*." *Communication in Statistics, Theory and Methods* 35(12): 2275–2286.

Schwarzer, Ralf, and Matthias Jerusalem. 1995. "Generalized self-efficacy scale." In *Measures in Health Psychology: A User's Portfolio. Causal and Control Beliefs*, edited by John Weinman, Stephen Wright, and Marie Johnston, 35–37. Windsor: NFER-NELSON.

Scott, William A. 1955. "Reliability of content analysis: The case of nominal scale coding." *Public Opinion Quarterly* 19(3): 321–325.

Scott-Tennent, Christopher, and María González Davies. 2008. "Effects of specific training on the ability to deal with cultural references in translation." *Meta* 53(4): 782–797.

Seeber, Kilian G., and Dirk Kerzel. 2012. "Cognitive load in simultaneous interpreting: Model meets data." *International Journal of Bilingualism* 16(2): 228–242.

Seeber, Killian G. 2013. "Cognitive Load in Simultaneous Interpreting: Measures and Methods." *Target* 25(1): 18–32.

Setton, Robin, and Manuela Motta. 2007. "Syntacrobatics: Quality and reformulation in simultaneous-with-text." *Interpreting* 9(2): 199–230.

Shaffer, Juliet Popper. 1973. "Testing specific hypotheses in contingency tables: Chi-square partitioning and other methods." *Psychological Reports* 33(2): 343–348.

Shapiro, S.S., and M.B. Wilk. 1965. "An analysis of variance test for normality (complete samples)." *Biometrika* 52(3/4): 591–611.

Shaw, Sherry, Nadja Grbić, and Kathy Franklin. 2004. "Applying language skills to interpretation: Student perspectives from signed and spoken language programs." *Interpreting* 6(1): 69–100.
Shrout, Patrick E., and Joseph L. Fleiss. 1979. "Intraclass correlations: Uses in assessing rater reliability." *Psychological Bulletin* 86(2): 420–428.
Sieber, Joan E., Rebecca Iannuzzo, and Beverly Rodriguez. 1995. "Deception methods in psychology: Have they changed in 23 years?" *Ethics & Behavior* 5(1): 67–85.
Siegel, Sidney. 1956. *Nonparametric Statistics for the Behavioral Sciences*. New York: McGraw-Hill.
Sijtsma, Klaas. 2009. "On the use, the misuse, and the very limited usefulness of Cronbach's alpha." *Psychometrika* 74(1): 107–120.
Sim, Julius, and Chris C. Wright. 2005. "The kappa statistic in reliability studies: Use, interpretation, and sample size requirements." *Physical Therapy* 85(3): 257–268.
Simmons, Vani N. et al. 2011. "Transcreation of validated smoking relapse-prevention booklets for use with Hispanic populations." *Journal of Health Care for the Poor and Underserved* 22(3): 886–893.
Skidmore, Susan Troncoso, and Bruce Thompson. 2013. "Bias and precision of some classical ANOVA effect sizes when assumptions are violated." *Behavior Research Methods* 45(2): 536–546.
Smith, M. Brewster. 2000. "Moral foundations of research with human participants." In *Ethics in Research with Human Participants*, edited by Bruce D. Sales and Susan Folkman, 3–10. Washington, DC: APA.
Spearman, C. 1904. "The proof and measurement of association between two things." *American Journal of Psychology* 15(1): 72–101.
Specia, Lucia, Nciola Cancedda, and Marc Dymetman. 2010. "A dataset for assessing machine translation evaluation metrics." *Seventh International Conference on Language Resources and Evaluation*, Malta. 3375–3378.
Spurrier, John D. 2003. "On the null distribution of the Kruskal-Wallis statistic." *Journal of Nonparametric Statistics* 15(6): 685–691.
Steel, Robert G.D. 1961. "Some rank sum multiple comparisons tests." *Biometrics* 17(4): 539–552.
Steiger, James H. 1980. "Tests for comparing elements of a correlation matrix." *Psychological Bulletin* 87(2): 245–251.
Steiner, Erich. 2012. "Methodological cross-fertilization: empirical methodologies in (computational) linguistics and translation studies." *Translation: Corpora, Computation, Cognition* 2(1): 3–21.
Sterba, Sonya K. 2006. "Misconduct in the analysis and reporting of data: Bridging methodological and ethical agendas for change." *Ethics & Behavior* 16(4): 305–318.
Stevens, James P. 1984. "Outliers and influential data points in regression analysis." *Quantitative Methods in Psychology* 95(2): 334–344.
Stevens, S.S. 1946. "On the theory of scales of measurement." *Science* 103(2684): 677–680.
Stoline, Michael R. 1981. "The status of multiple comparisons: Simultaneous estimation of all pairwise comparisons in one-way ANOVA designs." *The American Statistician* 35(3): 134–141.
Streiner, David L. 2003. "Starting at the beginning: An introduction to coefficient alpha and internal consistency." *Journal of Personality Assessment* 80(1): 99–103.
Sturges, Herbert A. 1926. "The choice of a class interval." *Journal of the American Statistical Association* 21(153): 65–66.

Sun, Sanjun, and Gregory M. Shreve. 2014. "Measuring translation difficulty: An empirical study." *Target* 26(1): 98–127.
Sun, Sanjun. 2016. "Survey-based studies." In *Researching Translation and Interpreting*, edited by Claudia V. Angelelli and Brian James Baer, 269–279. New York: Routledge.
Tabachnik, Barbara G., and Linda S. Fidell. 2012. *Using Multivariate Statistics*. 6th Edition. Boston: Pearson.
Tamariz, Leonardo, Ana Palacio, Mauricio Robert, Erin N. Marcus. 2013. "Improving the informed consent process for research subjects with low literacy: A systematic review." *Journal of General Internal Medicine* 28(1): 121–126.
Tang, Wan, Hua He, and Xin M. Tu. 2012. *Applied Categorical and Count Data Analysis*. Boca Raton, FL: Chapman & Hall/CRC.
Tavakol, Mohsen, and Reg Dennick. 2011. "Making sense of Cronbach's alpha." *International Journal of Medical Education* 2: 53–55.
Terrell, Colin D. 1982a. "Significance tables for the biserial and the point biserial." *Educational and Psychological Measurement* 42(4): 975–981.
Terrell, Colin D. 1982b. "Table for converting the point biserial to the biserial." *Educational and Psychological Measurement* 42(4): 983–986.
Thompson, Bruce. 1994. "Guidelines for authors." *Educational and Psychological Measurement* 54: 837–847.
Thompson, Bruce, and Tammi Vacha-Haase. 2000. "Psychometrics is datametrics: The test is not reliable." *Educational and Psychological Measurement* 60(2): 174–195.
Thourlby, William. 1978. *You Are What You Wear*. New York: Sheed Andrews and McMeel.
Thye, Shane R. 2000. "Reliability in experimental sociology." *Social Forces* 78(4): 1277–1309.
Timarová, Šárka, and Heidi Salaets. 2011. "Learning styles, motivation, and cognitive flexibility in interpreter training." *Interpreting* 13(1): 31–52.
Timarová, Šárka, Ivana Čeňková, Reine Meylaerts, Erik Hertog, Arnaud Szmalec, and Wouter Duyck. 2014. "Simultaneous interpreting and working memory executive control." *Interpreting* 16(2): 139–168.
Tinsley, Howard E.A. and David J. Weiss. 1975. "Interrater reliability and agreement of subjective judgments." *Journal of Counseling Psychology* 22(4): 358–376.
Tippett, L.H.C. 1925. "On the extreme individuals and the range of samples taken from a normal population." *Biometrika* 17(3/4): 364–387.
Tomarken, Andrew J., and Ronald C. Serlin. 1986. "Comparison of ANOVA alternatives under variance heterogeneity and specific noncentrality structures." *Quantitative Methods in Psychology* 99(1): 90–99.
Toothaker, Larry E., and De Newman. 1994. "Nonparametric competitors to the two-way ANOVA." *Journal of Educational and Behavioral Statistics* 19(3): 237–273.
Tufte, Edward R. 1990. *Envisioning Information*. Cheshire, CT: Graphics Press.
Tukey, John W. 1949. "Comparing individual means in the analysis of variance." *Biometrics* 5(2): 99–114.
Tukey, John W. 1977. *Exploratory Data Analysis*. New York: Pearson.
Tukey, John W. 1993. "Graphic comparisons of several linked aspects: Alternatives and suggested principles." *Journal of Computational and Graphical Studies* 2(1): 1–49.
Turner, Jean L. 2014. *Using Statistics in Small-Scale Language Education Research*. New York: Routledge.
Van der Laan, Paul, and L. Rob Verdoren. 1987. "Classical analysis of variance methods and nonparametric counterparts." *Biometrical Journal* 29(6): 635–665.
van Someren, Maarten W., Yvonne F. Barnard, and Jacobijn A.C. Sandberg. 1994. *The Think Aloud Method: A Practical Guide to Modelling Cognitive Processes*. London: Academic Press.

Vermeiren, Hildegard, Jan Van Gucht, and Leentje De Bontridder. 2009. "Standards as critical success factors in assessment: Certifying social interpreters in Flanders, Belgium." In *Testing and Assessment in Translation and Interpreting Studies*, edited by Claudia V. Angelelli and Holly E. Jacobson, 297–329. Amsterdam: John Benjamins.

von Hippel, Paul T. 2005. "Mean, median, and skew: Correcting a textbook rule." *Journal of Statistics Education* 13(2): np.

Walker, Susan Noble, Madeleine J. Kerr, Nola J. Pender, and Karen R. Sechrist. 1990. "A Spanish language version of the Health-Promoting Lifestyle Profile." *Nursing Research* 39(5): 268–273.

Wanzer, Melissa Bekelja and Ann Bainbridge Frymier. 1999. "The relationship between student perceptions of instructor humor and students' reports of learning." *Communication Education* 48(1): 48–62.

Welch, B. L. 1947. "The generalization of 'Student's' problem when several different population variances are involved." *Biometrika* 34(1–2): 28–35.

Welch, B.L. 1951. "On the comparison of several mean values: An alternative approach." *Biometrika* 38(3/4): 330–336.

Wells, Craig S., and John M. Hintze. 2007. "Dealing with assumptions underlying statistical tests." *Psychology in the Schools* 44(5): 495–502.

Wendt, Hans W. 1972. "Dealing with a common problem in social science: A simplified rank-biserial coefficient of correlation based on the U statistic." *European Journal of Social Psychology* 2(4): 463–465.

Wilcox, Rand R. 1987. *New Statistical Procedures for the Social Sciences: Modern Solutions to Basic Problems*. Hillsdale, NJ: Lawrence Erlbaum Associates.

Wilcox, Rand R. 1995. "Three multiple comparison procedures for trimmed means." *Biometrical Journal* 37(6): 643–656.

Wilcox, Rand R. 1998. "How many discoveries have been lost by ignoring modern statistical methods?" *American Psychologist* 53(3): 300–314.

Wilcox, Rand R. 2005. "New methods for comparing groups: Strategies for increasing the probability of detecting true differences." *Current Directions in Psychological Science* 14(5): 272–275.

Wilcox, Rand R. 2012. *Introduction to Robust Estimation and Hypothesis Testing*. 3rd edition. Amsterdam: Academic Press.

Wilcox, Rand R., and H.J. Keselman. 2003. "Modern robust data analysis methods: Measures of central tendency." *Psychological Methods* 8(3): 254–274.

Wilcox, Rand R., Charlin L. Ventura, and Karen L. Thompson. 1986. "New Monte Carlo results on the robustness of the ANOVA F, W, and F* statistics." *Communications in Statistics—Simulation and Computation* 15(4): 933–943.

Wilcoxon, Frank. 1945. "Individual comparisons by ranking methods." *Biometrics Bulletin* 1(6): 80–83.

Wilkinson, L. and The APA Task Force on Statistical Inference. 1999. "Statistical methods in psychology journals: Guidelines and explanations." *American Psychologists* 54(8): 594–604.

Wilks, S.S. 1935. "The likelihood test of independence in contingency tables." *Annals of Mathematical Statistics* 6: 190–196.

Winner, Larry. 2006. "NASCAR Winston Cup race results for 1975–2003." *Journal of Statistics Education* 14(3). n.p.

Wu, Dekai, and Kuanyin Xia. 1995. "Large-scale automatic extraction of an English-Chinese translation lexicon." *Machine Translation* 9(3/4): 285–313.

Yau, Nathan. 2011. *Visualize This: The Flowing Data Guide to Design, Visualization, and Statistics*. Indianapolis, IN: Wiley Publishing.

Yudes, Carolina, Pedro Macizo, and Teresa Bajo. 2011. "The influence of expertise in simultaneous interpreting on non-verbal executive process." *Frontiers in Psychology* 2: 309.
Zimmerman, Donald W. 1996. "Some properties of preliminary tests of equality of variances in the two-sample location problem." *Journal of General Psychology* 123(3): 217–231.
Zimmerman, Donald W. 1998. "Invalidation of parametric and nonparametric statistical tests by concurrent violation of two assumptions." *Journal of Experimental Education* 67(1): 55–68.
Zimmerman, Donald W. 2004. "A note on preliminary tests of equality of variances." *British Journal of Mathematical and Statistical Psychology* 57(1): 173–181.
Zimmerman, Donald W. 2011. "A simple and effective decision rule for choosing a significance test to protect against non-normality." *British Journal of Mathematical and Statistical Psychology* 64(3): 388–409.
Zimmerman, Donald W. 2012. "A note on consistency of non-parametric rank tests and related rank transformations." *British Journal of Mathematical and Statistical Psychology* 65(1): 122–144.
Zimmerman, Donald W., and Bruno D. Zumbo. 1993. "Rank transformations and the power of the Student t test and Welch t' test for non-normal populations with unequal variances." *Canadian Journal of Experimental Psychology* 47(3): 523–539.
Zipf, George. 1949. *Human Behavior and the Principle of Least Effort*. Oxford: Addison-Wesley Press.
Zwischenberger, Cornelia. 2015. "Simultaneous conference interpreting and a supernorm that governs it all." *Meta* 60(1): 90–111.

Appendix A: Guide to selecting a statistical test

Tests of differences

Dependent variable	Independent variable	Type of test	Test name and page number
Continuous	Categorical variable to define two groups	Parametric	*t*-test (99)
		Nonparametric	Mann-Whitney *U*-test (100)
	Categorical variable to identify two conditions for the same participants	Parametric	Paired *t*-test (104)
		Nonparametric	Wilcoxon signed-ranks test (107)
	Categorical variable to define three or more groups	Parametric	One-way analysis of variance (ANOVA) (111)
		Nonparametric	Kruskal-Wallis test (133)
	Categorical variable to identify three or more conditions for the same participants		Repeated measures ANOVA (136)
	Two or more categorical variables		Factorial ANOVA (151)
	At least one variable to define groups and one continuous		Analysis of covariance (ANCOVA) (165)
Categorical	Categorical		Chi-squared test of homogeneity (169)

Tests of relationships

None	Two continuous variables	Parametric	Pearson's *r* (180)
		Nonparametric	Kendall's τ (190)
Continuous	One continuous variable		Simple linear regression (217)
	Two or more variables		Multiple linear regression (228)
Count data	Any number of variables		Poisson regression (236)

Index

adjusted R^2 231, *see also* coefficient of determination
Agresti-Pendergast test 150
alternative hypothesis 5–6, 73, 79, 81, 113–14, 119–23, 169–70
analysis of covariance, *see* ANCOVA
ANCOVA 165–6, 234
Anderson-Darling test 60
anonymity 19–21, 23
ANOVA: factorial (independent) 151–5; mixed 163–4; multivariate 150; one-way 110–24, 131–2, 136–42; repeated measures 136–45, 161–3, 235; two-way 157–61
Anscombe Quartet 66–7, 182–3
asymmetry 50–1
attenuation 194
authorship 243–5
autocorrelation 220

backward elimination, *see* model selection
bar chart 52, 159
Bartlett's test 117
Bayesian statistics 248
Belmont Report 15
beneficence 15–19
beta (β) coefficient 222–5, 236
binary correlation 193, *see also* correlation
binary logistic regression, *see* regression, logistic
Bonferroni correction 125, 135–6, 147, 149, 156, 162–3
bootstrapping 109
box-and-whisker plot, *see* box plot
box plot 48, 53–4, 67, 89, 116, 124, 159
Brown-Forsythe test 117, 150
Brunner-Munzel test 109

carryover effect 7, 105, 145, 198
categorical data 23–4, 27, 40, 52, 56, 167–9, 175–6
causality 4, 150, 187, 189–90, 215
census 10–11, 71
Central Limit Theorem 63–4, 78–9, 101–2, 119, 181, 190
central tendency 41–6
CFA, *see* confirmatory factor analysis
chi-squared (χ^2) distribution 65
chi-squared (χ^2) tests: goodness-of-fit 174–5, 236; homogeneity 169–72; independence 169–72
CLT, *see* Central Limit Theorem
coefficient of determination (R^2) 188–9, 225, 231
coercion 13, 16
Cohen's d 80, 96–8, 109
Cohen's kappa (κ) 195, 207–11, 214
collinearity 228, 234
confidence interval 60, 72–3, 80–1, 96–8, 100, 106, 108, 125–7, 183–6, 190, 201, 209–10, 224–5, 245–8
confidentiality 19–20, 23
confirmatory factor analysis 33
conflict of interest 241, 244–5
content analysis 170, 210–11
contingency table 169, 171, 174–5
Cook's distance 68, 233
correction for tied observations 83, 103
correlation 179–93, 215, 229
counterbalancing 106
covariance 49–50, 182–3
Cramér's V 172–3
Cronbach's alpha (α) 195–6, 199–205
cross tabulation, *see* contingency table

data transformation 27–8, 61, 63–4, 68, 184, 219, 226–7, 233, 236
data visualization 51–6
debriefing 17–18
deception 16–17, 21, 245
degrees of freedom 49, 65, 75–7, 122–3, 138–42, 153, 161
dependent variable 4–5, 111–12, 137, 156–8, 165, 215–18, 225–6, 231
discrete variable 23–4, 58, 233
dispersion 46–50
dummy variable 23–4, 228, 232, 234
Dunnett's test 125, 127–8, 132
Dunn-Nemenyi test 136
Durbin-Watson test 220

EFA, *see* exploratory factor analysis
effect size 77–9, 96–8, 103, 106–8, 128–30, 133, 136, 144, 147, 155–6, 163, 172–3, 225, 231, 245–8
epsilon squared (ε^2) 128–9
eta squared (η^2) 128–9, 144, 155–6, 163
ethics, *see* research ethics
experimental research 6–7
exploratory factor analysis 33, 35
extrapolation 55, 226, 228
extreme observation, *see* outlier

F-distribution 65, 76, 141, 201
F-test, *see* Fisher's F-test, Welch's F-test
fabrication 242
factor analysis 31–3
factorial ANOVA, *see* ANOVA, factorial
falsifiability
falsification 242–3
Fisher's exact test 172–3, 175–6
Fisher's F-test 114–17, 119–24
Fisher's Least Significant Difference test 149
fixed effect 164, 234–5
Fleiss's kappa 210–11
Fligner-Policello test 109
forward selection, *see* model selection
frequencies 24, 40–1, 52, 56–7, 170–1, 208, 236–7
Friedman's test 146–7

G-test 175–6
Games-Howell test 132–3, 156, 163
Gaussian distribution, *see* normal distribution
Gauss-Markov theorem 238
generalizability 8, 10–12

generalizability theory 196, 212
Greenhouse-Geisser adjustment 137–8, 142, 161–2

Hedges' g 96–7, 109
heteroscedasticity 92–3, 99–101, 104, 117, 131–2, 219–20, 227
histogram 45, 52–3, 58, 89–0, 92, 175
Hodges-Lehmann estimator 103
homogeneity of variance, *see* homoscedasticity
homoscedasticity 91–3, 106, 114–17, 137–8, 181, 219–20, 226–7
Honestly Significant Difference test, *see* Tukey's Honestly Significant Difference (HSD) test
Hotelling's T^2 test 150
HSD, *see* Tukey's Honestly Significant Difference (HSD) test
human participants 9, 11, 14–15, 18

ICC, *see* intraclass correlation coefficient
independence, assumption of 92, 115–16, 137, 169–70, 220, 234
independent variable 4–5, 7–8, 111–12, 151–2, 154–5, 161–2, 215–19, 224, 226–32, 236–8
inferential statistics 23, 39, 41, 70–1, 90, 92, 194, 205, 218
informed consent 10, 15, 17–20
Institutional Review Boards 14, 21, 195
interaction effect 145, 153–5, 157, 159–63
interannotator agreement, *see* reliability, intercoder
intercoder reliability, *see* reliability, intercoder
internal reliability, *see* reliability, internal
Internet-mediated research 20–1, 34
interpolation 226
interquartile range 48, 54
interrater agreement, *see* reliability, intercoder
inter-rater reliability, *see* reliability, intercoder
interval data 26–8, 31–2, 45–6, 52, 180, 190, 193, 212
intraclass correlation coefficient (ICC) 212
IQR, *see* interquartile range
IRB, *see* Institutional Review Boards

Jonckheere-Terpstra test 150
justice 15–17

Kendall's tau (τ) 190–1
Kolmogorov-Smirnov test 60, 69
Krippendorff's alpha (α) 206, 211–13
Kruskal-Wallis test 119, 132–36
kurtosis 51, 61–2

leptokurtosis 51, 62
Levene's test 92, 117, 138
likelihood ratio test, see G-test
Likert-type scales 26, 31–2, 45, 47, 61, 145, 197–200
linearity 218, 226–7
linear regression, see regression
line graph 55–6
logistic regression, see regression, logistic

M-estimation 68, 109, 149
Mahalanobis distance 68
main effect 154–5, 157–8, 160–3
Mann-Whitney U-test 93–4, 100–4, 135–6
MANOVA, see ANOVA, multivariate
Marascuilo's procedure 173
Mauchly's test 138, 161
McNemar's test 176
mean 41–4, 63–4, 77, 79–81, 114, 119–22
mean squared error (MSE) 122, 126–7, 221
measurement error 59, 67, 71, 194, 206
median 43–5, 47–8, 51, 68, 81–3, 102–3, 107–8, 133–5
meta-analysis 117, 148, 246–7
mixed ANOVA, see ANOVA, mixed
mixed effect model 163–4, 233–5
mode 45–6
model selection 216, 231–2
MSE, see mean squared error
multicollinearity 228–9
multiple linear regression 192, 217, 228, 231, 236
multivariate ANOVA, see ANOVA, multivariate

Newman-Keuls test 149
NHST, see null hypothesis significance testing
nominal data, see categorical data
nonlinearity 25, 190, 226–7
nonmaleficence 15; see also beneficence
normal distribution 59–61, 63–4, 76, 78, 184
normality assumption 59–64, 78–9, 93–4, 100–1, 106, 118–19, 132, 135, 146, 181, 190

null hypothesis 5–6, 73–5, 83, 91, 132, 230
null hypothesis significance testing 73, 77, 245–6, 248

observational research 6, 8, 152, 166, 215
omega squared (ω^2) 128–30, 133, 155–6, 163
one-way ANOVA, see ANOVA, one-way
operationalization 3–4, 10, 23, 29
order effect 7, 105–6, 145, 162
ordinal data 24–7, 46, 52, 82, 190
outliers 42–4, 47–8, 51, 54, 63, 66–9, 76, 118, 181–3, 232–3, 243

p-value 73–5, 77, 84, 103, 123–5, 148–9, 231–2, 246
paired t-test, see t-test, paired
pairwise comparisons 113–14, 124–7, 132, 142, 156
parameter 9–11, 39, 71–2, 217–18
partial correlation 191–2, see also correlation
partial-eta squared (η_P^2) 144, 150, 155–6
Pearson's r 180–90, 197
phi coefficient (φ) 173
plagiarism 242–3; see also authorship, self-plagiarism
platykurtosis 51
Poisson distribution 66
Poisson regression, see regression, Poisson
polynomial regression, see regression, polynomial
population 9–13, 16, 39, 59–61, 63–4, 70–72, 155, 164–5, 217
post hoc tests 124–7, 132–3, 142–3, 147, 156
power 60, 73–5, 77–8, 91, 98, 105, 114, 130–1, 150, 152, 156, 161, 194
precision 22–3, 35, 77
principal component analysis 35

QQ plot 61–2, 118
Quantile-Quantile plot, see QQ plot
quantiles 47–8, 61, 118
quasi-experimental research 7–8, 152, 166
questionnaire, see survey

R^2, see coefficient of determination
random effect 164–6, 234–5
random variable 53, 58, 63, 101, 164, 170
range 47–8
rank transformation 28, 68, 82–3, 104, 166
rank-transformed Welch test 103–4

rANOVA, *see* ANOVA, repeated measures
refutability, *see* falsifiability
regression 55, 68, 76, 215–38; logistic 193, 235–6; mixed effects 234–5; multiple 217, 230–1, 236; multivariate 238; polynomial 227; Poisson 236–7
reliability 28–31, 193–213; intercoder 194–6, 206–13; internal 30–31, 195–6, 198–205; split-half 199; test-retest 195–8
repeated measures ANOVA, *see* ANOVA, repeated measures
repeated measures designs 7, 105, 137, 161–4
replication: experimental 83, 97, 202, 246, 248; statistical 152, 194, 196
representativeness 9–13
research design 6–8, 16–17, 87, 92, 145, 165
research ethics 9, 13–21, 241–5, 248
research hypothesis 5–7
research misconduct 241–4
research question 3–7, 9, 34
residual error 76–7, 115–16, 119, 122, 126, 128, 133, 135, 137, 139–40, 212, 218–23, 226–7, 233, 235
respect for persons 15
risk 15–18, 20
robustness 6, 43, 117, 166

sample size 63–4, 78, 98, 130
sampling 7, 9–13, 67, 92, 94; error 10–11, 71, 89, 161
Satterthwaite's correction 100
scatterplot 54–5, 63, 67, 181–2, 218–20, 223, 226–7, 232–3
Scheffé's test 149
scientific fraud, *see* research misconduct
Scott's pi (π) 208, 211
scree plot 33
self-plagiarism 243–4
Shapiro-Wilk test 60, 69, 93, 119, 137, 175
skewness 43, 50–1, 61, 66, 104, 118, 193
Spearman's rho (ρ) 191–3
sphericity 137–38, 141–2, 161–2
spurious correlation 187, 191
standard deviation 10, 48–50, 59, 63–4
standard error 64, 210, 221, 224–5, 228
statistical software 34–5
Steel's test 136
Steiger's z-test 186
stepwise selection, *see* model selection
Student's *t*-test, *see* *t*-test, Student's

Sturges' formula 53
survey design 29–35, 145, 170, 193–205
survey items 24, 30–3, 195, 198–203
survey translation 31, 204

t-distribution 64–5, 76
t-statistic 64–5
t-test 90–100, 224–5; one-sample 79–81; paired 88, 104–7, 142; Student's 90–5; Welch's 99–100
test-retest reliability, *see* reliability, test-retest
trend analysis 143
triangulation 6, 8, 206, 248
trimming 68, 181, 243
Tukey's Honestly Significant Difference (HSD) test 125–6, 132, 148, 156
two-way ANOVA, *see* ANOVA, two-way
Type I error 73–4, 77, 91–4, 113–14, 116, 125, 131–2, 146–7, 149
Type II error 73–4, 77, 91, 93, 105, 194, 228

unbiasedness 84

validity 28–31, 194, 201–5
variance 48–50, 65, 76, 99–100, 128, 200, 212, 219, 221; heterogeneous, *see* heteroscedasticity; homogeneity of, *see* homoscedasticity
variance inflation factor (VIF) 229
VIF, *see* variance inflation factor

Welch's *F*-test 133–4, *see also* ANOVA
Welch's *t*-test, *see* *t*-test, Welch's
Welch test, rank-transformed, *see* rank-transformed Welch test
Wilcoxon matched-pairs signed-ranks test 88, 106–8
Wilcoxon rank-sum test, *see* Mann-Whitney *U*-test
Wilcox's *Z*-test 150
winsorization 68, 181, 233
within-subjects design, *see* repeated measures designs

Yates correction 172
Yuen-Welch test 150

z-score 60–1, 64, 67–8, 185, 229
z-statistic 102–3, 108
z-transformation 184, 186
Zipf's law 101

# Taylor & Francis eBooks

Helping you to choose the right eBooks for your Library

Add Routledge titles to your library's digital collection today. Taylor and Francis ebooks contains over 50,000 titles in the Humanities, Social Sciences, Behavioural Sciences, Built Environment and Law.

Choose from a range of subject packages or create your own!

Benefits for you
- Free MARC records
- COUNTER-compliant usage statistics
- Flexible purchase and pricing options
- All titles DRM-free.

Benefits for your user
- Off-site, anytime access via Athens or referring URL
- Print or copy pages or chapters
- Full content search
- Bookmark, highlight and annotate text
- Access to thousands of pages of quality research at the click of a button.

REQUEST YOUR FREE INSTITUTIONAL TRIAL TODAY

Free Trials Available
We offer free trials to qualifying academic, corporate and government customers.

eCollections – Choose from over 30 subject eCollections, including:

Archaeology	Language Learning
Architecture	Law
Asian Studies	Literature
Business & Management	Media & Communication
Classical Studies	Middle East Studies
Construction	Music
Creative & Media Arts	Philosophy
Criminology & Criminal Justice	Planning
Economics	Politics
Education	Psychology & Mental Health
Energy	Religion
Engineering	Security
English Language & Linguistics	Social Work
Environment & Sustainability	Sociology
Geography	Sport
Health Studies	Theatre & Performance
History	Tourism, Hospitality & Events

For more information, pricing enquiries or to order a free trial, please contact your local sales team:
www.tandfebooks.com/page/sales

Routledge — Taylor & Francis Group | The home of Routledge books

www.tandfebooks.com